# Hedgemaids and Fairy Candles

# Hedgemaids and Fairy Candles

## The Lives and Lore of North American Wildflowers

Jack Sanders

Illustrated by Dawn Peterson

Ragged Mountain Press
Camden, Maine

First paperback printing Fall 1995

Published by Ragged Mountain Press

10 9 8 7 6 5 4 3 2 1



Library of Congress Cataloging-in-Publication Data
Sanders, Jack, 1944–
Hedgemaids and fairy candles: the lives and lore of North American wildflowers / Jack Sanders.
p. cm.
Includes bibliographical references and index.
ISBN 0-07-057233-X
1. Wild flowers—North America. 2. Wild flowers—North America—Folklore. I. Title.
QK110.S25 1993
582. 13' 097—dc20 92-47408
CIP

Questions regarding the content of this book should be addressed to:
Ragged Mountain Press
P.O. Box 220
Camden, ME 04843
207-236-4837

Questions regarding the ordering of this book should be addressed to:
The McGraw-Hill Companies
Customer Service Department
P.O. Box 547
Blacklick, OH 43004
Retail Customers: 1-800-822-8158
Bookstores: 1-800-722-4726

A portion of the profits from the sale of each Ragged Mountain Press book is donated to an environmental cause.

*Hedgemaids and Fairy Candles* is printed on 60-pound Renew Opaque Vellum, an acid-free paper that contains 50 percent recycled waste paper (preconsumer) and 10 percent postconsumer waste paper.

Illustrations of summer wildflowers appear on the first two pages of the color insert; late summer and fall wildflowers are shown on the last two pages.

Printed by R.R. Donnelley
Text Design and Illustrations by Dawn Peterson
Production by Molly Mulhern
Page Layout by Faith Hague
Edited by Jim Babb, Dorcas Susan Miller, and Pamela Benner

To my wife, Sally, who helped me with this project in countless ways over many years; to Betty Grace Nash, who encouraged me to keep at it; to Jim Hodgins, who published many of my essays in the pages of *Wildflower* magazine; and to Newton's pal, who introduced me to the fine folks at Ragged Mountain Press, this book is dedicated.

# Contents

## LATE SUMMER AND FALL



**Color plates of selected wildflowers appear following page 120.**

# Introduction

A wag once called wildflowers "weeds with a press agent." Whether they are "weeds" or "wildflowers," nothing in nature does more to beautify our world. Their countless colors and endless designs can be found almost anywhere the sun hits the earth—from fields to woods, deserts to ponds, and even in junkyards, dumps, and cracks in concrete.

What is a wildflower? Nothing more than a blooming plant that can survive without our help. More than 10,000 kinds exist in North America, many of them rare and limited in territory, hundreds of them abundant and widespread. They range from odd-looking orchids whose locations are whispered only among trusted friends, to weeds that pop up in every lawn and garden and keep herbicide manufacturers in business.

Many common wildflowers are natives that were here long before humans walked the earth, while many others have been deliberately or accidentally imported from Europe, Africa, or Asia. Frequently, native plants are either more common or more rare today than they were when the Europeans arrived and began redesigning the surface of the continent. The colonists gave the plants more or less of what they wanted. As forests were cleared, sun-loving species found new habitats—and often made enemies with the very farmers who had given them light. But as wetlands were drained or filled for fields, habitats of many species were eliminated, and those plants were often made rare or rarer.

This book covers natives and immigrants with equal interest, a fact symbolized by the title, *Hedgemaids and Fairy Candles.* Hedgemaids is one of the numerous names applied to ground ivy, a lowly Old World plant of open fields that has found the New World much to its liking. Fairy candles is a common and probably better name for black cohosh, a tall, majestic native of our woodlands. Hedgemaids took well to the North American landscape as it was opened by agrarian settlers for fields and yards, while fairy candles have survived our tree-felling tendencies and still stand tall in many of our eastern woodlands.

Our most common wildflowers are often called weeds. One definition of a weed is a plant growing profusely where it is not wanted. I may be accused of being a press agent, but I think of weeds not as pests, but as the most successful wildflowers. Yes, there are a few villains—ragweeds and poison ivy chief among them. But weeds that are exceedingly common in field, lawn, or garden are simply wildflowers that are able to adapt and survive better than others. Often, they are among the most highly evolved plants on the evolutionary scale.

Wildflowers come in myriad designs. The form, size, color, scent, positioning, and other characteristics of the blossoms all result from eons of evolution. Botanists have figured out the purpose of some of the often intricate floral patterns, usually aimed at luring or guiding insects. Others remain mysteries. No matter what the design, wildflowers are always interesting and usually beautiful.

Those who came before us appreciated wild plants, if not as decorations, then at least for their practical uses, alleged or proven. Commonplace field or roadside flowers that few today could name might well have made valued medicines for your great-great-grandmother. That weed in your lawn may have been cherished by the Indians, who seemed to find a use for almost anything that sprouted from the earth. Some of our weediest wildflowers have been cultivated since ancient times for medicines, foods, flavorings, scents, dyes, ropes, and even sources of wines and cordials.

Many books have been written by herbalists and naturopaths on how to use plants to heal or to improve health. Almost half of the medicines in use today employ substances first found in nature, so no doubt there is validity to the use of some plants to treat some ailments. This book merely points out uses to which plants have been put, however, and does not recommend or endorse any plant as a treatment for any illness.

Nor is this book a substitute for a good field guide, several of which are listed in the bibliography. Rather, it picks up where field guides leave off, describing what is interesting about the plants you have already identified, such as their natural history, folklore, habitats, horticulture, uses, origin of their names, and even their place in literature. I have tried to include many of the widespread and most recognized species you are apt to find on a walk or in your backyard, and I have deliberately excluded plants found only in such restricted environments as the seashore or high mountains. While the blossoms of many trees and shrubs could be considered wildflowers, this book covers only herbs—plants whose above-ground parts die back in the winter or after their season of life.

Like birds and other creatures of nature, wildflowers have ranges. The preponderance of plants in this book are found east of the Rockies, both in the United States and southern Canada. Most species range out to the states bordering the Mississippi. Quite a few live coast to coast. Like other creatures, however, wildflowers change their ranges, often heading westward and occasionally eastward. For the sensitive, less adaptable species, ranges tend to grow smaller. Some plants have become so rare that they are

*BLOOM COUNTY, by Berke Breathed. © 1982, Washington Post Writers Group. Reprinted with permission.*

hardly ever found outside special wildflower preserves, the zoos of the plant world.

Of course, uncommon plants should not be picked. Nor should they be dug for transplantation—unless they are certain to be destroyed by a bulldozer or some other machination. They are uncommon usually because they are sensitive to their surroundings, which are difficult to duplicate, or because they have been overpicked or overdug. If you want to try growing rare or fussy flowers, do it with stock from a reputable nursery or with a few seeds gathered from the wild ones you have found. Certainly, plenty of flowers can be picked for bouquets or dug for transplanting without endangering the species' or colony's survival. Oddly enough, these flowers—such as daisies, asters, and goldenrods—are also the ones that usually look best decorating a dining room table or adding color to the backyard.

But whether you see them in your yard, on a roadside, or way off in the woods, enjoy wildflowers for the marvelous creations they are. They have been around far longer than humans, despite our carelessness and callousness. And they bring color and beauty to a world that needs both.

## ~ Spring

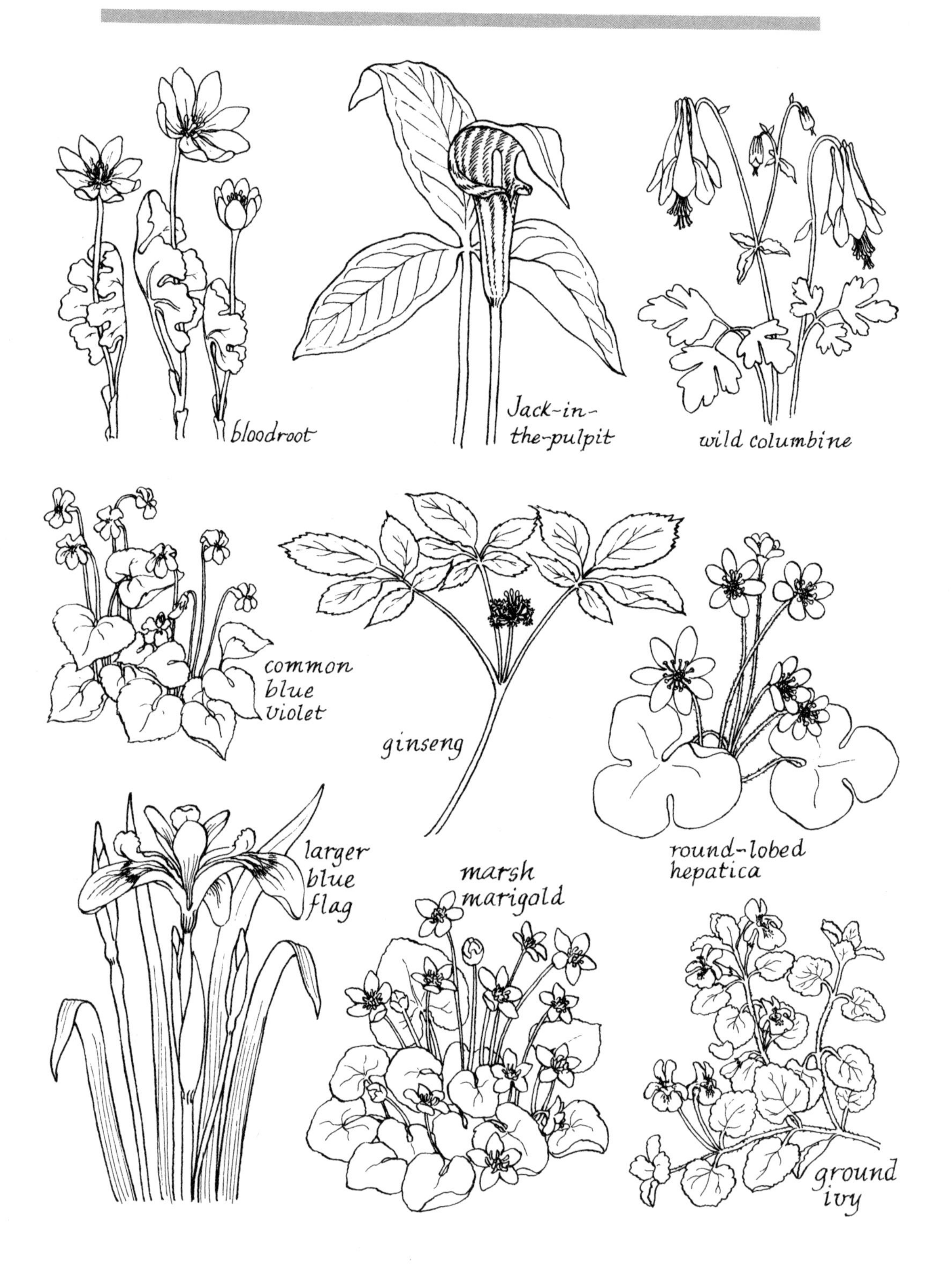

bloodroot
Jack-in-the-pulpit
wild columbine
common blue violet
ginseng
round-lobed hepatica
larger blue flag
marsh marigold
ground ivy

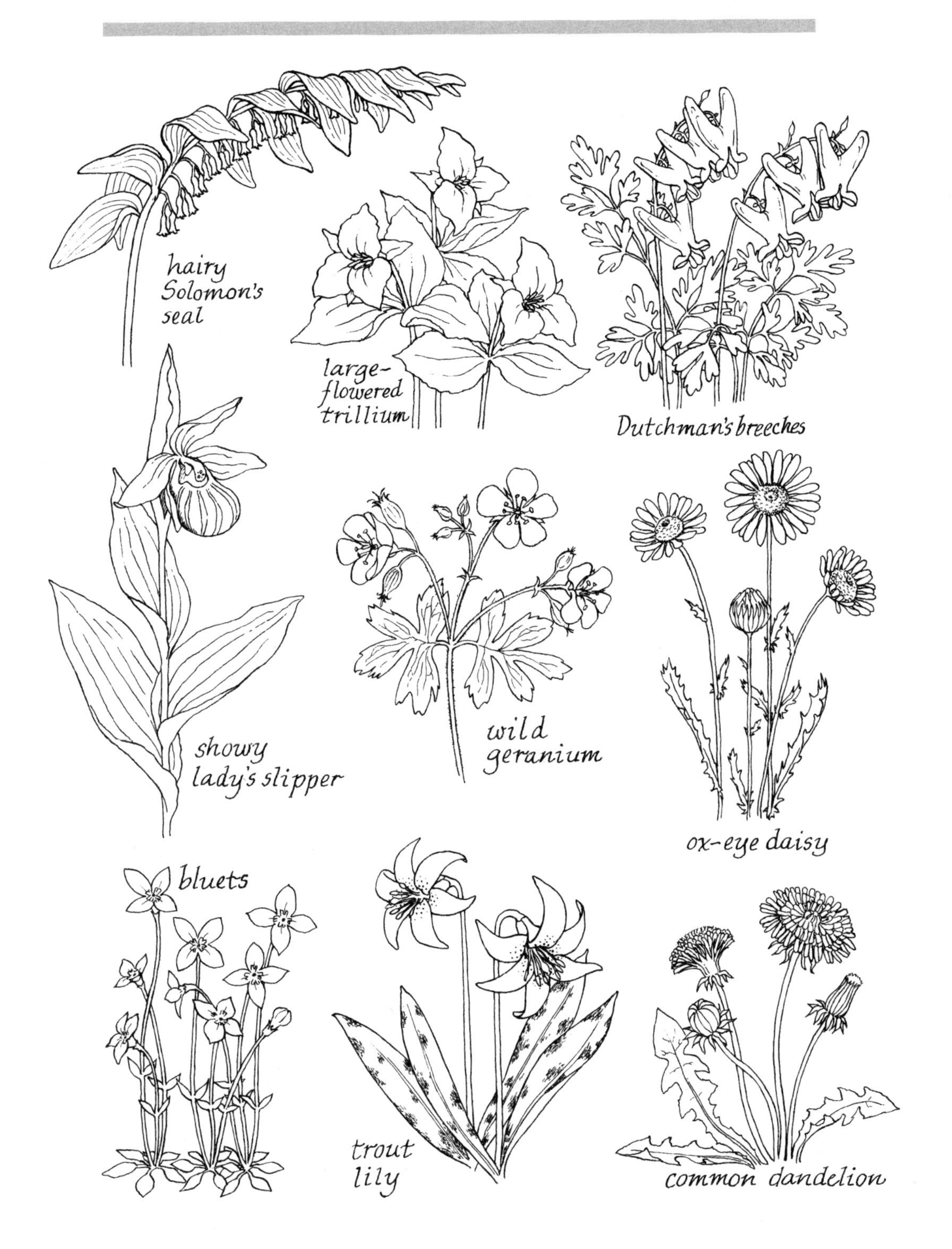
hairy Solomon's seal
large-flowered trillium
Dutchman's breeches
showy lady's slipper
wild geranium
ox-eye daisy
bluets
trout lily
common dandelion

**Skunk Cabbage**
*(Symplocarpus foetidus)*

# *The First Flower of Winter*

In much of North America, skunk cabbage has earned the popular reputation as the first flower of spring. It might be more accurate, however, to call it the first flower of winter. "The skunk cabbage may be found with its round green spear-point an inch or two above the mould in December," reported naturalist John Burroughs. "It is ready to welcome and make the most of the first fitful March warmth."

Henry David Thoreau observed that almost as soon as the leaves wither and die in the fall, new buds begin pushing upward. In fact, he counseled those afflicted with the melancholy of late autumn to go to the swamps "and see the brave spears of skunk cabbage buds already advanced toward the new year."

People living in colder parts of North America have long watched for skunk cabbage as a sign of spring. The tip of the plant's spathe or sheath begins to push through the still-frosty earth and to stand tall when the first faint breaths of warmer air begin blowing. This process can occur in January with an unusually long January thaw—a "goosethaw" as some New Englanders call it—or it can occur as late as March.

## *Bees and Bugs*

Skunk cabbage, *Symplocarpus foetidus*, is both an unusual and an important plant. Tiny and fetid (whence the Latin specific name), the flowers are located on a thick, round spadix hidden within the large green and purple spathe.

Insects, particularly bees, profit from the early blossoms. In March, when the weather gets warm enough to awaken them, bees must look far and wide for food. Skunk cabbages are out in force in bogs and swamps, providing plenty of pollen until early tree flowers, like maples, appear.

Bees visit skunk cabbage in desperation, for the flower's odor—which naturalist Neltje Blanchan describes as combining "a suspicion of skunk, putrid meat, and garlic"—is not attractive to them. Also, because the spathe is designed for smaller insects, bees occasionally get entrapped and the flower becomes their tomb.

The fetid odor is, however, delightful to certain varieties of flies, which detect the smell from long distances and continue transporting pollen when bees have gone on to sweeter-scented blossoms. Sometimes hundreds of flies can be seen swarming around the plants.

Skunk cabbage also attracts certain kinds of carrion beetles, which usually dine on the thawing corpses of animals that died over the winter. Beetles crawl about in the pollen that falls to the base of the spadix inside the sheath and also wander about the flower-bearing spadix itself, no doubt looking for the source of that mouth-watering aroma. Thus tricked, they pick up a few grains of pollen to fertilize the next plant that similarly fools them. According to scientists, the smooth and slippery interior of the spathe keeps beetles from wandering across parts of the plant barren of pollen.

Despite such designs aimed at attracting the "right" insects and protecting pollen for them, skunk cabbages are apparently susceptible to pollen theft by slugs, which are also attracted to the plant. In addition, certain kinds of spiders spin their webs at the entrance of the spathe, catching insects that are supposed to be pollinating the flowers.

### *Summertime Shelter*

After the flowers come the leaves, which by midsummer are usually huge—clusters up to several feet wide. These natural umbrellas provide shelter for various creatures, including birds, frogs, and lizards. The yellowthroat, a variety of warbler, sometimes builds its nest in the hollow of a skunk cabbage, using the foul odor to mask the bird's scent and to discourage investigation by four-footed predators.

This native American plant has a long history of medicinal use. American Indians dressed wounds with a powder obtained from the dried roots, used the huge leaves as poultices, and used root hairs to treat toothaches. The Delaware made a tea for whooping cough from the root and epileptics among them chewed the leaf to avoid seizures. The Nanticoke used skunk cabbage in a cold medicine. Micmacs sniffed bundles of leaves to relieve headaches, though botanical explorer Peter Kalm found that the smell gave him a headache. Skunk cabbage has also been employed to treat asthma, rheumatism, hysteria, dropsy, and other maladies.

One of the more unusual medicinal uses for the plant was in tattooing, an art practiced on the ill by such tribes as the Menomini. Skunk cabbage powder was mixed with pigments and other ingredients, moistened, and then inserted into the skin with a sharp fish tooth. The resulting designs were not so much decorative as they were charms to prevent the return of diseases.

Some Indians made a flour from the dried roots and ate the early spring leaves, which had first to be dried or repeatedly boiled to remove the mouth-blistering calcium oxalate. In large enough doses, skunk cabbage can cause nausea, vomiting, dizziness, and temporary blindness. Yet, though acrid and even toxic to humans, the raw roots are reportedly relished by bears.

Skunk cabbage thrives from Canada to the Carolinas and beyond the Mississippi. Because it is widespread and eye-catching, it has gained a variety of folk names, including skunkweed, polecat weed, meadow cabbage, fetid hellebore, rockweed, swamp cabbage, Midas ears, parson in a pillory, clumpfoot cabbage, polkweed, and collard.

Scientists have disagreed over how the plant should be categorized and named, with some authorities calling it *Spathyema foetida* and others *Ictodes foetidus* (with *Ictodes* meaning "skunk oil"). *Symplocarpus*, the name that has been pretty much settled upon today, is from the Greek words for "connection" and "fruit," descriptive of the closely clustered balls of red berries that appear in late summer.

Dr. Harold Moldenke of the New York Botanical Garden wrote in 1949 that the skunk cabbage's nearest relatives are in Malaysia, where the genus is more common. This distance suggests that when the Northern Hemisphere was warmer, ancestors of our skunk cabbage may have worked their way up the east coast of Asia, across to Alaska via the Aleutians, and headed south. Subsequent ice ages cut the plant's range, and the long line between *Symplocarpus foetidus* and those East Asian ancestors was broken. A similar plant, the yellow skunk cabbage

(*Lysichitum americanum*) of the Pacific Coast states, may share those same ancestors.

### *Beauties*

The flower structure is typical of the Arum family, one of the smallest and most primitive clans of flowering plants. Unlike other large wildflowers, the blossoms are not symmetrical, fragrant beauties. Nonetheless, some people have noticed that the flower-bearing spadix, when removed from the sheath, is not unattractive. In fact, Nelson Coon, in his *Dictionary of Useful Plants*, calls the flower an example of "beauty within the beast," and says he often decorates his dining table with a bouquet of skunk cabbage flowers in the spring. A doctor who lives near me grows skunk cabbages in pots to give to her friends each spring in celebration of the new season.

The showy clusters of leaves are also decorative additions to wet areas. The plants, once established, are long-lasting. Though it is hard to imagine wetlands that lack skunk cabbage, if yours do and you would like some, simply dig up a smaller-size plant in the spring or stick some of the late summer berries into the moist soil.

If you are like Thoreau, you may find hope in the December buds of this well-known plant.

**Round-lobed Hepatica**
*(Hepatica americana)*

## *The Gem of the Woods*

*Blue as the heaven it gazes at,*
*Startling the loiterer in the naked groves*
*With unexpected beauty; for the time*
*Of blossoms and green leaves is yet afar.*

So an unknown poet once described an encounter with one of the first of the truly beautiful spring wildflowers. Made uncommon by overpicking and overdevelopment, the pastel blossoms of hepatica nonetheless can still be found in many woods, clustered in colonies that push through the dead leaves, sometimes even before the snow has melted.

Round-lobed hepatica (*Hepatica americana*), the more common of the two native hepaticas, is a flower of variety. Its blossoms may show up in any of several colors, including white, pink, lavender, purple, and blue, each in a pastel shade that seems too delicate for the harsh weather of April. The flowers may bear from six to eight sepals that look like petals.

The blossoms may or may not be scented. Naturalist John Burroughs, who called hepatica "the gem of the woods," noted its fragrance in several of his essays. "This flower is the earliest, as it is certainly one of the most beautiful, to be found in our woods, and occasionally it is fragrant," he wrote in *A Bunch of Herbs.* "Group after group may be inspected, ranging through all shades of purple and blue, with some perfectly white, and no odor be detected, when presently you will happen upon a little brood of them that have a most delicate and delicious fragrance." Elsewhere he wrote that more often than not scent will be found in white flowers, but that one year after a particularly severe winter almost every blue hepatica he came upon was scented—another of the little unexplained peculiarities that make wildflowers so fascinating.

### *The Liverwort*

The three-lobed leaves of hepatica resemble a liver, and it is not surprising that *Hepatica* comes from the Greek word for "liver." These furry leaves take on a rusty, liverlike color when they dry up later in the season. Leaves remain on the stem through winter and are not replaced by fresh ones until after the plant blooms.

Centuries ago people used the shape or form of a plant as a sign of its medicinal properties; this practice was known as "the doctrine of signatures." Thus, herbs with leaves that were ribbed like a snake's flesh were often used to treat snakebites, and a European version of hepatica was used as a cure for liver ailments. "It is a singular good herb for all diseases of the liver, both to cool and cleanse it, and helps inflammations in any part, and the yellow jaundice," wrote Nicholas Culpeper, a noted seventeenth-century English herbalist who also recommended it for the "bites of mad-dogs."

Some herbals still list hepatica as a remedy for kidney, liver, and bladder ailments and for certain gastric problems, but most modern herbalists consider it useful only for coughs. Hepatica tea has long been used as a treatment for bronchitis and as a diuretic. (A once-popular laxative, called Sal Hepatica or "liver salt," did not use the plant, just the name.) In the mid-1800s a popular patent medicine called "Dr. Rogers' Liverwort and Tar" was used to treat lung afflictions.

The Chippewas used hepatica as a treatment for convulsions, especially in children. They called the plant *gabisanikeag,* which means "it is silent," possibly a reference to its effect on convulsing people. Other American Indians used it to try to straighten crossed eyes. Perhaps the most peculiar use was practiced by the Cherokee, who feared dreams about snakes. Individuals would drink a tea made of hepatica and walking fern. The tea would make them vomit, but would also, supposedly, banish snake dreams. The fresh plant is said to be irritating to the skin and large amounts taken internally can cause poisoning.

### *Other Names*

The use and shape of the leaves and the flower itself have led to a variety of folk names, including liverwort, liverleaf, heart-leaf liverwort, liver-moss, mouse-ears, spring beauty, crystalwort, golden trefoil, ivy flower, herb trinity, and squirrel cup. Sharp-lobed hepatica (*Hepatica acutiloba*), the only other North American species, has a point at the tip of each lobe.

Round-lobed hepatica prefers acid soils. The plant thrives in woodlands, particularly favoring sites under oak trees, and it may also be found in more sunny environs such as pastures. It is widespread, growing west to Manitoba and into Alaska as well as down into northern Florida. Sharp-lobed hepatica likes neutral or slightly alkaline soil and is common in the central United States.

Hepaticas are members of the Crowfoot, or Buttercup, family, and fewer than a half-dozen species are known in the world. The next of kin is the anemone, which can often be found blooming at the same time in the same places. In fact, hepatica was once classified under the genus *Anemone,* and through the years round-lobed hepatica has been known to scientists by at least four names: *Anemone hepatica, Hepatica hepatica, Hepatica triloba*, and the modern *Hepatica americana.* Just in case you care, some authorities suspect that sharp-lobed hepatica may be merely a race of the round-lobed species.

Although I have seen hepatica flowers as early as mid-April, I am told of their appearance in Connecticut in late March. Some observers claim it is the earliest flower of spring, excepting what one author describes as "the plebeian skunk cabbage that ought scarcely be reckoned among true flowers." Burroughs said that in some years he found coltsfoot first, while in others he has found hepatica first. In my yard, coltsfoot usually blooms in March.

F. Schuyler Mathews participated in the debate, noting that some people felt the trailing arbutus was the earliest flower in New England. "I have found the hepatica in some seasons earlier than the trailing arbutus, but this is a matter of personal experience," Mathews wrote. "William Hamilton Gibson asserts positively that the flower is really the first to appear, and I believe he is quite right. It is the easiest thing in the world to pass the hepatica without noticing it, so closely does it snuggle among the withered leaves; on this account, I am inclined to believe it comes and goes quite undiscovered, while the conspicuous arbutus never fails to attract attention."

When the buds push through the leaves—or even snow—they bear many little hairs. "Someone has suggested that the fuzzy little buds look as though they were still wearing their furs as a protection against the wintry weather which so often stretches late into our spring," wrote Mrs. William Starr Dana.

### *Self-fertilizing Flower*

The flower, incidentally, can fertilize itself and does not require visiting insects for pollination. Considering the dearth of insects in the north in March or April, that is not surprising. Some early flies, bees, and butterflies do visit the flowers. The color of the small blue azure butterfly, among the first of its kind to emerge each year, is not unlike the pastel blue found in many hepaticas.

The temptation for woodland walkers to pick this flower is great because it is so colorful among the bleak, dead remnants of last season, and so full of promise of flowers to come. Yet picking is one reason we do not find it more often in our woods and so should be avoided. Hepatica has survived because it is hearty, it spreads readily, and—when left alone—it thrives. Hepaticas can be successfully transplanted, but should never be removed from the wild unless threatened with certain destruction.

Hepatica is considered easy to grow from seeds, which appear a little later in the spring. Use a small bag to grab and handle the tiny seeds, and plant them immediately in appropriate soil. The seeds will germinate in the fall and send up two little seed leaves the next summer. The following spring, the plant should grow to about six inches and produce attractive blossoms at just about the time you are anxious to see the first flowers of the season.

**Wood Anemone**
*(Anemone quinquefolia)*

# *Flowers of the Wind*

Early spring is the windy season, when nature sweeps away the cold and snow and awakens long-sleeping roots with gusts of warmer air. Among the first plants to stir under these beckoning blasts is the appropriately named windflower, also known as wood anemone. This plant and its closely related cousin, rue-anemone, seem too small and delicate to force through the recently thawed earth and survive. Yet on inspection, the wood anemone seems ideally designed to bear the brunt of the strongest spring winds.

"The practical scientist sees in the anemone, trembling and bending before the wind, a perfect adaptation to its environment," noted Neltje Blanchan, a turn-of-the-century naturalist. The plant is "anchored in the light soil by a horizontal rootstock [and is] furnished with a stem so slender and pliable no blast can break it."

Anemones not only are adapted to the harshness of wind but actually take advantage of stiff breezes. Spring clouds often accompany the wind, and when the sky is cloudy, the white flowers nod. Breezes jar pollen loose and carry it to blossoms nearby and below, thus fertilizing flowers without the need for bees or other insects whose numbers are slim so early in the season. Blossoms consequently have no nectar and little scent, devices that other plants use to attract visitors.

## *Windy Ways*

Anemone is based on the Greek word for "wind," whose root word means "breathes" or "lives," and is the same root from which words like "animated" and "animal" stem. Some authorities say the generic name means simply "wind" because the flower was believed to bloom when the wind blows. Other authorities are more specific, maintaining that anemone is a combination of *anemos*, meaning "wind," and *mone*, meaning "habitat," suggesting that the plant lives in windy places. Still other authorities say the genus was named for Anemone, a nymph whom Zephyr loved but who was transformed into a flower by the jealous Flora. Take your pick.

Anemones are members of the Buttercup, or Crowfoot, family, which has about 1,100 species in thirty-five genera worldwide. The genus, *Anemone*, has some 85 species, about 25 of which are found in North America, mostly in colder climates.

## *Gay Circles*

Wood anemone, *Anemone quinquefolia*, is usually found growing in woods, particularly around the roots of trees. Although the flower is solitary, plants usually cluster together, probably to effect pollination by wind. William Cullen Bryant observed:

*Within the woods,*
*Whose young transparent leaves scarce cast*
*A shade, gay circles of anemones*
*Danced on their stalks.*

Wood anemone is more common in the East, and is found from Nova Scotia down into the Georgia highlands and westward to Minnesota. *Quinquefolia* describes the leaves that often, but not always, come in sets of five; in many anemones, leaves are only in threes. The plant's folk names include woodflower, mayflower, nimbleweed, and wild cucumber.

Rue-anemone is often confused with the wood anemone. Both have white, similarly shaped flowers that bloom at the same times and in the same places. Wood anemone has clusters of three to five, deeply cut leaves while rue-anemone has roundish leaves with three to five tips. In addition, wood anemone sends up single flowers while rue-anemone has a single cluster of several blossoms. Both species can have between five and ten petal-like sepals, though neither has petals; wood anemone usually bears five sepals and its cousin, usually six. Found from Ontario and New Hampshire as far south as Florida and as west as Kansas, rue-anemone is monotypic, a species with a genus all to itself.

Bryant's "gay circles of anemones" may have been rue-anemone, often found growing near—even intermixed with—the wood anemone. Rue-anemone is *Anemonella thalictroides*—literally, "little anemone thalictrumlike," thalictrum being the generic name for the meadow-rues, summer-blooming plants that have leaves very similar to those of rue-anemones. (*Thalictrum* itself means "a plant with divided leaves.") Rue, incidentally, has nothing directly to do with sorrow or regret, as in the English noun and verb, but is from the Latin, *ruta*, or the Greek, *rhute*, words that refer to a bitter herb.

## *Elaiosomes*

Anemones are among the many spring woodland plants that make use of ants to spread their seeds. The seed casings bear tasty protuberances called elaiosomes. The ants haul the seeds to their nests, eat the elaiosomes, then discard the seeds in an unused tunnel, where they can sprout in a protected environment. (See Violets: Love in the Springtime.)

For some anemones, such as the European wood anemone, protection may be important. The embryo is not developed when the seed leaves the plant, but forms slowly during the fall and winter and is ready for germination in spring.

Among the many North American members of the genus are such eastern woodland species as the thimbleweeds, *A. virginiana* and *A. cylindrica*, named for their thimblelike seed clusters, and Canada anemone, *A. canadensis*. All look like bleached buttercups and were popular with Indian medicine men. More showy are the beautiful pasque flowers of the western prairies, so called because they bloom around Easter. *A. patens* is a handsome white flower, cuplike and much bigger than the eastern anemones. The western pasque flower, *A. occidentalis*, a mountain species of the Pacific states and British Columbia, has large yellow flowers.

## *Life and Death*

Anemones have a long history of recognition, for better or worse. Windflowers were said to have sprung from the tears of Venus, goddess of love, when she was grief-stricken over the death of her young lover, Adonis. In another legend, Anemos, the wind, used the flowers to herald the coming of spring. Romans carefully picked the first anemone of the year, offering a prayer to protect themselves from fevers.

Crusaders are said to have returned from the Middle East with the beautiful poppy anemone, *A. coronaria.* The sudden appearance in Europe of this red-and-white flower gave rise to tales of its having sprung from drops of Christ's blood, and it became a popular flower in the gardens of medieval monasteries. The flowers have graced gardens for centuries, and *A. coronaria* is the parent of many colorful cultivated anemones.

Some people even believe that Christ spoke of the poppy anemone when he said, "Consider the lilies of the field . . . even Solomon in all his glory was not arrayed like one of these," since the beautiful flower grew in great numbers in the rather bleak hills of its native Palestine.

## *Carrying the Plague*

Oddly enough, European peasants avoided some anemones as if they carried the plague. When peasants came upon a field of these flowers, they would hold their breath and run by, fearing that they would fall ill if they inhaled the vapors. Egyptians considered the flowers a symbol of sickness. The Chinese planted these "flowers of death" on graves.

Nonetheless, old herbalists found the plant useful for headaches, gout, leprosy, eye inflammations, and ulcers. Anemones are generally acrid plants, and many species are said to be somewhat poisonous, but Nicholas Culpeper extoled the bitterness in urging that the plant be chewed to relieve headaches. "And when all is done," he wrote, "let physicians prate what they please, all the pills in the dispensary purge not the head like to hot things held in the mouth."

Indians of Quebec used anemone tea for just about any ailment, while other Indians employed it in treating boils, lung congestion, and eye illnesses. Virgil J. Vogel, in *American Indian Medicine*, reported that the Meskwakis burned seeds to make a smoke that was supposed to revive unconscious persons. Certain Ojibwas used the plant to soothe and prepare their throats for singing.

Modern authorities usually advise against such practices because the plant has some poisonous constituents. Linnaeus reported that underfed cows died from eating European wood anemone, *A. nemorosa*, a closely related species.

## *Culture*

Though not endangered, neither the wood anemone nor rue-anemone is particularly common. These plants should never be picked or transplanted unless transplanting will protect them from certain destruction. If you wish to try to establish them, use seeds acquired in the spring or from a wildflower seed house. Plant wood anemone seeds in the spring and rue-anemone in the fall. Both species favor slightly acid soils in situations similar to those found in open deciduous woods—not too dry and not too wet.

Whether you enjoy them in your garden or in the woods, these two native anemones—true and rue—are sure signs that more spring wildflowers are on their way. I have seen anemones blooming as early as April 15—and as late as May 15. Only skunk cabbage, coltsfoot, arbutus, certain violets, and hepaticas (which are related) may appear earlier in my woods.

Perhaps we can be more happy about seeing them than winter-weary Nathaniel Hawthorne, who wrote his fiancée in 1841: "There has been but one flower found in this vicinity—and that was an anemone, a poor, pale, shivering little flower that had crept under a stone wall for shelter."

**Coltsfoot**
*(Tussilago farfara)*

# *A Roadside Cough Medicine*

In the Northeast, big, bright bunches of yellow and orange heads rise from the ground at the time of the equinox, returning color to the land and offering assurance that the drabness of winter is ending. These flowers belong to coltsfoot, a hearty import from Europe that is marching across the northern United States and southern Canada. The plant grows along highways and in some of our poorest soils. One sizable patch near my house, for example, does well in a roadside shoulder composed chiefly of salty sand that has accumulated from years of sanding during winter storms. These plants seem to require only open sunlight and moist ground.

At a distance, the flowers of coltsfoot are often mistaken for those of the dandelion, but viewed up close, the flowers are distinctly different. Coltsfoot has many yellow rays surrounding an orangish disk, while dandelions have only small tubes with rays. Coltsfoot has a stout stem covered with hairy, scalelike projections, while the dandelion has a slender, smooth stem. Also, coltsfoot blooms well before the leaves emerge, while dandelions show flowers and leaves at the same time.

## *One of a Kind*

In fact, no flower is really like that of *Tussilago farfara.* The plant is the only species within its genus and thus forms a monotypic genus. Coltsfoot's native territory is northern Europe, North Africa, and Asia. In North America, it seems to be pushing westward from the Atlantic Coast states and provinces into Minnesota and beyond, favoring cooler climates and blooming in March or, if the winter has been harsh or late, in early April.

Few people associate the roundish leaves, which appear later in the spring and last until early fall, with the flowers that bloomed months earlier. The leaves are rather large and similar to the hoofprint of an unshod horse, earning the plant its name. Coltsfoot has a bad reputation among farmers in England, where it sometimes infests plowlands. The wide leaves come up at about the same time as grain, and can blanket large areas of fields.

Coltsfoot, though, has largely been considered a friend. In fact, in 1971 Czechoslovakia issued a commemorative postage stamp in its honor. For many years its leaf was the symbol for apothecary shops in France. A concoction from coltsfoot served as a popular cough remedy, for the plant contains mucilage, which coats and soothes an irritated throat. The generic name is based on the Latin, *tussis*, and means "cough dispeller." Robitussin, a patent cough medicine, uses the same root word.

When youngsters in New England came down with a cough or cold, they ate coltsfoot candies, made by boiling down a mixture of fresh leaves and water, removing the leaves, adding lots of sugar, boiling the mixture to a thick syrup, and dropping the syrup by the spoonful into cold water. In a popular liquid form of the medicine, a mixture of leaves and water was boiled down and honey added for flavoring.

Strange as it may seem, asthmatics used to smoke coltsfoot to gain relief. "The fume of the dried leaves taken through a funnell or tunnell, burned upon coles, effectually helpeth those that are troubled with the shortnesse of breath, and fetch their winde thicke and often," wrote John Gerard. Gypsies long used the dried leaves as a tobacco. The leaves were also important in the concoction of an English pipe mixture called "British Herb Tobacco."

Although the plant was employed mainly for respiratory problems, Nicholas Culpeper, another early herbalist, listed all sorts of maladies it would address, among them "St. Anthony's fire" and "burnings." "[It] is singular good to take away wheals and small pushes that arise through heat, as also the burning heat of the piles or privy parts, cloths wet therein being thereunto applied," he wrote. Coltsfoot was used to treat diarrhea, insect bites, inflammations, leg ulcers, and phlebitis. Dried leaves were brewed as an aromatic tea, and the ashes obtained by burning the leaves were once used to season foods.

Studies in Japan have found, though, that the flowers cause liver tumors in rats. The plant is best used for nonmedicinal purposes. In the past Scottish Highlanders stuffed mattresses with seed hairs, while English peasants used to soak leaves in a saltpeter solution to produce a taper that burns as bright as a torch.

Coltsfoot is an important bee plant, providing nectar early in the season when there are few other flowers. Coltsfoot can self-pollinate, though, so it does not depend entirely on bees to perform this service. Self-pollination occurs when flowers close up, pressing male and female parts together.

### *A Study in Survival*

Coltsfoot is a study in highly evolved survival techniques. The flowers flourish at a harsh time of the year when temperatures may vary dozens of degrees, often dipping below freezing. The stalk, or "scape," is covered with hairy scales to retain heat and insulate against icy blasts. Some scientists think these scales are tinged red to enable the plant to absorb the sun's heat better.

As the stalk arises, the closed flower head is usually turned toward the ground, as protection against both cold and rain. When the plant blooms, the head straightens and faces the sun. The flower closes at night and stays closed on cold or cloudy days, conserving heat and displaying the blossom only when insects are likely to appear.

The disk is composed of about forty tightly packed florets, shaped like upside-down bells. These florets serve the male function of giving off pollen. The numerous ray florets around the outside of the disk possess female parts, and project pollen-catching stigmas. Thus, an insect drawn to the bright flower wanders around the disk, easily extracting nectar from the conveniently compact florets and picking up pollen. The insect then takes off for another flower, lands on the rays (which act as landing strips), and brushes against ray-flower stigmas. The stigmas rake off pollen and become fertilized. Coltsfoot, a typical Composite, has thus used its colony of two different flowers to efficiently attract, reward, and extract payment from an insect.

When sufficiently fertilized, the head folds up and again droops for protection. Disk florets, rays, and bracts quickly die, focusing all the plant's energy on developing seeds. A few days later the head stands up again and opens a dandelionlike "clock" of fuzz-topped seeds, ready for spring breezes to catch and carry them to distant fields. Coltsfoot seeds have been known to travel more than 8.6 miles.

While seeds are important for creating new colonies, coltsfoot can also expand by sending out underground runners. These runners can establish new plants even if they are broken off from the parent plant, so it is difficult to eradicate a colony simply by digging or plowing it up.

Though the task of the flower is now complete, the season has hardly begun. As flowers die, leaves appear. They grow only a few inches off the ground but are up to ten inches across. At first the leaves wear a coating of "fur" on their upper surface to protect them from the cold, but this fur is shed as the weather warms. (Cottony hair under the leaf, retained to keep moisture and dust away from the breathing pores, or "stomata," was once gathered by English villagers for tinder.)

The chief function of these large leaves is to manufacture food to store as starch in the roots, nourishment for the next year's flowers. The leaves also provide shade, cutting off light to other plants that might want a homesite, and preventing evaporation from the moist ground—the plant likes wet feet. And finally, the leaves collect rain and direct it down the stalk to the roots below.

### *Farmyard Names*

Its medicinal properties have earned coltsfoot its other common name, coughwort, but the plant has a whole farmyard full of folk names including horsefoot, horsehoof, dovedock, sowfoot, colt-herb, hoofs, cleats, ass's-foot, bull's-foot, foalfoot, foalswort, ginger, clayweed (reflecting the habitat it likes), butterbur, and dummy weed. One of its oldest names is *Filius-ante-patrem*, Latin for "son before father," because the flowers show up before the leaves do. *Farfara*, incidentally, is an old word for the white poplar tree, whose leaves are similar to those of coltsfoot. (Coltsfoot is sometimes applied to our marsh marigold, which is not related. Sweet coltsfoot, *Petasites*, is related and is usually found in more northern climates.)

Coltsfoot is a perennial that is easy to establish. Obtain seeds from freshly opened clocks and plant them in wet, clayish soil. The plant will grow and spread quickly. Although a century ago coltsfoot was so uncommon that even North American wildflower experts had trouble figuring out what it was, it now grows widely in the cooler East. In the coming decades, it will probably work its way across the continent and maybe even into southern states.

Spring flowers bring color to eyes accustomed to the monotony of brown and white. For splashes of lively color after the snows melt, coltsfoot can't be beat, an opinion no doubt shared by Alfred Williams, who in the last century wrote:

*A thousand years will come and go,*
*And thousands more will rise,*
*My buried bones to dust will grow*
*And dust defile my eyes.*
*But when the lark sings o'er the world*
*And the swallow weaves her nest,*
*My soul will take the coltsfoot gold*
*And blossom on my breast.*

**Bloodroot**
*(Sanguinaria canadensis)*

# A Bloody Early Bloomer

Perhaps it is because we have been so long without flowers that the earliest seem to be among the most beautiful: exotic, orange-red columbines; dainty, pastel hepaticas; bright, golden coltsfoot; deep, ivory anemones; and pure, white bloodroot. It is ironic that a flower named for so strong a color bears petals that are pure white, but "blood" refers to the orange-red juice, which can be seen in the reddish stem and on your fingers if you pick one.

Bloodroot rises from the cold earth as soon as it can. "It is singular how little warmth is necessary to encourage these . . . flowers to put forth," wrote John Burroughs in 1871. "It would seem as if some influence must come on in advance underground and get things ready, so that, when the outside temperature is propitious, they at once venture out. I have found the bloodroot when it was still freezing two or three nights a week. . . ."

I have found bloodroot flowers as early as April 13 in Connecticut, but they are more common at the beginning of May. Flowering requires a lot of work for a plant, and work requires energy and food. Bloodroot and other early bloomers can put on their floral shows so early because they have stored food over the previous season in their thick roots, corms, or bulbs. Most plants that flower in late spring, summer, or fall rely on food produced in the current season.

## Endearing Arrival

Bloodroot's arrival is almost endearing. Both the budded stalk and the plant's single leaf arise together, but in no ordinary fashion. The leaf is wrapped around the stem and bud, like a mother protecting its baby with a cloak. As the bud is ready to blossom, it pushes itself a bit higher so that when the petals open, they are still given a degree of protection by the enveloping leaf.

And well they should be protected. The petals, from seven to twelve of them, are so delicate that the blossoms often last only a day or two before a strong wind or a heavy spring shower rips them away. Probably for this reason, bloodroot has never evolved into a particularly popular garden plant. "This is the reason why some of our most beautiful wild flowers are not cultivated by florists," wrote naturalist F. Schuyler Mathews in 1901. "It does not pay to spend much time over such ephemeral lives."

Mathews could not have known that one freak bloodroot plant, found in the Midwest around 1950, would produce a variety whose flowers are more durable. "Peony flowers" or double bloodroots (*Sanguinaria canadensis multiplex* or *florepleno*) have all descended from that one plant.

## *A Poppy*

As its shape suggests, *Sanguinaria canadensis* is a member of the Poppy (*Papaveraceae*) family, a small group of some 115 species in twenty-three genera, found mostly in north temperate zones. The name refers to the orange red, bloodlike color of its juice, and to a portion of its range; it was probably first identified in Canada. The only member of its genus in the world, bloodroot is nonetheless widespread, found wild from Nova Scotia to Florida and as far west as Manitoba and Nebraska. It has been exported to Europe, where it also does well.

Bloodroot is also known as coon root, snakebite (from its poisonous characteristic), sweet slumber (it was used to induce sleep), red root, corn root, turmeric, and tetterwort.

The plant's juice is so abundant and such a potent dye that several wildflower manuals warn against picking the flowers because the fluid will stain everything it touches. Indians knew this, and used the juice mixed with animal fat to paint their faces (whence another name, Indian paint), dye baskets, decorate weapons and implements, and color clothing. Colonists were quick to follow suit. With alum as a mordant, or stabilizing agent, they used bloodroot to dye cloth—particularly wool—a reddish orange hue. Even the French imported bloodroot as a dye.

## *Medicinal Uses*

Medicine men in various tribes noticed that, when injured, the plant "bled" like a human, and they took this as a sign that bloodroot was good for treating ulcers, ringworm, and other skin afflictions. After learning of these uses, a London physician of the mid-nineteenth century concocted a treatment for skin cancers by mixing bloodroot, zinc chloride, flour, and water. The treatment, used extensively at London's Middlesex Hospital, eventually fell out of use, but was resumed in the 1960s for minor cancers of the nose and ear.

The juice's color may have also led to its widespread use among the Algonkian nations as a blood purifier. Calling the plant "puccoon" or "paucon," a name that refers to the red juice, some tribes used it to treat cramps, stop vomiting, induce abortions, and even repel insects. According to Gladys Tantaquidgeon, a Mohegan who recorded folk medicines of Indians of the northeastern United States, "For general debility, a pea-sized piece of root is taken every morning for thirty days."

The plant contains protopine, also found in opium, and the powder and tinctures obtained from the rootstock have also been used by North Americans for several centuries to treat a variety of ailments. *Ladies' Indispensable Assistant* (1852) said bloodroot "is excellent in coughs and croup. It is an emetic, and narcotic; produces perspiration, and menstrual discharge; is good in influenza, hooping cough, and phthisic [lung disease]. It is good in bilious complaints, combined with black cherrytree bark, also in cases of scarlet fever and catarrh." Indians and colonists would put a few drops of the juice on a lump of maple sugar, which they would suck to relieve coughs and sore throats. Sugar was necessary because the taste is said to be so nauseating that it can cause "expectorant action."

Some modern herbalists warn that if juice gets on the skin it may cause an allergic reaction similar to that of poison ivy. Modern herbals describe its uses, but often warn that the plant is so strong that it should not be used without medical supervision. An overdose can kill a person, though its taste is so awful it is hard to believe anyone could swallow that much without causing that "expectorant action."

Medicine men and herbalists alike apparently overlooked bloodroot's chief modern use. In 1983, Vipont Laboratories began using an extract of bloodroot in Viadent toothpaste and mouth rinse. The American Dental Association said that the extract, called sanguinarine, was a promising plaque-fighter. A former surgeon general of the Army Dental Corps called it "the best thing that's happened since fluoride. What fluoride has done in fighting tooth decay, this material will do in preventing gum disease."

Bloodroot is a fine, early spring plant for rich woods or shady borders. Although it transplants readily in the spring, it is not overly common in many areas and should not be removed from natural habitats, unless the locality is in danger of destruction or has an overabundance of plants. It is better to obtain seeds, which have a good germination rate. Because they will self-sow fairly readily, the plants can, in good situations, form large colonies. If the weather is not too harsh, blossoms can last for a week or more.

### *Trickery*

Bloodroot flowers manage pollination by trickery. The blossoms have no nectar, but their inviting petals and bright yellow anthers (the part of the stamen that bears the pollen) attract insects, which transfer pollen picked up during their hopeless search for sweets. The visit is not a total loss for bees and other pollen-eating insects.

After writing an article on bloodroot for *Wildflower* magazine, I heard from an Ontario enthusiast who said flowers bloom in his area long before bees are around to be tricked. His observations indicated the plants readily self-pollinate. "This is corroborated to some extent by examination: The stamens form a tight ring around the stigma and it is quite easy for the pollen, ejected from their sacs, to hit the stigma." No doubt, the colder the climate, the less likely this early bloomer is to be visited by bees. Like other flowers, especially at this time of year, they are apparently able to produce seed with or without insect help.

**Common Dandelion**
*(Taraxacum officinale)*

## *Our Tulips in the Grass*

To many homeowners the dandelion is little more than a prolific, pesky weed. To others, however, this abundant yellow-flowering plant provides not only beauty, but food, drink, medicine, and even inspiration for poetry.

Perhaps no one has praised the dandelion better than Wallace Nutting, the noted turn-of-the-century photographer and author. "The dandelion is the greatest natural agent of decoration in our part of America," he wrote in *Connecticut Beautiful* in 1923. "In some fields it is so abundant that there is no more than enough grass visible to give it a setting. . . . It is so thoroughly at home that we feel it to be the most prominent and persistent native American, whatever its origin. Coming as it does in the early spring, it clothes an entire landscape with its gorgeous color, and rejoices the heart of man. . . . It is our tulip in the grass."

Among our thousands of species of wildflowers, the common dandelion may be the most common; probably its only close competitor is the common chickweed. Not only are its numbers great, but its flowering season is one of the longest of any of our plants. I have seen plants blooming in every month of the year in Connecticut, though finding one in January or February is rare.

### *Where'd It Come From?*

Most authorities report that the common dandelion came here from Europe, but originated in Asia Minor. It spread like wildfire across the continent, as it has across most of the civilized world. Even the most casual observer of flora knows why. The dandelion's highly efficient system of transmitting seeds makes use of the wind, which can carry its fuzz-topped fruits long distances in a stiff breeze.

Besides ensuring the species' survival, these seeds provide entertainment for millions of children. What youngster has never blown or waved the seed-laden stalks and watched with glee as the "fuzzies" floated off? Years ago, children used to "tell" the hour of the day by counting the number of times they had to blow before all of the seeds would separate from the head, or by counting the number of seeds remaining after one good blow. That's why the fuzz-heads are often called "clocks" and the plant is sometimes called "blowball."

Maidens would blow at the ball, and the remaining seeds would foretell the number of children they'd have when they were grown and married. Girls would play "he loves me, he loves me not" while boys would play the "she" version, blowing the clocks down to the last seed.

Another favorite pastime of children, particularly girls, was making chains, bracelets, and curls from the scapes, or hollow flower stems. Charles F. Millspaugh, a scientist, employed his technical training to describe this pastime in *American Medicinal Plants* in 1892: "The curls are formed as follows: a split is started in four directions at the smaller end of a scape, into which the tongue is deftly and gradually inserted, causing a slow separation into sections that curl backward, revolutely, being kept up to their form by the tongue, when the scape is curled to the end it is drawn several times through the operator's mouth and partially uncurled into graceful ringlets."

James Russell Lowell was much less technical. "My childhood's earliest thoughts are linked with thee," he wrote in "To the Dandelion":

*Dear common flower, that grow'st beside the way,*
*Fringing the dusty road with harmless gold*
*First pledge of blithesome May,*
*Which children pluck, and, full of pride uphold,*
*High-hearted buccaneers, o'erjoyed that they*
*An Eldorado in the grass have found,*
*Which not the rich earth's ample round*
*May match in wealth, thou are more dear to me*
*Than all the prouder summer-blooms may be.*

### *Little Flowers*

Unless you inspect the dandelion closely, you may think the bloom is just a mass of yellow petals or "rays." Each of the hundred or more rays is actually a tiny, tube-shaped flower. Long, straplike rays extend from the top, outside edge of those tubes.

Thus, one dandelion flower is actually a composite of many little ones, which is why the plant is a member of the huge Composite family. Composites are considered among the most advanced and successful family of flowers, and surely the dandelion is no exception.

Like many Composites, dandelions open in the morning and close in the evening. The head closes quickly with the first few drops of rain, perhaps a remnant of a stage in its evolution when it needed to protect its nectar and pollen. Closing the flower head helps to preserve heat on cool, early spring nights. Its tightly shut appearance has given the flower one of its less attractive folk names, swine's snout.

It is interesting to observe that dandelion flowers are usually only a little higher off the ground than the surrounding vegetation. In a frequently cut lawn or on waste ground without much vegetation, they tend to stay low; in a field, their scapes will send them up twelve to eighteen inches off the ground—whatever is needed to best catch those seed-dispersing breezes.

### *Apomixis*

Unlike most Composites, dandelions do not need their showy displays to attract insects, though insects will visit them. The genus is apomict; that is, it produces seeds without pollination. Because such seeds are genetically identical to the parent plant, apomixis tends to make life tough for botanists because countless "mini-species" of the genus are created. Every time a significant mutation occurs and a plant successfully produces seeds that spread and germinate, a new "species" is born.

While most texts identify only a handful of dandelion species in a given area, expert botanists can find enough differences to identify hundreds of species. In England alone, more than 150 dandelions have been identified.

You, too, can notice different types or subspecies. For example, in dry open fields at higher elevations, dandelions tend to have small flowers; in waste places, such as along roadsides, they tend to be large and coarse; and in wetlands, they often develop red leaf-veins.

When each dandelion's blooming period is completed, the flower head folds up for several days and then reopens wide with its array of "fuzzies" to catch the wind. When the seeds have blown away, a smooth, rounded, white button remains, the inspiration for such names as monk's head and priest's crown. These names refer to the Medieval custom of tonsure, in which the top of a priest's or monk's head was shaven clean as a sign of his eschewing vanity and other worldly ways.

The dandelion has also been called milk gowan by the English, reflecting the whitish juice that also made an impression on the Chippewas, who called it by a name that meant "milk root." That "milk" is sticky and contains latex. The Russians have done considerable experimentation with hybrids of the Russian dandelion or chew-root (*Taraxacum kok-saghyz*), which it is said can yield three or four times the latex of ordinary dandelions. In the United States there have been experiments with making rubber from our dandelions, but none has proved commercially feasible.

Other names include doon-head, puffball, yellow gowan (gowan is an Old World daisylike flower), Irish daisy, cankerwort, and lion's tooth.

### *The Lion and Its Teeth*

"Dandelion" is a corruption of the French *dents de lion*, tooth of the lion, a name that is applied to the plant in almost every European tongue. Experts disagree on the origin of the name. Most think it is related to the deeply toothed leaves that could be said to resemble lions' teeth. Some, however, maintain the name is connected with the flower's color, which is the same as the yellow used for heraldic lions.

Common dandelion, *Taraxacum officinale*, is one of three *Taraxacum* species found in North America, and one of about two dozen known in the world. The generic name is from the Greek, meaning "to disquiet," probably referring to its ancient medicinal use as a stimulant. *Officinale* is a Latin word that means "a shop where things are sold," and suggests that herbalists kept this plant among their wares. Botanists never seem satisfied with a name, though, and this species has also been known off and on since 1753 as *Leontodon taraxacum*, with *Leontodon* meaning literally "lion's tooth."

While our word for the plant is from the French, the French have often called the plant *pissenlit*—politely translatable as "wetting the bed"—because children believed that eating or even picking the flowers would cause them to wet their beds at night. Perhaps it's one of the hazards of curl making.

## *Remedies*

The bed-wetting belief may have been connected with the fact that since the Middle Ages, the root was used as a diuretic in the treatment of liver and kidney disorders. One modern British herbalist maintains the plant is far better as a diuretic than drugs chemically produced by pharmaceutical companies. According to Mr. Millspaugh, the dandelion "is one of those drugs, overrated, derogated, extirpated, and reinstated time and again by writers upon pharmacology."

Indeed, dandelion's deep-growing root has had many uses besides sparking the ire of homeowners and keeping herbicide manufacturers in business. The root has been an ingredient in many patent medicines for dyspepsia, constipation, gallstones, insomnia, dropsy, and jaundice. Culpeper, the Elizabethan herbalist, even claimed "This herb helps one to see farther without a pair of spectacles."

The roasted and ground root has been used for dandelion coffee, and some feel it improves the taste of real coffee when added to the ground beans. Euell Gibbons maintained that the roasted root produces the best-tasting coffee substitute found in the wild on this continent. Many people dig up the roots in spring and slice them into salads or boil them as one would a parsnip, to which they are alike in consistency but not in taste.

The deep root is important in survival, for it enables the plant to go far down in the earth for water and thus to withstand dry spells that would kill other plants or make them dormant. The deep root also makes it difficult for animals or humans to dig or pull up the plant and subsequently eat it. In these respects, and in the root's popularity as food and drink, the plant is much like its cousin, chicory.

## *Good Eating*

Young leaves have long been used in salads and are still sold in some grocery stores. Many people boil the leaves and serve them like spinach. "Young dandelion leaves make delicious sandwiches, the tender leaves being laid between slices of bread and butter, sprinkled with salt," wrote Maude Grieve in *A Modern Herbal* in 1931. "The addition of a little lemon juice and pepper varies the flavor. The leaves should always be torn to pieces, rather than cut, in order to keep the flavor."

A friend of mine boils the fresh spring leaves about six minutes until they are tender, then mixes them with some salt pork that has been rendered with a little garlic. "It's super," she says. Bradford Angier, who wrote *Feasting Free on Wild Edibles*, liked his leaves scrambled with eggs. Apaches were said to be so fond of dandelions that they would search for days to find enough to satisfy themselves—an amount that was said to exceed belief.

It should be emphasized that only the young leaves are used; older mature leaves are too bitter to eat unless they are boiled twice, changing the water after the first boiling. True dandelion-leaf aficionados, doing what the chicory and endive fans do to produce "witloof," keep roots in the cellar, forcing them in winter or even year-round to obtain blanched, tasty leaves for salads. A hundred years ago many seed catalogs carried dandelions, even some "improved" hybrids.

## *Underground Babies*

Dandelions are able to bloom so early in the season, often long before the last frost, because the flowers are formed at the top of the root and are protected by several inches of soil. As soon as the weather turns nice for a bit, the buds, all ready to go, shoot up and open. The flower heads are popular as food, even before they're "born." These subterranean buds are boiled and served with butter and seasoning. Buds and blossoms may also be prepared by dipping them in batter and frying them as fritters, although Gibbons insisted that developing buds dug from beneath the ground tasted better than ones that have seen the light of day.

The blossoms are often used to prepare an excellent wine. I have never had the patience to make dandelion wine, but have been given several bottles of homemade stock over the years. It was a thick, rather sweet, and tasty concoction.

### *Nutritious*

The consumption of sundry parts of the dandelion dates back to ancient times. Its popularity may be related not only to its flavor and availability, but also to recognition of its food value. Ancient Egyptians were known to prescribe the plant for various ailments that were probably caused by dietary deficiencies. Today it is known that the plant is rich in vitamins and minerals, especially in Vitamin A.

Animals also find the dandelion a tasty treat. Birds, of course, eat the seeds, as do small animals, such as mice. Rabbits, pigs, and goats enjoy the entire plant. While cows usually shun the plant because of its rather bitter-tasting juice, it has been said that when cows eat dandelions, their milk production will increase.

For bees and dozens of other kinds of insects, the dandelion is an important supply of food, not because it produces abundant nectar but because it blooms at the edges of the season when other flowers are scarce.

To poet Lowell, however, dandelions were much more than food and medicine. He concluded his poem:

*How like a prodigal doth nature seem,*
*When thou, for all thy gold, so common art!*
*Thou teachest me to deem*
*More sacredly of every human heart,*
*Since each reflects in joy its scanty gleam*
*Of heaven, and could some wondrous secret show,*
*Did we but pay the love we owe,*
*And with a child's undoubting wisdom look*
*On all these living pages of God's book.*

Without a doubt, the dandelion is no ordinary weed, if we only "with a child's undoubting wisdom look." Berke Breathed's famous comic strip character, Opus, has long shown this wisdom. When life becomes too stressful, Opus seats himself among the flowers in a lawn, taking a "dandelion break." He is a penguin of good taste.

**Wild Columbine**
*(Aquilegia canadensis)*

## *An Elfin Beauty*

Few plants have generated as much admiration as American columbine. "Our columbine is at all times and in all places one of the most exquisitely beautiful of flowers," wrote John Burroughs, one of its many fans. Europeans had long ago admired its beauty, importing American columbine to their gardens in the early 1600s after it was first collected by John

Tradescant, a noted naturalist of his time. In a 1940s survey of hundreds of North American naturalists, American columbine ranked as the seventh most popular native wildflower.

This much-praised plant is infrequently seen, since it prefers remote locations like rocky cliffs and outcroppings. It is not unusual to find a clump of plants growing from a handful of soil in a pocket on a huge boulder.

Yet columbine suffers from human intervention through habitat destruction and destruction of individual plants. Too often people who are lucky enough to find columbine succumb to the temptation to pick it. Or, out of misplaced pity, they try to dig it up and move it from its barren, rocky home to some crowded garden, where it loses some of its natural attractiveness and probably the proper habitat for continued good health.

"It contrives to secure a foothold in the most precipitous and uncertain of nooks, its jewel-like flowers gleaming from their lofty perches with a graceful insouciance which awakens our sportsmanlike instincts and fires us with the ambition to equal it in daring and make its loveliness our own," wrote Mrs. William Starr Dana. "Perhaps it is as well if our greediness be foiled and we get a tumble for our pains, for no flower loses more with its surroundings than the columbine."

Lest those who have never seen American columbine (*Aquilegia canadensis*) confuse it with the garden varieties, there is no real comparison. "Although under cultivation the columbine nearly doubles its size," wrote Neltje Blanchan, "it never has the elfin charm in a conventional garden that it possesses wild in nature's."

Nor do cultivated varieties, most of which descend from a European species, possess the color or fine form of wild columbine. No other wildflower in the eastern United States has the same scarlet color, brightened by a sort of translucence. This rich exterior is complemented by a bright, yellow interior and yellow around the mouth.

### *Clever Design*

The color and shape of the blossom are part of nature's clever design, long in evolution. Each flower consists of five long tubes or spurs that hold nectar deep inside and away from thieving insects. These tubes are longer in native wild species than in European or cultivated varieties. The common Continental wild columbine is blue, a color that attracts bees; bees can easily reach into the shorter tubes to extract sweets.

American columbine, however, is red, a color that attracts ruby-throated hummingbirds. Not coincidentally, hummingbirds are the only creatures that can easily suck nectar from the flowers and, in so doing, pollinate them. The yellow opening and interior are said to guide the bird into the flower. Ms. Blanchan went so far as to suggest in 1900 that probably to the hummingbird "and no longer to the outgrown bumblebee, has the flower adapted itself." Although some bees, wasps, and other insects cheat the system by nibbling through the end of the spur to get nectar, only the largest, strongest, and largest-tongued insects can draw nectar from the tube.

Hummingbirds, incidentally, are not found in Europe. It is interesting to note, too, that many of the columbines in the western United States are white, yellow, or blue—colors that do not attract hummingbirds. These varieties use insects for pollination and consequently many have evolved shapes more convenient for bees and flies. While American columbine is tubular, many western columbines are more open, with a display of beckoning petals. In addition, these western flowers are positioned horizontally, convenient to insects, while American columbine dangles flowers upside down, which is fine for hummingbirds.

### *A Buttercup*

Few people would guess that this oddly shaped flower is a member of the Buttercup family and that it is closely related to anemones and hepaticas, which bloom a bit earlier in spring.

*Aquilegia* is a small genus of fifty species worldwide, but limited to north temperate zones. While easterners have only one native, *A. canadensis*, some fifteen or twenty species live in the West, particularly in the Rockies where they find the kind of cold they seem to like. Colorado's state flower is Rocky Mountain blue columbine, *A. caerulea.*

*Aquilegia* may come from the Latin for "eagle" because of a fancied resemblance of the flower's spurs to an eagle's talons. Or it may be a combination of *aqua*, "water," and *lego*, "to collect," a reference to the nectar-holding spurs.

A bird of peace, not of war, figures into the common English name. Columbine is from the Latin, *columba*, meaning "dove." Some people say the name stems from an imagined likeness of the flowers—probably of a European species—to a flight of doves. Others say the resemblance is to a circle of doves or pigeon heads, a design commonly painted on dishes and other circular objects long ago.

Other folk names for the plant include culverwort (from the Saxon, *culfre*, meaning "pigeon" and *wyrt*, "plant"), rock bells, honeysuckle, rock lily, bells, meeting houses, cluckies, and Jack-in-trousers—a name that sounds rather risqué and may well be.

### *Poisoning the Kids*

Years ago New Englanders used to honor veterans, especially on Memorial or Decoration Day, by garnishing their graves with wild columbine and other flowers that would produce a red, white, and blue combination. The plant has some medicinal history, although few people today would think of picking one to make a lotion for sore mouths or throats.

"The seed taken in wine causeth a speedy delivery of women in childbirth," wrote the English herbalist Nicholas Culpeper. The common European or garden variety (*A. vulgaris*) was once fairly frequently used in Europe for this and other ailments—until physicians found that children were being poisoned by overdoses and that other herbs served their purposes better and more safely.

Young Meskwaki Indians mixed ripe seed capsules with smoking tobacco to improve the tobacco's smell. They believed that the seeds smoked or added to a potion yielded a sort of love perfume, handy when courting. Other groups of Indians ate the roots and used the seeds for a tea to treat headaches and fever.

We might better use the seeds in establishing and spreading this uncommon perennial. Columbine favors dry, not too rich, rocky woods and outcroppings with a soil pH of 5 to 7.5. The plant spreads well from seeds that can be gathered in July or purchased from wildflower nurseries, some of which also carry plants. Columbine should never be transplanted from the wild unless it is threatened with certain destruction.

Remember to plant columbine in an area that is like its natural situation. "Nothing is daintier or more beautiful than the color effect of this graceful blossom among the gray rocks of a hillside pasture," said F. Schuyler Mathews. Once it is established, you, too, might be able to feel a little of the healing properties that Ralph Waldo Emerson once described: "A woodland walk, a quest for river-grapes, a mocking thrush, a wild rose or rock-living columbine, salve my worst wounds."

**Dutchman's Breeches**
*(Dicentra canadensis)*

# *Rude Little Trousers*

Some wildflower enthusiasts seem almost to swoon over Dutchman's breeches, an uncommon and unusual species that was once subject of fiery debate. John Burroughs counted it "among our prettiest spring flowers," though I prefer the description of the author who called it one of the "daintiest."

What you call a flower can be a matter of controversy, especially if you lived in Victorian times. For it was then that one Dr. Abbott raged: "To think that such a plant should be called 'Dutchman's breeches'! If this abomination were dropped from *Gray's Manual*, perhaps in time a decent substitute would come in use." Dr. Abbott offered "dicentra," the generic name, as an alternative.

Although he admitted the name is "rather rude," F. Schuyler Mathews defended its use. Unlike *dicentra*, a Latin word that would be "enigmatic or meaningless" to most Americans, "Dutchman's breeches means something, and it does not seem quite abominable if we look at it from the right point of view. I like the name because of its Knickerbocker flavor, and although it is suggestive of a bit of rude humor, it is not without a certain poetic significance," he wrote.

The flowers are, after all, peculiar things, much like the garden bleeding hearts to which they are closely related. However, they lack the color of the cultivated *Dicentra* and bear flowers that are mostly white with a bit of yellow. And they are shaped like a pair of old-fashioned knickers.

But to some Victorians, talking about the clothing that covered that part of the body was not the stuff of garden club meetings, and even Mr. Mathews (perhaps knowing that the original meaning of "breech" is "buttocks," or "rump") admitted that "breeches . . . sounds a bit unrefined." He added, though, that if we were to use the more proper "pants," we would lose the flavor of the name. Imagine Henry Hudson clothed in "Dutchman's pants," he said. "Presto! all the poetry attached to the romantic vigils in the Catskills is gone."

Incidentally, Dutchman's breeches—worn, not grown—could be sizable affairs. Mathews tells the story of a settler who persuaded some Indians to sell for a pittance all the land that would be enclosed by a pair of these voluminous trousers. The Indians thought they had the best of the deal until the Dutchman sliced up his ample drawers into narrow strips, sewed them end to end, and made a ribbon that enclosed several acres.

### *Folk Names*

The unusual form of the flowers has generated a variety of folk names that show how one shape can conjure up different ideas: soldier's cap, white hearts, eardrops (because they hang like earrings), monk's head, butterfly banners, kitten breeches, bachelor's breeches, and little boy's breeches. Another old-fashioned name is "boys and girls," which children used when they found Dutchman's breeches with its similarly shaped but pinkish sibling, squirrel corn.

Scientists were not so imaginative. Their name is *Dicentra cucullaria*, which simply describes the plant as two-spurred and hooded.

*Dicentra* is a small genus of only sixteen species worldwide, all native to North America and Asia. Dutchman's breeches is the type species, the plant theoretically most typical of the genus and the one from which the genus was named.

*Dicentra* in turn belongs to the small Fumitory family of only five genera and 170 species. Dutchman's breeches are widespread in the northern United States from the Atlantic to the Dakotas and Kansas, and out along the Columbia River in Washington, Idaho, and Oregon. Squirrel or turkey corn (*D. canadensis*), which has a pink "waistband" instead of a yellow one, has a similar range, though not as western. Squirrel corn is named for its yellowish kernel-like bulbs, perhaps a delicacy for squirrels and wild turkeys. The West Coast has several colorful species, including bright pink bleeding heart (*D. formosa*).

### *Strange Form*

Why these flowers evolved so strange a form must be left to conjecture. The shape does have its advantages. Each upside-down blossom is sealed from the effects of rain or wind on pollen. The blossom is also protected from invasion by most crawling or small, flying insects that might steal nectar without carrying pollen to the next flower. In fact, only the long, strong tongue of female bumblebees is said to be able to reach from the flower's bottom opening up into each of the two long spurs to lap up the sweets, picking up and depositing pollen in the process.

Like columbine and jewelweed, though, Dutchman's breeches are not perfect vaults. Certain wasps, carpenter bees, and even bumblebees have learned to chew holes through the tips of the spurs to gain direct access to the nectar.

Dutchman's breeches are early spring arrivals. "As soon as bloodroot has begun to star the waste, stony places, and the first swallow has been heard in the sky, we are on the lookout for Dicentra," wrote Burroughs. The flowers have been seen in bloom in my part of western Connecticut as early as April 18 and as late as mid-May.

### *Elfin Trousers*

The plants favor rocky hillsides of open woods, often forming sizable colonies. Mabel Osgood Wright once described "a bed among rocks of much-cleft silver-green foliage, set with flower-sprays of two-pointed white and yellow bloom that might be pairs of elfin trousers hung out to bleach." Dutchman's breeches like limestone regions but, paradoxically, their soil should be rich woodland humus, neutral to slightly acid.

The bulbs transplant easily, but because the plants are uncommon—mostly because their favorite habitats have been developed or damaged by development-related erosion—they should be left alone unless threatened with certain destruction. You can gather seeds in late spring, but do not sow them until September.

Unlike many of the wildflowers described in this book, Dutchman's breeches have no notable history as a practical plant. The species has never been popular as a food or a medicine, although one of its old-time names, colicweed, suggests that it may have been used to treat that ailment. There is also record of its use for skin infections and as a tonic and a diuretic.

Perhaps the fact that it is somewhat toxic and narcotic has limited its use. The plant is unpopular with farmers whose grazing cattle could suffer convulsions, even death from eating too many of the leaves. Ranchers called it "staggerweed" because of the effect it had on livestock. You might want to consider this information when planting *Dicentra* of any sort in a yard frequented by small children who like to stuff strange things into their mouths.

One of *Dicentra*'s constituents is a poppy-like hallucinogen, which may explain its unusual use by the Menomini Indians of upper Michigan and Wisconsin. According to a 1923 paper by Huron H. Smith, Dutchman's breeches "is one of the most important love charms of the Menomini. The young swain tries to throw it at his intended and hit her with it. Another way is for him to chew the root, breathing out so that the scent will carry to her. He then circles around the girl, and when she catches the scent, she will follow him wherever he goes, even against her will." Do perfume manufacturers know about this?

While Dr. Abbott considered the name an abomination and Burroughs called it "absurd," the name can also be annoying. When writing about the plant, the mind asks whether to say, "The Dutchman's breeches is . . ." or "the Dutchman's breeches are . . ." If you come across only one, do you have a Dutchman's breech? Not, I suppose, unless you can wear a pair of pant.

**Trout Lily**
*(Erythronium americanum)*

## *A Lily by Any Other Name . . .*

Anyone writing a book on the origin of the folk names of American plants would have a field day with *Erythronium americanum.* Our earliest-blooming member of the Lily family is commonly and widely known by at least three very different names: trout lily, adder's tongue, and dog's tooth violet.

Trout lily has several interpretations. The name may come from the fact that the plant flowers in mid-April, just as trout season opens. It is more likely, though, that the name stems from the leaves, whose purplish blotches resemble the markings on some kinds of trout, and from the fact that the plant is often found near woodland streams in which these fish live.

Dog's tooth violet, really an inappropriate name, may have evolved because the plant blooms when the woods are full of violets. Also, the pointed corms are shaped somewhat like a tooth. In her book on flower names, Mary Durant says there is no real logic to this one, and it probably came from the European variety, *E. dens canis*, whose roots may better resemble a dog's choppers.

Adder's tongue is the most confusing name. Some authorities feel that the spots on the leaves are similar to markings on certain snakes. Other authorities liken the plant's twin leaves to the forked tongue of a snake. The name was probably inspired by the appearance of the leaves, which pop out of the soil. "Whoever sees the sharp purplish point of a young plant darting above the ground in earliest spring . . . at once sees the fitting application of 'adder's tongue,'" said a turn-of-the-century writer.

If you do not like any of those possibilities, you can always select from among yellow lily, yellow bells, yellow snowdrop, rattlesnake tooth violet, rattlesnake violet, yellow snakeleaf, lamb's tongue, deer's tongue, snake root, star-striker, and scrofula root. (Scrofula is a skin disease once treated with this plant.) If the English names are not bad enough, trout lily's Latin name seems equally off the beam. *Erythronium*, from a Greek word, is an allusion to the color red. While the trout lily we know is hardly red, other species within the genus are of that color, including *E. dens canis.*

John Burroughs preferred fawn lily, partly because he thought the leaf mottling resembled the markings on a young deer. "It is a pity that this graceful and abundant flower has no good and appropriate name," he lamented in the 1890s. "It is the earliest of the true lilies, and it has all the grace and charm that belong to this order of flowers. . . . In my spring rambles I have sometimes come upon a solitary specimen of this yellow lily growing beside a mossy stone where the sunshine fell full upon it, and have thought it one of the most beautiful of our wild flowers. Its two leaves stand up like a fawn's ears, and this feature with its recurved petals, gives it an alert, wide-awake look."

### The Droppers

Burroughs was also interested in the root system. Trout lily deeply embeds its corms and roots, while most members of the lily clan grow bulbs and roots near the surface. The trout lily seeds, which appear in June, do not germinate until early the next spring, creating little corms that grow near the surface. Young corms produce several threadlike droppers, which head down at an angle of about forty-five degrees. (Some misguided ones may surface and then dive, which explains the white "threads" that appear in trout lily groves.) At the end of each dropper—several inches lower in the ground and up to ten inches away from the mother—a new little corm is formed from food sent down the line by the parent. Eventually the line withers away. Each offspring produces only one leaf, aimed at making food to send droppers down even farther the next year.

This pyramid scheme may continue several years, and someone has calculated that after four years a typical seed will have produced nine plants with corms as deep as seven or eight inches, even deeper if the soil is loose and loamy. When the descenders hit hard soil, they stop diving and the corms begin producing flowers. Though the flowers stand only an inch or two above the surface, trout lilies actually grow from six to ten inches tall; most of the plant is under the surface.

Why the unusually deep collection of corms constructed in such a fashion? Some botanists believe the system amasses a great deal of stored food to produce flowers bearing the best-quality seeds. At any rate this growth pattern explains why we find large, dense colonies of trout lily leaves with relatively few flowers. Most of those leaves spring from nonflowering corms and are there only to manufacture food. These groves of trout lilies are valuable in nature because they help to tie together the delicate forest floor, especially in wet areas, thus preventing erosion.

### Growing Them

You can acquire plants by digging up a few shallow corms from a colony. The young, pencil-shaped corms should be planted at least four inches deep in loose soil with plenty of mulch. They do best in semishaded soil that is at least slightly damp. But plan to be patient; you may have to wait up to four years for a flower to appear. Meanwhile, however, you will have an ever-increasing supply of the handsome, mottled leaves that make a fine spring ground cover. Seeds, produced in small numbers, can be gathered in June or July, but will take up to six years to form blooming corms. Nursery stock plants are often available.

While the East has only two native species of *Erythronium* (the other is the white trout lily *E. albidum*), western states and provinces have more than a dozen types, including yellow fawn lily (*E. grandiflorum*), which blooms brightly from sagebrush and clearings in the mountains just after the snow recedes. Many western varieties can be successfully grown anywhere from corms or seeds; a good wildflower horticulture book will provide the details. Some are very limited in area, however, such as the mother lode fawn lily (*E. tuolumnense*) of the western Sierra Nevada, and should not be removed from their native habitat.

Some eighteen species of *Erythronium* live in North America, mostly in cool or mountainous states as well as Canada. The eastern trout lily is probably the most widespread, ranging from New Brunswick to Florida and westward to the Mississippi and into Arkansas and Nebraska.

### *Looking Down*

Trout lily's blossoms have a faint scent not unlike that of tulips. The flowers are closed at night but open each morning, with the petal-like yellow sepals curving backward. As in many of the lilies, trout lily flowers point groundward, a position that may serve two purposes. The central flower parts are protected from rain that could wash away pollen and insect-drawing nectar. The position also helps to keep certain kinds of crawling insects from robbing the nectar, which is provided for flying insects that are more skillful at spreading pollen from bloom to bloom. An ant, for instance, is likely to slip and fall off the smooth interior of the flower before reaching the prize. Actually, the ant would also have difficulty negotiating the smooth, slender flower stalk.

European herbalists began using *Erythronium* plants long before the settlement of North America, but today even European herbals consider our native *E. americanum* the best of the genus for medicinal use. Its chief internal use is to produce vomiting. Its leaves have long been employed as a poultice to treat ulcers and tumors, as well as scrofula. Some tribes of Indians, such as the Winnebago, ate the bulbs, probably well cooked. The leaves of the trout lily were also used by Indians to brew a tea that was said to relieve stomach pains. Cows also love the twin leaves—perhaps to soothe their twin stomachs!

**Common Blue Violet**
*(Viola papilionacea)*

# *Love in the Springtime*

Asked to name a favorite spring wildflower, few people would pick the violet. This spring classic is well loved, but it has become so common in gardens and lawns that most people don't consider it wild. Yet the forest floor and open field are the usual haunts of our most common native violets. Unlike their garden-born brethren, however, they are sometimes so small and unassuming that the woodland walker might miss them pushing demurely but firmly through the brown carpet of last year's leaves.

Even if your careful eye does spot an early violet, you might have trouble finding its name, for the world of violets is a jumbled one. More than 75 species exist in North America, most of them natives. However, interbreeding has created numerous new forms and varieties, some of which only the most dedicated botanist could identify. Dr. Harold N. Moldenke estimated in the 1940s that about 300 species, varieties, and natural hybrids of violets were living north of Mexico, with the Northeast being home to 132 of them. While that number is enough to tax the best taxonomist, were we to go south of the border, we would find hundreds more, some so big they are classified as shrubs.

The violet would seem to need no description, since even kindergartners can count it among the handful of flowers they readily recognize. Nonetheless, few admirers of any age probably take the time to look closely at the blossom, which has five petals: two upper, two lateral, and one bottom. The two sets act as flags to attract pollinating insects while the bottom petal is the landing strip. In many species small veins of color, which to us are just decorations, act as arrows, directing the insect to a nectar-laden spur at the rear of the bottom petal. These guides are much more visible to the ultraviolet-sensing eyes of bees. Some species have hairs near the nectar opening, giving the insect something to grab onto while pushing its head inside. Functioning like our eyelashes, these "beards" also prevent rain or dew drops from getting in and diluting the nectar. Most varieties of violets also turn toward the ground at night or when it is cloudy, another defense against spring rains and dew.

### *Insect Tricks*

When visiting most flowers, a bee must touch an anther to pick up the pollen on it. Not so in violets. As the insect wiggles in for a drink, it jiggles loose grains from the partly hidden anthers overhead; pollen dusts the insect's back. (Various flowers that attract small bees have similar, hidden anthers to prevent larger insects such as bumblebees from making pollen a meal instead of a cargo.)

If few people pay close attention to the pretty blossoms, even fewer notice the other flowers, the ones that never bloom. Called cleistogamous flowers, they appear lower on the plant, sometimes under the ground and often later in the season so that even if they are noticed, they are usually considered buds, pods, or defective flowers. In fact, while they never open, they contain all the necessary parts to produce fertile seeds. This system may have developed because so many violets flower early in the season when insect pollination is more chancy than in the warmer, bee-filled months. Not all violets produce these nonblooming flowers. Some summer violets with showy blossoms can easily attract bees and moths and do not appear to need back-up cleistogamous flowers.

Once seeds are ripe, another insect may stop by to do its job. Some species of ants harvest and "plant" violets and certain other spring wildflowers in a symbiotic relationship called "myrmecochory"—literally "ant farming." They are drawn to the seeds by small protuberances, called elaiosomes, that contain attractive oils and possibly sugars. The ants carry the seeds, sometimes as far as seventy yards, to their nests where they consume the little treats. The shell, however, is too hard to open, so ants discard the seed proper, often in an unused tunnel in the nest. Here, amid nutrients provided by the soil and accidentally by the housecleaning ants, the seed has a much better chance of producing a plant than does one dropped on the forest floor, where it may be eaten by foraging birds and rodents. Among other spring bloomers that get a helping hand from ants are bloodroot, anemones, wild ginger, hepaticas, and trilliums. The phenomenon is much more common among plants of forests than those of field and meadow.

## *Myth and Medicine*

Violets have long been important in mythology and herbalism, two traditions that often intermix. John Gerard said that the very name of the plant stems from Greek mythology. One story he relates says that *viola*, the old Latin word for the plant as well as the modern generic name, may have come from the Greek, *Ione* or *Io*. Io, one of Zeus' lovers, evidently picked the wrong god to fool around with because Zeus' wife became jealous. To protect Io, Zeus turned her into a white heifer and created sweet-scented violets for her to graze upon.

Greeks treasured violets and Athenians considered them the symbols of their city. According to legend, when Ion, the founder of Athens and another possible source for *viola*, was leading his people to Attica, he was welcomed by naiads, water nymphs who could inspire men. The naiads gave him violets as a sign of their good wishes, and the flower became the city's emblem. Rare was the Athenian house without violets growing in the garden; violets decorated the altars, decorated brides, and decorated busts. The last could be taken as a bit of an embarrassing memorial, for violet wreaths were sometimes employed, by the Romans at least, to relieve hangovers. (One could wonder at Aristophanes' reporting that the people of Athens were proud to be known as "violet-crowned Athenians.") On the more practical side, Greeks also used the plants to help induce sleep, to strengthen the heart, and to calm anger.

Romans acquired much of their culture from the Greeks, and with it came an appreciation of this plant. Like Greeks, they decorated banquet tables with thousands of violets in the mistaken belief that the flowers could prevent drunkenness. Ironically, the Romans often also drank a wine made from violet blossoms.

Perhaps more appropriate was the flower's use as a symbol of innocence and modesty. Romans often placed violets on the graves of small children. Even to Shakespeare's time, they were associated with death. "I would give you some violets," said Ophelia to Laertes, "but they withered all when my father died." It was also once believed that the soul leaving the body would take the form of a flower. Later in *Hamlet*, after Ophelia dies, Laertes hopes that violets will grow from her grave: "Lay her i' the earth, and from her fair and unpolluted flesh, may Violets spring."

Medieval Christians believed violets were once strong, upright flowers until one day on Mount Calvary, the shadow of the cross fell upon them. Forever after they bowed in shame at what mankind had done. Probably in connection with this legend, violets were often used in Good Friday ceremonies. However, while the violet is usually styled as being modest, Sir Walter Scott once characterized it as a boastful queen of the forest flowers:

*The Violet in her greenwood bower,*
*Where Birchen boughs with Hazels mingle,*
*May boast itself the fairest flower*
*In glen, in copse, or forest dingle.*

### *Caporal Violette*

A small boy from France did much to spread violets into modern gardens. As a child on Corsica, Napoleon Bonaparte loved the sweet-scented violets that grew there. Josephine wore them on her wedding day, and, though he was not always faithful to her and eventually divorced her and married again, Napoleon always gave her a bouquet of violets each year on their anniversary. She, in turn, maintained an extensive garden of violets which, of course, became the rage in France.

After Napoleon was banished to Elba, he declared: "I shall return with the violets in spring." As a result, the flower became the symbol of his followers, who called him "Caporal Violette" or "Le Père Violet." And after his defeat at Waterloo, Napoleon is supposed to have visited the grave of Josephine, picked a few violets, and placed them in his locket, where they were found six years later when he died.

Later Napoleon III adopted the violet as the symbol of his regime. The day he met his future wife, Eugenie, she reportedly expressed her favor of him by wearing a violet gown and violets in her hair. Naturally, she carried the flowers at her wedding and received bouquets of them on their anniversaries.

Because of all the Napoleonic interest in violets, France became a leader in developing and cultivating new varieties of violets and pansies. "Pansy," in fact, comes from the French, *pensée*, meaning "thought" or "sentiment," as in those anniversary bouquets. "There's rosemary, that's for remembrance; pray, love, remember; and there is pansies, that's for thoughts," said Ophelia.

Others had also been charmed by violets. Mohammed considered them his favorite flower. A tenth-century English herbalist said the blossoms could chase away evil spirits. Ancient Britons used the flowers as a cosmetic, says Maude Grieve, adding that Celtic women mixed violets and goat's milk to concoct a beauty lotion. Writing about violets, herbalist Gerard was almost ecstatic: "There be made of them garlands for the head, nosegaies and poesies, which are delightfull to looke on and pleasant to smel to. . . . Yea, gardens themselves receive by these the greatest ornament of all, chiefest beauty, and the most excellent grace, and the recreation of the minde which is taken hereby cannot be but very good and honest; for they admonish and stirre up a man to that which is comely and honest. . . ."

The violet's use as a medicine was extensive from the sixteenth century on, and many herbalists highly recommended it for such problems as insomnia, epilepsy, pleurisy, impetigo, ulcers, jaundice, eye inflammations, and rheumatism. It was widely used as a mild laxative and as a cough medicine because of its ability to lubricate the linings of the alimentary canal with a soothing coating. Among the few plants to contain salicylic acid, the chief ingredient in aspirin, certain violets have found use as pain relievers. As Culpeper put it, they were useful "in cooling plasters, oyles, and comfortable cataplasms or poultices. A drachm weight of the dried leaves or flowers . . . doth purge the body of choleric humours and assuageth the heat if taken in a draught of wine or other drink."

Perhaps its most interesting medicinal use, mentioned in several herbals right up to modern times, has been as a treatment for cancers, such as those of the tongue, skin, and colon. Mrs. Grieve records one case in which a man was supposedly cured of colon cancer in nine weeks, during which time he had consumed almost all the leaves from a nursery bed of violets covering an area equal to 1,600 square feet.

Violets, which contain a good deal of sugar, have found their way into the culinary world, especially in confections. The flowers have been popular crystallized and served as a candy or a cake decoration. Syrups and even marmalades are made from the pectin-rich flowers, which were also added to gelatins and salad dressings for both color and flavor. Gerard tells of "certaine plates called sugar violet, violet tables, or plate, which is most pleasant and wholesome, especially it comforteth the heart and the other inward parts." Violet plate (plate being a thin confection) was once carried in drugstores as a sort of cough lozenge. The flowers have also been used as a food dye, particularly in candy making. (Violet, like rose, has become so well known as a flower that the word is also a color.)

Though somewhat bitter when raw, the leaves were used in salads and in fritters. Added to soup they functioned as a thickener. Captain John Smith reported in 1612 that violets found in Virginia were good in salads and broths. Modern research has shown that these old violet-eaters had the right idea. The basal leaves of the common blue violet (*Viola papilionacea*) have, in the springtime, five times more vitamin C per 100 grams than the equivalent weight of oranges, and 2½ times more vitamin A than spinach has.

### *Famed Europeans*

Many of the uses as well as much of the lore of violets sprang up around *Viola odorata*, the sweet-scented violet. A native of the Mediterranean region, the species has been so popular it spread far and wide as a garden escape, and is found coast to coast in North America. The deep purple flower is so sweet that an oil from it is used extensively in the perfume industry, though some authorities say that the scent tends to numb the olfactory sensors after a short time. Because of its scent, this species was also used to grow many hybrids.

Even more widely used in hybridizing is *V. tricolor*, known by a host of names including heartsease, bird's eye, bullweed, pink-eyed John, godfathers and godmothers, and wild pansy. The fondness people had for it is shown in other, more colorful folk names, including some of the most verbose names ever recorded: love-lies-bleeding, love idol, cuddle me, call-me-to-you, meet-me in-the-entry, kiss-her-in-the-buttery, kit-run-in-the-fields, three-faces-under-a-hood, and Jack-jump-up-and-kiss-me. It is the ancestor of our garden pansies, which are nothing but overblown violets. The small blue, yellow, and white flowers, common wild in Europe and found as garden escapes here, were revered by early Christians who saw in their three colors a symbol of the trinity; hence, it was often called herb trinity.

As for the name "heartsease," that may have stemmed from its old use as a medicine to treat heart disease; people believed God had given the plant heart-shaped leaves to mark it for that use. The name may also come from its ancient use as an aphrodisiac and a love potion. As the latter it played a major part in Shakespeare's *A Midsummer Night's Dream*, its use described by Puck:

*Yet mark'd I where the bolt of Cupid fell:*
*It fell upon a little western flower,*
*Before milk-white, now purple with love's wound,*
*And maidens call it love-in-idleness . . .*
*The juice of it on sleeping eye-lids laid*
*Will make or man or woman madly dote*
*Upon the next live creature that it sees.*

### *Native Violets*

While it might be said that Europe has the most famous and spectacular violets, North America has the greater variety, six times as many as the Old World. Ours come in purple, blue, yellow, and white, and sundry shades and combinations thereof. They also come in two forms, those whose flowers and leaves rise directly from the underground root, and those with stems bearing the leaves and flowers. Violets are certainly popular; Illinois, New Jersey, Rhode Island, and Wisconsin have made them their state flowers. No other genus has been so honored so often.

Perhaps the most popular of the natives is the birdsfoot violet (*V. pedata*), which inhabits woods and dry fields across the eastern half of the United States and southern Canada, bearing handsome violet and lilac-purple flowers. The namesake leaves are unusual, deeply cut like the claw of a bird and much like the buttercups called crowfoot. Often birdsfoot violet blooms a second time in a season, surprising many an autumnal walker.

It is said that John Bartram, the first famous American botanist, was inspired to pursue botany instead of farming by one day finding a colony of birdsfoot violets at the edge of a field. That night he dreamed of the flower and the next day announced that he was hiring a manager for his farm and heading for Philadelphia to study botany. He mastered Latin in only three months so he could deal with the nomenclature, and over the years he sent more than 200 species of plants to Europe, many of them identified and named because of him. Plants whose names recall Philadelphia (*Lillium philadelphicum*, *Erigeron philadelphicus*) or Pennsylvania (*Polygonum pensylvanicum*, *Silene pensylvanica*) were probably so named because Linnaeus got the specimens from Bartram.

Another well-known species is blue marsh violet (*V. cucullata*), one of spring's earliest. It favors woodland swamps, but according to the late U.S. senator George Aiken, does well in ordinary gardens or makes a good seasonal ground cover. "Royal in color as in lavish profusion, it blossoms everywhere—in woods, waysides, meadows and marshes . . . from the Arctic to the Gulf," said Neltje Blanchan. This is one of the bearded violets that attract small bees. Another is the palm or early blue violet (*V. palmata*), which is so thick with foliage that it, too, makes a good cover. The long-blooming dog violet (*V. conspersa*) is a light-blue, almost white species of wet woodlands. Whether the flowers or the animals should feel insulted, I don't know, but the name reportedly is a belittling reference to the flower's lack of scent.

Among the white violets, the sweet white (*V. blanda*) is known for its scent, though it is not nearly as strong as *V. odorata*. The sweet white violet bears very clear markings. "The purple veinings show the stupidest visitor the path to the sweets," said Ms. Blanchan. Other white violets include the lance-leaved (*V. lanceolata*), primrose-leaved (*V. primulifolia*), and the Canada (*V. canadensis*). The last, found coast to coast, has purple-tinged petals. This species has been called a violet in the process of evolving from white to purple, which Sir John Lubbock and other scientists have considered the most advanced flower color.

Some scientists believe that after green, yellow was the first color developed by flowers. There are many kinds of yellow violets in North American woods, particularly on the West Coast, where at least a dozen yellow species are found. All the continent's yellow violets, like the downy yellow (*V. pubescens*), the smooth yellow (*V. pensylvanica*), the prairie yellow (*V. nuttallii*), or the round-leaved (*V. rotundifolia*), have at least a tad of blue, purple, or brown, usually as part of the insect guidance system. The round-leaved violet is one of our earliest wildflowers. But in the Northeast at least, it comes long after the bluebird, despite the poetry of William Cullen Bryant, who employed his profession's license when he wrote:

*When beechen buds begin to swell,*
*And woods the blue-bird's warble know,*
*The yellow violet's modest bell*
*Peeps from the last year's leaves below.*

**Plantain-leaved Pussytoes**
*(Antennaria plantaginifolia)*

# *Sweet and Everlasting*

The everlasting tribe of the Composite family is appropriately named. Some of the most common varieties seem to be almost year-round plants, green-leaved and undaunted by winter, even in the north.

Best known of the everlastings are pussytoes, among our earliest bloomers. From late April through May, they send up odd, whitish puffs from basal rosettes of furry green leaves that lie on the ground and seem alive all winter. They are usually found in large colonies, with the plants interconnected by underground runners, and when in bloom make patches of old lawns or field appear almost as if some of winter's snow had been left behind.

Looking like their namesake toes, the small fuzzy flowers shoot up on long, downy stems. These furry heads and stems are said to entangle the legs of crawling insects, discouraging them from stealing nectar or pollen. The flower heads consist of tight clusters of tiny tubular yellowish flowers, which grow long, hairlike extensions that later carry the seeds away. Pussytoes are among the few plants that have both male and female flowers, growing in separate colonies close to one another. The males, shorter than the twelve- to eighteen-inch-high females, produce pollen that small bees and flies transfer to the loftier females.

Although the floral tubes contain nectar, pussytoes do not rely on insect visits to produce seed. If the female fails to be fertilized, it can still develop seeds on its own, though their quality is said to be not as good.

### *A Flower for Children*

Pussytoes make a yard interesting. They are also among the plants that grass fanatics attack with herbicides in their quest for the putting-green lawn. In fact, many writers on flowers ignore them or, as F. Schuyler Mathews does, disparage them. "There are great patches of straggling white seen in the meadows through April," he wrote at the turn of the century, "and one wonders, from the distance of a car window in the swiftly passing train, what the 'white stuff' is—leastwise, I have been asked such a question. But it is only [pussytoes], and scarcely merits attention, unless one wishes to examine its peculiar fuzziness through a little microscope."

Yet, for children, pussytoes can be a treat. When little, my two boys were always entertained by the similarity of the flowers to a cat's paw, and even felt an affection for the colonies of them that appeared on one lawn we would pass while walking to school together. They knew, too, that these flowers were a sign that winter was over and warmer days were on their way. One year, the owner of the pussytoed yard hired a lawn-care service that laid down weed killer. The next spring, the boys searched in vain for the old colony. In the years that followed, the pussytoes never returned. The poison worked well.

Fortunately, some people would rather have pussytoes than lawns of poisoned perfection, and there are still plenty of old lawns where pussytoes abound each spring. The flowers usually come up and die down before the grass needs much mowing, and the basal leaves stay low during the year, not minding the mower's visits.

Pussytoes have gone by many different names over the years, including early everlasting, ladies' tobacco, dog toes, four toes, love's nest, Indian tobacco, poverty weed (many plants that frequent poorer soils are so called), white plantain, pearly mouse-eared everlasting, and plantain-leaf everlasting. The plant is found from Quebec to Florida and west to Texas.

Pussytoes are known to the botanist as *Antennaria plantaginifolia. Antennaria* comes from the resemblance of the pappus (the hairs that carry the seeds) to an insect's antennae, while *plantaginifolia* means the leaves are shaped like those of plantain.

The genus *Antennaria* contains about eighty-five North American species, though some botanists count far fewer species, but many varieties and subspecies. *Antennaria* belongs to the Composite family, which includes such common flowers as daisies, asters, and dandelions.

Closely related to members of the *Antennaria* genus—and once included in it—is pearly everlasting (*Anaphalis margaritacea*), a common summertime plant of the open fields. *Margaritacea* means "pearly," describing the shape and color of the flowers. Under a magnifying glass, the yellow-eyed, fuzzy white flowers bear a surprising resemblance to the blossoms of the much larger pond lily. *Anaphalis*, an ancient Greek word for a similar plant, has only one representative in North America, and some thirty-five in Europe and Asia.

Pearly everlasting is also called Indian posy, silver leaf, life-everlasting, moonshine, cottonweed, none-so-pretty, lady neverfade, silver button, and ladies' tobacco. It ranges across North America from the northern states to Alaska and Newfoundland.

Pearly everlasting was once widely used by Indians and colonists to treat dysentery, heart diseases, paralysis, bronchitis, and as poultices for sprains, bruises, boils, and "painful swellings." Mohegans treated colds with a tea made from the leaves. Some tribes soothed sore throats and relieved hoarseness with it, and medicine men even claimed that chewing everlasting made the user want to sing. The dried leaves were also widely smoked, both for enjoyment and to relieve headaches and asthma.

### *Fresh Drawers*

The names "everlasting" or "live-forever" were applied first to European species. When picked they maintained a nice scent for many months and were used to freshen chests and drawers in Elizabethan England. Colonists also used them. "Ladies are accustomed to gather great quantities of this life everlasting and to pick them with the stalks," wrote Peter Kalm on visiting Philadelphia in 1748. "Ladies in general are much inclined to keep flowers all summer long about or upon the chimneys, upon a table or before the windows, whether on account of their beauty or because of their scent . . . [The plant] was one of those which they kept in their rooms during the winter because its flowers never altered."

Both pussytoes and pearly everlasting favor poorer soils, and pussytoes are most often found in old lawns that have not been fattened with expensive fertilizers. Transplanting is easy. Just dig up a wad of plants in May and put them, with a shot of water, in a sunny area where they will not be overnourished or get too wet.

Most people who have everlastings don't mind sharing them—including the weed-freaks, who'd love you to haul them all away. *De gustibus non est disputandum*—there's no accounting for taste.

**Tall Buttercup**
*(Ranunculus acris)*

## *Bitter Beauties*

Buttercups are famous flowers. Almost everyone recognizes them, even toddlers. Natives of both Europe and America, they can be found across the continent, and most are common and colorful additions to our landscape. But few people realize that buttercups can be dangerous as well as beautiful.

Buttercups, also called crowfoots, are a large genus of primitive plants, most of which bear yellow flowers from May to September. Occasionally you will see half-white and half-yellow blossoms and rarely all white ones. More than 80 species live in North America and more than 300 worldwide, though botanists disagree on whether some are species or just varieties of species.

The genus, called *Ranunculus*, is sizable and significant enough to have lent its name to *Ranunculaceae*, the Crowfoot, or Buttercup, family of about thirty-five genera and 1,100 species around the world. The family includes anemones, hepaticas, delphiniums or larkspurs, snakeroots, columbines, wolfbanes, and bugbanes. *Ranunculus* is Latin for "little frog"; most buttercups, like most frogs, like moist places.

### *A Basic Flower*

Botanists consider buttercup flowers to be one of our simplest designs on the evolutionary scale. Flowers started out as modified leaves, and most early ones were green, greenish white, or greenish yellow. Many of the first flowers were merely petals or sepals emanating from a collection of male stamens and female pistils.

Most modern flowers, which developed as insects developed, evolved specialized forms suited to particular insects. Composites developed compact, sweet, and attractive blossoms; some orchids evolved elaborate methods of directing visitors through passages and past pollen-giving and -receiving devices; milkweeds employ outright trickery to gain fertilization.

But like magnolias, also primitive flowering plants, buttercups stayed with a basic collection of bright petals, pistils, and stamens, with no special arrangement to manage pollinators. Like many other yellow flowers, they are designed to attract all sorts of insects, including bees, flies, wasps, and even beetles. One German scientist found some sixty-two different species of buttercup flowers. Both white and yellow are "the democratic colors," wrote Clarence Moores Weed. "Blossoms of these colors—except those pollinated by night-flying moths—generally have nectar which is easily accessible and are visited by a great variety of insects." Thus buttercup blossoms, sometimes mounted singly on tall plants, other times appearing in great numbers, get their share of the action and, as is obvious from their numbers, are quite successful at not only surviving, but multiplying.

Among the most common of our buttercups is *Ranunculus acris*, the tall, common, or meadow buttercup, an import from Europe that now ranges from coast to coast. Growing six or more feet high at times, this buttercup is found in moist fields, along roadsides, and in lawns, where mowers may limit its height, but not its ability to thrive and blossom. The plant's leaves have many slender, pointy lobes, and the design looks somewhat like a large bird's foot—giving rise to its name, crowfoot. It is quite possible that Shakespeare wrote of this flower in *Love's Labor's Lost*:

*When daisies pied and violets blue,*
*And lady-smocks all silver-white,*
*And cuckoo-buds of yellow hue*
*Do paint the meadows with delight.*

### *Bitter History*

As delightful as the flowers may look, the plant's specific name, *acris*, means "bitter." Herein lies much of the buttercup's fame in folklore and folk medicine, for nearly all species are acrid to one degree or another, sometimes painfully so. Some buttercups have been known as blister plant for centuries. Indeed, European beggars used to rub buttercup juice on their skin to grow sores so that passersby would take pity on them and give them food or money. Anne Pratt, a nineteenth-century British writer on wildflowers, reported, "Instances are common in which the wanderer has lain down to sleep with a handful of these flowers beside him, and has awakened to find the skin of his cheek pained and irritated to a high degree by the acrid blossoms' having lain near it."

Maude Grieve wrote, "Even pulling it up and carrying it some little distance has produced considerable inflammation in the palm of the hand." She added, "Cattle will not readily eat it in the green state and if driven from hunger to feed on it, their mouths become sore and blistered." Nonetheless, sneaky folks in ages past fed buttercup blossoms to cows to add a golden tint to the cream and butter produced from the milk, just as today marigold petals are fed to chickens to give their flesh a more marketable golden hue.

A nineteenth-century scientist reported that, as an experiment, a slice of the rootstock of the bulbous buttercup (*R. bulbosus*) was placed on a person's palm. It began to cause pain within two minutes. The sample was removed, but ten hours later, a sizable blister had appeared. The blister eventually became an ulcer and took some time to heal. More entertaining is the following description, reported by Charles F. Millspaugh in *American Medicinal Plants*: "A lady who applied the bruised plant to the chest as a counter-irritant, became ill-humored, fretful, cross, and disposed to quarrel, and suffered from soreness and smarting of the eyelashes some time before its action was felt at the region nearest the application."

The Mohawks believed that it was unhealthy to have too much water in the blood. They would remedy the situation by mixing buttercup, poison ivy, and water, and placing a bit of the mixture on the skin. A sore would form and from it would run "surplus water." This practice explains why Mohawks called buttercups by a word that meant, "the plant which makes a hole."

It is quite possible that the bitterness of buttercups evolved as a defense against being eaten by the creatures who graze in meadows and swamps. As noted elsewhere, milkweeds and chrysanthemum daisies developed this defense against insects and other herbivores.

### *Accursed*

Perhaps the most powerful of our buttercups is cursed crowfoot, *R. sceleratus.* The ancient Greeks used this plant to remove tumors and other growths. Swallowing just two drops of the juice is said to be enough to kill a person by severely inflaming the alimentary canal. *Sceleratus* is a Latin word with a variety of meanings, none of them too friendly. While it meant "ungodly," "irreligious," "wicked," or "unnatural," the word also was used in the sense of "sharp," "nipping," or "biting," which is probably how it came to be attached to this buttercup, and not through some sinister employment of the past.

While the buttercup is an attractive flower, especially in large numbers, you need not risk blisters gathering them. The petals of most picked flowers soon fall off, making them ill-suited for bouquets. Yet despite such shortcomings, the buttercup has endeared itself to people through the centuries. During the Middle Ages, it was worn by lovers at betrothal time. In many cultures, sighting buttercups was said to be good luck. And what child has never picked a buttercup and placed the blossom under a playmate's chin to see whether the companion likes butter?

The shiny, waxy surface that is able to reflect light onto chins is the result of a high starch content in the cells on the petals' surface. This flashy outfit is no doubt aimed at catching the eye of passing insects and drawing them to its rather rich store of nectar. Probably because of the starch and the sweets, early settlers used to pickle the flowers. American Indians of the West ground seeds of certain species as an ingredient in flour and used roots to create a yellow dye.

### *Poison for Poisons*

In medicine, buttercups were chiefly used to remove warts and other unwanted growths. The *Ladies' Indispensable Assistant,* a guide to the housewife published in 1852, said the buttercup is good "for corns on the feet." But it was also employed as an external relief from headaches. (Perhaps its pain—worse than the ache—diverted attention from the head!) Europeans used to bind buttercup leaves to the wrists of persons suffering from fevers and pneumonia, and one Englishman in the 1790s claimed to cure cancer with it. A tea made from the plant was a folk treatment for asthma in the United States during the last century.

Ironically, buttercups were once employed as an emetic on people who had swallowed a poison; the effect on the stomach was so quick and violent that it would cause people to vomit instantly. Said one nineteenth-century writer, "It is . . . as if Nature had furnished an antidote to poisons from among poisons of its own tribe."

Modern herbalists usually recommend against use of buttercups as any kind of medicine, considering the plants to be too dangerous. Even John Gerard warned about them in the sixteenth century: "There be divers sorts or kinds of these pernitious herbes comprehended under the name of Ranunculus or Crowfoote, whereof most are very dangerous to be taken into the body, and therefore they require a very exquisite moderation, with a most exact and due manner of tempering; not any of them are to be taken alone by themselves, because they are of a most violent force, and therefore have the great nede of correction."

But if you are a fisherman who favors live bait, some of that "violent force" may be harnessed to help you. According to an early nineteenth-century herbalist, if you pour some buttercup tea on ground containing worms "they will be forced to rise from their concealment." That's probably more practical than using it for headaches, fevers, or asthma.

**Celandine**
*(Chelidonium majus)*

# *A Golden Poppy*

You walk into the doctor's modern office. He inspects your problem—a wart on the sole of your foot. Then, instead of scratching out a $40 prescription to be filled by the local pharmacy, he writes the word "celandine" and tells you to go pick some. Frequently squeeze its orange-yellow juice on your wart, he says.

This treatment seems strange, something from another century and not the recommendation of a twentieth-century physician. Yet there are doctors today—at least one in my neighborhood—who prescribe celandine to treat warts, just as herbalists did in ancient Greece and Rome, and during the Middle Ages. For centuries, celandine has been considered one of a few dozen herbs essential to the basic collection of any practitioner of botanic medicine, and it was used to treat nearly two dozen major kinds of disease. It is also a widespread and colorful wildflower whose greens are among the first to appear each spring.

## *Colorful Medicine*

Celandine is famous for its plentiful and brightly colored juice, which can irritate the skin and should be handled with care. The juice has been described as strong and disagreeable in odor, and its taste persistent and nauseating. "A drop of this acrid fluid on the tip of the tongue is not soon forgotten," wrote Neltje Blanchan.

The potent liquid includes several alkaloids, one of which is narcotic and quite poisonous in its pure state. The juice had found many medicinal uses, especially as a treatment for eye problems. Wrote John Gerard, a sixteenth-century herbalist, "The juice of this herbe is good to sharpen the sight, for it cleanseth and consumeth away slimie things that cleave about the ball of the eye and hinder the sight. . . ." Nicholas Culpeper, an herbalist of the seventeenth century, added that it is "one of the best cures for the eyes. . . . Dropped into the eyes the juice cleanseth them from films and cloudiness that darken the sight, but it is best to allay the sharpness of the juice with a little breast-milk." Culpeper said, "Most desperate sore eyes have been cured by this only medicine," adding a question that seems easy to answer: "Is not this far better than endangering the eyes by the art of the needle?"

Because celandine's orange juice looks like bile, herbalists of old treated liver ailments with it. The plant was used to improve the blood, cure wounds, and promote perspiration (to cleanse the body of poisons or "bad humors"). It was also used to treat jaundice, eczema, scrofula, piles, toothaches, corns, itches, and ringworm. The powdered root was placed on a decayed or loose tooth to make it fall out. "Celandine is a very popular medicine in Russia where it is said to have proved effective in cases of cancer," reported Maude Grieve.

Donald Law, a modern British herbalist, says gypsies used to put celandine in their shoes and keep it there when they walked, claiming that it not only kept the feet fresh but also cured jaundice. Dr. Law, who is very enthusiastic about herb and folk medicine, connects the gypsy practice to a theory that every part of the human body has a corresponding pressure point on one of the feet. He notes that gypsies are descended from the Chinese and that the Chinese practice acupuncture. "The gypsy remedy may be wiser than we think," he says.

## *A Gypsy*

Celandine itself is a gypsy. A native of Europe and Eastern Asia, it was probably brought to North America for use as a medicine and dye. Around the turn of the century, celandine was found only locally along the East Coast, but it has since proved the prediction of Ms. Blanchan who said, "Doubtless it will one day overrun our fields, as so many other European immigrants have." The plant has now traveled across the Mississippi and will no doubt continue its westward migration into states with cool or cold winters.

Celandine can be found in almost any situation, from poor to rich soils, from open fields to woods, from fairly dry to moist ground. It seems to prefer shaded rich soils; roadsides by woods are a favorite haunt. Along a country road near my home, several celandine plants live fifteen feet off the ground, rooted in the rot of a limb-hole in a living tree.

Celandine also has a long blooming season. I have seen its yellow, four-petaled flowers as early as May 1, and plants will bloom throughout the summer and into the fall. Its leaves are among the last to fold up and die in late fall and early winter; they have been seen healthy and green in late December in Connecticut. Celandine is also among the earliest herbs to come to life in late winter or early spring. I have found them, juice flowing, in late February, and one observer has seen their leaves coming up under the ice in late January.

Most plants disdain crawling insects and in fact develop sometimes elaborate defenses to keep them away. Not celandine. Like some other woodland plants, such as violets, celandine has evolved "myrmecochory" to entice ants to plant its seeds. (See Violets: Love in the Springtime.)

## *The Swallows*

Celandine is a word of peculiar etymology, with at least two theories for its origin. The word comes from the Greek, *chelidon*, meaning "a swallow." Pliny, the Roman writer, traced it to the tradition that the flowers bloomed when the swallows (of Europe) arrived and that the blossoms faded at their departure. Gerard disputed this theory, pointing out that in southern Europe, celandine blooms year-round. He maintained the name stemmed from the mistaken belief that swallows used the plant as an eyewash for their young.

Among celandine's many folk names are swallowwort, felonwort, wartweed, sightwort, tetterwort, killwort, garden celandine, and, in one of the more entertaining accidents of plant nomenclature, wartwort. Wort, of course, is an Old English word for plant. A "tetter" was a skin disease; a "felon" was a finger or toe infection, not a criminal.

To the botanist, the plant is *Chelidonium majus*, meaning simply "greater celandine." The name differentiates it from lesser celandine, which is, in fact, a member of the Buttercup family and not a *Chelidonium* at all. (Wordsworth celebrated lesser celandine when he wrote, "There's a flower that shall be mine, 'tis the little celandine." The sculptor of the Wordsworth memorial in Grasmere church in the Lake District of England was no botanist, however, and mistakenly portrayed greater celandine on the monument.)

Actually, *Chelidonium majus* has no brothers and sisters in the entire world. Like bloodroot, it is the only species in its genus. Celandine in turn is a member of the small Poppy family of twenty-three genera and about 115 species worldwide, and one of only a few poppies found wild in the eastern United States.

**Marsh Marigold**
*(Caltha palustris)*

## *Friends of the Farmer*

To the old New England farmer, the sight of marsh marigolds or cowslips was a noteworthy event several times over. The yellow flowers, which appear from mid-April to mid-May, are the first bright sign that the growing season has finally arrived. Swamps, woodland streams, and moist fields light up with their abundance. As John Burroughs described it, they give "a golden lining to many a dark, marshy place in the leafless April woods, or [mark] a little water-course through a greening meadow with a broad line of new gold. One glances up from his walk, and his eye falls upon something like fixed and heaped up sunshine there beneath the alders, or yonder in the freshening field." To some Indian tribes, the plant was called by a name that translates almost poetically as "opens the swamps."

Marsh marigold has long been a symbol of spring. Centuries ago, English peasants threw the flowers on the thresholds of cottages and farmhouses and wove them into garlands as part of May Day festivals.

To many a woods-wise farmer, however, the marsh marigold had a more practical value. The shiny, kidney-shaped leaves were gathered young and boiled from ten minutes to an hour, producing greens that some New Englanders would insist are better than spinach and that American Indians had long enjoyed as a vegetable.

Boiling, incidentally, removes acrid irritants that could be poisonous and that cause grazing livestock to avoid the plant. In this respect, it is much like the buttercup, and indeed the acrid chemical may be the same as that found in so many *Ranunculus* species. Some people say young plants have less or none of the poisonous constituent.

The penny-wise farmer would grab not only the leaves, but also the blossoms, which years ago were peddled on city street corners. They were, after all, the first big and bright wild flower of the season, and they were common and free to any who would get wet feet to pick them. Farmhouse rooms, too, were decorated with lush bouquets of the sweet-scented blossoms.

### *Fit-stopping Gas*

In some areas, including Virginia, people picked and pickled the buds as a substitute for capers. Herbalists used the plant to treat several maladies, such as warts, anemia, and fits. Some herbals mention its use for clearing the throat and bronchial passages, but Charles F. Millspaugh, in *American Medicinal Plants*, observed, "The medical history of this herb is very sparse and of no consequence; it has been used in cough syrups which would, without doubt, have been fully as efficacious without it." Some American Indians treated scrofulous sores with the plant, and the Chippewas used it as a postpartum medication for mothers.

One nineteenth-century physician even noted, "It would appear medicinal properties may be evolved in the gaseous exhalations of plants and flowers, for on a large quantity of the flowers' . . . being put into the bedroom of a girl subject to fits, the fits ceased."

### *Mary's Gold?*

Commonly called either marsh marigold or cowslip, the plant is neither a marigold (as in the garden *Calendula*) nor a true cowslip (an English primrose). The origins of both names, however, are interesting.

There are two theories about "marigold." Some authorities say it is derived from the church festivals in the Middle Ages, when the flower was one of several devoted to the Virgin Mary, hence "Mary-gold." Mrs. William Starr Dana, however, noted that the Anglo-Saxon word for marsh is "mere" (pronounced with two syllables) and suggested that the word is a modern English equivalent of "marsh-gold." As reasonable as that may sound, the *Oxford English Dictionary* favors the former derivation. But here we go from the sublime to the ridiculous. Cowslip literally means "cow slop," which is to say, cow dung. The English cowslip frequents meadows and pastures, as does its namesake. And if the ground is moist enough, marsh marigold joins them.

Marsh marigold is native to North America, Europe, and Asia. A flower so early, common, and bright is bound to pick up many names, and this one is no exception. The plant is called king cups, water blobs, May blobs, mollyblobs, horse blobs, bull's eyes, leopard's foot, great bitterflower, water gowan, meadow gowan, Marybuds, verrucaria, solsequia, water dragon, capers, cowlily, soldier buttons, palsywort, water-goggles, meadowbouts, crazy bet, gools, drunkards, water crowfoot, and meadow buttercups.

Blob originally meant "bubble," but because bubbles are round, blob came to be used for other things that are round, such as drops, fruit, flowers, and eventually a science fiction movie monster. Gowan is based on an Old Norse word for gold. *Verrucaria* is Latin, meaning "cure for warts," while *solsequia*, also from Latin, means "sun-follower"; the flowers open in the morning and close at night. "Winking Marybuds begin to ope their golden eyes," wrote Shakespeare. Drunkards, an old Devonshire name, stems from a belief, especially among children, that the scent of the flower encouraged drunkenness because the wetland-loving plant seems to drink so much water.

The final two names on the list are technically more fitting than the two commonly used ones, for the plant is a member of the Crowfoot, or Buttercup, family. The flowers, bearing five to nine petal-like sepals, are quite similar to those of common buttercups. Like buttercups, as well as the related anemones and hepaticas, they are early bloomers that do not mind chilly northern climes.

### *Swamp Cups*

To the scientist, marsh marigold has but one name, *Caltha palustris*. *Caltha* is from the Greek for "cup" or "goblet." The word, descriptive of the flower's shape, was also the name the Romans used for true marigold. *Palustris* is from the Latin for "swamp." *C. palustris* is the type species of a small genus of temperate and arctic plants, only three of which can be found in North America, and about fifteen worldwide. Marsh marigold grows from Labrador to Alaska, and south into the Carolinas and Nebraska. The other two natives, both bearing white sepals, live in the mountains of western North America.

Marsh marigolds, incidentally, are among the few wildflowers that can grow in the middle of a stream. The plants probably gain a foothold when the water is low. Later, when the stream becomes swift with current, the flowering plants present an unusual sight.

Marsh marigold is ideal for anyone who happens to have a moist, swampy spot that is sunny in springtime. The soil need be wet only in the spring, for the roots of the plant, whose leaves disappear by summer, can survive in places that become fairly dry later in the year. The location must be quite moist at least from March through May, however, and it is best if the ground is damp year-round.

Marsh marigold can be introduced with seed obtained from healthy flowers, though it will take several years to get mature, blooming plants. The species self-sows and multiplies fairly rapidly from seed. If you have access to a large colony, you can transplant at any time. (Do not take plants where they are not common or where they should be encouraged to spread.) Marsh marigolds are susceptible to winter kill, especially if they are unsheltered, so mulching the transplant area in late fall or sticking a pail or basket over the crown of a plant for the winter helps assure survival.

Survival is naturally encouraged by the design of the flower itself. Unlike most blossoms of its family and of similar shape, marsh marigolds have not one, but many sources of nectar. Nectar is available next to each of the many pistils around the flower center. Consequently, bees and early flies wander all around the treasure trove of sweets, carrying pollen to many of the stigmas.

Bees buzzing around marsh marigolds was an unforgetable image for John Moore, a twentieth-century British novelist and naturalist. Describing an English soldier stationed in Korea, he wrote that the young man, remembering springtime in his homeland, thought about finding "kingcups by the river so shiny you'd think the bees could see their faces in them."

**Larger Blue Flag**
*(Iris versicolor)*

# *Born to the Purple*

Blue flag, one of our more majestic and unusual midspring wildflowers, is a member of a regal family that has impressed both naturalists and gardeners through the ages. Yet the plant received only a mediocre review from none other than Henry David Thoreau. "How completely all character is expressed by flowers," the essayist wrote. "This is a little too showy and gaudy, like some women's bonnets. Yet it belongs to the meadow and ornaments it much."

Without doubt, the blue flag is showy, but that is part of its means of survival. At a time of year when many blossoms vie for the attention of nectar-hunting pollinators, the showy, big blossoms are flags for passing bees. The flowers give insects plenty of room to land and have ample veining to guide them inside.

## *Nature's Mechanism*

Blue flag's blossom has evolved to move pollen from flower to flower. Bees cannot help rubbing against pollen-bearing anthers located overhead, positioned so that grains cannot fall onto the stigma, self-fertilize, and create poor-quality seeds. The sticky stigma is situated so that bees will deposit pollen from other flowers.

A turn-of-the-century plant naturalist, appropriately named Clarence M. Weed, found that irises are particularly susceptible to thievery. While adapted to large bumblebees, they are also visited by all sorts of flies, skipper butterflies, moths, and other insects that usually do not transfer pollen. Nevertheless, the iris has plenty of nectar to go around, and it is perhaps no accident that the flag is a denizen of wet places—swamps and moist fields—making production of large amounts of nectar easy.

The leaves, too, are specially designed. Grasslike and vertical, they allow the sunlight to penetrate into a tightly packed colony of plants. What's more, unlike broad-leafed plants, the iris can assimilate light on both sides of its leaf, not just on the upper surface.

Larger blue flag is one of the most visible and most representative of the wild irises east of the Mississippi River. Although not rare today, *Iris versicolor* was more plentiful in the days when there were more pastures and swamps. Many of these wet areas have been drained, filled, or bulldozed for fields and, more recently, subdivisions and shopping centers. Blue flag's blooming season in the Northeast runs from late May through June. When they are undisturbed, the plants are often found in impressive colonies. Blue flag may be found in shaded swamps or open meadows, but almost always where their roots can remain moist year-round.

Wild irises are not common, and the flowers should not be picked, no matter how tempting. Although blue flags are perennials and spread from rhizomes, they also depend on their seeds for propagation. Besides, said Mabel Osgood Wright, "This iris must surely be seen in its home to be known in anything but outline. If many flowers of wood and field lose quality away from their surroundings, the herbaceous flowers of moist lands and waterways do so in far greater degree."

## *Regal History*

The iris has had a lofty and regal history. Henry Wadsworth Longfellow wrote of the flower:

*Born in the purple, born to joy and pleasance*
*Thou dost not toil nor spin*
*But makest glad and radiant with thy presence*
*The meadow and the lin.*

The name comes from the Greek goddess, Iris, who was a messenger between humans on Earth and gods on Mount Olympus. Wherever she went, Iris trailed a rainbow, and whenever the ancient Greeks saw a rainbow they took it as a sign that Iris was delivering a message. Thus, "iris" came to mean "rainbow" and reflects the variety of colors sported by various species. One of Iris's duties was to guide the souls of dead women to the afterworld, so Greeks often planted the flowers next to graves.

The ancients considered the iris a symbol of power and majesty. Egyptian kings used the design of the blossom on their scepters and placed it on the brow of the Sphinx, believing its three major petals to be symbols of faith, wisdom, and valor. Modern use of the symbol may trace back to Clovis, a sixth-century king of the Franks. According to one legend, his army was trapped by a larger force of Goths, backed up against the Rhine River near Cologne. As he searched for a way to escape, Clovis noticed in the distance a large colony of golden irises extending far out into the river. He realized that the water was shallow enough for his troops to cross and escape. In another version of the tale, Clovis was able to sneak across the river and attack the rear guard of the Goths by finding flags growing in a shallow area. In either event, Clovis eventually conquered the Goths and adopted the iris as his family's badge. (For a similar reason, the Scots took the thistle as a national symbol; see Thistles: Watch Your Step.)

Perhaps knowing this tradition, King Louis VII of France selected the iris as his house emblem when he was a young Crusader. It thus became the *fleur-de-lis*, *fleur-de-lys*, or *fleur-de-luce*, all corruptions of *fleur-de-Louis*, "flower of Louis." There is no connection with *lis*, the French word for "lily," though in *The Winter's Tale*, Shakespeare spoke of "lilies of all kinds, the fleur-de-luce being one." Our blue flag, a different species from the white iris of Louis, is sometimes called the American fleur-de-lis. The flowers are commonly called flags because Louis, Clovis, and other rulers in Europe frequently employed the design on flags, banners, and crowns.

Less regal are some of the other folk names for our own *Iris versicolor*: poison flag, liver lily, snake lily, dragon flower, and dagger flower. Some of these names refer to the shape of the blossom (dragon) or the leaf (dagger); the Old English word for the plant was *segg*, which was a small sword. Other names reflect the plant's long history as a medicinal herb.

## *Food and Drug*

*Iris versicolor* has probably been used in medicine more extensively than any other member of its clan. Indians dug the roots from wild plants and even cultivated colonies near ponds. They used the root as an emetic, a cathartic, and a poultice, and also treated stomach problems and dropsy with it. Members of some Western tribes carried the root of another species to prevent snakebites.

"It is excellent in removing humor from the system, much more so than the outrageous mercury and much more safe," said the *Ladies' Indispensable Assistant.* The advice did not suggest that a clown would turn dour; this "humor" was a bodily fluid, and the writer presumably referred to a "bad humor" that would cause sickness.

The rhizome, or creeping rootstock, contains a powerful, acrid resin, so strong that many modern authorities on herbs warn against its internal use. Some herbalists in the past, however, considered the plant valuable in treating chronic vomiting, heartburn, liver and gall bladder ailments, sinus problems, colic, gastritis, enteritis, syphilis, scrofula, skin diseases, and even migraines. Drugs called Iridin or Irisin, used as diuretics, were once produced from the plant, which was long listed in the *U.S. Pharmacopoeia*, a catalog of accepted drugs. Modern research indicates the root may have the ability to increase the rate at which fat is converted into waste, and an iris has been used in India as a treatment for obesity.

Various species, particularly European ones, are known as "orris root." After drying a few months, their roots gain a sweet scent, not unlike that of violets. Ground into powder, these roots were once made into little pomander balls that were carried by the wealthy as a perfume. This same powder was also carried by witches, who, it was said, induced abortions with it.

In the nineteenth century, growing *Iris florentina* was a major industry in parts of Italy, particularly the Chianti section of Tuscany, which shipped the dried rootstock to Florentine perfumeries. Florence, whose city seal bears an iris, is still a center of interest and hosts the International Iris Trials, a competition for iris growers. Iris roots are still used as fragrances in fancy soaps, cosmetics, and liquid perfumes.

There is a theory that an Italian dish got its name from the iris. According to the story, one type of iris was called *machaironion* in Greek. The root of this species was ground with flour to create a pasta later called "macaroni."

The French, who enjoy all sorts of drinks made from plants, once used roasted iris seeds as a coffee. The leaves have been used to make a green dye, and the root, to make black dye and ink.

### *Many Varieties*

There are at least 36 species of irises in North America, some of them garden escapes native to other continents. One botanist claimed that in southeastern United States alone, nearly 100 different species can be found, many of them in southern Florida. Worldwide, more than 150 species grow in the north temperate zone, much to the pleasure of gardeners specializing in this handsome genus.

Irises are in turn members of the Iris family (*Iridaceae*), which consists of nearly sixty genera and 1,000 species worldwide. The family includes much more modest relatives, small blue-eyed grasses of spring fields. Many irises bear a resemblance to orchids, and it is not surprising that the Iris family is fairly closely related to the Orchid family (*Orchidaceae*).

*I. versicolor* ranges from the East Coast to Wisconsin and from Canada south to Virginia. Western blue flag (*I. missouriensis*), the most widespread of several beautiful western species, is found from British Columbia to southern California and eastward into the Dakotas and Colorado. Almost all irises are showy and colorful. They come in blue, purple, lilac, orange, white, and yellow hues, providing a shocking contrast to their verdant homes in wooded wetlands and meadows.

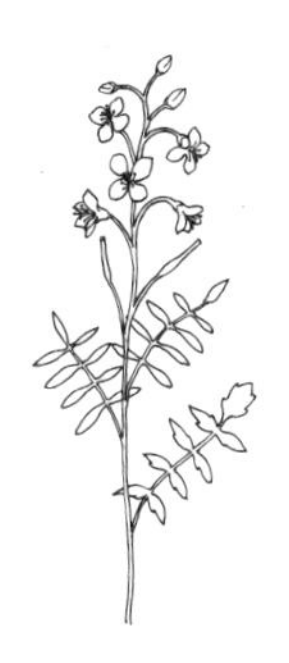

**Cuckoo-Flower**
*(Cardamine pratensis)*

# *The Cuckoos of Spring*

They're called cuckoo, and perhaps with good reason. The friendly, almost jovial little flowers spring up in surprising places with surprising speed. They may also disappear for a year or two, only to return suddenly en masse.

Cuckoo-flowers are one of our earliest mustards, a delightful member of the cress clan that inhabits moist ground in the spring. The flowers have the typical, four-petaled form of mustards; the family is called *Cruciferae* for the crosslike appearance.

The plants appear in swamps, spring pools, and meadows from late April through May. My first meeting with cuckoo-flowers occurred on the main street of town. Dozens of these plants sprang up one year from a large puddle in a lawn not four feet from the highway. I did not recall seeing them the year before, and they did not show up during an unusually dry spring the year after. But the following year they were back—and have been almost every year since—apparently reacting to normally moist springs.

I took several plants and stuck them in a wet corner of my yard, and they have reappeared yearly in steadily increasing numbers. They are quite attractive, especially in large colonies, providing a somewhat uncommon splash of pink (when seen close up) and silver-white (when seen from a distance) in early spring. The flowers are nice when added to bouquets of dandelions, celandines, and other common spring flowers. Unless, that is, you believe in "little people." English country folk held that cuckoo-flowers belonged to the fairies and should not be picked. Taking them into the house was bad luck.

Cuckoo-flowers, which are easily transplanted or grown from seed, can liven up a wet section of your yard. In fact, you can create active flower beds in wet areas from March through late autumn. If you plant coltsfoot and marsh marigolds for early spring, blue flags for late spring, purple lobelias and cardinal flowers for late summer, and purple asters for fall, you will have a lovely progression of moisture-loving plants. All of these flowers are perennials and most will spread.

## *"Nearly Worthless"*

*Cardamine pratensis*, type species for its genus, is sometimes called meadow bittercress and is closely related to the various cress and bittercress mustards, most of them spring water-lovers. Some forty-five species of *Cardamine* can be found in North America. Some authors say *C. pratensis* is native to this continent while others maintain it is an import from Europe; it is also found in Asia. West Coast *Cardamine* species include Brewer's bittercress (*C. breweri*) and western bittercress (*C. oligosperma*), both widespread in the Pacific states.

Unlike some of its more popular relatives, the cuckoo-flower "is an insignificant and nearly worthless salad plant," wrote Dr. E. Lewis Sturtevant in *Edible Plants of the World.* "It has a piquant savor and is used as watercress." Nonetheless, the plants were once cultivated in France and probably in colonial America, and are a good source of both potassium and iodine.

Cuckoo-flower was better known as a medicine. Linnaeus selected the name *Cardamine*, meaning "heart-strengthening," because some members of the genus were used as heart sedatives. Cuckoo-flower, however, was more popular years ago as a treatment for hysteria and epilepsy. While some people might suspect its use in treating such disorders is the source of "cuckoo," the origin is the European bird. The plant flowers "when the cuckowe doth begin to sing her pleasant notes without stammering," wrote Gerard. *Pratensis* means "meadow," referring to the plant's usual home.

Other names for the plant include *flos cuculi* (or frock flower), May-flower, cuckoo-spit, lady-smocks, milk maids, and smick-smock. The frock and smock names refer to the fancied resemblance of the blossoms to clothing, and one author goes so far as to say the smocks are spread out on the sunny grass to bleach.

Unlike most mustards, which tend to be white or yellow, cuckoo-flowers are often pink, lilac, violet-pink, or white. En masse, however, as they are often found in England, they appear lighter; hence Shakespeare's line from *Love's Labor's Lost*, "lady-smocks all silver white." These words helped British novelist and country essayist John Moore realize that Shakespeare was real. "During an Easter holiday when I was about sixteen," he wrote in *The Season of the Year*, "I went to Stratford on Saint George's Day and bicycled home beside the Avon meadows where the cuckoo-flowers of a laggard spring looked like silvery pools left behind by a March flood. Seeing those 'lady-smocks all silver-white,' I realized that Shakespeare had been a boy here. He suddenly ceased to be the author of things we read at school; he jumped clean out of the curriculum and landed in life itself. He had seen the lady-smocks as I had seen them; we had shared the same experience. Moreover, he had seen them here."

Years later, in some professor's Shakespeare text, he ran across a footnote that said lady-smocks are not silver-white but pale mauve and "could not therefore have been intended." "So much for academic criticism!" said Moore. "The don had clearly never been to Stratford and looked down upon the river-meadows in April."

**Jack-in-the-Pulpit**
*(Arisaema atrorubens)*

# *The Silent Preacher*

He is found where the ground is damp and shady. He stands short or tall, depending on his food. He was a friend of many Indians and is a foe of certain insects. He may become a she, and then a he again. He might even kill you. His name is common, but his stage makes him famous.

He is Jack-in-the-pulpit, one of our strangest-looking flowering plants, common from Nova Scotia and New England to Texas. The plant is well known, although some people mistake it for a pitcher plant. While it is shaped somewhat like that insectivorous species and often contains trapped insects, Jack-in-the-pulpit lives off nutrients in the ground, not on the corpses of its accidental victims.

The common folk name is perfect. The long spathe looks like an old-fashioned pulpit, complete with overhead baffle to amplify and project sermons throughout the church in the days before public address systems. For the plant, however, the hood is simply an umbrella, preventing the vertical, tubelike spathe from filling with rainwater that could drown the flowers or wash away their pollen.

"Jack" is the spadix, the clublike, flower-bearing stick that stands erect in the pulpit with just the tip protruding to survey his "congregation." Jack was a common colloquialism for "fellow" or "guy," especially in England.

## *Hot Stuff*

Jack-in-the-pulpit is a member of the Arum family, a small group of primitive flowering plants whose name comes from the Arabic word for "fire." Anyone who has tasted the raw root quickly understands the meaning. The root contains crystalline calcium oxalate, a powerfully bitter substance that burns so badly it can cause blisters. Schoolboys used to dare their comrades to take a bite of the root, with results the taster would long remember. What was a joke among pupils was serious business for young men of certain American Indian tribes, however. Without complaint or hesitation, they had to eat one of the fiery roots before they could officially enter manhood. Both trick and ritual were dangerous. A calcium oxalate crystal bears many microscopically small but sharp needles that cut and poison the flesh. If the root gets to the back of the mouth, it can cause enough swelling in the throat to suffocate the victim.

Jack-in-the-pulpit is what one herbalist calls ' violently acrid" in taste. "In its fresh state, it is a violent, irritant to the mucous membrane, when chewed burning the mouth and throat," said English herbalist Maude Grieve. "If taken internally, the plant causes violent gastroenteritis, which may end in death." Despite this ability to poison, the dried and powdered root has been used in small doses to treat croup, whooping cough, malaria, bronchitis, and asthma. Chippewas employed it for sore eyes, and Mohegans of Connecticut concocted a liniment and a throat gargle from it. Osages and Shawnees made a cough medicine from it, while Pawnees applied the powdered root to their heads to relieve headaches—or at least provide a real reason for the pain!

The American Indians long ago discovered that one of the chief constituents of the root is starch. They also found that roasting the roots or corms, or drying them for at least six months, removed the acridity. ("How can men have learned that plants so extremely opposite to our nature were eatable and that their poison, which burns the tongue, can be conquered by fire?" wondered explorer-naturalist Peter Kalm in 1749.) The roots were peeled and ground into a powder from which bread was made. The chocolate flavor is nice, said Adrienne Crowhurst in *The Weed Cookbook*, but she wondered whether it was worth all the bother to prepare. Shredded root that had been boiled along with berries was mixed with venison by certain Indian tribes. Bradford Angier, in *Feasting Free on Wild Edibles*, tells how to make Jack-in-the-pulpit cookies, flavored with hazelnuts. Lee Allen Peterson's *Field Guide to Edible Wild Plants* mentions potato chips made from the roasted root.

Because of its popularity among American Indians, Jack-in-the-pulpit is also called Indian turnip, the rootstock being shaped somewhat like that of the turnip. The plant's generic name is *Arisaema*, a Greek word that refers to the red-blotched leaves of some European species, or perhaps to the purple stripes on the native plant's pulpit. Our most common species of Jack-in-the-pulpit is *Arisaema triphyllum*, *triphyllum* referring to the three-leaved clusters, one or two of which accompany each flower.

Jack-in-the-pulpit is found in moist woods or wood edges, frequently inhabiting the borders of wetlands, and is sometimes used by those who study soil conditions as a sign of nearby swampland. As the soil becomes wetter or more poorly drained, you are apt to find Jack-in-the-pulpit's cousin, skunk cabbage, another member of the Arum clan. Jack-in-the-pulpit grows from less than a foot to three feet tall, depending on the nutrients and water supply available to it.

### *Visitors*

The plant is so constructed and colored that insects, especially fungus gnats, are drawn down the spathe to the base of the spadix, which bears the tiny flowers. The floor of a chamber at the base of the tube is covered with pollen. After it has descended and picked up pollen, an insect has a hard time leaving. It cannot climb up the spadix because of a projecting ledge, nor up the slippery tube. The only exit is a small flap at the base, where the two sides of the pulpit come together. Insects that are persistent, small, and strong can find the door and squeeze through it. Larger flies are sometimes trapped. The plant often contains insect corpses, leading some scientific observers to wonder whether the Jack-in-the-pulpit is evolving slowly over the eons into an insect-eating variety like the pitcher plant or the Venus flytrap.

The spathes vary in color. Most are deep purple, vertically striped white or greenish. Others are almost pure green. Some authorities say the males are green while the females are purple. Others say green plants are simply sterile, which makes sense if the purplish, meaty color is designed to draw flies, as it is in the related skunk cabbage. An old legend that the purple color comes from the blood of Christ at the crucifixion inspired a nineteenth-century poet:

*Beneath the cross it grew:*
*And in the vase-like hollow of the leaf*
*Catching from that dread shower of agony*

*A few mysterious drops, transmitted thus*
*Unto the groves and hills their healing stains*
*A heritage, for storm or vernal shower*
*Never to blow away.*

### *Sex Changes*

Dr. Harold N. Moldenke of the New York Botanical Garden reported in his 1949 book, *American Wildflowers*, that Jack-in-the-pulpits start out life as males, then become females, then may revert to the male state. The young plant stays male a couple of years or until it has gained enough strength and food-storage capacity to take on the tougher job of being a female. As in mammals, where the task of feeding young before and after birth requires a special ability and good health, the job of producing seeds requires extra strength and sound health in the plant, which must put aside food, not only for itself, but also for its offspring. (Seeds are, after all, largely stored food or "meat." Many seeds are nutritious, which is why we eat grains like wheat, corn, and rye, and all sorts of nuts and seed-carrying berries.)

Sometimes a plant will remain male for many years because it lacks the proper food, moisture, or light to develop into a strong female. Or, a female may revert to the male state if conditions change. A transplanted female, for example, might need all of its strength to heal wounds that may have occurred in the move, and to adapt to new surroundings. If it cannot produce seeds, it may revert to being a male.

The unusual characteristics of this plant have generated most of its folk names: marsh turnip, pepper turnip, wild turnip, bog onion, brown dragon, starchwort, dragon root, devil's ear, cuckoo plant, priest's pintle, and wake-robin. The last name, also applied to the red trillium, refers to the fact that in some areas the plants bloom at about the time that the robins return, from late April through May.

Some authorities today list three Jack-in-the-pulpits: swamp, or small, Jack-in-the-pulpit (*A. triphyllum*); woodland Jack-in-the-pulpit (*A. atrorubens*, meaning "dark red"); and northern Jack-in-the-pulpit (*A. stewardsonii*). Other authorities believe that *A. atrorubens* and *A. stewardsonii* are just variations of *A. triphyllum.* To add to the confusion, some authors consider *A. atrorubens*, instead of *A. triphyllum*, to be the correct name of the chief North American species.

Telling the varieties apart is often difficult. Swamp Jack-in-the-pulpit has one three-parted leaf, while woodland Jack-in-the-pulpit usually has two. Northern Jack-in-the-pulpit is similar looking and is found in bogs in Pennsylvania and New Jersey, and perhaps in states and provinces to the north.

Green dragon (*A. dracontium*) is also in this genus. The species is readily recognized by its long spadix, or tongue, which extends way beyond the spathe. Green dragon plants were once used to poison vermin.

Jack-in-the-pulpit is easily grown in a rich, shady spot. You can dig up and move whole plants or, better yet (and to avoid unnecessary sex changes), find some of the bright red berries that appear on the spatheless spadix by August and September, and plant them about an inch under the surface. The berries, which come in clusters and are at first bright green, are delicacies for pheasants and other woodland birds, but may be somewhat toxic to humans.

Jack-in-the-pulpit's germination rate is very good. Flowering plants usually appear the next year, occasionally in two years. The plants are hardy as well as long-lasting and, while not colorfully showy, they add a touch of the exotic to any spring wildflower garden.

**Large-flowered Trillium**
*(Trillium grandiflorum)*

# *Dead Meat*

Our native red trillium has received mixed reviews from those who study and write about wildflowers. Although the plant is both handsome and unusual, it exudes an odor that has cost it admirers, but gained it a peculiar method of survival.

*Trillium erectum* is one of the most recognized members of this family of two dozen or so North American species. Possibly because the flowers are strange-looking and showy, and they grow in the woods, many people believe them to be rare. Actually red trillium is as common as any forest flower. It is safeguarded because it is not excessively finicky about habitat and because its odor dissuades people from picking the blossoms. Found from Canada to North Carolina and westward to the Mississippi, red trillium dwells in rich, cool woodlands, preferably with some evergreens nearby. Often they are found on hillsides.

The purple red flowers of mature plants are about six inches above the ground and tend to nod a little so that the blooms are partially hidden. Linnaeus created the name *trillium* to describe the "threeness" of the plant. Each plant has three leaves; each flower has three petals and three sepals; each ovary has three cells; and each berry has three ribs. Rarely, four-petaled flowers are found.

Plants of the genus are also called wake-robin because many of them bloom when robins arrive in the spring. Another folk name, birthroot, recalls its use by Indians and early colonists to promote birth. Indians recognized other medicinal properties in the plant, using it as an antiseptic, astringent, and expectorant. They also used it to restrain gangrene, control hemorrhages, and treat heart palpitations. They boiled the leaves in lard and applied them to ulcers and tumors. In Canada, people once thought that chewing the root would serve as an antidote for rattlesnake bites; this action was taken despite the root's reported terrible taste. For skin ailments, such as sore nipples, the trillium-based medicine was often "injected" into the skin with jabs of a dog whisker. Today, its value as a medicine is debated by herb experts.

## *A Stinker*

One of its more colorful names—one that my son Ben loved when he was young and hates now that he is older—is stinking benjamin. Benjamin, however, was not a person. The word is a corruption of the word "benzoin," or the earlier form, "benjoin," a substance obtained from Sumatran plants and used in the manufacture of perfumes and incense. (Our native shrub, the spicebush, noted for its strong spicy scent, bears the Latin name, *Lindera benzoin.*) There is, however, no perfume made from red trillium, and the name was probably meant to amuse. But for apt humor, one can't beat the much more earthy and colorful moniker, "wet-dog trillium."

Other names include Indian balm, purple trillium, beth-flower (a corruption of "birth-flower"), bumblebee root, herb trinity, trinity lilies (for they are members of the large Lily family), lambs quarters, nosebleed (it was used to stop that condition), red benjamin, true-love, and ground lily.

Some wildflower enthusiasts have seemed insulted that so showy a blossom would be so malodorous. "It repels us by its unpleasant odor. . . . Altogether we are inclined to believe that the plant has too great an idea of its own importance," wrote one turn-of-the-century author. Neltje Blanchan described the bloom as an "unattractive, carrion-scented flower . . . resembling in color and odor raw beefsteak of uncertain age." But she did more than belittle the plant. She studied the flower and found that while most flying insects ignored it, the common green flesh-flies that are also found in garbage and on dead animals were attracted by the scent and color. The flies apparently feed on pollen, since the flowers have no nectar. In the process, the insects pick up enough grains to pollinate subsequent flowers. Thus, trilliums look and smell like rotten meat for a good reason.

Trilliums bloom in April and May and are generally easy to transplant in any season. Care should be taken, however, to include a good-sized ball of soil with the roots. Transplants may not bloom for a year or two after being moved. I once acquired some small bulbs from a lot being bulldozed for a new house, and although they grew leaves each year they did not blossom until three or four years later. The plants had to mature, storing enough food to push up flowers early in the season. Trillium seeds are generally successful at producing plants, but will not give flowering plants until at least the third year after sowing.

### *Other Trilliums*

Trilliums are found in various shapes and shades through much of North America, and some wildflower enthusiasts specialize in collecting the more showy white and pink varieties. The late U.S. senator George Aiken of Vermont was an expert trillium gardener. He wrote in *Pioneering with Wildflowers*, "For a beginner in growing wildflowers, there is hardly a family more satisfactory than the trilliums. They grow wonderfully well in hardwoods shade and rejoice in a plentiful supply of leafmold. All may be propagated from seed." Senator Aiken grew at least a dozen varieties in Vermont, including species from California, the Rockies, and even a rare yellow variety from a Tennessee mountain. All of the plants seemed to do well.

Some nurseries carry large white trilliums and dwarf trilliums (*T. grandiflorum* and *T. nivale*), both of which are attractive and long-lasting. While the range of white trillium is supposed to include Connecticut, I have never seen one in the wild in my hilly town. Along one of our lakes, however, is a wood that belonged to the large estate of a woman who was prominent in the local garden club years ago. Each spring those woods are dotted with white trilliums that she had no doubt planted thirty, forty, or more years earlier. We can enjoy them today because the woman left her estate to the town as a park.

The Pacific Coast has several native species, including the widespread western trillium (*T. ovatum*), which has pink or white flowers.

Many people think painted trillium (*T. undulatum*), with white petals "painted" with red-pink near the center, is the finest-looking trillium; it was ranked sixth out of more than 1,000 candidates in a 1940s poll of favorite

North American wildflowers. Painted trillium ranges from Nova Scotia to the mountains of Georgia, but seems to be rather uncommon in the southern two-thirds of its range, probably because it has been picked or bulldozed almost into extinction in more populated areas. Like most trilliums, it has a mild fetid odor. But for stinking, none comes close to old Ben.

**Water Speedwell**
*(Veronica anagallis-aquatica)*

# *Diamonds in the Rough*

The suburban yard is often the object of a strange fanaticism. People who plant fancy and expensive flowers in beds and borders collectively spend millions of dollars on chemicals to kill the flowers that grow in their grass. They classify giant, often cumbersome, and sometimes bizarre-colored hybrids as beautiful and desirable, while small, delicate blossoms are attacked with costly, perhaps dangerous chemicals in order to produce a putting-green lawn.

Why is an acre of sameness, of monotonous green grass so desirable? Wouldn't an acre of green concrete or green pebbles be easier to maintain? Why not install Astroturf?

A grass lawn, regularly mowed but otherwise left on its own, can become a wild garden dappled with different shades of green and spotted with pink, purple, yellow, blue, and white. Many varieties of wildflowers creep into an unpoisoned lawn, along with pretty mosses, colorful lichens (if you have some rocks), and unusual mushrooms—all mixed with the usual grasses.

## *Always Interesting*

To me this variety of color and form is far preferable to a rolled, aerated, fertilized, and poisoned carpet of perfection. No matter where you walk or sit, in a natural lawn you will find something interesting—an orchidlike gill-over-the-ground, a pastel blue speedwell, a dense cluster of heal-all, a starlike chickweed, a shiny buttercup, and, yes, even a bright yellow dandelion, the most dread invader for lawn perfectionists.

Several dozen varieties of wildflowers will do well in a lawn that is regularly mowed and possesses halfway decent soil. Probably my favorite fingernail lawn flowers are the speedwells, represented in natural lawns by at least a half-dozen common species. All have the same general form: three larger petals—at each side and at the top of the blossom—and one small petal pointed groundward. Each blossom also has two stamens that protrude from the center and bend toward opposite directions, like two stalked crab's eyes.

Among the most common of the speedwells

is, suitably enough, common speedwell, *Veronica officinalis.* This spring and early summer flower is blue with a hint of red, a shade described by the Chinese with a word meaning "the sky after rain." To Tennyson the color was special. He wrote of spring in his poem, "In Memoriam":

*Bring orchis, bring the foxglove spire,*
*The little speedwell's darling blue,*
*Deep tulips dashed with fiery dew,*
*Laburnums, dropping-wells of fire.*

After a visit to England, where common speedwell is native, John Burroughs called it "the prettiest of all humble roadside flowers I saw. It is prettier than the violet . . . a small and delicate edition of our hepatica, done in indigo blue and wonted to the grass in the fields and by the waysides. . . . I saw it blooming with the daisy and buttercup upon the grave of Carlyle. The tender human and poetic element of his stern, rocky nature was well expressed by it."

Common speedwell is a native of both Europe and Asia Minor. Like many other plants now common in North America, it made the trip across the Atlantic with settlers or later immigrants. It is a perennial, and owes its success to its ability to spread by underground runners and to produce seeds without help. While insects like bees will cross-pollinate, the flower can also self-fertilize as it withers and its two protruding stalks bend inward, allowing the pollen-bearing anthers or "eyes" to touch the pollen-catching stigma.

Common speedwell was employed in the Old World to treat skin diseases, scrofula, wounds, hemorrhages, and coughs. It was also used as a diuretic and expectorant. "It wonderfully helps all those inward parts that need consolidating and strengthening," wrote Nicholas Culpeper. "It cleanses and heals all foul or old ulcers, and fretting or spreading cankers."

Its English name, which dates back to at least the 1500s, may have been related to a belief that the plant was quick in curing. Another theory says the name reflects the fact that the colorful corollas fall off and fly away soon after the flowers are picked. In other words, speedwell is used in the sense of "So long!" or "Good-bye!"

### St. Veronica

There are also two theories about its Latin generic name, *veronica.* The name may have stemmed from the Greek words, *phero*, meaning "I bring," and *nike*, "victory," because of its supposed curative properties. The more common explanation, however, is that the name comes from St. Veronica. As Neltje Blanchan described it, "An ancient tradition of the Roman Church relates that when Jesus was on his way to Calvary, he passed the home of a certain Jewish maiden who, when she saw the drops of agony on his brow, ran after him along the road to wipe his face with her kerchief. This linen, the monks declare, ever after bore the impress of the sacred features—*vera icona*, the 'true likeness.' When the church wished to canonize the pitying maiden, an abbreviated form of the Latin words was given to her, St. Veronica, and her kerchief became one of the most precious relics at St. Peter's where it is said to be still preserved. Medieval flower lovers, whose piety seems to have been eclipsed only by their imaginations, named this little flower from a fancied resemblance to the relic."

While European speedwell is probably the species most often seen here, there are native American species. Among the best known and most widespread is *Veronica virginica*, culver's root, a plant of moist woods and thickets. It was widely used in the nineteenth century to purge the bowels, but was eventually found to be too potent. The Chippewas called the plant *wisugidjibik* or "bitter root" and treated scrofula with it—just as Europeans had done with their own species. The Chippewas also used it to stop nosebleeds.

Unlike most of our imported species, culver's root is a tall plant, growing to seven feet and looking far different from the dainty lawn and field speedwells. In fact, some botanists classify it under a different genus, labeling it

*Leptandra virginica.* It has also borne such colorful and unusual names as oxadaddy and quitch. Culver recalls an early American physician who used it. Like all speedwells, it is closely related to the genus *Digitalis,* the foxgloves of medicinal fame.

Another native, American brooklime, *V. americana,* may be found in and about brooks and swamps from coast to coast. A succulent plant that grows upright to nearly a foot, it has been used in salads, though some think its taste is too bitter. Leaves of common speedwell were once used in England as a substitute for tea, though one nineteenth-century authority said it was "more astringent and less grateful than tea." Other names for the plant include lluellin, fluellein, Paul's betony, groundhele, gypsy weed, and upland speedwell. Lluellin and fluellein, once common names in England, were corruptions of the Welsh name of the plant, *Ilysiau Llewelyn* or "Llewelyn's herb." Llewelyn was a thirteenth-century Celtic prince of Wales conquered by Edward I; the event gave England control over the Welsh territory.

*V. officinalis* is the type species for the genus *Veronica,* a large group of some 300 species found throughout the world. About 30 species live in North America, including many small varieties such as corn speedwell (*V. arvensis*), bird's eye speedwell (*V. chamaedrys*), slender speedwell (*V. filiformis*), and the beautiful blue-and-white thyme-leaved speedwell (*V. serpyllifolia*). Most of these plants love lawns, blooming in the spring or early summer in varying shades of blue. Several European species have become popular as border and rock garden plants, and are sold in many nurseries. One of the largest-flowered species is Cusick's speedwell (*V. cusickii*), a native found in Pacific Coast alpine meadows and bearing half-inch, blue-violet blossoms. Most of the eastern and alien varieties have quarter-inch or smaller flowers. Veronicas in turn are members of the Figwort family of 165 genera and 2,700 species worldwide, including mulleins, toadflaxes, snapdragons, turtleheads, beardtongues, and monkeyflowers.

Although they may be invaders, and some people consider them pests, the speedwells can help you have a lively, colorful lawn. People pay fortunes for small diamonds; here are living equivalents, diamonds in the rough, that are absolutely free.

**Hairy Solomon's Seal**
*(Polygonatum pubescens)*

## *The Several Seals of Solomon*

In the cool air of a shaded wood, amid the fresh spring ferns and the shoots of summer's plants, we find our several Solomon's seals, both true and false. Often growing side by side, they are as much a part of spring in eastern North America as asters are of fall. They are odd, primitive-looking plants that seem more at home with dinosaurs than with the automobiles whose woodland roads they frequently line. They rise straight from the soil, then lean over almost parallel to the ground, with leaves spread out like the fronds of uncut ferns.

While true and false Solomon's seals are similar in general leaf form and placement, and both are members of the Lily family, they belong to separate genera and bear very different flowers.

Perhaps our most common true Solomon's seal is *Polygonatum biflorum*, whose tubular, yellow-green flowers hang singly or, more often, in pairs from under the stem. The position is no accident. Nature intended the flowers to face the ground because the location makes it difficult for rain or for many types of crawling insects to invade the store of nectar. Yet higher species of bees, which pollinate the flowers, have no difficulty landing on the blossoms and gathering sweets and pollen.

In the summer, *P. biflorum* forms dark blue berries which, like the flowers, dangle from the stem. By planting these berries, either whole or mashed, in rich, slightly acid, dry soil, you can easily introduce the plant to shaded spots around your yard. Solomon's seals can also be transplanted in the spring, but only from places where the they are common or threatened with destruction.

Once established, *Polygonatum* enlarges into great clumps and also multiplies from seed. A wildflower gardener reported that she acquired about a dozen roots of great Solomon's seal and within about five years had more than 500 shoots coming up in her garden.

Great Solomon's seal (*P. commutatum* or *P. giganteum* or *P. canaliculatum*) is probably more desirable for decoration, but less common than *P. biflorum*. It can reach a height of five or more feet. Great Solomon's seal has two to eight flowers, rather than one to two, growing from each leaf axil. Unlike the smaller species, it is hairless, prefers neutral soil, and blooms in June instead of May in my neck of the woods.

## *The Seal*

The origin of the name, Solomon's seal, has been much debated by those who research such things. In the most common explanation, the name is derived from the fact that the rootstock bears indentations that look like the impressions of a signet ring, as if it had been pressed into hot wax. These scars occur when the previous year's above-ground growth dies down to the roots; the approximate age of the plant can be determined by counting the number of scars. Legend has it that the depressions resemble Hebrew letters, and were originally set in the rootstock by King Solomon as testimony to its medicinal values.

Another theory is that slicing the root transversely reveals a shape similar to the Hebrew alphabet character employed as a seal of approval by King Solomon. Still another folktale says that seal refers not so much to the scars as to the fact that the root was used to heal up or seal fresh wounds or broken bones.

Mary Durant, in her book *Who Named the Daisy? Who Named the Rose?*, has her own theory. The name was introduced to Europe in the early Christian era, she wrote, when the desire to see symbols in wild things was strong. The six-pointed Star of David was commonly called Solomon's seal, so the six-pointed flower picked up the same name. However, while the name survived, its origin based in the flower design was forgotten. When people in more modern times tried to figure out where the name came from, they turned to the roots, using the marks upon them or their use in treating wounds as the explanation.

*Polygonatum* is Greek for "many kneed," referring to the joints of the zig-zag stem. *Biflorum* refers to the two-flowered characteristic of the small Solomon's seal. *Commutatum* means "changes" or "changing," probably because great Solomon's seal is a rather variable plant. Perhaps this is why there seems to be such a variety of scientific names for it.

The English folk names for smaller Solomon's seal include sealwort, conquer-John, hairy Solomon's seal, and dwarf Solomon's seal.

The larger species is called sealwort and smooth or giant Solomon's seal.

### *Hastie Fists*

A European variety, *P. multiflorum*, is similar in chemical composition to our species, and its root has been used for treating lung ailments, "female complaints," stomach inflammations, broken bones, piles, and poor complexions. For a long time it was an ingredient in beauty creams. Because the French used it to heal wounds, they called it *l'herbe de la rupture*. It was employed, like jewelweed, to wash skin that had come in contact with poison ivy. Indians mashed the root and, warming it with water, made a poultice with it to treat bruises, sores, wounds, and black eyes. Midwestern Indians used great Solomon's seal to relieve headaches.

John Gerard noted in his 1597 *Herbal*: "The roots of Solomon's seal, stamped while it is fresh and greene and applied, taketh away in one night or two at the most, any bruse, blacke or blew spots, gotten by falls or women's wilfulness in stumbling upon their hastie husband's fists, or such like."

Five species of *Polygonatum* live in North America. *P. biflorum* is probably the most widespread, as it is found from southern Canada to Florida, and out to Texas and Nebraska. Great Solomon's seal is almost as widespread.

### *Why False?*

Like true Solomon's seals, *Smilacina racemosa*, false Solomon's seal, is a member of the large Lily family. The plant bears plumes of white flowers in lacy terminal clusters. False Solomon's seal is found from coast to coast in southern Canada and from Georgia to Arizona. It saw limited use as a medicine and as a source of starchy food, obtained from the root. The young shoots of both false and true Solomon's seals have long been cooked like asparagus, not surprising since both plants are closely related to asparagus, another lily. False Solomon's seal is also called wild spikenard, false spikenard, Solomon's plume, Job's tears, and goldenseal.

"The false Solomon's seal is, in my estimation, even more beautiful than the true," writes F. Schuyler Mathews in *Familiar Flowers of Field and Garden*. "Its spike of fine white flowers is like the *Spiraea japonica*; besides, its wavy bright green leaf with the parallel veining is particularly graceful. Most wildflowers, like the true Solomon's seals, have rather insignificant blossoms; but there is nothing meager about the bloom of this little plant. It deserves cultivation and, in truth, if it is transplanted to a position in the garden similar to its natural environment, it will flourish most satisfactorily."

Perhaps its name has helped prevent it from being popular with gardeners. "It is a shame that any aspersion of falsity should attach to it," said Mathews. "Why should not a plant so deserving have its own good name? We might as well call a Frenchman a false Englishman."

Mrs. William Starr Dana wrote, "A singular lack of imagination is betrayed in the common name of this plant." Added Neltje Blanchan: "As if to offer opportunities for comparison to the confused novice, the true Solomon's seal and the so-called false species—quite as honest a plant—usually grow near each other. Grace of line, rather than beauty of blossom, gives them both their chief charm."

At least one audience appreciates false Solomon's seal as much as it does true Solomon's seal. Woodland birds, which do not discriminate on the basis of our poorly chosen names, eat the berries of both.

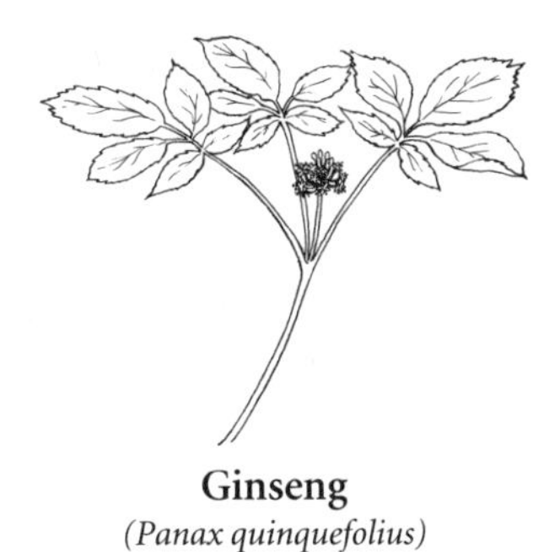

**Ginseng**
*(Panax quinquefolius)*

# *The Dwarf and His Big Brother*

As its very name suggests, dwarf ginseng is not a spectacular plant. It is, nonetheless, one of those early spring flowers that woodland trekkers delight to find amid the blanket of brown leaves. The plant bears a little cluster of white, fluffy blossoms that an author of the last century described as "one feathery ball of bloom."

Dwarf ginseng likes rich woods, where it blooms in April and May, springing from a small round ball of a root (whence its other common name, ground nut). "One must burrow deep, like the rabbits, to find its round, pungent, sweet, nut-like root, measuring about half an inch across, which few have ever seen," wrote Neltje Blanchan.

Dwarf ginseng's scientific name is *Panax trifolium*, meaning "all-healing" and "three-parted leaves." The specific (second) name distinguishes it from *P. quinquefolius*, the better-known American ginseng, which has five-parted leaves. *Panax* means "panacea," referring to true ginseng's reputation around the world for magical powers to cure any ailment and to lift the spirits of those who consume it.

### *Bigger Brothers*

True ginseng, also native to North America, is most often found in the northern Midwest, but it used to be much more common and widespread than it is today. As far back as the turn of the century, wildflower writers reported that it was disappearing from the continent's woods, not because of disease, but because of nature's worst enemy, humans.

The problem arose because of its wide medicinal use in China, where a closely related species, *Panax schin-seng*, was being depleted. The Chinese turned to North America, and in 1876 alone, 550,000 pounds of American ginseng were exported from the United States to China. Ginseng was so precious that several get-rich-quick books were written about hunting and growing the plant. One ginseng grower, A. R. Harding, wrote in 1936 that ginseng root under cultivation was bringing between $5 and $10 a pound, amounting to thousands of dollars per acre. In his book, *Ginseng and Other Medicinal Plants*, he mentioned a grower who bragged of having collected some 5,500 ginseng roots from the woods in a single season. Cultivating ginseng was never lucrative, though, because the plant is susceptible to disease and because it requires six years to develop a mature root from seed.

Pickers decimated the population of ginseng, or sang, as it was sometimes called. Today, ginseng is on many no-pick or endangered lists, and it has been making a slow comeback. Although the old market had faded and collecting it requires more work than most people are now willing to invest, in remoter parts of the United States, such as Appalachia, sang diggers are still at work, fetching up to $125 a pound for the wild root.

To complicate matters, a new interest in ginseng supplements appeared in the early 1990s. *The Wall Street Journal* reported in October 1992 that sales of ginseng pills, such as Ginsana, had jumped 170 percent in the past year, far outstripping sales increases in other over-the-counter supplements, such as multivitamins, vitamin C, and vitamin A. Ginsana, made by a Swiss pharmaceutical firm, is being promoted as a substance that helps build physical endurance.

### *Aphrodisiac*

The Chinese have respected and used ginseng root to treat just about every possible ailment. Roots shaped like a human being are the most prized. In fact, a particularly humanlike root was said to be literally worth its weight in gold.

Aside from using it to treat sundry diseases and ailments, the Chinese found ginseng valuable as an invigorating tonic, and even as a love potion. "Considering the population of China, who can quarrel with its reputation as an aphrodisiac?" asks herbalist John Lust.

Ginseng is believed to be a corruption of the Chinese *schin-seng, schin-sen*, or *jin-shen*, meaning "manlike" or "man-plant." The name refers to the tendency of some Chinese (as well as North American) ginseng roots to grow in the shape of the human body. Even certain American Indians called it *garantoguen*, which is supposed to have had the same or similar meaning.

Among the Indians, the Meskwakis, or Fox, of Wisconsin made a love potion from ginseng; Penobscot women in Maine steeped the root to obtain a fertility drink. The Creeks of Alabama drank the same solution as a cough medicine. The Delaware and Mohegans considered it a cure-all tonic. Some modern herb fans still recommend chewing the root or drinking the tea to reduce stress and tension. While many authorities seem to believe that ginseng has no real medicinal value, the recently issued Peterson's *Field Guide to Medicinal Plants: Eastern and Central North America* says, "Research suggests it may increase mental efficiency and physical performance, aid in adapting to high or low temperatures and stress (when taken over an extended period)."

Ginsengs are members of the Ginseng family (*Araliaceae*), which has some fifty-two genera and more than 475 species worldwide. The family includes our two *Panax* species and several members of the *Aralia* genus, among them wild sarsaparillas and the spikenards. None of these plants is noted for its beauty, but most have histories of being used as medicines.

Before you consider following the Chinese and using ginseng to spice up your life or increase your endurance, consider Charles F. Millspaugh's description of the physiological actions of a sizable dose: "Ginseng causes vertigo, dryness of the mucous membranes of the mouth and throat, increased appetite, accumulation of flatus with tension of the abdomen, diarrhoea, decreased secretion of urine, sexual excitement, oppression of the chest and a dry cough, increased heart's action and irregular pulse, weakness and weariness of the limbs, increased general strength, followed by weakness and prostration, somnolence, and much chilliness." Take care!

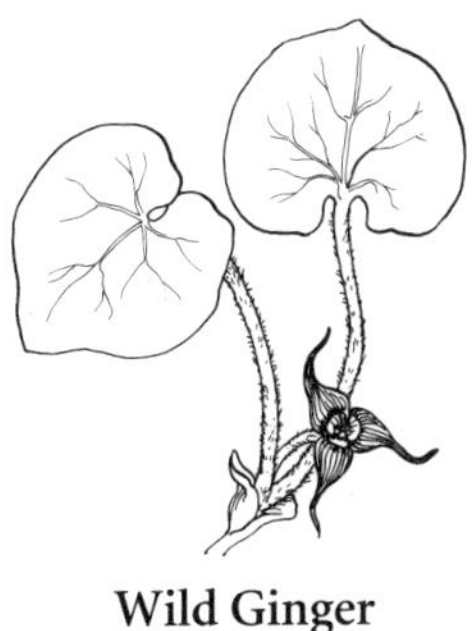

**Wild Ginger**
*(Asarum canadense)*

# *An Overlooked Crank*

Certain flowers might be grouped under the head of 'vegetable cranks,'" wrote Mrs. William Starr Dana. "Here would be classed the evening-primrose, which opens only at night; the closed [bottle] gentian, which never opens at all; and the wild ginger, whose odd unlovely flower seeks protection beneath its long-stemmed fuzzy leaves, and hides its head upon the ground as if unwilling to challenge comparison with its more brilliant brethren."

Wild ginger flowers do indeed grow from the base of the plant, lying on the ground under heart-shaped leaves, and most spring hikers never know that the blossoms are there. But the plant's posture may be for mundane reasons rather than eschewing competition, as Mrs. Dana wrote. The flower stays low because the ground is the source of insects that visit and pollinate it.

## *Insect Friends*

As an early bloomer, wild ginger attracts early spring flies that come out of the ground looking for the thawing carcasses of winter-killed animals. These flies are probably drawn to the flower by its carrion-colored, brownish red hue, and to the pollen, much of which they eat but some of which they transfer to other blossoms. The cuplike shape of the flower also provides flies with a shelter from the cold winds that are common in April and early May in the North.

Wild ginger is a native North American plant and is not related to the common flavoring herb of the tropics. Its rootstock, however, does have a similar taste. In fact, the powdered root was widely used as a flavoring substitute for real ginger in the late 1700s and early 1800s, and Canadians used it as a spice throughout the nineteenth century.

"I know one person who will not drink a cup of tea without a sprinkle of wild ginger on it," wrote George Washington Carver, famous for his research on peanuts but who was also interested in many native wild foods. He not only employed the powdered root as a flavoring, but considered the leaf the "acme of delicious, appetizing, and nourishing salads."

For woodsmen of the past century, wild ginger provided a rare sweet treat. Pieces of the root were cooked in thick sugar-water for long periods—some recipes call for simmering it off and on over three or four days. The resulting candied root is said to be delicious, and the left-over gingery syrup was a treat on flapjacks and fruits. The root was also used as a fragrance; an oil obtained from it was once an ingredient in expensive perfumes.

Wild ginger, *Asarum canadense*, belongs to a small genus of some twenty species found in the north temperate zone worldwide. The plant ranges throughout the northern states and the provinces, from the Atlantic to the Plains. A dozen other species may be found in North America, including three in the far West, among them the exotic-looking long-tailed wild ginger (*A. caudatum*), ranging from British Columbia and western Montana south to central California. Each of its "petals" tapers to a long, whiplike end.

The genus *Asarum* is in turn a member of the small Birthwort family, which has only six genera and 200 species worldwide. It is a rather independent clan, not closely related to any other in the plant world. That is not surprising, since wild ginger's ground-hugging flowers are unlike any others you are apt to see. They are among our few brownish red flowers, and their three-part, cuplike form makes them seem primitive, almost prehistoric.

*Asarum*, incidentally, is an ancient Latin word whose original meaning is unknown. An old Latin dictionary, published in 1835, defines the word as "the wild foalsfoot or wild spikenard," giving Pliny as the source of this information.

### *An Antibiotic*

The Indians, who rarely overlooked a plant of possible value, made use of wild ginger as a medicine and a flavoring. According to one authority, the women of a certain tribe drank a strong asarum root tea as a contraceptive. Others used it as a heart medication. But its most common uses among American Indians and early settlers were more to be expected. It was a popular carminative—something that removes flatulence—and was used to relieve stomach and intestinal cramps, colic, and upset stomachs.

Many tribes of American and Canadian Indians used wild ginger on fresh meat and fish, on older meat, and on foods being preserved for later use to render these foods safe for consumption. Meriwether Lewis reported its use as a poultice to treat an open wound suffered by one of the members of the Lewis and Clark expedition in 1806. These uses make sense in light of the fact that two antibiotic substances have been found in the roots of wild ginger. According to a 1970 study, wild ginger is an active agent against a broad spectrum of bacteria and fungi.

The Chippewas, incidentally, called the wild ginger *namepin*, which translates as "sturgeon plant," possibly because lake sturgeon (*Acipenser fulvescens*) is dark olive above and reddish below, similar to the combination of colors found on the flower. The plant is sometimes called "sturgeon potato." The Montagnais Indians of Newfoundland called the plant by a name meaning "beaver his food."

Eastern wild ginger is a curious, rather attractive herb. Growing up to a foot in height, the plant bears pairs of large, heart-shaped leaves, designed to capture what sunlight makes its way through the forest canopy. The plant likes slightly moist, rich soil, and spreads slowly, eventually producing a handsome and full woodland ground cover. Unfortunately, it is not a common plant, and some states even include it on their protected list. While it transplants easily, wildflower gardeners should not take it from its natural habitat unless it is threatened by destruction. It is preferable to buy the plants from a reputable wildflower nursery, meaning that the nursery does not sell plants stolen from the wild.

The fuzzy leaves begin to come up in late March and by mid- to late April, the flowers are usually out. Blossoms generally last until mid-May or later. Unlike some other spring flowers, the foliage does not die down in midsummer and remains lush until well into the fall, as the plant processes and stores food to send up next spring's growth.

Wild ginger is also known as Indian ginger, colic root, heart-leaf, heart-snakeroot, Vermont snakeroot, Canada snakeroot, false coltsfoot, and asarabacco (an old European name for another, apparently similar plant). "Ginger," incidentally, is a word of ancient origin. The *Oxford English Dictionary* traces it back to *srngavera*, a Sanskrit word that may have meant "horn body," referring to the shape, color, texture, and arrangements of the root of the true ginger. Over many centuries and through several languages, it became "ginger."

**Early Saxifrage**
*(Saxifraga virginiensis)*

## *The Rock Crushers*

Saxifrage is a name that seems at once ridiculous and appropriate. The plant—at least, many of the most common native species—is small, its flowers are tiny, and its aspect rather delicate. Yet, saxifrages thrive on mountains and in the Arctic, and the name means "stone breaker." The little plants do not possess amazing powers of strength, but are so called because people thought that the plants, which make their homes on stone outcroppings, caused the cracks and crevices in which they live.

### *Tiny But Many*

Early saxifrage (*Saxifraga virginiensis*) is common on hills and mountains of the cooler states east of the Mississippi. The flowers are among the smallest early spring blossoms, for each five-petaled flower is only a quarter of an inch across. Years ago, some botanists used the generic name, *Micranthes*, or "small flower," instead of *Saxifraga.*

But what it doesn't have in size, early saxifrage makes up for in numbers. Each stalk bears a cluster of from six to twelve or more blossoms, and the plants in turn form colonies, whose hundreds of blossoms make an attractive sight. It is their colonizing and love of rocky places that make saxifrage a favorite among rock flower gardeners who specialize in native species. The flowers appear as buds before the stem is much above the basal rosette of roundish leaves. As the stalk grows, the flowers bloom and continue blossoming as the stem gets taller, as high as nine inches.

Saxifrage is one of the numerous wildflowers that protects its nectar and pollen from hungry ants and other wingless critters with hairy, sticky stalks. The feet of the insect become entangled in fuzz, encouraging the creature to look elsewhere for nourishment.

*S. virginiensis* is one of 70 or so members of the genus found in North America, and 250 worldwide. The Rocky Mountains are a favorite haunt of the genus, and about 25 species can be found there. Purple saxifrage (*S. oppositifolia*) is native to the Rockies above 9,000 feet as well as to the European Alps. Scientists suspect that glaciers carried the plant from common arctic ground south to these disparate locations.

Saxifrages are in turn members of a sizable family—like the genus, it's called Saxifrage (*Saxifragaceae*)—that is closely related to roses. The Saxifrage family has some twenty-five genera in North America, among them the mitreworts, stonecrops, heucheras, currants, gooseberries, and even yard shrubs like mock orange and hydrangeas.

### *Cold Climates*

Many North American saxifrages favor cool or downright cold climates. Naturalist John Burroughs, in the summer of 1899, visited Alaska and found many specimens there. At Port Clarence, on the Bering Straight, he stood with excitement on the flower-covered tundra.

> *How eagerly we stepped upon it; how quickly we dispersed in all directions, lured by the strangeness! In a few moments, our hands were full of wild flowers, which we kept dropping to gather others more attractive, these, in turn, to be discarded as still more novel ones appeared. . . . Soon I came upon a bank by the little creek covered with a low, nodding purple primrose; then masses of shooting-star attracted me; then several species of pedicularis, a yellow anemone, and many saxifrages. A complete list of flowers blooming here within 60 miles of the Arctic Circle, in a thin layer of soil resting upon perpetual frost, would be a long one.*

Such is the ability of some members of the species to thrive in harsh climates.

Saxifrages are among the few native plants that seem to have little or no history of special uses. The plants were not used as a medicine, a dye, or a scent source. However, the greens of various species—such as the lettuce saxifrage, (*Saxifraga micranthidifolia*) of eastern mountains, and swamp saxifrage (*S. pensylvanica*) of eastern and midwestern wetlands, have seen some use as salad ingredients or as boiled vegetables. Several unrelated British plants are called saxifrages, not because they are similar to the genus, but because they are said to have the ability to break up stone in the bladder. Some authorities say that *Saxifraga* was similarly derived. The roots of some species bear pebble-like tubers, a sign under the "doctrine of signatures" that it could treat bladder stones.

Other names for our *S. virginiensis* include spring saxifrage, may-flower, sweet wilson, and everlasting—the last, apparently, because the flowers may bloom for three weeks or longer.

Early saxifrage is easy to grow in dry woodland soils, in sun or in shade. In the wild, the plant is often found near rocks that are wet in the spring. Seeds collected in July and planted any time can be used to start saxifrage near rocks. Or, if you have access to a large colony of plants, one or two specimens can be divided off to establish a new colony. There are also dozens of saxifrages, both from the wild and hybridized, on sale for gardens, especially rock gardens. A double form of the European meadow saxifrage (*S. granulata*) is known as pretty maids and figures in the popular nursery rhyme:

> *Mary Mary quite contrary*
> *How does your garden grow?*
> *With silver bells and cockleshells*
> *And Pretty Maids, all in a row.*

**Ground Ivy**
*(Glechoma hederacea)*

# *The Girl on the Ground*

Although it is among our most common wildflowers, many people overlook ground ivy, or hedgemaids, when they walk through a field, an open wood, or their backyard. Yet this small, creeping plant is both beautiful and interesting. It has an unusual reproductive technique, an ability to adapt and spread, a history of intriguing uses, and many odd names.

Ground ivy is one of our earliest spring wildflowers. I have seen it bloom as early as April 6 and, though it is basically a spring flower, I have upon occasion found it blooming well into September.

Its kidney-shaped leaves, like those of true ivy, are usually green all year round. Ground ivy is actually a mint, very closely related to catnip—so closely that some authorities place it under the same genus as catnip and call it *Nepeta hederacea.* Both catnip and ground ivy have aromatic leaves. Ground ivy's scent has been called "pleasant" by one writer and "disagreeable" by another. It is a matter of taste, as much among cats as people, for I've seen one of our cats take pleasure in rolling in a colony of fresh ground ivy while the other ignored it.

*Glechoma hederacea*, now generally accepted as the correct name, describes the plant as being similar to another mint and to an ivy. (*Glechoma* is Greek for "pennyroyal" and *hederacea* means "ivy-like.") The species spread from Europe both west and east to cover North America and Asia, including Japan. Farmers hated it because most livestock would not eat it, horses were said to get sick from it, and fields would be overtaken by it.

Almost every old yard has a patch of this hearty perennial somewhere. People who favor putting-green lawns find it a pest while people who like a variety of greenery encourage it to grow, especially in dampish, shaded places around the bases of trees, at borders, or in corners around the house. Ground ivy spreads rapidly, for it is able to root at nodes as it creeps along the ground, so you should trim it to keep it in check. I cut mine back with the lawn mower.

Ground ivy may be unappreciated because it bears such tiny blossoms. Yet a close examination reveals a marvelous flower, reminiscent of an Easter orchid, with its beautiful purple-crimson color, spotted here and there with darker purple. If the blossoms came in giant size, gardeners would surely prize them.

## *Double Guarantee*

The flowers are more than pretty, though, for they are unusually designed to guarantee fertilization. The plant has both male and female flowers. The male flowers are larger and have both stamens and pistils, though not at the same time, and the females have only a pistil. This dual-sex arrangement is found in several members of the Mint family, including thyme and marjoram. Pollen-bearing male blossoms may be bigger to attract bees to them first. When the nectar is spent, the bees then go out of their way to squeeze into the smaller female flowers, thus carrying pollen to the female pistils.

That isn't all. The large, male flowers are actually hermaphroditic. At first they contain four pollen-bearing stamens and an immature pistil. Later, the stamens die and the pistil enlarges, ready to accept pollen from other, fresher flowers. No wonder ground ivy so successfully spreads its numbers and range!

Though a pest to lawn freaks and some gardeners, ground ivy has been an important plant for many centuries in Europe and is rather well liked there today. John Burroughs, a nineteenth-century American naturalist, once challenged Englishmen to "compare our matchless, rosy-lipped, honey-hearted, trailing arbutus with his own ugly ground ivy." Trailing arbutus may be more beautiful, but owing to its scarcity nowadays, it can rarely be appreciated.

## *Making Merry*

As is usual with plants of popular history, a long list of folk names has developed, including such mouthfuls as gill-go-over-the-ground, lizzy-run-up-the-hedge, robin-run-in-the-hedge, and gill-go-by-the-hedge, as well as gill, gillale, tunhofe, turnhoof, hayhofe, hove, cat ivy, cat's foot, robin-runaway, gill-run-over, crow victuals, wild snakeroot, and field balm. For its fans at least, one of its nicest names is ground joy.

Perhaps the most popular use of ground ivy was in the production of beer and ale, producing names such as alehoof—literally, "ale ivy." Long before the discovery of the value of hops, Saxons used ground ivy to clarify, flavor, and preserve beer and ale. One of the plant's other common names, gill-over-the-ground (and variations thereof), is said to have come from the French word, *guiller*, which means "to ferment." The word also means, suitably enough, "to make merry."

Some authorities, however, believe that "gill"—short for gillian—is used as the common British word for "girl," prompting other folk names such as hedgemaids and haymaids. This latter usage may have arisen from a misunderstanding of the original meaning of gill. The plant has become hermaphroditic in name as well as in physiology, though, for in many places, particularly the western United States, it is called creeping Charlie.

Since the Middle Ages, herbalists have used ground ivy to treat so many maladies that it would appear to stock an entire apothecary shop. The herb was best regarded as a cure for prolonged coughs, such as from consumption. Gill tea, a popular cough medicine among English country folk, consisted of an infusion of ground ivy in boiling water, with the bitterness reduced by adding sugar, honey, or licorice. Said to be mildly stimulating and good for the appetite, the tea was also drunk as a refreshment.

Herbalists used ground ivy to treat pulmonary problems, sciatica, gout, kidney ailments, digestive difficulties, hysteria, diarrhea, bruises, and—taken as snuff—nasal congestion and headaches. Gypsies made a sort of first aid ointment from it, and painters drank the tea to treat lead poisoning. In olden times, wrote John Gerard, it was "commended against the humming noise and ringing sound of the ears, being put into them; and for them that are hard of hearing." Nicholas Culpeper expressed the same thing more colorfully: "The juice dropped into the ear doth wonderfully help the noise and singing of them, and helpeth the hearing which is decayed."

If you have a spot of dampish, shaded ground that could use a pretty cover, try ground ivy. If you don't have any growing on your property—and this may be the case in newer subdivisions whose lawns have not had time to be "invaded"—dig some up from a field or obtain some from a friend. It will grow quickly and spread rapidly, but you can easily control it by mowing. And despite its name, you can plant ground ivy in hanging baskets, where it does quite well.

Then, if you catch a cold, you'll be able to have a fresh spot of gill tea.

**Showy Lady's Slipper**
*(Cypripedium reginae)*

## *The Slipper and Its Chamber*

Lady's slippers are among those special wildflowers whose locations are whispered only to trusted people. It's not just that they may be rare, but also that they *look* rare.

Indeed, wildflower enthusiasts are usually careful to catalog, mentally at least, the locations of these largest of our orchids. One May, when I was looking for some yellows and pinks to photograph, I asked a couple of knowledgeable friends who immediately remembered where they had seen yellow lady's slippers twenty years earlier. We went to the spot in deep moist woods and, sure enough, they were still there.

The pink lady's slipper proved more elusive. My friends recalled a favorite colony from a decade or two earlier, but when we drove to the place, we found houses instead of flowers. We checked several other localities without success. Then another flower-watcher told me they were blooming in a somewhat remote, hilly section of the town. We drove up and—lo and behold!—several fine plants were standing, not in deep, distant woods, but in a clearing four feet from the pavement of the road.

### *Where?*

Other people have found lady's slippers in various habitats. Asa Gray, the noted botanist, said the pinks could be found in dry or moist woods, particularly near evergreens. F. Schuyler Mathews usually saw them "among withered leaves that lie under birch, beech, poplar, and maple," but admitted, "Nature is not always regular in her habits." W. T. Baldwin, author of a nineteenth-century book on New England orchids, reported, "The finest specimens I ever saw sprang out of cushions of crisp reindeer moss high up among the rocks of an exposed hillside, and again I have found it growing vigorously in almost open swamps, but nearly colorless from excessive moisture." Mr. Baldwin quoted an Adirondacks resident as saying they have a "great fondness for decaying wood, and I often see a whole row perched like birds along a crumbling log." Mrs. William Starr Dana found them in little shelves on cliffs. "It has a roving fancy and grows up hill and down dale," said William Hamilton Gibson.

That fancy depends to a great extent upon the nature of the soil, which must be quite acidic. The soil must contain a certain type of fungus, with which the lady's slipper species have an unusual but vital symbiotic relationship. Unlike most seeds, the minute, dustlike lady's slipper seeds contain no food to allow them to grow. Rhizoctonia fungi attacks and digests the outer cells of the seeds and, if things balance out just right, the inner cells escape digestion, absorb nutrients the fungus obtained from the soil, and germinate.

The symbiosis with the fungus does not end at germination. The protocorm, or baby corm, continues to obtain minerals and other soil nutrients through Rhizoctonia or other fungi. The fungi, in turn, takes from the seedling foods that are photosynthetically manufactured. These sensitive and complex relationships make native orchids of all kinds relatively uncommon, and make growing them from seed virtually impossible outside a laboratory. What's more, it sometimes takes years for a lady's slipper to become a mature plant.

About ten species of lady's slippers live in North America, and some two dozen are found worldwide. They belong to the genus *Cypripedium*, Greek for "Venus's shoe" or "sock." In medieval Europe, the plant was called "the Virgin's shoe" or "the shoe of Mary" (*Calceolus marianus*). The French still sometimes call it *soulier de Notre Dame*, "shoe of Our Lady." In North America, the plant is widely known as moccasin flower.

### *The Labellum*

These and other names suitably describe the main part of the flower, called the lip or labellum. This saclike structure is designed to attract insects, particularly bees. The roundish opening at the top is surrounded by veinlike lines that attract and direct the insect's eye. In many species, the long sepals or wings also help insects find the opening. The flower's scent, described by some as heavy and oily, also draws in passing bees.

The edge of the circular hole is inflected or lipped downward. Once inside, a bee finds it difficult to escape and instead explores the chamber. The chamber is lined with hairs—many secreting a sweet nectar—that lean toward an opening at the rear. The trapped bee works its way through the nectar toward the beckoning light at the opening. To escape, the bee must rub against first the stigma, which is built like a comb to remove pollen, and then against the anthers, which give up pollen in a semiliquid but quick-drying form. When the bee visits another lady's slipper, the stigma rakes off the previous deposit of pollen, thus fertilizing the blossom, and the anther pastes on a new load. Big bumblebees, which have difficulty squeezing through the narrow exit, will sometimes give up and simply chew their way out of the sac, defeating the ingenious mechanism. Others simply die, entombed.

In hunting for nectar, bees must be careful not to waste energy, for part of what they collect is used for their own fuel. Beating those wings so rapidly is a high-energy task. If the search requires too much time, the insect will consume most or all of what it collects, and fail its colony. Consequently, bees are attracted to flowers in which pollen collection is easiest. For example, members of the Composite family, like daisies and sunflowers, and of the Pea family, such as the clovers, draw bees with close-packed, nectar-filled tubes. Some flowers, like lady's slippers, monkshoods, lobelias, and certain gentians, are difficult to get in or out of, so they must offer an extra rich store of nectar as a reward for all the work. Otherwise, they would fail in the competition with other flowers to attract pollinating insects, and the species might not survive. But recent research has shown that lady's slippers are in their own league with respect to pollination.

Douglas E. Gill, a University of Maryland zoologist, spent sixteen years studying 3,000 pink lady's slippers in a national forest, and found that only one-third of the plants flowered during that time. Of those 1,000 flowers, only 23 were successfully pollinated. In other words, once a bee has visited one lady's slipper, it is not likely to visit another.

How can the species survive? Since the average life span of a plant is 20 years, and some plants may live for 150 years, lady's slippers have a long time to turn out one successful flower. And once that flower is pollinated, it produces some 60,000 seeds.

### *Pink and Yellow*

Most lady's slippers bloom in May and June with the yellow (*Cypripedium calceolus pubescens* or the smaller *C. calceolus parviflorum*) usually a week or so earlier than the pink (*C. acaule*). The two differ not only in color, but leaf positioning. Pink lady's slipper has brown sepals (sometimes called the "shoestrings" of the slipper) and leaves that rise from the base. Yellow lady's slipper bears purplish sepals and has clasping leaves right up its stalk.

It is difficult to say which is the less common of the two. I have seen more of the yellow than of the pink, while others maintain that the pink is easier to find. Neither should be picked, of course, and unless they are in certain danger from the likes of bulldozers, attempts should not be made to transplant them. While transplants may survive for a season or two, more often than not they die because of some imperfection in their new surroundings. Even buying from nurseries may be a mistake, not only because the plants will probably die, but also because they are probably stolen stock. Thousands of lady's slippers are being taken illegally from the wild, often from parks and preserves, for resale to nurseries. The reason is simple: horticulturists have been unable to figure out how to grow these plants from seeds, and reproduction by division is a slow process. Purchasing stolen plants only encourages their eradication in the wild.

Not everyone would want them in the garden. Alice Morse Earle, who wrote books on life in colonial times, said at the turn of the century, "I have never found the lady's slipper as beautiful a flower as do nearly all of my friends, as did my father and mother, and I was pleased by Ruskin's sharp comment that such a slipper was fit only for very gouty old toes."

### *Bounty Hunters*

Most writers, however, have found the lady's slippers attractive, probably in part because they are so exotic and unusual. In the nineteenth century, Europeans went wild over orchids, sometimes offering thousands of dollars for new species. That encouraged botanical bounty hunters to comb the jungles and mountains of the world in search of elusive species that might be cultivated in European hothouses. New discoveries would be sent from some far-off land to England, France, or Germany, only to spark new searches. One lady's slipper, *C. fairrieanum*, arrived in England from the Himalayas in the 1850s, but soon disappeared from the flower show scene, prompting someone to offer a $5,000 reward for a new specimen. Expedition after expedition over the next half century searched in vain for the Lost Orchid. According to A. W. Anderson in *How We Got Our Flowers*, a surveying crew accidentally rediscovered it near the Bhutan-Sikkim border in 1904.

In an amazing case of plant genocide, a German who bought specimens of the newly discovered *C. spicerianum* around 1870, then paid to have the species eradicated in its native territory in northeastern India so that he could sew up the market.

While the rose-and-white showy lady's slipper usually wins the most praise for beauty among the natives of North America, Mabel Osgood Wright admired the yellow moccasin flower. "How the eye loves to linger upon yellow flowers!" she wrote. "Of the three primary colors, yellow always seems to me the most harmonious under all conditions, from the first marsh marigold to the last brave wand of goldenrod. . . . Roughly speaking, without attempting a census, it seems to me that taking the year through, the majority of landscape flowers are yellow." Incidentally, orchids come in many colors, but you will never find a blue one among the more than 5,000 known species worldwide.

Yellow lady's slipper has also had its practical side. Cypripedin, a resinoid substance obtained from its rhizome (rootstock), was once listed in the *U.S. Pharmacopoeia* and was employed in the treatment of hysteria because it was believed to be a gentle tranquilizer. Lady's slipper tea is still recommended in some modern herbals for nervous headaches. Indians treated toothaches with the plants. Too much of it, however, can cause hallucinations.

Other names for the yellow lady's slipper include whippoorwill's shoe, yellows, slipper root, Indian shoe, Noah's ark, duck, nerve root, and American valerian. (European valerian, no relation to *Cypripedium*, is also and more commonly used to treat nerve disorders). Yellow lady's slipper ranges from coast to coast as far south as Georgia and Texas in higher elevations. Pink lady's slipper was once considered a monotypic North American species, going under the name of *Fissipes acaulis*, the generic name meaning roughly "split-lip." Now pink lady's slipper is just another *Cypripedium*. It has been called some of the above names as well as camel's foot, squirrel's foot, two-lips, Indian moccasin, and old goose. This species is more eastern, and does not range beyond the Mississippi River.

There are several West Coast species. California lady's slipper (*C. californicum*) has yellow-green and white flowers, up to fifteen on a stem. Mountain lady's slipper (*C. montanum*) has one to three white and dull purple flowers. And clustered lady's slipper (*C. fasciculatum*), which blooms as early as April, has greenish yellow flowers with brown veins.

### *The Queen*

The most attractive of the *Cypripedium* clan is no doubt the showy lady's slipper, whose pink slipper is accented with white sepals. *C. reginae* tends to favor colder locales in the eastern mountains and in southern Canada and the northern states, especially around the Great Lakes. It is the largest and most colorful of the lady's slippers, and its Latin name suggests that it is the queen of the clan.

Once ranked second in a poll on the most beautiful flowers of the continent, showy lady's slipper has suffered because it is choosy about habitat and has been overpicked and overdug. A century ago, Mrs. Dana predicted that this species would eventually become extinct. She wrote of a secret place near Lenox, Massachusetts, where showy lady's slipper was growing. To her dismay a local boy discovered the spot and proceeded to uproot the flowers and sell them by the dozen in nearby towns. Perhaps it is natural justice that the tiny hairs on the leaves and stems of this and other lady's slippers can give molesters a good, poison ivy–like rash.

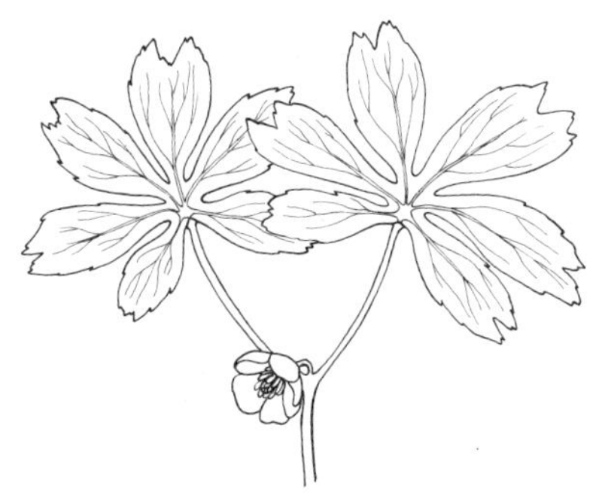

**May Apple**
*(Podophyllum peltatum)*

# *The Green Umbrellas*

In midspring, certain warm rich woods are covered with what children used to call green umbrellas. Sometimes vast colonies of these plants unfold their pairs of large leaves across the forest floor.

Though not as common as they once were, May apples persist in many woods from Texas, Kansas, Minnesota, and Ontario eastward. The pretty flower, with six to nine waxy white petals, springs from the crotch of the leafstalks, but it is often downturned and hidden from view by the leaves. When a plant has only one leaf, no flower appears. The scent of May apple is usually described as unpleasant; John Burroughs called it sickly sweet.

The fruit, not the flower, has attracted the most interest. The large, egg-shaped, yellow berry has always fascinated people, especially children. The berry is edible, and farmers' boys used to relish its taste, variously described as sweet to mawkish to insipid.

The fruit's scent is also strong. Charles F. Saunders, in *Edible and Useful Wild Plants*, observed, "When green it exhales a rank, rather repulsive odor, but when fully matured, all that is changed into an agreeable fragrance, hard to define—sort of a composite of cantaloupe, summer apples, and fox grapes. Brought indoors, two or three will perfume a whole room."

Captain John Smith tasted May apple in Virginia in 1612, reporting it as "a fruit that the Inhabitants call Maracocks, which is a pleasant wholesome fruit much like a lemond." Explorer Samuel Champlain was introduced to it by the Hurons in 1619 and said it tasted more like a fig. Early settlers of Rhode Island found it "a pleasant fruite," and it was eaten by many, despite a well-recognized laxative effect. Naturalist Euell Gibbons was fond of May apple. In *Stalking the Wild Asparagus*, he described how to make May apple marmalade, which he called ambrosia, and said a shot of May apple juice in lemonade does wonders for the flavor.

## *Pigs and Boys*

The berry was so popular that a nineteenth-century writer once took a few facetious shots at the eminent botanist, Asa Gray, for saying that pigs and boys ate the harmless fruit. "Think of it, boys!" exclaimed William Hamilton Gibson, "and think of what else he says of it: 'ovary void, stigma sessile, undulate, seeds covered with lateral placenta each enclosed in an aril.' Now, it may be safe for pigs and billygoats to tackle such a compound as that, but we boys like to know what we are eating, and I cannot but feel that the public health officials of every township should require this formula of Dr. Gray's to be printed on every one of these big loaded pills, if that is what they are really made of!"

Despite the plant's name, berries appear in August or September. Although the ripe berries are edible, the leaves and roots are quite poisonous if eaten raw. In fact, some tribes of American Indians used the poisonous parts to commit suicide. "The root is a very effective poison which the Savages use when they cannot bear their troubles," wrote botanist Michel Sarrazin in 1708. Two years later, A. T. Raudot reported that Huron women "are very subject to poisoning themselves at the least grief that betakes them; the men also poison themselves sometimes. To leave this life they use a root of hemlock or of citron [May apple], which they swallow." Menominis and Iroquois made insecticides from May apple to kill the likes of potato bugs and corn worms.

Despite its toxicity, herbalists and physicians have long used extracts of the tuberous root to treat several maladies, though its main use has always been as a cathartic—a vigorous laxative. "Its greatest power lies in its action upon the liver and bowels," said Maude Grieve. "[It] is a powerful medicine exercising an influence on every part of the system, stimulating the glands to healthy action. It is highly valuable in dropsy, biliousness, dyspepsia, liver, and other disorders."

May apple was listed as an official drug in the *U.S. Pharmacopoeia* until 1930 and had been commonly prescribed. American scientists in the 1950s experimented with using a May apple extract to treat paralysis, and a 1976 report said it showed promise in the treatment of certain types of cancers. It is still an ingredient in purgative medicines and for treatment of intestinal worms, and in the 1970s Abbott Laboratories had a hard time getting the 300,000 pounds it needed yearly because few people were growing it as a crop. The Food and Drug Administration has approved use of etoposide, derived from May apple, for certain cancers. Modern herbals recommend its use only under medical supervision or suggest avoiding it altogether.

Botanists call May apple *Podophyllum peltatum*. The generic name is from *podos*, "foot," and *phyllon*, "leaf." *Peltatum*, the specific name, also describes the leaf and means "shield-shaped." It appears that the taxonomists could not agree on just what shape it really has.

### *Mandrake*

The plant's second most common name is American mandrake, though it is not related to the true mandrake, a southern European plant with purplish flowers, said to possess magical properties (hence, "Mandrake the Magician," once a well-known comic strip). Homer D. House wrote, "Mandrake relates in no way to the mandrake or mandragora of the ancients and, not withstanding its poisonous character, it is a very respectable herb in comparison with the traditions of the mandrake of the ancients, described as flourishing best under a gallows with a root resembling a man in shape, uttering terrible shrieks when it was torn from the ground, and possessing the power to transform men and beasts."

May apple's folk names, mostly referring to the fruit, include Indian apple, hog apple, devil's apple, vegetable mercury, vegetable calomel (calomel was a cathartic chemical), wild lemon, wild jalop (jalop is a Mexican morning glory used as a purgative, a medicine more drastic in its effects than even a cathartic), ground lemon, Puck's foot (a reference to the forest fairy in *A Midsummer Night's Dream*), duck's foot, and raccoon berry (raccoons must have tastes similar to pigs and boys).

May apple is native to both North America and Japan. The plant is a member of a tiny genus of only four species worldwide; the other three species are Asian, indicating the movement must have been from there to here across the Bering Strait. The genus in turn is a member of the small Barberry family, which includes the popular shrub.

May apples may be grown in the wildflower garden (the French imported them for their gardens in the eighteenth and nineteenth centuries) and they make a good seasonal woodland ground cover, especially if you have some slightly acid soil (pH 4 to 7). They may be transplanted in summer from root divisions from large, healthy colonies. Seeds can be removed from the pulp of the ripe berry in early fall and sown then. Do not place May apples next to smaller, delicate woodland species. May apples spread both by seed and by creeping roots, and they will soon blanket your woods, choking out anemones, hepaticas, and violets. But if there is nothing better in or about your trees, May apple is a fine ground cover. Keep in mind that young children may be attracted to the berries before they ripen, when they may be harmful to eat. Perhaps May apple is safer for pigs than for boys.

**Common Fleabane**
*(Erigeron philadelphicus)*

# *No Bane for Fleas*

Many of our common weedy wildflowers are Europeans that tagged along with early settlers and became well established here. Some weeds, like certain species of fleabane, have gone the other way, taking a bit of the New World to the Old.

Fleabanes are flowers of spring and summer fields and lawns that often look like daisies or asters. The agrarian settlers who felled the virgin forests and opened the ground to the sky probably made these plants much more common than they were before the colonists arrived. Fleabanes love open land and bright sun. Fleabanes, wild carrot, black-eyed Susans, chicory, red clover, and other native and imported flowers of sunny seasons often blanket old fields.

Fleabane is a misnomer. A naturalist of a few centuries ago said one of the genus was commonly called fleawort in England because "the seeds are so like fleas." Bane, based on an Old English word for killer, may have replaced wort perhaps because of the plant's similarity to the true common fleabane (*Inula dysenterica*) of Europe, a cousin of our elecampane. In England people used to burn the dried leaves of common fleabane, whose smoke would supposedly drive away fleas and other insects. Or, they would hang the dried plant around rooms for the same reason.

### *Dogbane?*

Our native fleabanes have probably never been successfully employed to combat fleas. That any of them "drive away fleas is believed only by those who have not used them dried, reduced to powder and sprinkled in kennels, from which, however, they have been known to drive away dogs," wrote Neltje Blanchan in *Nature's Garden.*

In fact, most of our fleabanes have been of little practical use except to decorate the landscape and provide honey for bees. Horseweed, more formally known as Canada fleabane (*Erigeron canadense* or *canadensis*), is an exception. Though it is named for Canada, the plant is found from there through eastern and central states into Central and South America south to Argentina.

In many places horseweed has lost its flea bane name, probably because it lacks the most characteristic feature of the well-known fleabanes—dozens of long rays that surround the yellow central disc in daisylike fashion. In fact, many people coming upon horseweed would probably assume the flowers are buds about to bloom. The short rays are upright, much like a ready-to-open flower, and are hardly visible except close up.

Horseweed picked up its equine name either because of its supposed resemblance to a horse's tale or because it was widely used by American Indians and settlers as a treatment for such horse diseases as strangury. Kentucky horsemen were using it by 1830. It is also known as butterweed (probably a variant of bitterweed, which it is also called), coltstail (the flower's shape), prideweed (the stem is very straight and upright), bloodstanch (it was used to stop hemorrhages), and fireweed (it often inhabits burnt-out ground).

This last name indicates one of its rarely noticed, but important services. Though horseweed is a coarse plant that looks as a true weed ought to look and spreads by floating, fuzz-topped seeds, its habits are as unassuming as its flowers. It survives best in barren soil where little else is growing, and once stronger, more aggressive perennials arrive, horseweed disappears. By this time, the plant has served its purpose of providing a temporary ground cover, with roots that held soil in place and leaves that shaded the soil and retained moisture. When it died at the end of the season, it added nutrients to the soil for next year's crop of whatever plants show up. Those who have seen the effects of erosion or have watched topsoil blow away in the wind will appreciate horseweed, a sort of vegetable Band-Aid for Mother Earth.

### *Retribution?*

Noticed by explorers as early as 1640, horseweed was soon introduced into Europe. In 1653 it was growing in the Botanic Gardens of Paris, and thanks to its air-borne seeds, only a few years later it was all over Paris and its suburbs. By 1881, John Burroughs reported, "Our fleabane has become a common roadside weed in England." Today, it can be found spreading through Asia, South Africa, Australia, and even the Pacific islands.

Charles F. Millspaugh said jokingly that horseweed was sent overseas "in part to recompense Europe for the miserable dock weeds she has sent us." It was more likely exported as a medicinal plant, for old herbals mention it as a treatment for kidney stones, diabetes, dropsy, diarrhea, and dysentery. It was also used for lung and tonsil disorders. The Chippewa, Catawba, Ojibwa, Meskwaki, and Houma Indians employed horseweed for stomach pains and "diseases of women." The Crees on Hudson's Bay treated digestive problems with a tea made from the plant. Many tribes used both its flowers and leaves as tobacco.

In modern times, the oil extracted from horseweed has been used commercially as a flavoring for candies and soft drinks, but never to a degree where the plant has been grown as a noteworthy crop.

### *Young and Old*

Fleabanes are members of the genus *Erigeron*, a name that has been explained in various ways by various authorities. Maude Grieve says the word means "soon becoming old." "In many of the species, the plant, even when in flower, has a worn-out appearance, giving the idea of a weed which has passed its prime," she wrote. Edwin Rollin Spencer, in *All About Weeds*, understood the translation differently, believing it to refer to the fact that seeds appear and ripen quickly after the flower blooms.

Mrs. William Starr Dana says *Erigeron* is a combination of the words for "spring" and "an old man," an "allusion to the hoariness of certain species which flower in the spring." Still another theory says the word means "early old" because, while the seeds are in effect baby plants, they are wearing beards like old men.

*Erigeron* is a widely distributed genus, but most members—at least 140 species—are native to North America. Most *Erigeron* species are found in the Midwest and West north to the Arctic. Philadelphia or common fleabane (*E. philadelphicus*), one of the earliest and most common species, is a tall, slender plant that blooms from May to September across the entire continent. Its flowers, each bearing 100 to 150 rays, are often tinted pink or lavender when in bud, but sometimes lose color when they open. This fleabane is one of several North American species from which larger, more colorful cultivars have been developed. In the nineteenth century, Philadelphia fleabane was considered better than Canada fleabane for treating urinary disorders.

Daisy fleabane (*E. annuus*) blooms a little later, appearing first in June and lasting through the summer. The flowers, bearing forty to seventy rays, are slightly smaller than those of Philadelphia fleabane, and like other fleabanes, may be tinged with pink, though they're usually white. This plant is also called sweet scabious, lace buttons, and white top. Lesser daisy fleabane (*E. strigosus*) is like the above except that its leaves along the stem have very few if any teeth. Both daisy fleabanes may have dozens of blossoms per plant. West Coast species are commonly called daisies instead of fleabanes; even Philadelphia fleabane is called Philadelphia daisy out West. Seaside daisy (*E. glaucus*) lives on coastal bluffs, while Coulter's daisy (*E. coulteri*) and dwarf alpine daisy (*E. pygmaeus*) live in mountainous regions.

Robin's plantain (*E. pulchellus*), which is found east of the Mississippi from the Gulf into Canada, has only a few large flowers and mostly basal leaves. The rays are bluish, violet, or lilac flowers, making it look "like a blue aster out of season," said F. Schuyler Mathews. In cooler areas, Robin's plantain, coltsfoot, and dandelion are some of the earliest of the huge Composite family to bloom each year. Like its namesake, robin's plantain is one of those sure signs that spring is here.

**Ox-Eye Daisy**
*(Chrysanthemum leucanthemum)*

# *A Flower Loved and Hated*

When poets wrote of the snows of June, with spring fields as white as after a midwinter's blizzard, they were writing not of weather, but of the ox-eye daisy. This plant with white flowers, which immigrated with the colonists, took over whole crop fields and gardens. Its population peaked during the height of the American agricultural era, and today is seen in not nearly the numbers for which it was once known.

Few people these days can recall when whiteweed was feared and hated for its tendency to overtake fields and gardens. Prolific and difficult to eradicate, the daisy was as much an abomination to farmers as it was and still is a favorite of children and lovers. So despised was this plant among the Scots, who called them gools, that they appointed gool-riders to see that the daisies were removed from wheat fields. The farmer found to have the biggest crop of gools had to pay a fine of a castrated ram.

In North America the love-hate relationship with the daisy began sometime after Europeans arrived. In precolonial North America, the East was a land of forests; there were few sun-loving, field-filling flowers. Even after the first settlers cleared off the valleys and ridges in New England, the Atlantic states, and Canada, their fields were relatively free of weeds, white or otherwise. Eventually, however, sun-lovers invaded from Europe. Later, sun-loving natives of the Plains and prairies, such as black-eyed Susan, came eastward.

Together they created many backaches for farmers, who had no fancy weed killers and were forced to fight the invaders by hand. Most of the aliens came mixed with crop seeds from the old countries while some snuck rides in ballast, in the hay used in packing, or on the bottoms of muddy boots. Still others were actually invited, to fill gardens that would supply kitchens or medicinal concoctions. One source of the daisy, it is said, was the German fodder used to feed the horses of British troops during the Revolution.

Now the farms are disappearing in parts of our continent, especially the East. The fields have turned into subdivisions or returned to woodland. The sun-loving daisy has lost many of the haunts where it had thrived. A field full of them as white as snow is becoming a rare sight, in my part of Connecticut at least.

A plant as persistent and as hardy as ox-eye daisy could hardly be wiped out by the monumental changes in society during the past half century, or even by the invention of powerful herbicides. There are still plenty of places where clumps of daisies appear each June with black-eyed Susans, St. Johnswort, hawkweeds, evening-primroses, and other denizens of poor and mediocre soils. That, in fact, is an attribute of the daisy much to be admired: It inhabits and beautifies waste places where few plants survive and which might otherwise be rather drab.

### *Contradiction*

The ox-eye daisy may seem a simple flower, but it is actually rather complex and contradictory. Its name is not even its own. Daisy means "day's eye" and was coined to refer to a pinkish English flower that closes at night and opens in the sunlight. Our ox-eye daisy remains open around the clock, and has been better called moon daisy. "The flower, with its white rays and golden disc, has small resemblance to an ox's eye, but at dusk it shines out from the mowing-grass like a fallen moon," wrote Marcus Woodward, an English naturalist.

Then there is its scientific name, *Chrysanthemum leucanthemum*, which literally translates as "golden flower, white flower." The type species for the genus is an all-yellow flower, which explains the generic name. While our daisy is more known as a white flower, its scientific name is appropriate, for each daisy blossom is really a bouquet of flowers of both colors. The deep-yellow center disc is composed of hundreds of tiny fertile yellow florets, while the twenty to thirty white rays or "petals" are sterile flowers. The rays have, in evolution, given up their reproductive function and parts in order to serve as decorations to draw insects to the pollen-bearing center flowers, an arrangement common in the Composite family. The rays also serve as handy landing pads for arriving insects.

"Because daisies are among the most conspicuous of flowers and have facilitated dining for their visitors by offering them countless cups of refreshment that may be drained with a minimum loss of time, almost every insect on wings alights on them sooner or later," observed Neltje Blanchan in *Nature's Garden*. One tiny, black, centipedelike creature appears to live on the flower heads. To feast on the nectar, it inserts almost the full length of its narrow body into the tubes. It is unusual to find daisies without these creatures crawling around the discs, and they may be adapted by nature to live only on these plants.

### *Right Conditions*

With all of their florets per blossom, each daisy plant produces a huge number of seeds, one reason why they have survived so well since being brought to North America. The daisy seems also to like our environment better than that of its native Europe, where the plants are said to be not as numerous.

Daisies will grow, however, only if conditions are right. Some years ago I transplanted several daisies into rich soil exposed to partial sunlight in my yard. Although most survived for one season, none came up the next year. Two years later, I discovered a daisy blooming happily in another part of the yard with poorer soil. By the natural spread of seeds and the survival of those that found a fit place, the plant began to establish itself. Later efforts at transplanting proved more successful; I put them in the poorest soil in the yard, but a spot well drained and sunny, and they began a small colony.

The daisy blooms primarily in late May and June, although healthy plants in ideal conditions will produce blossoms through July and August, and into September. The flowers are long lasting, and fine for picking for bouquets.

### *A Bane of Bugs*

A native of both Europe and Asia, the ox-eye daisy is a member of a genus that has more than 100 species worldwide. Many of the popular garden chrysanthemums are descended from Chinese and Japanese species. Certain Oriental members of the genus, called the pyrethrum daisies, are displeasing to insects and are used as a commercial source of pyrethrum, a popular natural insecticide. Even our daisy appears to have built-in protection from herbivorous insects, most of whom seem to shun its bitter juice. English country folk knew this. They mixed the plant with the straw bedding of farm animals and hung it from the ceilings of their homes to chase away insects, including fleas.

Although some eighteen species of *Chrysanthemum* are found in North America, including the common feverfew (*C. parthenium*) and the corn marigold (*C. segetum*), few are native. In fact, probably the only native North American chrysanthemum species are found at or near the Arctic Circle. The ox-eye daisy is by far the most widespread member, found in almost every state and province, though they are less common in the South.

A plant as widespread and as well known as this one is bound to generate a good deal of folklore and folk names. Almost everyone knows the "He loves me, he loves me not" litany with which one learns the fate of a romance by plucking a daisy's petals. It is also said that dreaming of daisies in spring or summer will bring good luck but such dreams at other times of the year foretell bad fortune. Eating the roots is supposed to stunt a child's growth, but eating three of the blossoms after a tooth extraction means one will never have another toothache. Children used to construct something called white-capped old women out of them and to make daisy chains. English children used to pluck the flower heads, slide them onto pieces of straw, and wear them in hats like the plumes that garnished helmets of knights of old.

In folk medicine, the plant has had many uses. "The ancients dedicated it to Artemis, the goddess of women, considering it useful in women's complaints," said Maude Grieve. After the establishment of Christianity, ox-eye daisy became the plant of St. Mary Magdalen and was called the Maudelyn or Maudlin daisy. It has served as an antispasmodic, diuretic, and tonic (such as for night sweats), and in the treatment of whooping cough and asthma. The daisy was also used for soothing bruises, wounds, and ulcers. "An ointment made thereof doth wonderfully help all wounds that have inflammations about them, or by reason of moist humours having access unto them are kept long from healing," wrote herbalist Nicholas Culpeper. English country folk also added extract of daisy to ale to treat jaundice.

In Italy, the young leaves, though small, were eaten in salads. Linnaeus, who gave the plant its scientific name, reported that sheep, horses, and goats eat the plant, but cows and pigs avoid it as bitter. Cows have been known to eat daisies, perhaps out of desperation, and dairy farmers are said to dislike the flavor it gives milk. John Burroughs, the naturalist and essayist, wrote, "The ox-eye daisy makes a fair quality hay if cut before it gets ripe."

Ox-eye daisy is also known as great ox-eye, golden marguerites, daisy, horse gowan, butter daisy, field daisy, dun daisy, button daisy, horse daisy, bull daisy, midsummer daisy, poorland daisy, maudlinwort, Dutch morgan, moon flower, moon penny, poverty weed, white man's weed, herb margaret, and dog blow.

Even among scientists, it has had a few names. *Leucanthemum vulgare*, a term first applied in 1778, was used as late as the 1940s. One authority identified it in 1949 as *Leucanthemum vulgare* var. *pinnatifidum*, which roughly translates as "common white flower with featherlike leaves." *Chrysanthemum leucanthemum*, which dates from 1753, is probably a better scientific name, and it certainly has more charm. I believe it is one of the most mellifluous that botanists have devised. Try it out loud!

**Wild Geranium**
*(Geranium maculatum)*

# *Splashes of Springtime Purple*

In the wildflower world, May seems to be a month of whites, yellows, and greens. There are few purples or blues, especially among the medium- to large-blossomed herbs. One common and beautiful exception is the wild geranium, a flower whose varying shades and hues of light rosy-purple enliven many semi-shaded, moist places through much of North America.

Wild geranium is a true geranium, much different from pelargoniums, those showy plants of summer flower boxes. The miscasting occurred in the eighteenth century when pelargoniums were first imported as garden flowers from South Africa. Thus wild geranium (*Geranium maculatum*) is a rather silly name, meant to distinguish our native plant from false "geraniums" from another continent. Perhaps wild geranium would be better called by one of its other names, such as cranesbill or alumroot.

*G. maculatum* is one of thirty or so species of geraniums found in North America. Several species are imports. Early in this century, one Siberian species was found in eastern North America along roadsides in parts of New York City, of all places. *G. carolinianum*, a bushy, white-flowered native considered a pest, is found in woods and fields from coast to coast. The smaller, deeper-purple dove's foot geranium (*G. molle*), so called because of its leaf shape, is an import that has become widespread but not exceedingly common.

Known from New England to Alabama and west to Nebraska, wild geranium is found growing, often luxuriantly, in open woods and along shaded roadsides where there is at least some seasonal moisture. Plants are a foot or two tall, and usually grow in groups so that they take on a shrubby appearance, sometimes creating low hedges. The fairly large, toothed, five-part leaves are somewhat mottled with brown; hence the specific name, *maculatum*, meaning "mottled."

Wild geranium has acquired many names here and in Europe, to which it was exported as a medicinal herb. It has been called storksbill, alum bloom (alum was a common styptic chemical), chocolate flower (the color of the dried medicinal root powder), crowfoot, old maid's nightcap (flower shape), shameface (presumably, the color of the flower, like an embarrassed face), rockweed (it is often found near stone walls), and sailor's knot (probably the seed pod's shape).

*Geranium* means "crane." Both the generic name and the common name, cranesbill, refer to the plant's seed case, which has been likened in shape to a crane's long beak. This shape serves a function. When the fruit is ripe, the long pod pops open and catapults seeds into the air. Naturalist William H. Gibson calculated that some of the tiny seeds are fired more than thirty feet. Perhaps it is not surprising that geraniums are fairly closely related to jewelweeds, which have a similar seed-shooting technique, though a totally different flower shape. Such propulsion, of course, helps to ensure the spread of the plant into new territories.

When it lands on the ground, the seed continues to move. It has a tail, called an awn, which curls when it is dry and straightens when it is wet. Some botanists suspect the tail-twisting motion propels the seed along the ground until it becomes stuck in a small hole or crack. At this point, the motion may help push the seed into the ground. The amazing ability to crawl into a protected spot helps the seed to find a good place to germinate and to escape from mourning doves, quail, chipmunks, and other animals that eat it.

### *A Discovery*

A European geranium, very similar to *G. maculatum*, alerted German scientist Christian Konrad Sprengel to the fact that insects are responsible for pollination in many kinds of flowers—shocking news in the 1780s. Sprengel advanced the theory, also novel at that time, that every part of a flower has a distinct purpose. He determined that the hairs around the inside of the geranium's corolla serve to stop raindrops and dew, preventing them from watering down the nectar that attracts insects. He also figured out that the little, deeper-purple veins in the petals help guide insects to the nectary.

The pollen, incidentally, is an unusual color. While most pollen is orangish, the pollen of wild geranium is bright blue. "Seen through the microscope, this blue pollen is quite a curiosity," wrote F. Schuyler Mathews in 1895.

Besides being an attractive plant, recommended in most wildflower horticulture books, *G. maculatum* has long been valued as a medicine. Because of the large amount of tannin in its leaves, it has been employed chiefly as an astringent and styptic. Leaves and roots have been used to treat diarrhea, cholera, gonorrhea, neuralgia, toothaches, hemorrhages, sore throats, and gum diseases. Certain American Indians mixed it with grape juice as a mouthwash for youngsters with thrush, a mouth disease. Added to a mixture of milk and sugar, it was a popular gargle for children. Indians also valued it for "looseness of the bowels," and more modern authors warn that the plant can cause just the opposite problem, constipation.

**Bluets**
*(Houstonia caerulea)*

# *A Wee Bit of Spring Snow*

The fresh green fields of May are often dotted with little blossoms called bluets, a dainty name for a dainty plant. Only half an inch or so across, its four-petaled flowers are bright sparkles that may appear in large numbers and in several shades ranging from white to blue. "Millions of these dainty wee flowers, scattered through the grass of moist meadows and by the wayside, reflect the blue and serenity of heaven in their pure, upturned faces," wrote Neltje Blanchan. "Where the white variety grows, one might think a light snowfall had powdered the grass or a milky way of tiny floral stars had streaked a terrestrial path."

Although found from Canada to Florida and west to the Mississippi, bluets are best known and most common in the Northeast. "No one who has been in New England during the month of May can forget the loveliness of the bluets," wrote Mrs. William Starr Dana. "The roadsides, meadows, and even the lawns are thickly carpeted with the dainty enamel-like blossoms, which are always pretty, but which seem to flourish with especial vigor and in great profusion in this lovely region."

Both authors wrote their descriptions at the turn of the century when more of our land was devoted to agriculture. Like daisies, which used to whiten many an old field, bluets are less common today as subdivisions and woods have taken over land once used for grazing and growing. Yet, bluets can still be found on open land, especially near ponds and brooks. Usually they appear in small numbers and one often has to look carefully for their small, yellow-eyed blossoms.

Many years ago, W. Atlee Burpee, the horticulturist, saw the attractiveness of this little flower, which stays fresh long after picking, and he offered its seeds to the public as a cultivated flower. Perhaps gardeners prefer giant flowers (like giant cars, giant houses, and giant TV screens); it was a poor seller. At any rate, I have not seen bluets, also called Houstonia or Innocence, in many recent catalogs. A few nurseries still have the seeds, however, and various books commend it as excellent for shady rock gardens. This interest in the plant among gardeners may be spreading its range, locally at least, to well west of the Mississippi.

Bluets are members of the Madder family, a clan of mostly tropical plants containing 340 genera and more than 6,000 species. Best known in our territory are the open-field members of the family, such as bedstraw (see Bedstraws: Creepers for Runners) and wild licorice.

*Houstonia caerulea*, their Latin name, recalls the British botanist and physician, Dr. William Houston, who spent much of his short life gathering plant samples in Mexico and South America. He died in 1733 after an arduous collecting trek around the Gulf of Mexico. *Caerulea* means "sky-colored blue." (Cerulean frequently appears in translations of the *Iliad* and the *Odyssey*, describing the sky or even a woman's eyes.) Although the plant's name seems to indicate that the blue form is more common, I have more often seen the white variety, a color that may result from soil types where I live.

### *Two Forms*

*Houstonia caerulea* has two forms as well as two colors. On some flowers the stamens, tipped with pollen-bearing anthers, are low down in the flower tube and the pistils, topped with pollen-catching stigmas, stick out of the tube. On other flowers, the stamens stick out and the pistils are deep down. Each variation produces seeds of only its kind, and each grows in its own patch. The blossoms with tall pistils, however, usually must receive pollen from tall stamens, and short pistils must get pollen from short stamens. Small bees and butterflies do most of the pollination. Butterflies pick up pollen on just the right spot on their tongues to deliver it to stigmas of the corresponding height. This system of two-form flowers, called dimorphism, encourages cross-fertilization. Plants are not fertilized by plants in the same clump, and produce better-quality seeds.

Bluets are an excellent flower to add some springtime color to a small field or a section of lawn that is moist at least in the spring. You can obtain seed from nurseries or, if you have access to wild plants, you can divide off a few plants and they will multiply over the years. Plants can even be placed in pots and brought indoors to bloom through the winter.

Although they have little history of use as a food or medicine, bluets have acquired many folk names, mostly because of their good looks. They have been called Quaker ladies, Quaker bonnets, Venus's pride, bright eyes, angel eyes, blue-eyed grass (not to be confused with the six-petaled Sisyrinchiums that grow on grasslike stems), wild forget-me-nots, blue-eyed babies, nuns, little washer-woman, and star of Bethlehem (no relation to the garden variety with larger white flowers).

# ~ SUMMER

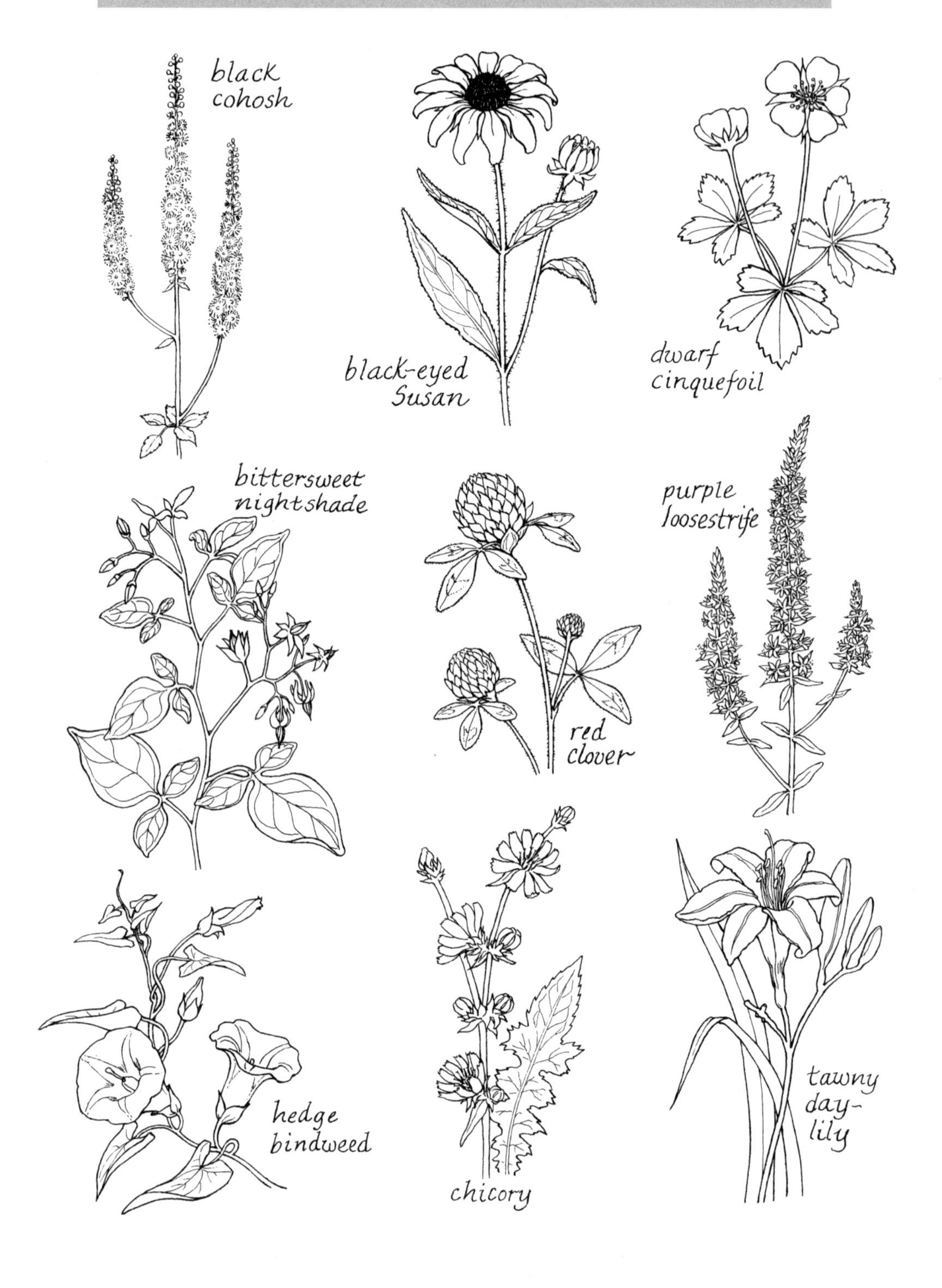

black cohosh
black-eyed Susan
dwarf cinquefoil
bittersweet nightshade
red clover
purple loosestrife
hedge bindweed
chicory
tawny day-lily

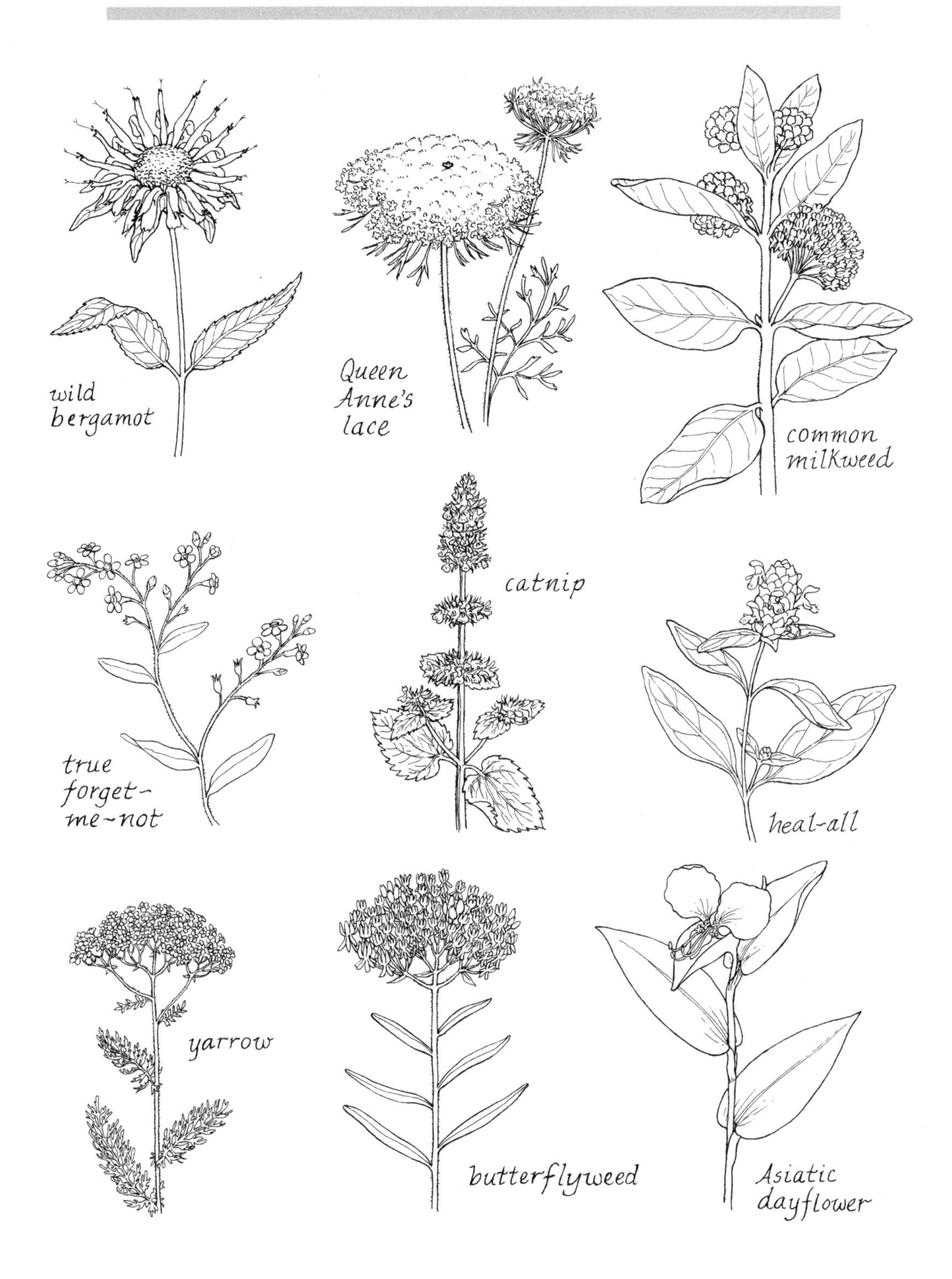
wild bergamot
Queen Anne's lace
common milkweed
true forget-me-not
catnip
heal-all
yarrow
butterflyweed
Asiatic dayflower

**Common Hawkweed**
*(Hieracium vulgatum)*

# *An Underground Pair*

When members of a floral family pick up names like king devil, grimm the collier, and devil's paint brush, one might suspect that the plants have sinister characteristics. In the case of hawkweeds, the suspicion is only partly true. While hawkweeds do tend to choke out other plants, they are nonetheless interesting, sometimes stunning wildflowers.

Hawkweeds have dandelionlike flowers that bloom from June through August. Some 300 species live worldwide, and about 56 in North America. Where they occur, they are often found in huge numbers. King devil (*Hieracium pratense*) and devil's paint brush (*H. aurantiacum*) are two quick-spreading members of the genus.

## *Two Devils*

King devil, which blooms in June, looks like a miniature dandelion on a tall, leafless, very hairy stem. The yellow flowers, smaller and with fewer petals than dandelions, bloom in clusters. They grow in fields and lawns, wherever it is open and sunny. If you cut them down with a mower, the flowers will pop right back up, with the speed and pugnaciousness of dandelions. These perennials spread by seeds and by stolons, shoots that embed themselves in the soil and start new plants.

Devil's paint brush, which blooms from around Memorial Day into August in loose clusters on long, hairy, leafless stems, is one of our most attractive flowers. Its shades of bright orange are similar to those of butterflyweed or wild columbine. "The midsummer meadows are ablaze with the brilliant orange-red flowers of this striking European weed," wrote Mrs. William Starr Dana. Said John Burroughs, "Its deep vivid orange is a delight to the eye. It repeats in our meadows and upon our hilltops the flame of the columbine of May, intensified."

## *Complete Possession*

Both plants are persistent, rapidly spreading weeds that have been a bane to farmers since their arrival from Europe in the nineteenth century, probably with crop seeds. Burroughs explained why in a report of his first discovery of masses of devil's paint brush in a New England field in August 1884. "They had been cut down with the grass in early July, and the first week in August had shot up and bloomed again. I found the spot aflame with them. Their leaves covered every inch of the surface where they stood and not a spear of grass grew there. They were taking slow but complete possession: they were devouring the meadow by inches. . . . The farmers were thoroughly alive to the danger, and were fighting it like fire."

What a shame such a beautiful, easy-to-grow flower can be such a pest. Neltje Blanchan considered devil's paint brush a plant worth acquiring. "Transplanted to the garden," she wrote, "the orange hawkweed forms a spreading mass of unusual, splendid color." It is easy to dig up and move, but heed Burroughs's warning about its tendency to spread. Since it sends off seeds through the air in the fashion of dandelions, do not be surprised to see it popping up elsewhere around the yard and neighborhood.

Devil's paint brush was also called grimm the collier (coalminer) because the black hairs on leaves and stems gave it the dirty look of a coalminer emerging from his mine. *Grimm the Collier* was a popular Elizabethan comedy.

### *The Hawks*

Hawkweeds get their English and Latin names (*hierax* means "hawk") from the old English belief that hawks swooped down to the earth to eat the juice of the plant to sharpen their eyes. These plants are also called hawkbits and speerhawks for that reason. *Pratense*, the specific name for king devil, means "of the field," while *aurantiacum* of devil's paint brush translates as "orange-red."

Hawkweeds were once popular in Europe for the treatment of lung disorders, for relief of stomach pains, for use as poultices, and for help with cramps and convulsions. American Indians of the Northwest once used a native species as chewing gum. It was even used for beauty treatments. "The distilled water [juice] cleanseth the skin and taketh away freckles, spots, or wrinkles on the face," wrote Nicholas Culpeper, the English herbalist, in 1649.

Many other hawkweeds can be found in North America. Two white-flowered varieties, white hawkweed (*H. albiflorum*) and western hawkweed (*H. albertinum*), may be found in the West.

The native rattlesnake-weed (*H. venosum*) of the East Coast has purple-veined basal leaves that are supposed to resemble the skin of the reptile. Many of our ancestors believed that God marked the creatures of nature, such as plants, to show how humans could use them. Thus, for generations, rattlesnake-weed was used to treat snakebites, and hence that specific name, *venosum.*

**Yellow Goatsbeard**
*(Tragopogon pratensis)*

# *The Geodesic Clock*

At a quick glance you might mistake this yellow, many-petaled flower for a common dandelion. Although it is closely related, goatsbeard is different and not nearly as common. Rising up to three feet in height, goatsbeard bears its single blossoms on stems with grass-like leaves. Perhaps because they are not as plentiful—or perhaps because they are more susceptible to mowers—they rarely appear in lawns. Instead they are found mostly along edges of moist woods and fields, frequently near roadsides.

The old flower head forms a blowball or "clock" of fuzz-topped seeds, larger and more like a ball than the blowball of a dandelion and having the appearance of a geodesic dome. This stunning puffball is the source of the plant's name. "The pappus, or feathery down crowning each seed, is very beautiful, being raised on a long stalk and interlaced, so as to form a shallow cup," wrote Maude Grieve. "By means of the pappus, the seeds are wafted by the wind and freely scattered."

In England, its native land, goatsbeard is called noonflower. The name describes one of the flower's undandelionlike characteristics—the blossom closes midday. Like chicory, a related flower that also fades in the sun, goatsbeard may stay open all day if the weather is cloudy. But unlike chicory, the blossom will reopen the next day. Its habit of closing early, apparently protection against the hot and desiccating rays of the sun, has earned goatsbeard other names, such as noontide and go-to-bed-at-noon. The habit also prompted Abraham Cowley to write in the seventeenth century:

*The goats beard, which each morn*
*abroad goes peep,*
*But shuts its flower at noon, and goes to sleep.*

Other names include buck's beard, star of Jerusalem, and Joseph's flower. The last name may stem from the common depiction of St. Joseph, husband of Mary, as a bearded, older man.

*Tragopogon pratensis*, its botanic name, means "goat's beard" and "of the meadow." The plant can be found in northern states east of the Mississippi and in southern Canada. *Tragopogon* is a small genus of about twenty-five Old World species, three of which have made their way across the Atlantic. Salsify (*T. porrifolius*) is a purple garden escape that is found locally throughout the United States and southern Canada; it is said to taste like oysters. Two additional species that have appeared in the Pacific Northwest may be hybrids of European imports. For instance, yellow salsify's specific name, *T. dubius*, may reflect the uncertain origin of this plant that is common throughout the Pacific states. Dandelions, hawkweeds, and chicory—all members of the chicory tribe of the Composite family—are closely related to Tragopogons.

### *Old Medicine*

In medieval Europe, goatsbeard was used as a medicinal plant, to treat—among other things—stomach disorders, breast ailments, and liver ailments. The milky juice was once a popular remedy for heartburn, a sort of liquid Tums. "A decoction of the roots is good for the heart-burn, loss of appetite, disorders of the breast and liver; expels sand and gravel, slime, and even small stones," wrote Nicholas Culpeper. "The roots of Goats-beard, boiled in wine and drunk, asswageth the pain and pricking stitches of the sides," said John Gerard.

The roots were once eaten in the fashion of a parsnip. "Buttered as parseneps and carrots [they] are a most pleasant and wholesome meate, in delicate taste far surpassing either parsenep or carrot," wrote Gerard. They have also been roasted and, like chicory roots, ground into a coffee substitute. Young stalks were cut up and boiled, like asparagus; in fact, they are said to have an asparaguslike flavor. The young basal leaves can be eaten either raw or boiled like spinach.

It is not easy to transplant goatsbeard; you must take care not to break its rather deep tap root. Instead, the next time you see one of those handsome domes, save some seeds to plant in a semishaded to sunny setting with moist, neutral soil. You will be rewarded for your efforts by goatsbeard's rather delicate flower and its unusual puffball.

**White Baneberry**
*(Actaea pachypoda)*

## *Plants to Twice Enjoy*

Although baneberry is often overlooked by wildflower fans, it is among the few plants whose ornaments can be enjoyed in two seasons for two reasons: It bears attractive flowers and, later, even more attractive berries.

Probably because the flowers are not big or plentiful, they have been almost ignored by many writers. F. Schuyler Mathews called the blossoms "not particularly interesting," and Neltje Blanchan dismissed them as insignificant. Many books on wildflowers, including one modern field guide, do not even mention baneberries.

Mrs. William Starr Dana, however, talked of gathering "the feathery clusters of white baneberry . . . when we go in the woods for the columbine, the wild ginger, the jack-in-the-pulpit, and Solomon's seal." Baneberry's flowers are delicately beautiful. During most of their appearance in May and June, the fluffy clusters are little more than stamens and stigmas, parts of flowers usually unnoticed in the fancier blossoms of other species. Like those of the closely related black cohosh or fairy candles, baneberry's petal-like sepals fall off soon after opening, leaving bunches of the bright, white fuzzies. Baneberries grow, bushlike, from one to three feet and are fairly common in and around the rich woods of the East.

## *Natural History*

Like May apple and goatsbeard, baneberry is better known for its fruits than for its flowers. The fruits appear in late summer or early autumn. Each white berry, which has a purple-black dot at the tip, sits at the end of a short, red stalk. The berries have inspired the plant's name and given it its fame, limited as that may be. They look "strikingly like the china eyes that small children occasionally manage to gouge from their dolls," wrote Mrs. Dana at the turn of the century. In New England, they are still commonly called doll's eyes or dolls' eyes. No one seems quite certain where to stick the apostrophe—is there one doll or are there many? One botanist avoids the problem, spelling it "dollseyes."

The clusters of berries are striking and attractive. Inside each waxy berry is a tightly packed and finely fitted set of seeds which, if planted in rich, humusy soil that will not dry out, should yield flowering baneberry plants in two years. If you are not patient enough to wait that long, try dividing the roots in late fall—or early spring if you know where some live. The perennial is not exceedingly common, so avoid transplanting whole plants.

Bane is an ancient English word that appears as early as Beowulf as "bona" or "bana," and that means "slayer" or "murderer." The berries are said to be poisonous. Just how poisonous they are probably depends on the person and the plant. Walter Conrad Muenscher's 1939 book, *Poisonous Plants of the United States*, reports that children have died from eating berries of the similar European baneberry (*Actaea spicata*), which Gerard described as having "a venomous and deadly qualitie." Professor Muenscher wrote that for our red baneberry (*A. rubra*), "eating six berries was sufficient to produce increased pulse, dizziness, burning in the stomach, and colicky pains." Yet Michel Sarrazin, an eighteenth-century French Canadian herbalist, observed, "It is thought that the fruit is a poison, which I don't believe, at least I know of no bad effects." Professor John M. Kingsbury's 1965 book, *Deadly Harvest: A Guide to Common Poisonous Plants*, does not even mention baneberries.

Whatever their effect on humans, big or little, it is best to keep baneberries away from tots who are apt to eat them, thinking they might taste as good as they look. Of course, it is important to make it clear to children that any wild berries could be dangerous and must be left alone.

## *Medicinal Uses*

North American Indians regarded baneberries as an important medicine, but use varied with season and aspect. Among the Ojibwas, for instance, red baneberry was considered a male plant—that is, good for men's ailments—at certain times of the year and a female plant at other times, depending perhaps on the size of the plant or the color of the berries. Chippewa women used white baneberry for menstrual difficulties while the men used red baneberry for diseases peculiar to them. Many Indians, such as Ojibwas and Potawatomis, took baneberry extracts to help with childbirth. Probably because it is said to affect the heart, the plant was also used as a substitute for digitalis. "It is said to revive and rally a patient when he is at the point of death," said a writer on Meskwaki medicines.

Maude Grieve reported that Indians considered the plants "a valuable remedy against snakebite, especially of the rattlesnake. Hence, it is—with several other plants—sometimes known as one of the 'rattlesnake herbs.'" Its use for this purpose was not widespread, probably because the plant may be as bad for you as the snakebite.

### *Names*

White baneberry, known as *Actea alba* or *A. pachypoda*, is a member of the Crowfoot, or Buttercup, family. *Actea*, a genus of only a half-dozen or so species worldwide, means "elder"; the leaves of some species resemble those of the elder tree. *Alba*, of course, means "white," while *pachypoda* means "thick-footed" or "thick-stalked" (just as pachyderm means "thick skinned"). Some botanists consider *A. alba* and *A. pachypoda* as separate species, but most modern authorities recognize only one white baneberry and now call it *A. pachypoda*.

Among its folk names are white cohosh, blue cohosh, whiteheads, necklace weed, white-berry snakeroot, grapewort, and herb-Christopher, the last referring to St. Christopher who was somehow associated with a similar plant in ancient times. Perhaps he used Britain's baneberry, the rather rare *A. spicata* found on limestone banks and called herb-Christopher, bugbane, and toadroot. Except for the fact that it has black berries, it is very similar to *A. pachypoda*. In fact, Linnaeus originally classified the American species as *Actea spicata alba*, meaning *alba* was a white variety of the species *A. spicata*.

Our white baneberry's close relative, red baneberry, bears bright berries of scarlet or crimson. *A. rubra* favors cooler climates, ranging from the upper East Coast as far south as Pennsylvania and west to the Pacific states, while white baneberry has been found from southern Canada to Georgia, though westward only to Missouri and Minnesota. Both have handsome berries, but the whites seem more striking because, for berries at least, white is less common a color.

**Tawny Day-Lily**
*(Hemerocallis fulva)*

## *Beautiful for a Day*

In early summer, highway departments roll out their machines and begin cutting roadside brush. But a person who appreciates beauty will lift the blade as it comes upon a patch of our most common member of the Lily family, tawny day-lily (*Hemerocallis fulva*).

The botanic name aptly describes the flower. *Hemerocallis* is Greek for "beautiful for a day" while *fulva* describes its tawny or orange-gray-yellow color. Each bloom lasts only one day, opening in the morning and closing forever around dark, much to the disappointment of people who pick them for bouquets. Fortunately, each tall stem bears many flowers and a colony of day-lilies stays bright with color for several weeks.

### *Natives of Asia*

Our wild day-lilies are natives of Asia, common in northern China, Siberia, and Japan. Members of the genus *Hemerocallis* were taken to England as early as the 1590s. It is said that North American sea captains brought them home to their wives after long journeys to the Orient.

Two of these imported species, tawny day-lily and yellow day-lily, are now found wild in North America. Yellow day-lily (*H. flava*) is sweet smelling, unlike the unscented tawny day-lily. *Hemerocallis* species differ from regular lilies (*Lilium*) in that they grow from fibrous rootstocks, or rhizomes, instead of from bulbs, and the flowers are presented irregularly on the stalk, rather than in some sort of symmetry, as is common with true lilies.

The plants have adapted well to our climate and have readily spread along moist, sunny or semisunny roadsides—almost anywhere that is not out-and-out arid in the eastern half of the United States and southern Canada. It is yet another example of an alien species taking a liking to its new home, and settling right in.

### *Living Antiques*

These day-lilies sometimes produce seeds, but the seeds are rarely viable. Instead, plants readily reproduce by dividing off rootstock to create new plants. It is interesting to speculate, as did Dr. Harold Moldenke in the 1940s, that millions of day-lilies in North America and Europe are actually still living parts of plants that grew in Asia centuries ago. Technically speaking, therefore, each plant you see along the roadside is hundreds of years old.

Day-lilies are easily transplanted by gently dividing old clumps, preferably in the fall. In fact, dividing helps provide room for the parent colony to "breathe" and allows it to produce more flowers. Although they will thrive in a variety of soils and sun exposures, day-lilies must be in well drained but not dry ground.

Other names for tawny day-lily include Eve's thread and, occasionally, lemon lily, though this is now used mostly for *H. flava.*

Day-lilies are the welcoming banners of summer. In most parts of their range, they begin blooming when summer arrives, though in more northern climates, they usually await the Fourth of July or thereabouts to start opening up.

### *Complete Food*

Although day-lilies have had no value in herb medicine, they are a veritable pantry of foods, and almost every part of the plant is eaten. In China and Japan, the buds or the newly opened flowers are picked, dipped in batter, and fried as fritters. Chinese chefs have long been fond of lily and day-lily flowers, calling them *gum tsum* or "golden needles" and preserving them by drying in air or salt, or by pickling.

Day-lily buds are also picked, boiled briefly, buttered, seasoned, and eaten like green beans. If the idea of eating buds or flowers seems unusual, remember that both broccoli and cauliflower are budding flower heads.

One way of preparing day-lilies is to collect the withering flowers late in the day and cook them slowly in butter and heavy cream seasoned with salt and pepper. The result is somewhat glutinous, but this glutinosity has led chefs to use the flowers as a thickening agent, as well as a flavoring, for soups and stews.

The young greens make a nice addition to salads, and the spring shoots are also good cooked like asparagus. Farmers in Connecticut used to chop up and boil the rootstock, serving it like potatoes. The flavor is said to be just as sweet as fresh corn.

The root, however, is better preserved as a source of the many little tubers that pop out around it as the plant divides; they are edible raw or roasted and have a nice nutlike flavor.

In the past forty years there has been much interest in developing hybrids of *Hemerocallis* species, of which there are more than a dozen (none native). In the 1950s a farmer in Texas was producing some 2½ million *Hemerocallis* plants each year.

Thanks to the hybridists, many of the twenty-five or so popular varieties belie their own name; they are now no longer beautiful for a day, but may last a week or more.

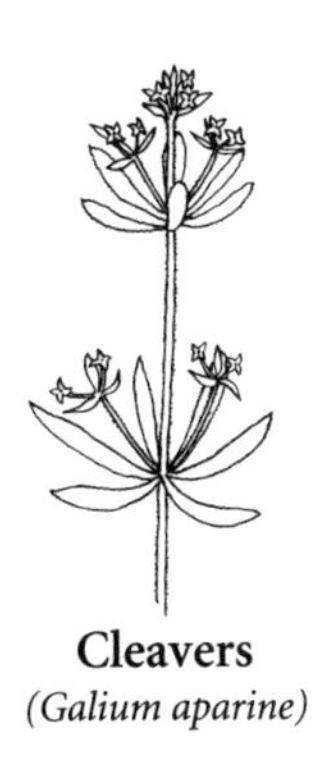

**Cleavers**
*(Galium aparine)*

## *Creepers for Runners*

Some wildflowers are more noted—and appreciated—for their foliage than for their flowers. Such are the bedstraws, common summer plants whose tiny blossoms often go unnoticed, but whose seeds can be all too noticeable and annoying.

Creeping, low, whorled-leafed plants whose favorite haunt is open fields, bedstraws are a large clan found worldwide. Some species, like fragrant bedstraw (*Galium triflorum*), range across North America, Europe, and Asia, from the Himalayas around the world to Japan. Few plant species can be found on so many parts of the planet, but many that are so widespread owe it to their exceptionally functional seeds.

"The most extraordinary thing about bedstraw is the way it catches on everything it touches," wrote F. Schuyler Mathews. The oval seedpods, covered with little hook-shaped hairs, have managed to hitchhike their way across three continents. In some species, such as the aptly named cleavers (*Galium aparine*), it is the hooked-haired stems that are more likely to grab hold of you, carrying the pods with them. In fact, *aparine* is from the Greek, "to seize." These hairs serve also to discourage some plant eaters, such as snails, from nibbling the leaves and stems.

Through the ages and around the world, different peoples have used different species of bedstraw for such varied purposes as medicine, cheese making, clothes dying, and—apparently—mattress stuffing. Yellow bedstraw (*G. verum*) was a popular remedy for gallstones and urinary diseases into this century, and was once used to treat epilepsy, hysteria, and internal bleeding. "An ointment is prepared which is good for anointing the weary traveler," said John Gerard.

## *An Old Dye*

Although maidens in Henry VIII's time believed wearing yellow bedstraw would turn their hair blond, the plant was used extensively to create a red dye. American Indians employed the closely related wild madder (*G. tinctorium*) for coloring red their feathers, porcupine quills, and other ornaments. French Canadians dyed clothing with the plant, which they called *tisavo jaune-rouge.*

One of the yellow bedstraw's chief uses was in the production of cheese. It not only curdled the milk in preparation for cheese making, but also, in some places, added color and sweetness to the product. Some hairy-stemmed varieties, like cleavers, were matted together and used as sieves to strain milk. *Galium*, the generic name, means "milk."

Bedstraw itself is an odd name whose origin has been traced to two possible sources: the old use of the dried plant to stuff beds or the belief that the plant was one of the "cradle herbs" mixed in the hay of the manger when Jesus was born in Bethlehem.

The genus *Galium* consists of around 250 species around the world, with some 75 in North America. The genus includes bedstraws, madders, wild licorice, and several cleavers. The *Galium* species are distinguished by their tiny white, greenish, purple, or yellow flowers with pointed petals. Leaves appear in whorls, usually of four, six, or eight. In general, the plants lie close to the ground, often forming mats.

Bedstraws are members of the Madder family (*Rubiaceae*) of some 340 genera and 6,000 species worldwide, mostly tropical. About the only other well-known genera within the family are the bluets (*Houstonia*) of spring and the imported woodruffs (*Aperula*), some of which are used to flavor wines.

Over the years the various bedstraws have picked up a myriad of names. Cleavers (*G. aparine*) has at least seventy recorded English names, including goosegrass, grip-grass, beggar-lice, cling-rascal, scratch-grass, stick-a-back, pigtail, liveman, sweethearts, and poorweed. Bedstraw seeds were once roasted as a coffee-substitute; the fact that true coffee is a related plant may explain why. The boiled young shoots, served with butter, have been eaten as a vegetable or, chilled, in a salad. The plant is consumed by just about all grazing mammals and fowl. Indians widely used it as a medicine. While their clinging nature has made cleavers unpopular with most people, mischievous youngsters have always loved to attach sprigs of them to the backs of unsuspecting comrades.

Yellow bedstraw has been called cheese-rennet, curdworts, bedflower, fleawort, yellow cleavers, and maidshair. Distilling its flower heads is said to result in a refreshing drink. Perhaps the best use of the plant was reported by Culpeper 400 years ago and might be noted by the recreational runners of today. "The decoction of the herb or flower," he wrote, "is good to bathe the feet of travellers and lacqueys, whose long running causeth weariness and stiffness in their sinews and joints."

So be kind to your lackey and give him a bedstraw bath.

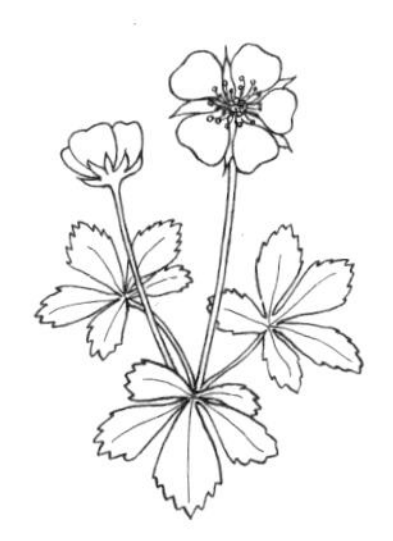

**Dwarf Cinquefoil**
*(Potentilla canadensis)*

# *A Rose by Another Name*

It is odd how some plants not only survive but thrive in parched or poisoned soil, and how they can produce some of our most attractive wildflowers. Dwarf cinquefoil, a creeping, thornless rose that many people see but few people notice, is a tiny yet pretty variety that can grow in these destitute areas. I have seen it creeping right up to the edge of highways from whose pavement drain salt, oil, gasoline, and other unpleasant substances. It also grows in fields and lawns, favoring dry soils.

In her column "The Excellence of Little" in *The West Hartford* [Connecticut] *News* some years ago, Jane B. Cheney noted, "The occurrence of this plant in waste places from Newfoundland down to the Carolinas is diagnostic of poor soil and dry soil. It does not take well to competition and itself dies out when soil is enriched. This characteristic is evidently particular to [dwarf cinquefoil] because many of the other species are large and reliable garden plants."

These dry-earth cinquefoils are nature's way of covering, even decorating, the more barren parts of our landscape. Like cacti, they spring from harsh, barren soils. As we allow more of the good topsoil to be eroded or scraped away, the cinquefoils are bound to become even more common. They are among those odd creatures of nature that thrive on our inability to handle our environment carefully.

## *Flower of Fives*

Cinquefoil is a French-based word meaning "five-leaved." The name should not be taken too literally, however, because the plant actually has single leaves deeply cut into five parts, not five separate leaves. The flower does have five, rounded yellow petals.

Cinquefoil leaves are similar in shape and form to those of wild yellow strawberries, and many people confuse the two plants. Yellow strawberries, however, have three-part leaves. The casual observer today is more apt to think cinquefoils are buttercups creeping along the ground. Those who know their flowers, however, will recognize the resemblance of the blossoms to those of wild roses. The flowers are flat, not cuplike as in the buttercups, and the petals lack the shiny surface of common buttercups. Dwarf cinquefoil may well be the most common of the wild roses—at least of the nonshrubby varieties.

*Potentilla canadensis* is one of more than 120 species of *Potentilla* found in North

America, the genus being most populous in the western and northwestern parts of the continent. Dwarf cinquefoil may be found as far west as Texas. It is also called five finger, finger leaf, barren strawberry, sinkfield (based on a misunderstanding of "cinque"), starflower, and running buttercups. The last name reflects the tendency for the low-lying plant to spread by slender runners.

Dwarf cinquefoil begins blooming at my Connecticut home as early as May 1, but the leaves spring from the ground long before that. I've seen them sprouting in February, just after a thaw. The plants flower until midsummer.

### *Many Varieties*

There are several other less common but still plentiful varieties of cinquefoil. Common cinquefoil (*P. simplex*) is another creeper, somewhat larger than *P. canadensis.* Unlike the latter, which has leaf-sections with flattish tops, common cinquefoil has pointed leaf tips. It's also called old-field cinquefoil because old fields are a favorite haunt.

Common silverweed (*P. anserina*), found along shores and streamsides from New England, the Great Lakes, and the West Coast up to Alaska, is also native to Eurasia, and has been used for centuries as a food and medicine. Rough-fruited cinquefoil (*P. recta*), a European import, is more upright, growing to two feet, with flowers that are up to an inch wide. Shrubby cinquefoil (*P. fruticosa*) is a sizable plant, up to three feet tall, with many leaves that give it the appearance of a shrub. It blooms coast to coast in the summer, and has been used as the parent for various garden plants, often ones with yellow-orange flowers. It favors meadows and shores of streams and ponds, and was once popular for a tea made from its leaves.

Robbins cinquefoil, also sometimes called dwarf cinquefoil, is a very rare and endangered member of the clan. You will not find *P. robbinsiana* creeping across your lawn. In fact, this species grows only in two windswept, mountainous sites in New Hampshire.

### *Potent Treatment*

Europeans called members of the genus five-leaf grass, *Fünffingerkraut, cinco en rama, quintefueille,* or *cinquefoglio* and considered them potent treatment (hence, *Potentilla*) for many ailments. Cinquefoils had been used since the time of Hippocrates for fevers and toothaches, as astringents, and on ulcers and cancers. The Greeks called the plants *pentaphyllon,* while the Latins labeled them *quinquefolium.* Both words—and most of the other foreign names noted above—mean the same as cinquefoil.

Herbalist John Gerard wrote 400 years ago that a European variety, *P. reptans,* "is used in all inflammations and fevers, whether infectious or pestilential, and in lotions, gargles and the like, for sore mouths, ulcers, cancers, fistulas, and other corrupt, foul, or running sores." On this continent *Potentilla canadensis* has seen limited use in folk medicine. Herbalist John Lust says it makes a good gargle and mouthwash, and a remedy for diarrhea. The bark of the root has been used to stop nosebleeds and other internal bleeding.

"Every time I see this humble poor-soil plant, I am amazed at the amount of experimentation which has gone on in the past to heal and cure people," wrote Jane Cheney in her column. "It is an impressive record of work, though I had rather have the science of today!"

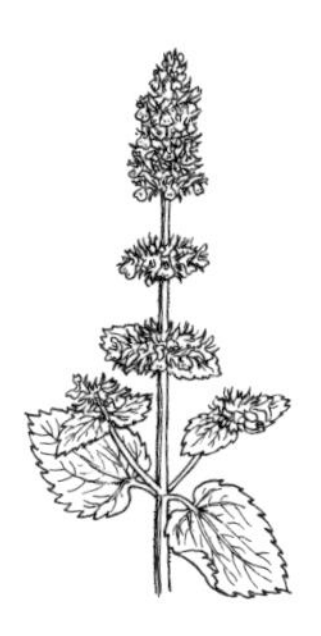

**Catnip**
*(Nepeta cataria)*

# *A Nip for the Kitty*

Catnip is a true curiosity among our common wildflowers. Its namesake characteristic has made it a widely known novelty. Who has ever owned a cat and never had a catnip toy?

Catnip is a member of the Mint family native to Eurasia. Probably due to its unusual qualities, the species has been carried around the world, and lives from coast to coast in the United States and southern Canada. In fact, it was so common here by the nineteenth century that Dr. Wooster Beach, in an 1857 book on plants and medicine, considered it a native. The weedy plant favors waste places, grows one to three feet tall, blooms in July and August, and has crowded clusters of mintlike, pale violet flowers.

Catnip has been put to many uses since ancient times. Pliny and Cicero recounted its effectiveness in treating scorpion bites. Through the centuries herbalists prescribed the flowering plant tops for fevers, colic, insanity, nervousness, bruises, headaches, and piles. It was supposed to relieve pain, induce sleep, and even eliminate nightmares. "It is generally used to procure women's courses . . . . Its frequent use takes away barrenness and the wind and pains of the mother," reported Culpeper. John Gerard found it "a present helpe for them that be bursten inwardly of some fall received from an high place, and that are very much bruised, if the juice be given with wine or meade."

Catnip was used especially for children's ailments. Many American youngsters of the eighteenth and nineteenth centuries drank catnip tea to reduce fevers, though their caring mothers would often sweeten the brew with honey. In a turnabout from the usual sequence of events, colonists apparently introduced Indians to the plant. The Chippewas were using it for fevers in the nineteenth century, calling it *gajungensibug*, which meant "little-cat leaf," probably because it could turn a staid old cat into a frisky kitten. The Delaware and Mohegans employed the tea to calm fretting babies. The Menomenis treated pneumonia with it, and the Ojibwas bathed the ill in catnip tea to raise the body temperature.

## *The Hangman's Brew*

One old English author reported, "The root when chewed is said to make the most gentle person fierce and quarrelsome, and there is a legend of a certain hangman who could never screw up his courage to the point of hanging anybody till he had partaken of it."

This is an odd reaction to an herb that was extensively used for centuries as a soporific tea, said to relax the drinker. Before the arrival of teas from China, English peasants brewed catmint tea, which one writer on herbs reports is "quite as pleasant and a good deal more wholesome" than Oriental teas. Naturalist Euell Gibbons recommended a spot of catnip tea with honey before going to bed, calling it "a pleasant nightcap." Indeed, the French used to serve the tea to retiring guests to help their digestion.

If you do not like the taste of catnip tea, you can always spread the plant's dried leaves around the house. Rats are said to hate the smell of the stuff, though one modern authority says it is of questionable value as a rat repellant.

### *The Cat's Meow*

Yet, for some reason, cats go crazy over catnip. Not just any catnip plant will do—it must be one with crushed or dried leaves. One of the hazards of transplanting catnip is that the plant bruises in the process. These bruises give off the plant's characteristic scent, attracting family or neighborhood cats who will frolic in the plants and may destroy them. On the other hand, cats will walk right past a catnip raised from seed or that has arrived uninjured. Thus, the old rhyme:

*If you set it, the cats will get it.*
*If you sow it, the cats don't know it.*

While cats may nip at the plants, the "nip" has nothing to do with biting. "Catnip" is the American bastardization of the British word, "catnep." "Nep," in turn, is an abbreviated form of the old Latin name for the plant, *nepeta*, which has also been used for its modern botanical name, *Nepeta cataria*. (*Cataria* is apparently bastardized Latin for "cat.") *Nepeta* comes from the Etruscan town of Nepete in northern Italy, now called *Nepi*, where the plant was supposedly first noted in ancient times or where it grew in particularly great profusion. The English used to say that something was "as white as nep," a reference to the whitish undersides of the leaves of catnep.

Anyone who doubts that this weedlike plant will transform an old cat need only crush a few leaves and toss them to kitty who will, as Neltje Blanchan wrote, "become half-crazed with delight over its aromatic odor." Gerard put it more quaintly: "Herbarists doe call Nep Herba cattaria & Herba catti, because cats are very much delighted herewith; for the smell of it is so pleasant unto them, that they rub themselves upon it, & wallow or tumble in it, and also feed on the branches and leaves very greedily." The closely related and more common ground ivy, or gill-over-the-ground (*Glechoma hederacea*), has a similar, but not as powerful effect on cats.

Catnip might also be called bee-nip. Both bees and beekeepers appreciate the plant, since its flowers generate large amounts of nectar that hive bees convert to a tasty honey.

Though it is usually found growing around parking lots, along dry roadsides, and in other waste places, catnip is a fairly attractive plant. In England, where it's commonly called catmint, it used to be popular for garden borders. It is a worthwhile plant to have around, if not for decoration, then for fun with your pet or for a spot of tea. But remember that if you transplant it, keep the family cat in the house for a day or two.

**Common Chickweed**
*(Stellaria media)*

# *It's for the Birds*

The normally staid, conservative Maude Grieve becomes expansive when describing the range of common chickweed in *A Modern Herbal*: "It has been said that there is no part of the world where the chickweed is not to be found. It is a native of all temperate and North Arctic regions, and has naturalized itself wherever the white man has settled, becoming one of the commonest weeds." Some authorities say it may be the most common flowering weed in the country, perhaps the world.

Common chickweed blossoms in lawns, gardens, and even sidewalk and parking lot cracks from as early as March to as late as November, and occasionally into December—even in New England. It thus has one of the longest blooming seasons of any wildflower of northern climes. In England's milder climate, it is said to bloom in every month of the year.

The white flower of common chickweed (*Stellaria media*) is distinctive. Its five petals are so deeply cleft that it almost looks as if there are ten narrow petals. This arrangement is typical of several chickweeds and stitchworts of the genus *Stellaria* that inhabit North America, mostly in lawns, fields, and waste places.

Chickweeds, like dandelions, are a scourge for those who want a putting-green lawn. Even television commercials for weed killers mention chickweed by name.

## *Bird Food*

Though lawn fanatics hate chickweeds, birds love them. Four centuries ago, John Gerard wrote in his *Herbal*: "Little birds in cadges [especially Linnets] are refreshed with the lesser chickweed when they loath their meat." Wrote Mrs. Grieve: "Both wild and caged birds eat the seeds as well as the young tops and leaves." Indeed, canary owners have been known to crawl on hands and knees, gathering the papery, seed-filled pods for their pets. One study of wildlife eating habits lists more than thirty common birds that eat *S. media*, but suggests that a complete inventory would be too long to publish. Thus, chickweed—like thistles, sunflowers, and berry-bearing plants—is good to have in the yard if you want to attract wild birds. Not surprisingly, the plant is called birdweed, chickenweed, chick wittles, cluckweed, and chicken's meat in England and America; *mouron des oiseaux* ("morsel for the birds") in France, and *Vogelkraut* ("bird plant") in Germany. An old Latin name, *morus gallinae*, meant "morsel for the hens."

Another set of names reflects the flowers' shape; *Stellaria* means "star." *S. media* has also been called starweed, starwort, star chickweed, and, in France, *stellaire.* Perhaps to give it a more native flavor over here, it is sometimes called Indian chickweed (though the Chippewas, who used this import in an eyewash, called it by a word meaning "tooth plant"). Other names include satinflower, skirt and buttons, white bird's eye, adder's mouth, and tongue grass (it looks like a snake's open mouth, complete with tongue), and winterweed (because of its long blooming season). Naturalist William H. Gibson tells of digging under snow and ice in England in midwinter and finding it blooming. Neltje Blanchan said, "Except during the most cruel frosts, there is scarcely a day in the year when we may not find the little starlike chickweed flowers."

### *Food and Medicine*

For a lowly lawn pest, chickweed has had quite a history of practical uses. C. P. Johnson, in *Useful Plants of Great Britain* (1862), found it "an excellent green vegetable, much resembling spinach in flavor and is very wholesome." Mrs. Grieve wrote, "The young leaves when boiled can hardly be distinguished from spring spinach, and are equally wholesome." Bradford Angier says the flavor is, to many people, less disagreeable than that of spinach. Herbalist John Lust reports that the plant contains significant quantities of Vitamin C and is a good source of phosphorus. It is also a good source of copper. However, because of its high nitrate content, says Barrie Kavasch, it should be eaten in moderation. Dr. E. Lewis Sturtevant, who headed the New York Agricultural Experiment Station in the late nineteenth century, noted, "This plant is found in every garden as a weed." Perhaps chickweed *belongs* in every garden.

As an herb medicine, chickweed has been used to treat ulcers, constipation, carbuncles, coughs, and hydrophobia. The crushed leaves were a popular poultice. If you believe Nicholas Culpeper, chickweed could cure a whole slew of problems. "The herb bruised, or the juice applied, with cloths or sponges dipped therein, to the region of the liver, doth wonderfully temper the heat of the liver, and is effectual for all impostumes and swellings whatsoever for all redness in the face, wheals, pushes, itch, or scabs, the juice being either simply used, or boiled in hog's grease; the juice of distilled water is of good use for all heat and redness in the eyes . . . as also into ears. . . . It helpeth the sinews when they are shrunk by cramps or otherwise, and extends and makes them pliable again." No wonder ancient herbalists lost many patients to the grave.

According to an old wives' tale, chickweed water was a remedy for obesity. But the good-humored Professor Lawrence J. Crockett observes that if that tale were true, chickweed would quickly disappear from overweight America. In modern herbals, chickweed's uses are limited. Mr. Lust offers a chickweed recipe for constipation and says it is good mixed with Vaseline to treat skin irritations. Joseph and Clarence Meyer recommend it only for external ailments.

### *Range and Survival*

Chickweed's range is remarkable. Describing exploration of southern New Zealand islands, Joseph Hooker (1817–1911) wrote: "On one occasion, landing on a small, uninhabited island nearly at the Antipodes, the first evidence I met with of its having been previously visited was the English chickweed; and this I traced to a mount that marked the grave of a British sailor, and that was covered with the plant, doubtless the offspring of seed that had adhered to the spade or mattock with which the grave had been dug."

The plant has clever ways to assure survival. In cold months when few flying insects are available for pollination, it produces cleistogamous flowers, which never open yet make seed. In warmer months, when its normal flowers compete with numerous larger and showier blossoms for the attention of insects, it produces nectar in great (for its size) quantities. Thus, it is pollinated by cross-fertilization, which produces a better quality of seed. As an annual *S. media* needs seeds in considerable numbers and with an excellent germination rate. That the species is so common and widespread is testimony to both the quantity and quality of seed.

The stem is from four to sixteen inches in length, but is weak, and the taller stems flop over, making the plant look like a creeper. When it flops, the plant sinks new roots, helping it to spread into dense carpets.

Dr. John Hutchinson, once head of the Botanical Museums at the Royal Botanical Gardens, found *S. media* "of considerable economic and biological interest, representing a high stage of evolution." As an example of its highly evolved systems, he cited the line of hairs that appears down only one side of the stem and on leaf stalks. "These carry out a special function," he said. "They are readily wetted by rain and dew and retain a considerable amount of water. This is conducted down to the leaf-stalks, where some of it is absorbed by the lower cells of the hairs, and any surplus is passed farther down to the next pair of leaves, and so on; the same process being repeated in each case." Chickweed does so well in fairly dry situations because it is able to make the best use of the water available.

Also common, especially in lawns, is the closely related mouse-ear chickweed (*Cerastium vulgatum*). A creeping plant whose fuzzy opposing leaves are shaped like the ears of a mouse, it grows throughout most of North America, including Alaska. The white, cleft-petaled flowers of mouse-ear chickweed are about one-quarter of an inch in diameter, while those of *S. media* are three-quarters of an inch wide.

About thirty species of *Stellaria* and twenty-five of *Cerastium* can be found on this continent, though—as is often the case—the imports seem to be most common and widespread. These two species are in turn members of the Pink family, which includes such common and oft-recognized flowers as ragged-robin, campions, catchflies, bouncing bet, and, of course, the pretty pinks themselves.

**Black-eyed Susan**
*(Rudbeckia hirta)*

## *Just a Pretty Face*

There is nothing special about the black-eyed Susan. It has no fragrance to speak of. It has little medicinal history. There is no real folklore attached to it. It is just an attractive, long-lasting flower that, as one writer observed, "many consider . . . the prettiest of all the wildflowers."

Black-eyed Susan, *Rudbeckia hirta*, is named for an eighteenth-century Swedish botanist. Olaus Rudbeck was a noted teacher at the University of Upsala in Sweden, where a country minister's son named Carl von Linne came to study medicine in the 1720s. Rudbeck took a shining to the young man and his interest in botany. Von Linne moved into Rudbeck's house and earned money by tutoring some of the prolific professor's twenty-four children.

The student, who later called himself Linnaeus, went on to develop the binomial system used to name all life forms by genus and species. For some reason known only to him, Linnaeus decided that coneflowers of North America should recall the mentor of his youth.

*Hirta* is Latin for "hairy," descriptive of the leaves and stalk. *R. hirta* is the type species for a clan of about twenty-five or thirty species usually called coneflowers; they are found throughout North America but mostly in the southern and western sections, including Mexico. Many coneflowers have bigger and more elongated center buttons—hence the name—than do black-eyed Susans. (Some authorities use black-eyed Susan when referring to a related plant, *R. serotina*, underscoring the difficulty of relying on common names.)

A native of the western plains and prairies, black-eyed Susan moved East in the 1830s, mixed with red clover seeds, much to the distress of farmers who did not like it befouling their fields. There are reports, too, that sheep and hogs have been poisoned by eating the plant, though it is hard to believe that anything as innocuous as a black-eyed Susan could harm the iron stomach of the omnivorous pig. Experiments on the tall, or green-headed, coneflower (*Rudbeckia laciniata*), long suspected by farmers of poisoning swine, found it caused little or no harm. Obviously, the plant likes its native land; it can now be found in just about every state and many provinces, favoring dry meadows, roadsides, and waste places, and often appears in great numbers. Black-eyed Susan is one of our most beautiful common wildflowers, ranking eleventh showiest in a 1940s poll of American and Canadian naturalists and botanists. Black-eyed Susan's bright yellow rays remain healthy for more than a month if the environment is right, making these flowers among our longest-lasting. The plants begin blooming in May or June, depending on how far north they are, and can still be flowering in October, if the weather remains mild.

### *Composites*

If you look closely at the cone or flower head, you will see that it is made up of hundreds of tiny seed-producing florets, which bloom in a ring around the cone, starting at the bottom and working up to the tip. Thus, each blossom is actually a composite of small, tightly clustered flowers and rays. The Composite family is the largest family of flowering plants, with more than 900 genera and 10,000 species throughout the world. The Composites are probably the most recent family to appear on the earth, and are among the most complex and highly developed of wild plants.

Black-eyed Susan's success at the business of survival is aided by its bright color, which attracts insects, its wealth of nectar that feeds them, and its abundance of yellow pollen. The pollen attracts short-tongued insects that can not get at the nectar, while the floret tubes hold nectar for insects—especially bees, butterflies, and moths—with tongues long enough to reach deep into the tubes.

Like other plants described in this book, the black-eyed Susan has many names, chiefly because it is so widespread and pretty. It is called yellow daisy, golden Jerusalem, English bull's eye, brown Betty, brown-eyed Susan, poorland daisy, and brown daisy.

Although *Rudbeckia hirta* has little history of use in herb medicine, American Indians such as the Chippewas employed tall coneflower (*R. laciniata*) to treat indigestion and burns. They called it *gizuswebigwais*, which means "it is scattering," perhaps a reference to its seeds or its tendency to multiply quickly in a field. Recent scientific research indicates that black-eyed Susan has some antibiotic properties, and may be useful in treating staphylococcus infections and for increasing the body's ability to ward off other kinds of infections.

### *Easily Acquired*

Black-eyed Susans are easy to transplant. Despite their liking for dry sandy soils, their roots do not go too deep. Instead, they have many tiny rootlets that form a clump and that, by their sheer numbers, are able to collect enough moisture for the plant. Black-eyed Susans are biennials and self-sow readily. They favor sun all or most of the day.

In their first year, the plants put up only a rosette of fuzzy leaves close to the ground. These leaves make and store enough food to send up the full-sized, mature, flowering plants the next year. If you transplant, make certain you get some of the immature basal-leaf-only plants, too, so you won't have alternating flowerless years. Do not pick flowers in the first year, but allow them to provide as much seed as possible to establish future plants.

Though many people would consider black-eyed Susan a weed, wildflower gardeners sometimes have trouble getting the plant to establish itself in their yards. Gardeners are either unaware that it is a biennial or they transplant it into rich soil. As the name poorland daisy suggests, black-eyed Susans thrive in poor soil, perhaps because the plants dislike competing for space—more of a problem in good soils than in poor ones.

Dr. A. F. Blankeslee, an American, has developed Gloriosa daisy (*Rudbeckia tetra*), an annual hybrid that is becoming popular with gardeners. Perennial Rudbeckias include the cultivars of *R. fulgida*, such as Goldsturm, Goldquelle, and Herbstsonne. Many of these plants are much larger than our wild *R. hirta*; they come with mahogany, orange, red, and gold flowers.

While many North Americans have waited until the development of hybrids to become interested in this genus, Europeans long ago imported wild black-eyed Susans for their gardens, and still grow them. Who could fault their good taste?

**Hedge Bindweed**
*(Convolvulus sepium)*

## *The Pretty Hedge-Binders*

People see it and say it looks like a morning glory, but few know it by its common name, bindweed. Yet from July into September, bindweed flowers can be found on vines climbing almost anything that is a few feet high—shrubs, fences, brush, fellow herbs, even garbage heaps.

Hedge bindweed has large, bell-shaped flowers that may be pink streaked with white or entirely white. The pink forms are particularly attractive. The "delicate pink flush is unequaled by the tint of many a highly cultivated flower," wrote F. Schuyler Mathews. In England, where the flowers of bindweed are among the largest native blossoms, country girls used to weave them into wreaths for their hair. They often called the plant bearbind or bearbine and would sing:

*Thy brow we'll twine*
*With white Bearbine*
*And 'mid thy glossy tresses*
*In sunny showers*
*Its wand'ring flowers*
*Shall wind their wild caresses.*

British naturalist Marcus Woodward, noting their short-lived glory, called the flowers "the just emblem of fleeting joys."

### *Glory's Cousin*

It is no accident that hedge bindweed looks like a morning glory, for it is closely related to our common garden climbers, including *Ipomoea purpurea* or *I. tricolor*, both natives of tropical America. Indeed, bindweed is often called wild morning glory, and it is a member of the small Morning Glory family (*Convolvulaceae*), which has about a dozen North American genera. Bindweed's flower is often hard to distinguish from that of the garden vine. There are some twenty-eight species of bindweed in North America, and it is often difficult to tell them apart.

None is as common or widespread as hedge bindweed, which is found not only in North America, but also in Europe and Asia. *Convolvulus sepium* literally means "entwining the hedge." The vines often climb up the stems of plants, and while they do not feed on them they can choke the host by binding the stem and strangling the plant. Moreover, bindweed's roots form a deep, dense mass that tends to drain the food supply from the soil, starving both host and neighboring plants.

In general, bindweed is not a wildflower that one would wish to introduce near a garden or important shrubs. It can, however, be an attractive vine on an otherwise dull fence or when mixed with tall, weedy, and hardy plants like goldenrods.

Like other vines, hedge bindweed inches its way upward by feeling what is ahead. The tip of the plant turns round and round until it strikes an object. Then, by a method not fully understood by scientists but believed to involve hydraulic pressure changes, the vine stem winds around the discovered object and proceeds onward and usually upward, reaching ten or more feet in length. In this way, it rises above the masses to catch those all-important rays of the sun and positions its flowers high for passing insects to see.

Hedge bindweed turns its tip counterclockwise as it searches for a foothold, and winds that way once something is found. A botanist once discovered that if the plant is turned in another direction, it will die unless it can disengage itself and rewind in its natural, counterclockwise direction. The hedge bindweed is a rapid climber when compared with other vines, and the stem can describe a complete circle in less than two hours.

### *Insect Friends*

Turn-of-the-century naturalist Neltje Blanchan observed, "Every floral clock is regulated by the hours of flights of its insect friends. When they have retired, the flowers close to protect nectar and pollen from useless pilferers," such as ants. Early in the summer, hedge bindweed blooms during the daylight hours when bees are active. However, an exception is nights with bright moonlight, when the flowers remain open and are visited by certain species of Sphinx moths, Ms. Blanchan said. "In Europe," she wrote, "the plant's range is supposed to be limited to that of the crepuscular moth [*Sphinx convolvuli*] and where that benefactor is rare, as in England, the bindweed sets few seeds; where it does not occur, in Scotland, this *Convolvulus* is seldom found wild." Members of a related genus in southern Florida, *Calonyction*, are called moon flowers or moon vines because they open in the evening to attract night-flying moths. (*Calonyction* is Greek for "Good night!") Later in the season, when the plant has already produced a good deal of seed and nectar-thieves are not so great a concern, bindweed flowers stay open well into the night, even when the moon is not full.

In North America, hedge bindweed apparently relies more on bees than on moths for pollination. The flowers, especially pink ones, are attractive to bees that are guided into the narrow tubular nectary by white stripes. The throat of the blossom is divided into five parts, and a cutaway of this area looks like the end of the barrel of a revolver.

Bindweeds, as well as other members of the Morning Glory family, play host to an unusual insect, the golden tortoise beetle (*Metriona bicolor*), which feeds on the leaves. According to Dr. Ralph B. Swain, an entomologist and author of *The Insect Guide*, the beetle can change the color of its shell from a dull reddish brown to a "glorious, glittering gold" in only moments. The glitter fades when the beetle dies, however, and the shell returns to a dull shade, much to the disappointment of collectors.

William Hamilton Gibson, a nineteenth-century lecturer on natural history, reported that this beetle, which is quick and hard to catch, has several colors. "Nor is [the] golden sheen all the resource of the little insect; for in the space of a few seconds, as you hold him in your hand, he has become a milky iridescent opal, and now mother-of-pearl and finally crawls before you in a coat of dull orange." Ms. Blanchan said the insect looks like "a drop of molten gold climbing beneath bindweed's leaves."

In southern states, another insect, the caterpillar of the yellow-banded wasp moth, is apt to be found on bindweeds. In fact, it is so common on plants of the Morning Glory family that it has been named *Syntomeida ipomoea.*

While hedge bindweed has made something of a pest of itself, field bindweed (*C. arvensis*—"of the field"), which bears equally pretty but smaller flowers, has been even more hated. Found coast to coast, it creeps across farmers' fields, sinking roots that are even deeper and more difficult to eradicate than those of hedge bindweed. Roots of this plant have been found six or more feet deep. One related North American species, *Ipomoea pandurata*, is called man-under-ground because its root system is said to be as large as a man. Weed expert Edwin Rollin Spencer reports that the plant can produce storage roots as long and as thick as a man's leg, and weighing up to thirty pounds! This huge root may reach down eight feet below the surface.

### *Many-named and Useful*

Being so common and widespread across three continents, hedge bindweed has picked up many folk names, among them lady's or old man's nightcap, hooded bindweed, bearbind (from the strength of its grip), great or greater bindweed (there is a small bindweed), bellbind, woodbind, pear vine, devil's vine, hedge lily, harvest lily, woodbine, creepers, and German scammony. Scammony, a name based on the Latin word for the herb, is a southern European member of the genus, used to produce a purgative widely sold in old apothecary shops. When *C. scammonia* was not available, *C. sepium* was used instead.

Some authorities maintain that many of our native bindweeds are not of the genus *Convolvulus*, but instead *Calystegia*. Theodore F. Niehaus's *Pacific States Wildflowers*, a Peterson guide, calls hedge bindweed *Calystegia sepium*, while Roger Tory Peterson's own *Field Guide to Wildflowers* uses the more widespread *Convolvulus sepium.*

While both scammony and hedge bindweed were used as purgatives in the Old World, jalap bindweed (*C. jalapa* or *Ipomoea purga*), a native of Central and South America, was used as such in the New World. Another tropical American species, *C. dissectus*, was used in the preparation of a Caribbean liquor, noyau. Still another, *C. rhodorhiza*, produced oil of rodium, "which is so attractive to rats as to cause them to swarm to it without fear, even if held in the hand of a rat-catcher," Maude Grieve maintained.

Of all the members of the genus, none is at once as useful and as popular as *Convolvulus batatas*, the tuberous-rooted bindweed. Though it is another tropical species, it often appears on dinner tables in North America, where it is known as the sweet potato.

**Chicory**
*(Cichorium intybus)*

## *The Roadside Peasant*

*Oh, not in Ladies' gardens*
*My peasant posy!*
*Smile thy dear blue eyes,*
*Nor only—near to the skies—*
*In upland pastures dim and sweet—*
*But by the dusty road*
*Where tired feet*
*Toil to and fro;*
*Where flaunting Sin*
*May see thy heavenly hue*
*Or weary Sorrow look from thee*
*Toward a more tender hue.*

Poet Margaret Deland paid this testimony to chicory, the common weed that often provides the only splashes of blue in summer countrysides filled with yellow, orange, pink, and white flowers. So common is it along the dusty road that, in Germany, it is called the *Wegewart* or "road plant."

Chicory is better known as a food than as a decoration. The Egyptians ate its basal leaves thousands of years ago and still do. In its European homelands it has been eaten since ancient times, though the plant probably was not cultivated until the 1600s. The Latin author, Horace, mentions its leaves as part of his own meager menu. In fact, chicory is related to several wild plants often used for salad greens in times past, including the dandelion, wild lettuces, and endive.

### *Popular Parts*

The leaves are good only when the plants are young. Some people place paper bags or other covers over the young plants to bleach the fresh leaves, keeping away the bitterness that develops as the chicory matures. The French dig up the roots and place them in dark cellars, forcing them during the winter. The resulting white shoots are picked for a salad called *barbe de capucin*, or "beard of the monk." In Belgium, chicory is a big crop, and Belgians consider the leaves one of their major exports.

The English and especially the French prize chicory for its root, which is roasted, ground, and flavored with burnt sugar to make a sort of coffee, or to add to coffee as a flavor enhancer. During the world wars, when real coffee was in short supply, many people used chicory instead. Even today, when coffee prices periodically go out of sight because of crop problems in South America or Africa, widely advertised national brands of coffee are openly padded with chicory, both to keep prices down and—say the labels—to enhance the product's flavor. In the southeastern United States, many people prefer coffee to which chicory has been added, favoring the touch of bitterness it adds. The practice has spawned a rather cumbersome and rarely used adjective, cichoraceous, meaning "coffee that tastes too much of chicory." The demand for the roasted roots in Europe is sometimes so great that the chicory itself is adulterated with wheat or even acorns.

Those who would experiment with chicory brew should dig up the deep roots, thoroughly clean them, and roast them in the oven until the roots break with a snap and the insides are dark. Grind the roasted root as you would coffee. In brewing, use a bit less of the grind than you would for coffee; chicory is stronger. (The young roots are also boiled and eaten like carrots, to which the root bears a resemblance.)

Some French authorities call chicory a contrastimulant, serving to "correct the excitation caused by the principles of coffee," said Maude Grieve. "It suits bilious subjects who suffer from habitual constipation, but is ill-adapted for persons whose vital energy soon flags."

During the seventeenth century, chicory and violet flowers were concocted into a faddish confection called violet plates (see Violets: Love in the Springtime). The flowers were also once used to make a yellow dye, while the leaves produced a blue dye—the opposite of what one might expect.

## *Medicine*

Chicory roots have medicinal properties as well, though the plant has never been very popular with herbalists. The roots have been used for jaundice, spleen problems, and constipation. The milky juice of the leaves and a tea made from the flowering plant are said to promote the production of bile and the release of gallstones. The leaves are also useful for gastritis, lack of appetite, and digestive difficulties, according to herbalists. They were also applied as a poultice to injuries.

Nicholas Culpeper seemed to find a use for just about everything that grew from the ground. He maintained that the plant, which he knew as succory, was "effectual for sore eyes that are inflamed, or for nurses' breasts that are pained by the abundance of milk." He added that it was good for those who "have an evil disposition in their bodies." On this continent, some tribes of American Indians quickly took to the newcomer, chewing its fresh, spongy root like a gum.

For most people, however, chicory is just a wildflower. The plants, which are three to four feet high, are sparsely leaved and not much to look at compared to the blossoms. The silver dollar-sized flowers, similar to hawkweeds and other Composites that lack the big center disks, are often described as sky blue—Emerson wrote of "succory to match the sky." As their brief life wears on, they turn pinkish and then white in death.

The flowers generally bloom in the morning, follow the sun, and fold up by noon on a bright day. On cloudy days or on days when the sun comes out and then is covered by clouds, they may not bloom at all, they may bloom and close early, or they may bloom all day.

Linnaeus, the Swedish botanist who set up the botanical naming and categorizing system, used chicory as one of several flowers in a floral clock. He determined that it opened regularly at 5 A.M. and closed at 10 A.M. The period varies with the month and with the country; in

England and the United States, the range is more like 6:30 A.M. to noon.

In legend the plant was once a beautiful maiden who refused the advances of the sun. In true male chauvinist fashion, he turned her into a flower, forcing her to stare at him each day and making her fade before his might.

With care, chicory can be transplanted to sunny gardens—or even better, to an open edge of the yard or to a field. It looks attractive if there is a good-sized colony of the plants. Chicory is a perennial, but like other common flowers of its type, such as the black-eyed Susan, it favors poor soils where competition is not too great and where its deep root can tap into water that other plants cannot find. Thus, unless you dig carefully, you will not get the entire root, and unless you transplant carefully, you will put it in a situation in which it will not grow well. It also likes soils with some limestone content.

Many wild plants will wilt for two or three days after transplanting. Water them once a day and they will soon straighten up. With some kinds of plants it may take a week or two, but if you have gotten enough root, chicory should survive.

### *Happy Immigrant*

Though not native to North America, chicory has made itself at home as few natives have. It can be found wild from New Brunswick to British Columbia, and south from Florida to California. The plant was probably imported as a hay crop—in Europe, it is still grown and valued as hay, and farmers who use it maintain that chicory is better than alfalfa because it produces more hay in a season.

While farmers might use reapers to cut their chicory, there was a time when only a golden sickle or a knife made from the horn of a stag could be used to cut the plant, which was harvested on certain special days not as food for livestock, but as an aphrodisiac for man. According to superstition, the plant was so powerful and sacred that if you talked while cutting it, you would die.

A plant as popular and as widely known as chicory is bound to accumulate a variety of names. They include wild succory (especially in England), French or Belgian endive, bunk, cornflower, coffeeweed, witloof, blue or ragged sailors, blue daisy, blue dandelion, and bachelor's buttons. Succory is from the Latin *succurre*, "to run under," referring to the deep roots. Witloof is based on a Dutch word meaning "white leaf," a reference to the practice of blanching the leaves. Blue sailor may come from a sailor's blue uniform, and ragged sailor may come from the flower's supposed typical aspect.

Its scientific name is *Cichorium intybus*. *Cichorium*, say some authorities, is Latin based on an Egyptian or Arabic word, *chikouryeh*, meaning simply "chicory." Other sources say it is from a Greek word meaning a root or salad vegetable. *Intybus* simply means "relating to chicory," and is also derived from an Arabic word for the plant. Some say that the words *intybus* and *endivia*, as in endive, both stem from the same Arabic word for the plant, *hendibeh*.

In Britton and Brown's *Flora*, chicory was the type species for a genus that included 8 species, all natives of the Old World. The authors also set up a Chicory family (*Cichoriaceae*) that included seventy genera and 1,500 species worldwide. Most are herbs, but two are trees native to the Pacific Islands. Family members included the dandelion, sow-thistles, blue lettuces, and hawkweeds. However, Gray and other authorities consider chicory merely another genus within the huge Composite family, though they do now often recognize a Chicory tribe of the Composite family.

### *Color for Cracks*

Like its cousin, the dandelion, chicory has an amazing ability to show up almost anywhere that is sunny. I have seen it appear between the cracks of sidewalks and parking lots, where no more than a sliver of earth is open to rainfall. A field full of these flowers is striking, especially in a season when large blue flowers are generally lacking. They remind one that fall, with its many blue asters, is not too far off. Though each blossom has a short life, chicory makes up for it with a long blooming season, from late June until early October.

Goldfinches love chicory seeds. One of the prettiest views I saw on a trip over the Skyline Drive in the Blue Ridge Mountains of Virginia was a flock of those bright yellow birds fluttering amid chicory's sky-blue flowers on a sunny, summer morn.

**Common Milkweed**
*(Asclepias syriaca)*

# *A Sweet Grabber*

"The common milkweed needs no introduction," wrote F. Schuyler Mathews in 1894. "Its pretty pods are familiar to every child, who treasures them until the time comes when the place in which they are stowed away is one mass of bewildering, unmanageable fluff. Then there are vague talks about stuffing pillows and all that sort of thing; but the first attempt to manipulate the lawless airy down usually results in disastrous confusion, and whole masses go floating away on the slightest zephyr." He adds, "Of course, there is more fun in chasing milkweed down than in patiently stuffing a pillow; so the milkweed has its own way and goes sailing off to scatter its seeds hither and thither."

Alice Morse Earle had fond memories of milkweed in her nineteenth-century childhood. "That exquisite thing, the seed of milkweed, furnished abundant playthings," she wrote in *Old-Time Gardens.* "The plant was sternly exterminated in our garden, but sallies into a neighboring field provided supplies for fairy cradles with tiny pillows of silvery silk."

## *Wild Cotton*

The references to stuffing pillows were no joke. Even the earliest colonists filled both pillows and mattresses with milkweed. "The poor collect it and with it fill their beds, especially their children's, instead of feathers," wrote Peter Kalm in 1772. The silky hairs, gathered before the seam of the pod splits and spreads the seeds, were mixed with flax or wool and woven to create a softer thread than either fiber yielded alone. "Place some bits of white sewing silk beside [this] sheeny silk of Nature, [and view them under a microscope] and the former will look like a coarse white rope," said Mathews.

A nineteenth-century magazine article reported that milkweed's "chief uses were for beds, cloth, hats, and paper. It was found that from eight to nine pounds of the coma [seed hair] . . . occupied a space of from five to six cubic feet, and were sufficient for a bed. . . . A plantation containing 30,000 plants yielded from six to eight hundred pounds of coma." During World War II, when there were shortages of all sorts of imported raw materials, milkweed seed fibers were used extensively as a substitute for Asian kapok in life preservers and for the linings of airmen's outfits. All these uses of the silky fluff have earned the plant such names as cottonweed, cottontree, silkweed, and wild cotton.

For a weed, this was a pretty handy plant in other ways. The French in Canada as well as some New Englanders in the eighteenth and nineteenth centuries ate the tender shoots like asparagus. French Canadians also made a "very good, brown palatable sugar," according to one eighteenth-century author, by gathering and processing the flower heads in the early morning when they were covered with dew. Paper is said to have been made from the fiber in the stalks of common milkweed. That fiber was also used to make a cheap type of muslin. Swamp milkweed's fiber was so strong, it was made into twine and cord. Rubber has been produced from various milkweed species, though commercial production has not been feasible.

American Indians made good use of milkweeds. The Chippewas cut up and stewed the flowers of common milkweed (*Asclepias syriaca*), eating them like jam. They believed that consuming the flower-jam before a big meal would allow a person to eat more food than usual. The Sioux, or Dakotas, used to boil the tender young seed pods and eat them with buffalo meat. (*Esclepain*, a constituent of milkweeds, is supposed to be a good meat tenderizer.) Some Indians used the buds as food. Hopi mothers who were nursing ate a kind of milkweed to increase the flow of milk.

Milkweed is bitter, though, unless it is properly prepared. Cooking requires several changes of boiling water, and the water must be boiling when it comes in contact with the plant. Putting pieces of milkweed in cold water and then turning on the heat will only serve to make the milkweed permanently unpalatable.

*A. syriaca* has been used to treat some of the same diseases as pleurisy root, which is no surprise because pleurisy root, also called butterflyweed, is a milkweed (see the next chapter). Milkweed root was used for typhoid fever, scrofula, and, in general, to help relieve inflammation of the lungs caused by a variety of ailments. Milkweed was imported to Europe by the early seventeenth century. Nicholas Culpeper, who called it swallow-wort, wrote, "The root, which is the only part used, is a counter-poison, both against the bad effects of poisonous herbs and the bites and stings of venemous creatures." One modern-day medicine for asthma still employs the plant. As late as the 1930s, the tuberous roots of common milkweed could be sold to commercial concerns for six to eight cents a pound, about the same price paid at the time for butterflyweed, which was then listed as an official drug in the *U.S. Pharmacopoeia.*

Milkweed also had an unusual medicinal use as an instant bandage. "The juice when applied to the skin forms a tough, adhesive pellicle [a thin film]," wrote Charles F. Millspaugh. "This has led to its use by the laity as a covering for ulcers and recent wounds."

It is no accident that *Asclepias*, the generic name, comes from Asclepius, the Greek hero of the medical art. On the other hand, *Syriaca*, meaning "of Syria" is probably an accident. This species is a native of America, though there are reports of it now growing wild in Syria. Perhaps Linnaeus mistook the country of origin while classifying and naming the plant in 1753. (He misnamed spotted jewelweed, a North American plant, with an African name—see Jewelweed: Nature's Toy and Salve). Or perhaps the plant had already been imported to Syria for a crop experiment and Linnaeus examined a specimen that had come from there. Some authorities do not believe that the first name applied to a plant is necessarily the best, and have preferred to use *Asclepias cornuti*, which was concocted in 1844. *Cornuti* means "horned" and may refer to the shape of the flower crowns or the seedpod.

North America can lay claim to 75 or more native species of milkweeds, some of them very difficult to tell apart. They represent more than half the known species in the world. *A. syriaca*, perhaps the most famous, is the type species for the genus and is found from Saskatchewan and Kansas eastward, and down into the highlands of Georgia. The milkweed genus is in turn a member of the Milkweed family (*Asclepiadaceae*) of some 220 genera and more than 2,000 species, mostly tropical. In fact, only 5 genera are found in North America. Several plants in these genera go by the name of milkweed, though they are not of the *Asclepias* genus.

### *Milk Trap*

As the name suggests, milkweeds are known for their milk. In common milkweed, this white juice, which oozes out of the stems and leaves when broken, contains sugar, gum, fat, and other compounds. It is both acidic and somewhat poisonous to animals. Like blood, it clots soon after exposure to air.

Few creatures, including livestock and insects, will eat the plants because of the acrid fluid. What is more, since milkweed depends on flying insects for pollination, it does not want ants and other crawlers robbing its nectar supplies. So when ants start creeping up the plant, tiny spikes in their feet pierce the green flesh, the flesh exudes the sticky fluid, and the fluid tangles the ants' feet. As an ant struggles to clean off the goo, it gets even more glued and becomes permanently stuck to the plant or it falls off. No system, however, is perfect. I have seen small ants, probably light-footed enough to avoid breaking the skin, make it to the top and dine on the sweets.

### *Saddlebags*

While some insects are thus kept away from the blossoms, others are attracted to the flowers, both by the color and by the sweet scent. Although milkweeds come in various colors, common milkweed tends toward a hue that is difficult to describe—Mathews insisted it is lavender-brown; Mrs. William Starr Dana said it is dull purplish pink; Neltje Blanchan called it "dull pale greenish purple-pink or brownish-pink"; Lawrence Newcomb describes it as brownish pink or greenish purple; and Roger Tory Peterson says it varies "in subtle shades of dusty rose, lavender, and dull brownish purple." Whatever the color, it and the strong sweet fragrance attract a wide variety of bees, butterflies, and moths. Often a half-dozen insects will roam the umbels at one time. Once the insects have landed, the plant uses an unusual strategy.

Each flower has a slippery surface. When an insect lands, its feet slide around—often down between one of the five nectar-filled points in a flower's crown. If that foot gets caught in a little slit, tiny pollen-coated devices called pollinia attach themselves. Ms. Blanchan said that these pollinia look like saddlebags, but they might also be likened to minuscule gnats with long amber wings. The pollinia drop off pollen as the insect visits other plants; eventually they fall away. If you watch closely as an insect crawls and often struggles around a freshly opened milkweed flower head, you may see one or several pollinia dangling from its legs.

It is hard to imagine a more clever device for plant reproduction, and you must inspect a flower with a needle and magnifying glass to really appreciate it. Ms. Blanchan, a great admirer of milkweed, wrote, "After the orchids, no flowers show greater executive ability, none [has] adopted more ingenious methods of compelling insects to work for them than milkweeds."

This system, like the sticky juice, is not perfect. Occasionally, bees, butterflies, and other insects can be found hanging dead from the flowers. Trapped in the pollinia-holding slit, they were attacked by spiders, ants, or beetles, or they were killed by heavy showers while struggling to get free.

### *The Butterflies*

A few insects make use of milkweeds in a different fashion. Caterpillars of milkweed butterflies (*Danaidae*)—the most common of which is the orange-and-black monarch—feed on the leaves, usually in small enough quantity so as not to harm the host. The ingested acrid juice of the plant makes both the milkweed caterpillar and the butterfly distasteful to hungry birds. Some species of butterflies that are not milkweed-eaters—such as the viceroy—mimic milkweed butterflies in color and design to take advantage of this strategy for survival.

Recent research has found that many common milkweeds contain potent, often poisonous substances known as cardiac glycosides. Digitalis, a cardiac glycoside obtained from foxglove, has been widely used in small quantities to make heart muscles perform more efficiently after a heart failure. Various plants containing these substances have been used since ancient times to poison the tips of arrows.

It is probably these powerful cardiac glycosides that make monarchs unpalatable. Birds almost immediately becomes nauseous and vomit for up to a half hour after eating a monarch. Most birds will simply bypass the monarch (and the look-alike viceroy) in the future. Some crafty birds, however, will catch a butterfly and sample a bit of the wing to see if it tastes bad, letting go it go if it is a monarch. In Mexico and Central America, where our monarchs spend the winter, there are birds such as grosbeaks and orioles that have learned which parts of the monarch contain the smallest doses of poison and eat only those parts.

The monarch is the best known of the milkweed butterflies, recognized by almost every schoolchild and frequently seen fluttering around patches of milkweed. The monarch caterpillar lives most or all of its life on the plant and then constructs its bright green chrysalis under a leaf. Once the butterfly emerges, it feeds on the flower's nectar—a good reason for the caterpillar to refrain from overeating the host.

### *Survival*

The dispersion of milkweed seeds on floating puffs of silk helps to ensure the plant's survival, something that seems certain in view of its large numbers and wide range. Survival is also aided by the roots, which common milkweed and other members of the genus sink deep into the ground. "Our milkweed is tenacious of life," wrote John Burroughs. "Its roots lie deep as if to get away from the plow."

Milkweeds are slow spreading and have not been really serious field pests. Farmers, though, dislike them because those roots are so hard to eradicate. Moreover, common milkweed has a mother plant, with the deepest roots, which sends out underground runners that sprout other plants nearby. Unless the mother root is killed, colonies cannot be prevented from starting and spreading.

Many people would just as soon have a patch of milkweed. They are handsome plants. The flowers have a sweet scent (Mathews said too sweet), and the blossoms attract beautiful butterflies and sometimes hummingbirds. The French, in fact, imported them to their gardens in the nineteenth century. Many people have found the dried pods attractive additions to dried flower arrangements or wreaths. The pods are sometimes gilded and often the insides are painted in a bright color.

Because of the deep roots, successful transplantation of mature plants is difficult. Attempt it only with small offspring of the mother plant in the spring. Better yet, grab a few pods in late August or September and plant seeds in fairly dry soil that gets plenty of sunlight. Seeds may be planted in the fall or spring.

There are many varieties of milkweed and some others should be mentioned. The flowers of swamp milkweed (*A. incarnata*) are smaller and less fragrant than those of common milkweed, but they are more beautiful. The specific name means "flushed with pink," but the color is actually deeper—a purplish red or magenta. The plant, which is widespread east of the Rockies, can be planted in gardens with moist soils. Purple milkweed (*A. purpurascens*), which is common east of the Plains, is also rich in color. Four-leaved milkweed (*A. quadrifolia*), unusual in that it favors shady forests instead of sunny fields, swamps, or roadsides, has pretty pink to lavender flowers. It, too, is found eastward of the Plains. A variety so red that it is called bloodflower (*A. curassavica*—"of Curacao") is common in the Gulf coastal states and southern California. White milkweed (*A. albicans*) favors the dry rocky deserts of the Southwest, while showy milkweed (*A. speciosa*), with its big, starlike, pinkish flowers, is found in a wide range of terrains from the central U.S. and Canada to British Columbia and California. There is also bright orange butterflyweed, a variety so handsome and interesting that it gets a chapter of its own (see the next chapter).

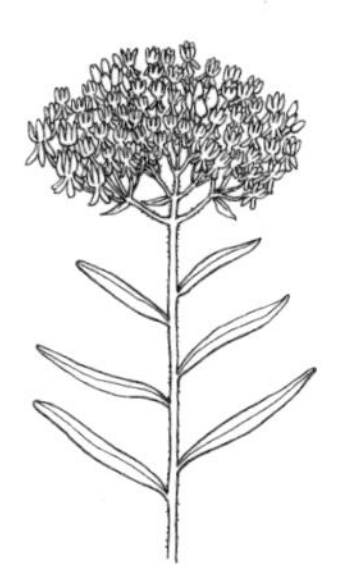

**Butterflyweed**
*(Asclepias tuberosa)*

## *A Neglected Beauty*

It is not shaped like a butterfly, nor does it act like a weed. Its common name comes instead from its ability to attract butterflies—indeed, the Delaware called the plant by a name that meant "where butterflies light." The bright, nectar-rich flowers attract many colorful species, including milkweed-loving monarchs, swallowtails, sulphurs, coppers, hairstreaks, and fritillaries, in addition to a wide selection of bees and other insects. Besides, few people would argue that butterflyweed sounds better than some of the plant's other common names.

*Asclepias tuberosa* is known as pleurisy root (because it was used to treat pleurisy), fluxroot (in medicine, a flux is a fluid discharge from the body), and chigger flower (the little biting mites are a similar color). It is also called white root, wind root, Canada root, orange root, Indian posy, swallowwort, and yellow milkweed. Of course, a plant with a striking flower and many purported medicinal uses is bound to collect many names.

And yet, despite such recognition, butterflyweed has strangely been ignored by many fancy-flower fans whose gardens would be much enlivened by its long-lasting, summertime color. At the 1876 United States Centennial Exhibition in Philadelphia, a bed of these flowers stirred considerable interest. Oddly enough, though the plant is a native of North America, the exhibited specimens had been grown in Holland and shipped over for the show. "Truly," wrote Mrs. William Starr Dana twenty years later, "flowers, like prophets, are without honor in their own country." In *The Floral Kingdom*, published in 1877, Cordelia Harris Turner bemoaned the fact that butterflyweed was a neglected beauty and predicted, "[It] will no doubt one day be extensively cultivated in and out of doors, as its perennial roots, besides its native attractiveness, will specially recommend it."

Mrs. Turner was a good judge of beauty, but a poor prophet. Butterflyweed can be found in few gardens and fewer homes, though it is hard to find a more beautiful and decorative flower. The bright, rich orange is as striking a color as can be found in a wildflower, and a yellow variant that sometimes appears is just as brilliantly hued. The color and design earned butterflyweed enough votes in the 1940s poll of naturalists and scientists to rank it as the fourth most showy wildflower in North America.

### *Significant Medicine*

Enough praise for the plant's appearance; butterflyweed has a long history of practical uses. An American Indian mound in Ohio, with remains dating from 700 B.C. to 1,000 A.D., contained textiles of butterflyweed fiber. In fact, many Indians, especially in the South, used the plant as a source of bow strings. Some tribes, such as the Meskwakis, obtained a red dye from it to use on baskets.

Among most Indian nations throughout much of North America, however, butterflyweed was best known as a source of medicine. Its thick root was used to treat various illnesses, such as pleurisy and rheumatism. The Delaware gave it to mothers after childbirth and Appalachian tribes employed it to induce vomiting. The Penobscots treated colds with it, and the Menominis and many others used it for all sorts of skin injuries, pressing the pulverized fresh root or blowing the powdered dry root into the wound.

Butterflyweed became a significant medicine among American physicians in the late nineteenth century, when it was widely used as an expectorant and to treat smallpox. The rootstock was considered a major or the major ingredient in at least a half-dozen medicines listed in *U.S. Pharmacopoeia*, the official catalog of acceptable drugs. Charles F. Millspaugh, in 1892, said it had received more attention as a medicine than any of the milkweeds, and listed at least fourteen uses, including treatment of dyspepsia, indigestion, dysentery, and eczema. According to John B. Lust, a modern naturopathy expert, the root has been recommended for colds, flu, and bronchial and pulmonary problems.

### *The Physician Asclepius*

Milkweeds in general are so noted for their medicinal properties that their generic name recalls Asclepius, a mythical son of Apollo, who was called the first great physician. Asclepius was so well loved by his patients that they eventually worshipped him as a god and erected temples to honor him. Asclepius, however, put beds in the temples and converted them into the first hospitals. As he visited patients, he carried a staff on which sacred serpents were wrapped. The serpents knew all the secrets of the earth and told him cures for diseases. Today this staff, called the caduceus, is the symbol of the medical profession.

According to Greek mythology, Asclepius became so good at his art that he could bring the dead back to life. He thereby incurred the jealousy and wrath of the gods, and Zeus eventually incinerated him with a thunderbolt. So much for pleasing the boss with good deeds.

Most parts of the butterflyweed are poisonous to some degree. Nonetheless, Indians of the West boiled the roots, possibly thereby removing the poisonous quality, and served the tubers as food. The Sioux made a sort of sugar from the flowers, and young seedpods were boiled with buffalo meat. Certain Canadian tribes were said to boil and eat the young shoots like asparagus.

Found from New England to Florida and west to Colorado and Arizona, butterflyweed blooms from mid- to late June in warmer parts of the country and in July in northern areas. The blossoms, which can last well into August and are among the longest-living of the wildflowers, are almost identical in form to their milkweed siblings. However, the brilliance of the orange makes the clusters or umbels glow like torches in a field on a summer's day, unlike the less bright purple, red, or white flowers of most milkweeds.

### *Finding Plants*

The plants are from two to three feet tall with fuzzy, many-leaved stems. They thrive in full sun, with well-drained soils—preferably sandy and not too fertile. Thanks to their deep tap root, which burrows far underground for water, they can withstand long dry spells.

The easiest and best way to grow butterflyweed is to acquire a plant from a generous friend or from some dry sunny waste place where it may be in danger, such as a field about to become a house lot. Take care to dig deeply to obtain as much of the thick white tuber as possible. Try, if you can, to collect smaller, younger plants; they are more apt to survive because the roots are smaller and less likely to be broken in digging. Butterflyweed transplants well, remaining perky and producing late-September seedpods similar to those on the familiar milkweeds.

I have planted and spread hundreds of seeds over the years, but have had no success in getting any to sprout in the yard, where they are probably eaten by birds and small rodents, and where my soil may be too rich for them. However, friends who have started the seeds indoors have had better luck.

**True Forget-Me-Not**
*(Myosotis scorpioides)*

## *Legendary Flowers*

If any flower could be considered a living legend, it would be the forget-me-not. In almost every major language, one can find a tale connected with the plant, and usually with the origin of its unusual name.

Denizens of lawns, meadows, pond shores, and brooksides—even brooks themselves—forget-me-nots are known to almost everyone as those pretty, little blue flowers with the white-and-yellow-ringed eyes. Their five, rounded petals and small, stem-top clusters have long symbolized friendship and loyalty, but have represented even more to many who have exchanged them over the centuries. They are "the sweet forget-me-nots that grow for happy lovers," wrote Tennyson.

The plant is called forget-me-not in many languages: *Vergissmeinnicht*, *nezaboravak*, *ne-m'oubliez-paz*, *forglemmegie*, etc. There are almost as many stories of the name's origin as there are languages. In one widely told tale, a knight was walking with his sweetheart alongside a pond or river when he saw some of these flowers growing on an island in the middle of the water. Foolish with love, he jumped into the water, armor and all, and managed to grab a bunch of flowers and toss them to his lover before sinking below the surface. His last words were: "Forget me not!" This story is also told in a version that has an armorless hero falling into the Danube and being swept away by the current.

In an equally depressing German legend, a young man in search of treasure is guided by a fairy to a mountain cave. He found the cave marked by forget-me-nots and began filling his pockets with the gold within. Pointing to the flowers at the cave's entrance, the fairy warned the boy to "forget not the best." The youngster ignored the fairy, continued to gather only gold, and was crushed in a cave-in. Related fables attribute to forget-me-nots the power to open caves with treasure inside.

One of the more sentimental tales tells of a boy and a girl who as children often played in the woods and fields. When the boy grew up, he decided to go off and make his fortune. As the two met to say good-bye, they promised to think of one another whenever they found one of the blue flowers that had been so common where they played as children. Years later the boy, now an old man, returned to the woods near his native village and ran into his childhood friend. Neither recognized the other till suddenly both spotted one of the blue flowers, both bent down to pick it, and their hands met. Thereafter, they called it forget-me-not.

The Persian poet Shiraz tells of a "golden morning of the early world, when an angel sat weeping outside the closed gates of Paradise. He had fallen from his high estate through loving a daughter of earth, nor was he permitted to enter again until she whom he loved had planted the flowers of the forget-me-not in every corner of the world. He returned to earth and assisted her, and together they went hand in hand. When their task was ended, they entered Paradise together, for one fair woman, without tasting the bitterness of death, became immortal like the angel whose love her beauty had won when she sat by the river twining forget-me-nots in her hair."

In a Christian legend, God named all the plants during the six days of creation, but one small blue flower could never remember what it was called. God forgave the flower's absent-mindedness and named it "forget-me-not." In a German version, God was handing out names to all the animals and plants after the creation. When he was nearly finished, he heard a little voice call out, "Forget me not, O Lord!" "That shall be your name," God replied.

In another Christian tale, Adam and Eve were leaving the Garden of Eden after their apple-eating escapade, and all the plants and animals were backing off in disapproval as they went by. All, that is, except a little blue flower that called out in a tiny voice, "Forget me not," the only friendly words spoken to them on that tragic day.

The ancient Egyptians believed that if they anointed their eyes with forget-me-nots during the month of Thoth, the ibis-headed god would create visions. A folktale maintained that the name of the plant was derived from the awful-tasting leaves—once sampled, they would not be forgotten. The flower has served as a sort of good luck charm, and was given to people starting a journey on February 29. It was also exchanged by friends on that day.

Poets have put the plant to good use, but none with quite as much license as Henry Wadsworth Longfellow. In "Evangeline," he wrote:

*Silently, one by one, in the infinite meadows of heaven,*
*Blossom the lovely stars, the forget-me-nots of the angels.*

That prompted the Rev. E. Cobham Brewer, in his *Dictionary of Phrase and Fable*, to comment dryly: "The similitude between a little light-blue flower and the yellow stars is very remote. Stars are more like buttercups than forget-me-nots."

### *Many Kinds*

Ten kinds of forget-me-nots inhabit North America. Among the most common are two species usually called simply forget-me-nots, though one is native and the other a European immigrant. Probably most common is the true forget-me-not (*Myosotis scorpioides*), widely called "true," possibly because it is the type species and best known of the clan. Its blossoms run from one-quarter to one-third inch in width on stems up to twenty-four inches high. A garden escape and native of both Europe and Asia, it is found locally from coast to coast along streams, in wet places, and even in fairly shady wood edges not noted for moisture. Other names for the plant include water forget-me-not, mouse-ear scorpion grass, marsh scorpion-grass, snake grass, and love-me.

The smaller forget-me-not (*M. laxa*) has blossoms one-fifth inch in width on stems about twenty inches high. *M. laxa*, a native, likes very wet situations and can be found growing in the middle of shallow brooks, sometimes choking them. It ranges from southern Canada to Georgia and west into the Rocky Mountains. Both are perennials that bloom from May to July, and are easily transplanted or acquired from nurseries.

*M. alpestris* is found in the Rockies from New Mexico into Canada. It, too, is simply called forget-me-not. In *A Field Guide to Rocky Mountain Wildflowers*, the authors observe that the plant blooms from late June through early August when the cow elk are migrating with their spring-born calves to higher summer ranges. While *alpestris* means "alpine," the flower called alpine forget-me-not is *Eritrichium elongatum*, found at altitudes of at least 9,000 feet in the Rockies. *Eritrichium* is a very closely related, look-alike species. Its name is Greek for "wool hair," descriptive of the hairiness of the plants.

Forget-me-nots are members of the Borage family, a clan of some 1,500 species in eighty-five genera, including heliotropes, cowslips (mertensia), puccoons, and buglosses. The genus *Myosotis* consists of about 35 species around the world. Not all have the typical blue flowers; the spring forget-me-not (*M. verna*), found from the East Coast into the Rockies, has white flowers—perhaps they are Longfellow's stars.

### *Scorpions of the Grass*

*Myosotis* means "mouse-ear," descriptive of the plant's leaves. *Laxa* is "open," referring to the looser racemes of flowers. *Scorpioides* reflects the fact that the raceme of blossoms tends to curl over in the fashion of a scorpion's tail. Employing the "doctrine of signatures," ancient herbalists decided that since forget-me-nots are shaped like scorpions, they must be good for treating scorpion bites and for centuries the herb was used for that purpose. People then reasoned that if it was good for scorpion bites, it was probably good enough for any bite, and eventually, any wound. "Dioscorides saith, that the leaves of scorpion grasse applied to the place, are a present remedy against the stinging of scorpions; and likewise boyled in wine and drunke, prevaile against the said bitings, as also of addars, snakes, and such venomous beasts," wrote John Gerard. "Being made in an unguent with oile, wax, and a little gum Elemni, they are profitable against such hurts as require an healing medicine."

It was the yellow ring around the center of the forget-me-not that helped lead Christian Konrad Sprengel (1750–1816), a German botanist, to conclude that outstanding markings on many kinds of flowers were signposts to lead bees and other insects to the nectar and pollen. He called these markings honey guides, or *Saftmal*. The yellow ring also forms a ridge around the opening and helps keep rainwater from getting into the flower's center tube, where it would dilute the nectar and damage the pollen.

Actually, forget-me-nots can produce seed without insect pollination because flowers can self-pollinate. (That pollen is amazingly tiny. Six thousand grains of it lined up would measure only an inch. In comparison, about 125 pumpkin pollen grains would measure an inch.)

### *True Blue*

Forget-me-nots have always been admired for their color. Although the shades will vary, the best blues of these flowers are said to come the closest of any flower to true blue. Says F. Schuyler Mathews: "Blue in a pure state does not exist on the petal of any flower, wild or cultivated. I might with justice except the familiar forget-me-not, whose quality of color is very nearly a pure blue."

Two naturalists remarked on seeing this color in the wilds of Alaska early in this century. John Burroughs, hiking there, observed, "The prettiest flower we found was a forget-me-not, scarcely an inch high, of deep ultramarine blue—the deepest, most intense blue I ever saw in a wild flower."

John Muir, in *Travels in Alaska* (1915), described the reverence an Alaskan held for this flower. "[He] proudly handed it to me with the finest respect and telling its many charms and lifelong associations, showed in every endearing look and touch and gesture that the tender little plant of the mountain wilderness was truly his best-loved darling."

No wonder the forget-me-not is the state flower of Alaska.

**Black Cohosh**
*(Cimicifuga racemosa)*

# *Candles of the Woodland Fairies*

Summer is the time of glory for the showy wildflowers of open fields. The woodlands, where flowers show their splendor in the spring, are almost void of blossoms by midsummer. So it's often surprising, even to someone familiar with wildflowers, to run across black cohosh brightly blooming in the dimly lit deciduous woods of July and August.

Although few American Indian names for plants are still in common use, cohosh is believed to come from an Algonquin word meaning "pointed." *Co-os* meant "pine tree" and the term refers to the plant's flower spikes. A less used, but more beautiful name suits the plant perfectly. Anyone who has ever seen its tall, furry, white racemes of flowers will know instantly why they have been called "fairy candles."

While sylvan fairies may have held sparkling candles that looked like these stamen-laden flowers, American Indians held *Cimicifuga racemosa* in high esteem, using it to treat rheumatism, pneumonia, croup, and asthma as well as "female complaints"—the plant is sometimes called "squawroot." Many tribes also brewed a tonic from the root. Perhaps because the flower heads eventually form pods with loose seeds inside, rattling like a rattlesnake, Indians used the plant to treat snakebite, giving rise to names such as black snakeroot and rattletop.

With the arrival of Europeans, cohosh's importance and reputation for curative powers

SUMMER

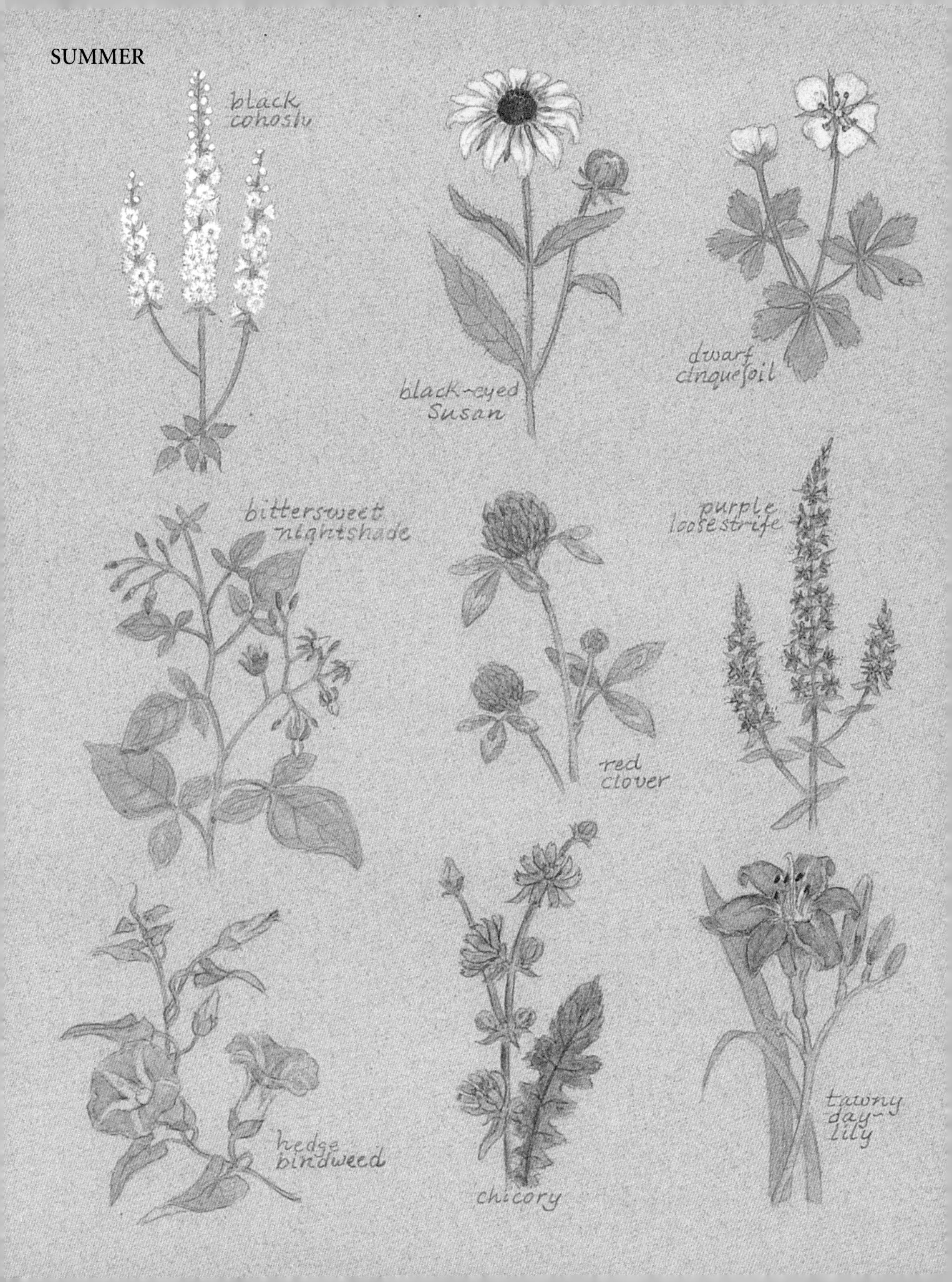

black cohosh
black-eyed Susan
dwarf cinquefoil
bittersweet nightshade
red clover
purple loosestrife
hedge bindweed
chicory
tawny day-lily

wild bergamot
Queen Anne's lace
common milkweed
catnip
true forget-me-not
heal-all
yarrow
butterflyweed
Asiatic dayflower

LATE SUMMER AND FALL

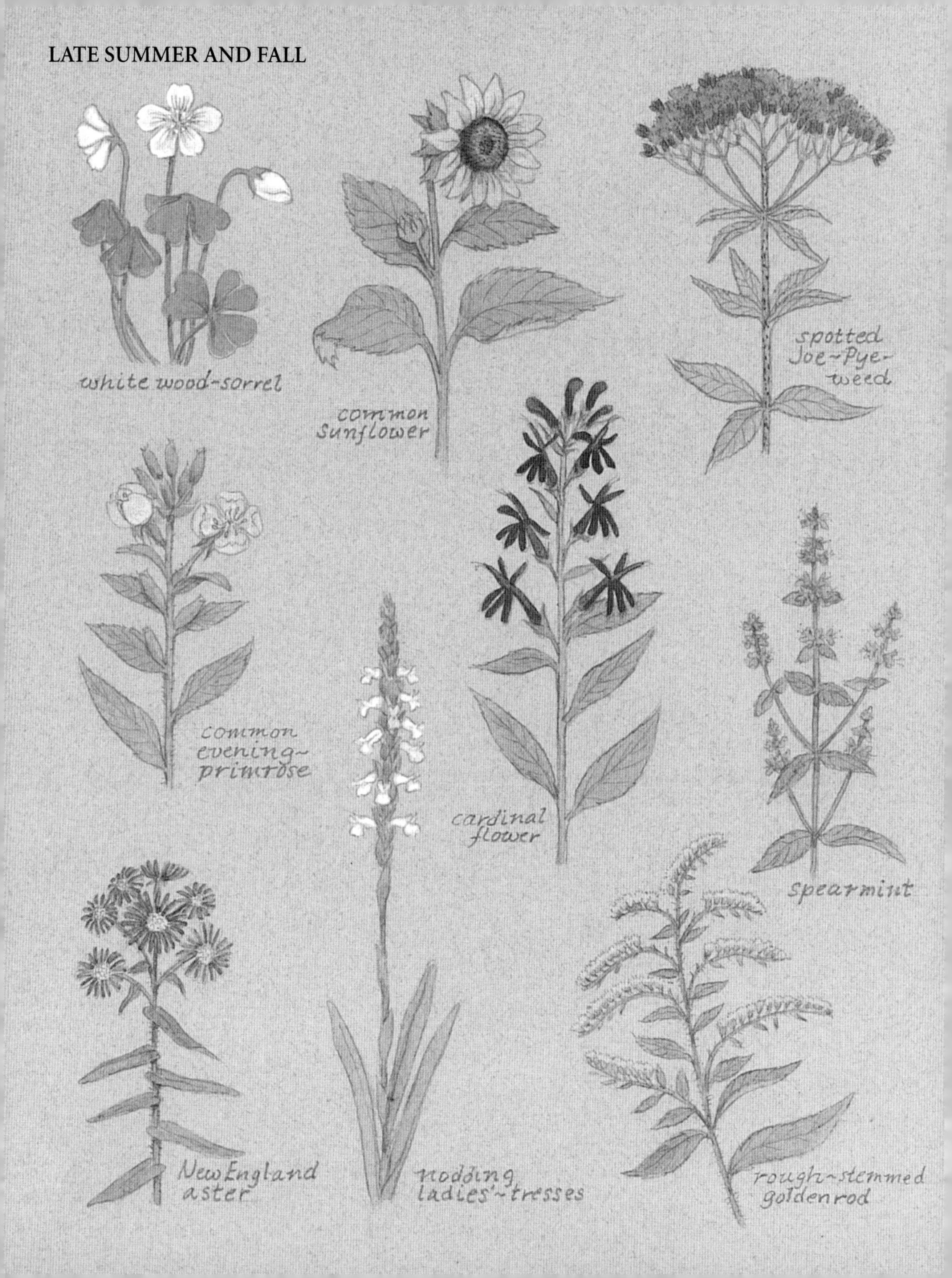

## LATE SUMMER AND FALL

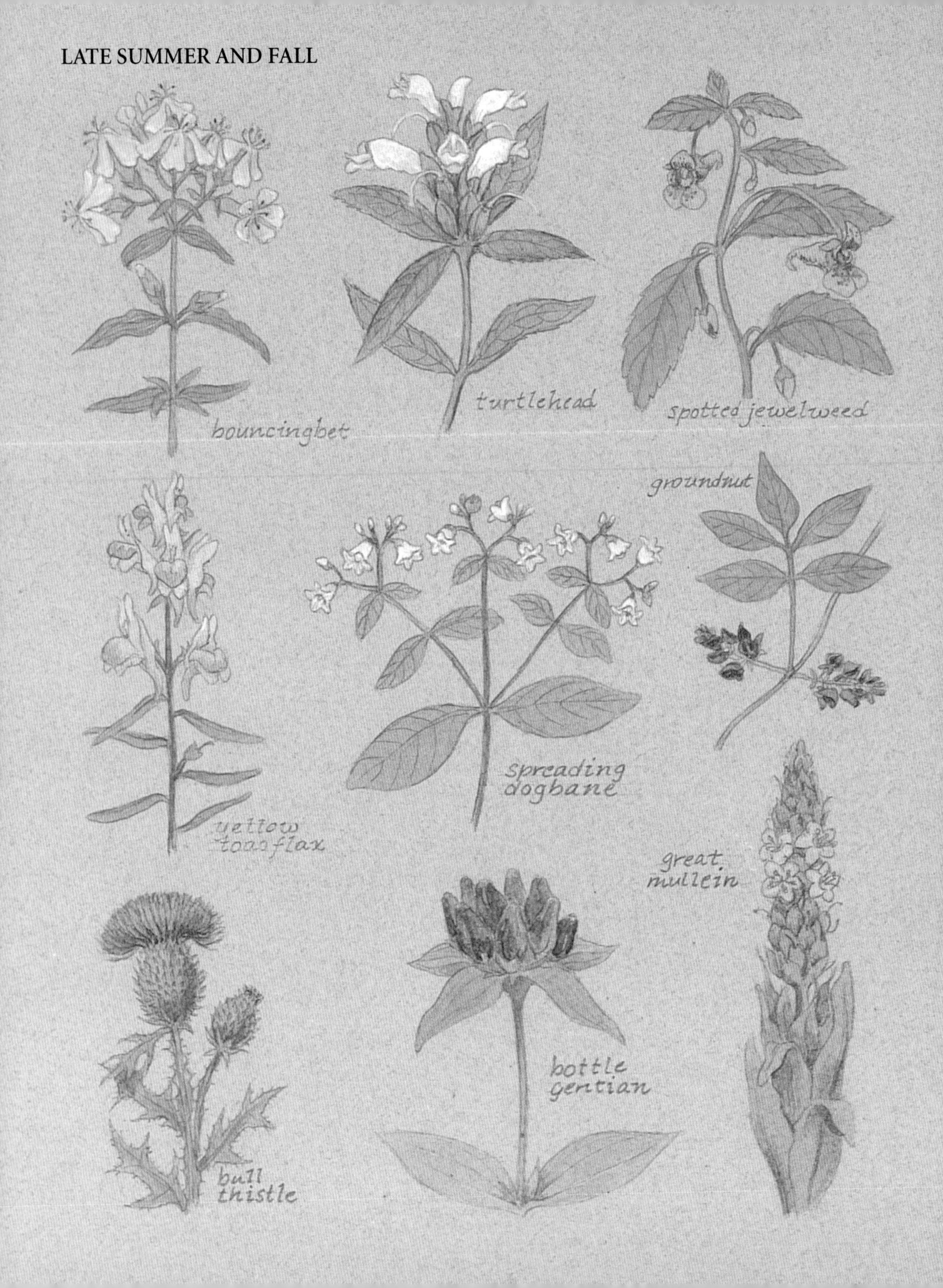

spread. The plant was used as a sedative, diuretic, astringent, and expectorant. It was also a treatment for whooping cough, consumption, bronchitis, diarrhea, and St. Vitus' dance (chorea).

Physicians of the nineteenth century used it to speed up a woman's labor. The plant would "stimulate the uterus and cause rapid painless expansion of the parts," wrote Charles F. Millspaugh, who listed many uses for the plant in his 1892 work, *American Medicinal Plants.* In general, he said quaintly, "It will be found in most cases to act with far more constant success in females than in males, as its action upon the female economy is marked and distinctive."

So important were medicines made from its blackish, gnarled roots that herbalists listed black cohosh in pharmacopoeias of Britain and the United States well into the twentieth century. While no longer so listed, the plant still appears in almost any modern herbal and is often recommended for dealing with menopause (it is said to contain estrogen and to have a calming effect) and high blood pressure.

### *Bane of Bugs*

Black cohosh was used not only for curing disease, but also for relieving another scourge—insect attacks. The fetid-smelling flowers, rubbed on the skin, served as a repellant to those little biting bugs of summer woods. From this use comes another common name, bugbane. Even the plant's generic name, *Cimicifuga,* reflects this function; *cimex* is Latin for "bug" and *fugare* is Latin for "to drive away."

The plant's unattractive odor can, however, have just the opposite effect. While its flowers bloom virtually alone in and at the edge of woods, the brighter, more plentiful species of the fields and other open spots attract the most plentiful pollinators, the bees. What bee would bother wandering off into the dark woods in search of an occasional blossom when such a wealth of nectar and pollen can be easily found in the open sunlight?

So the cohosh has turned to deception to attract the kind of insects that would be available to carry its pollen from blossom to blossom. The flower, which smells like carrion, lures carrion and meat flies that feed on the carcasses of forest creatures. (Trilliums and skunk cabbages of spring use this same technique.) You should use black cohosh as an insect repellent, then, only if you don't mind a fly or two stopping by to see if you are dead meat.

### *Summer Ghosts*

The fuzzy appearance of fairy candles comes from the numerous stamens on the many flowers along each spike. There are also small petals, but these fall off shortly after the blossoms open. The resulting fleecy wands, usually appearing in threes, sit atop plants that sometimes reach the striking height of nine feet. The fleecy flowers have inspired florid words from nature writers. "The tall white wands of the black cohosh shoot up in the shadowy woods of midsummer like so many ghosts," wrote Mrs. William Starr Dana. Neltje Blanchan called them "tall white rockets" and Frances Theodora Parsons observed, "If we chance to be lingering when the last sunlight has died away, and happen suddenly upon one of these ghostly groups, the effect is almost startling." Recommending them in her book *Old-Time Gardens,* Alice Morse Earle wrote, "The succession of pure white spires, standing up several feet high at the edge of a swampy field or in a garden, partake of that compelling charm which comes from tall trees of slender growth, from repetition and association, such as pine trees, rows of bayonets, the gathered masts of a harbor, from stalks of corn in a field, from rows of foxglove—from all 'serried ranks.' "

The unusual flower form is not surprising since the plant belongs to the Crowfoot family, a clan that includes flowers of such varied shape as common buttercups, larkspurs (delphiniums), mousetails, clematis, and columbines. The genus is small, consisting of fewer than a dozen species, mostly North American, and including the unscented but similar-looking American bugbane (*C. americana*) of east-central woods.

Black cohosh is by far the most widespread, ranging from New England to the Mississippi and south to Georgia. The plant's other names include richweed (because it favors rich soils), papoose root, rattleweed, rattleroot, rattlebox, tall bugbane, and bugwort. Three West Coast members of *Cimicifuga* are known, but rare. The false bugbane of the East and the Pacific Northwest, whose greenish flowers are small and dull, was once considered a *Cimicifuga* but is now called *Trautvetteria caroliniensis.*

Black cohosh is an ideal flower to plant along the edges of woods. It is attractive and long-lasting. It spreads fairly quickly under conditions it likes—shade; rocky, rich, moderately acid soil; and hillside locations. Try starting it from seeds, sowing them in August and September when they mature. Avoid transplanting from places where black cohosh is uncommon.

With a little luck, you'll keep the neighborhood fairies well lit and bug-free.

**Red Clover**
*(Trifolium pratense)*

## *Ubiquitous and Useful*

There is hardly a square yard of sunny ground that does not have some clover on it. Although many of these plants were not here three centuries ago, they are so common now that most flower-lovers do not even notice them, much less consider them worth noticing. Yet, observed close up or in large masses, clovers are attractive flowers, and some species are even spectacular. Moreover, many have been of immeasurable value to farmers through the ages, and without the clovers there would be many unhappy bees and a far poorer quality of honey than we now enjoy.

Clover is a doubly fitting name. It comes from *clava*, the three-pronged club used by Hercules in some of his Twelve Labors. All forms of clover are, of course, noted for their three-lobed leaves, a trait possessed by most members of the Pea family (and reflected in the "clubs" suit of cards). What's more, the weapon of the greatest hero of the Greeks and the strongest man of their mythology is somewhat symbolic of the fame and strength of these plants. Most were imported from Europe by farming settlers who knew their value not only as a food for horses, cattle, and other domestic animals, but also as a soil regenerator.

The roots of the clover and many other members of its family play host to certain bacteria that help to increase nitrogen in the soil. Farmers frequently plant clover in poor soil to enrich its nitrogen content and growing capacity. Once the plant has finished its season—or its life if it is an annual—the farmer can simply churn it into the soil, providing further enrichment as a green manure. Because of their popularity for such uses, imported species have spread to almost every corner of temperate North America.

## *The Pea Family*

The Pea family consists of more than 300 genera and 5,000 species worldwide, including indigos, trefoils, alfalfas, medics, vetches, wild beans, soy beans, peanuts, and, of course, peas themselves. True clovers, called *Trifolium* because of their three leaflets, include at least 275 species worldwide.

Nearly 100 Trifoliums are known in North America, but most occur in the western half of the continent. Only twenty or so clovers can be found in the East, and most of them are aliens. Though they may not be as common or widespread as the imports, the natives have many varieties. Among the most beautiful is the orange buffalo clover, which occurs throughout the central United States from Canada to the Gulf. Some of the prettiest natives, both common and rare, live along the West Coast. And some natives are very limited in range. One variety, *Trifolium virginicum*, is said to be found only on barren shale slopes of a few localities in the central Appalachians.

Most clovers have bushy, globelike clusters of white, yellow, purple, or red tubular flowers and the namesake three-lobed leaves. Some species have the occasional tendency to produce four or more lobes, whence the four-leaf clovers that some people treasure. The leaves in most species close up at night, a habit more commonly found in flowers than in their greenery, and one apparently designed to help retain heat in the cool night air.

## *Buxom Rural Things*

Clover is a kind of flower most appreciated in quantity. John Burroughs wrote, "Summer always comes in the person of June, with a bunch of daisies on her breast and clover blossoms in her hand. A new chapter in the season is opened when these flowers appear. One says to himself: 'Well, I have lived to see the daisies again, and to smell the red clover.' One plucks the first blossoms tenderly and caressingly. What memories are stirred in the mind by the fragrance of the one and the youthful face of the other! There is nothing else like that smell of clover. It is the maidenly breath of summer; it suggests all fresh, buxom, rural things, a field of ruddy blooming clover, dashed or sprinkled here and there with the snow-white of the daisies; its breath drifts into the road when you are passing; you hear the booming bees, the voice of bobolinks, the twitter of swallows, the whistle of woodchucks; you smell wild strawberries; you see the cattle upon the hills; you see your youth, the youth of a happy farm-boy, rise before you."

Burroughs was probably unaware that he was recording history when he wrote those words. The pastoral settings he described are becoming rarer almost daily, as parts of the United States become less agrarian, and once-farmed fields become lawns or woods. Even where farming is still strong, there is more reliance today on chemicals to do the jobs that nature—including plants like clover—once did.

Yet old-fashioned fields can still be found and the air over the flowers in them is full of bumblebees, honeybees, and butterflies, dipping and rising as they visit clover blossoms amid the daisies, milkweeds, fleabanes, St. Johnsworts, Queen Anne's lace, and other summertime field flowers. The nectar-filled tubes of red clover (*Trifolium pratense*) are designed for the larger bumblebees, who can easily open the tubes and reach down for a drink, picking up pollen along the way. Except for the long-tongued butterflies—robbers who do not pollinate—virtually no other insect except the bumblebee can reach the nectar of the red clover.

Clovers rely very heavily on bees for survival. Experiments have been conducted in which netting was stretched across a patch of white clover to keep away the bees, with the result that the plants produced only one-tenth the normal quantity of seeds. More dramatic was the experience of the New Zealanders who imported red clover for fodder and had a bumper crop of it the first season. But there were no bumblebees in New Zealand, and the entire crop failed to set seed. Realizing the problem, the New Zealanders imported fewer than 100 bumblebees and within a decade they were producing $1 million worth of red clover seeds annually, an example of the power of a symbiotic relationship.

Relying so heavily on bees for pollen transfer in the face of competition from so many other kinds of summer flowers, clovers, particularly white clover, have evolved an especially attractive nectar. Said to have a sugar content of more than forty percent, the liquid is so sweet that children used to pick and suck the blossoms. Burroughs describes the white clover as "the staple source of supply of the finest quality of honey," adding that celebrated European honeys "can hardly surpass our best products." Shakespeare called clovers "honey-stalks" and wrote:

*I will enchant old Andronicus*
*With words more sweet, and yet more dangerous,*
*Than baits to fish, or Honey-stalks to sheep.*

Red clover, while also full of sweets, draws in its visitors with the help of its scent and its color, shades of red being especially attractive to bumblebees.

Wildlife, too, has taken kindly to imported crop clovers. At least fifty species of birds and mammals feed on their foliage and seeds. Clovers constitute as much as twenty-five percent of the diet of such fowl as the ruffed grouse, prairie chicken, and mountain quail, and such mammals as marmots and woodchucks.

## *Clover Types*

Among the most prominent of our clovers, red clover is also called purple, meadow, honeysuckle, or broadleaf clover, as well as marlgrass, cowgrass, sugar plums, and knap. It stands up to two feet tall and produces deep red or purplish blossoms an inch or more around. It is interesting to watch bees move around a field of these flowers. The insects need to come no closer than a half an inch or so from a blossom before their sense of smell tells them whether its nectar has been cleaned out by previous visitors. Usually, it is the most attractive blossoms in full bloom that are bypassed by the bees, who seek out the freshly opened tubes of newer, less showy, but more food-filled heads.

*Trifolium pratense* (literally, "three leaves of the meadows") is the type species for the genus, and blooms coast to coast from around May until November along roadsides and wood edges, as well as in fields. Farmers used to say that an acre of clover would produce as much food for horses and cattle as four acres of grass. Red clover was once a leading hay crop and is still valued for its high protein and mineral content as well as its ability to revitalize fields. A few years ago, two million bushels of seed were being grown annually, mostly in Illinois.

Alsike or Alsatian clover (*T. hybridum*) may reach three feet, making it one of our taller clovers. It bears flowers that mix cream and deep pink florets such that the heads, often flat-topped, are striking in their brilliance, especially if you happen across a little colony of them on a sunny summer day. Sometimes called Swedish clover, this variety was imported as a popular fodder crop and blooms through much of the growing season in much of North America.

White clover (*T. repens*, meaning "creeping") is the common clover found in lawns that have not been poisoned with herbicides. Also called Dutch clover because it is native to northwestern Europe, white clover is particularly favored by bees and has long been used as a feed for livestock, even though scientists have found that the leaves contain some cyanide. White clover is also the kind on which you are most apt to find coveted four-leaf clovers, but you may also find five or six leaflets—even nine. The fascination with four-leaf clovers is said to hark back to the times when anything in nature that bore the shape of Christ's cross was considered sacred or magical. Even the three-leaf form had its religious significance, having been used, perhaps first by St. Patrick, as a symbol of the Holy Trinity ("three persons in one God").

The least hop clover, often called shamrock, bears the scientific name *T. dubium. Dubium* means "doubtful," indicating that it was uncertain at the time of its naming (1794) whether it was really a separate species. A European native now found throughout the United States and southern Canada, it bears small yellow blossoms, with from three to twenty florets per head as opposed to forty or more on the other species. Some say it is the true shamrock used by St. Patrick for his religious instruction.

Rabbit's foot clover (*T. arvense,* "of cultivated fields") is an unusual, though common, variety. Also called dogs and cats, pussies, hare's foot, or pussy clover, it has cylindrical gray and pink heads that are fuzzy like a rabbit's foot, making it a favorite of children. It inhabits waste places in most parts of North America except the Southwest, blooming in midsummer.

Varieties of *Melilotus* ("honey lotus") are called sweet clovers, although they are not true *Trifolium* clovers. Both white sweet clover (white melilot) and yellow sweet clover (yellow melilot) are tall—to ten feet—bushlike plants with the typical pealike flowers and elongated three-part leaves. Both have been used, dried and hanging, to sweeten rooms with their scent, and it has been reported that one of their chemical constituents, cumarin, is the same substance that flavors vanilla, a member of the Orchid family. This sweetness led to the use of the flowers in their native Europe to flavor snuff, pipe tobacco, and even Gruyere cheese. The flowers have also been an ingredient in a popular salve for skin sores. Both sweet clovers, which flower in June and July, are common throughout North America.

True clovers have little medical history. A tea from red clover was once used to treat whooping cough and other bronchial ailments, and some people enjoy the tea simply as a beverage, though they may add mint or other flavorings to liven it up. The plants have been credited with mystical powers in ages past. For example, witches were supposed to shun clover leaves, and all sorts of good luck—or even bad luck—was said to befall those who found clovers bearing more than the usual number of leaflets. Dreaming of clover is supposed to bring good fortune.

Sweet dreams!

**Wild Bergamot**
*(Monarda fistulosa)*

# *The Showy Mints*

Wild bergamot is one of the showiest of our early summer flowers. This aromatic plant, a perennial that grows three to five feet tall, has large, globelike blossoms from one to two inches wide. It is a denizen of dry, sunny localities, where it thrives as long as its tall, delicate stems are not disturbed by humans or machine. Fewer and fewer of these places remain, which is why the once plentiful plant is seen less frequently, at least in parts of the Northeast.

Wild bergamot is a native of North America. John Tradescant Jr. first noted the plant in the seventeenth century. (John was son of John Sr., who had been a gardener for King Charles I of England and who lent his name to the popular genus of spiderworts called *Tradescantia.*) The sharp citrus-and-mint smell of crushed bergamot leaves was apparently similar to that of bergamot oranges, grown around Bergamo, Italy, and gave rise to the plant's name.

To botanists, wild bergamot is *Monarda fistulosa*, a member of the Mint family. The generic name recalls another early plant scientist, Nicholas Monardes of Seville, Spain, a physician who in 1569 published a massive text on the medicinal values of New World plants. *Fistulosa* means "full of pipes," descriptive of the long florets.

Each flower head bears twenty to thirty of these florets, long tubular affairs containing enough nectar to satisfy the sweet tooth of many a flying creature. Dozens of varieties of butterflies and bees are drawn to the blossoms, whose pink, lilac, or purplish tints are particularly attractive to such insects, most of whom serve to pollinate the flowers. As a careful observer might suspect, bergamot can also be pollinated by hummingbirds. Its vials of nectar perfectly fit the long bills of the hummingbird, and a large colony of bergamots is almost sure to be frequented by these tiny birds.

The shape of the flower head, the hairs on its surface, and the construction of the florets all but prevent walking insects and those with short mouth parts from gaining a sip of the nectar. Despite these and other measures to stop pilfering by non-pollinating insects, however, there are always successful robbers. In this case, certain species of wasps chew holes in the base of each floret to suck out the nectar, without bothering to pick up any pollen.

Wild bergamot is easy to establish if you have a sunny, dry spot. It can be transplanted at almost any time of the growing season and can sometimes be acquired from places where plants are clearly threatened with extinction, particularly from roadsides that are likely to be mowed by highway crews. If you come across a colony that is not endangered, a few plants can be divided off so that you can leave most of the group intact. The few you take, if planted in the right spot, can spread fairly rapidly over the years. Since the stems are susceptible to breaking, place the plants where they are not apt to be brushed against or knocked over by people or animals.

Though perhaps the most common member of the clan, wild bergamot is not the flashiest. Gardeners may be familiar with another *Monarda* called bee balm, which is similar in form but bears bright red flowers. Despite its name it is probably less of a bee flower because its longer floral tubes allow only the biggest bees to get to the nectar. Bee balm is more suited to hummingbirds, whose favorite color is bright red.

Although many American wildflowers are garden escapes, bee balm is a native that has found its way into gardens. Explorer-botanists admired the plant greatly and took it back to Europe with them. Bee balm and a half-dozen cultivated varieties developed from it are still popular there, decorating the landscape with their white, purple, pink, or crimson flowers.

Bergamot and bee balm are perennials. My yard at one time had both species, growing about forty feet apart. One year the bergamot did not show up, a casualty apparently of a high water table brought on by some unusually wet summers. A year or two later, my small but growing colony of bee balm, whose rare rich red I had enjoyed each August, also failed to appear, even though it had been lush the year before. I was surprised. I decided that I must have miscalculated a spring run with the lawn mower and chopped off the young shoots. Two years later, however, in the very spot where the bee balm had been, a couple of plants bearing flowers almost the color of wild bergamot appeared and continued to reappear for several years. The flowers were redder than my bergamots had been, but not nearly the deep red of bee balm. Had there been some sort of cross-pollination before the demise of the bee balm, and my bergamot-looking plant was really an off-colored offspring of bee balm and some neighborhood bergamot? Or did the union take place years before between my two colonies, and the offspring's appearance was delayed by some happenstance of nature?

*Monarda didyma* (*didyma* means "in pairs," referring apparently to its pairs of opposing leaves) is also called Oswego tea, a name of pre-Revolutionary origin. In 1743, a botanist named John Bartram (see Violets: Love in the Springtime) was a member of a team of negotiators who traveled from Pennsylvania to upper New York state to make a treaty with the Indians. In the vicinity of Fort Oswego, Bartram came across the plant. He learned from the Indians that it was used in a tea to treat chills and fevers, and the name of the fort—the Indian word for the nearby river—became the name of the plant. Actually, it is likely that by the 1740s, many back-woods colonists were already brewing teas from the aromatic leaves of both bee balm and bergamot as a substitute for imported teas not readily available far from the coastal towns. After the famous Boston Tea Party, the plant became a widely used substitute for imported tea, at least until after the Revolution. If you want to try some, room-dry a bunch of leaves for a couple weeks and then steep about three-quarters of a teaspoon per cup in boiling water. After drying, these and other kinds of wild tea leaves should be kept in sealed glass jars stored in a cool, dark place.

Like the various mints to which they are related, Monardas have been used to flavor food. Leaves and young plant tips have been added to salads, cold drinks, and jellies, particularly apple jelly. An oil from the plants, said to smell like ambergris, has been used in perfumes.

Indians drank bergamot tea for headaches and sore throats, inhaled an oil extract to relieve bronchial congestion, used the leaves to treat acne, and applied fresh crushed leaves to soothe insect bites. Following the old "doctrine of signatures," some past herbalists believed that red bee balm was good for cleansing the red blood of impurities; some modern herbalists still vouch for this use.

The yellow and lavender-flowered spotted bee balm or American horsemint (*M. punctata*) was also popular with Indians from the East Coast to the Mississippi and into Texas and Arizona. It was used chiefly to treat fevers and stomach ailments. Thymol, an antiseptic in mouthwashes such as Listerine and in nose and throat sprays, has been obtained commercially from this plant as well as from bee balm.

About fifteen *Monarda* species, often called horsemints or lemonmints, can be found in North America. Wild bergamot ranges from the East Coast into Minnesota and Texas, while bee balm is more limited in native territory, growing in and about rich woods from New York to Michigan and down into Tennessee and Georgia. However, as a garden escape—a term usually applied to European species—bee balm is becoming more widespread and now is being found wild even on the West Coast. *M. menthaefolia*, called horsemint, bee balm, lemon mint and even wild bergamot, grows in and about the Rockies from Arizona to Manitoba and Alberta. Its flowers are more deeply purple or rose than the light pink or pale lilac of the eastern bergamot.

In southern California, the closely related red monardella (*Monardella macrantha*) attracts several kinds of tropical hummingbirds with its bright red flowers. Its generic name suggests it is smaller than a *Monarda*, and indeed, these are generally low-lying plants.

**Bittersweet Nightshade**
*(Solanum dulcamara)*

## *Beautiful, but Deadly?*

Nightshade. The word inspires images of villains, poisons, and death, of Gothic novels and Holmesian mysteries. But in the case of our climbing nightshade, the image is overplayed.

*Solanum dulcamara* is a common inhabitant of hedges, brush, and tall weeds. It is easy to identify. Each ovate main leaf has two smaller wing leaves jutting out at the base, and the small, purple-blue flowers have pointed, reflexed petals and a conical yellow beak. The flowers bloom in late spring and through the summer, while the berries appear in midsummer and into September. Nightshade is a native of Europe and Asia, but is found coast to coast in North America.

*Solanum dulcamara* is called climbing, bitter, or bittersweet nightshade. The Latin root for *solanum* means "quieting" or "healing" and is the same root from which our word "solace" comes. *Dulcamara* is a corrupted form of the word for bittersweet (or literally sweet-bitter). If you chew a leaf of *S. dulcamara*, the taste will at first be bitter, then sweet. This sensation is due to a substance called dulcamarine.

Solanine is a more active constituent. "It slows the heart and respiration, lessens sensibility, lowers the temperature, and causes vertigo and delirium, terminating in death with convulsions," one authority maintained many years ago. This substance, however, is found in small quantities and is not the same as the highly poisonous atropine contained in the related deadly nightshade (belladonna), the traditional weapon of mustachioed villains. In fact, modern authorities differ on whether eating berries or other parts of our climbing nightshade will do any more than cause a mild stomachache—if that.

Climbing nightshade has been used for centuries as an internal and external medicine (whence *solanum*). It has been an ingredient in preparations for kidney ailments, skin diseases, rheumatism, jaundice, and respiratory problems such as catarrh, asthma, and whooping cough. Gerard reported a rather specialized use for the plant: "The juice is good for those who have fallen from high places, and have been thereby bruised or beaten, for it is thought to dissolve blood congealed or cluttered anywhere in the intrals and to heale the hurt places."

Nicholas Culpeper, however, offered some of the most unusual uses: "It is good to remove witchcraft both in men and beast. . . . Being tied about the neck, it is a remedy for the vertigo or dizziness of the head, and that is the reason the Germans hang it about their cattle's neck, when they fear any such evil hath betided them."

## *Bright Berries*

Several authorities agree that the berries have proved toxic to some degree in children, and it is safest to remove the plants from places frequented by youngsters who will eat such things. At the least, it is a good idea to instruct children not to touch the berries. Actually, it is a good idea to warn youngsters against eating anything found outdoors. While most of our wild vegetation is harmless, a few plants can cause at least discomfort when consumed, and one or two might do more.

Often there are flowers and berries of various stages of ripeness, all on the same plant. The berries stand out. The fruits are at first green, then they turn orange, and finally they ripen to a bright, translucent red that almost glows in the sunlight. "I do not know any clusters more graceful and beautiful than these," wrote Henry David Thoreau. "They hang more gracefully over the river's brim than any pendant in a lady's ear. Yet, they are considered poisonous; not to look at surely. . . . But why should they not be poisonous? Would it not be bad taste to eat these berries which are ready to feed another sense?"

In his appreciative ecstasy, Thoreau perhaps overlooked the probable purpose of the bright color—to attract animals to eat the berries and thereby spread the species. Nightshade berries are popular with birds, which eagerly gobble them up. As nature takes its course, the indigestible seeds that were embedded in the berries are deposited, complete with fertilizer, perhaps miles away.

## *Timing*

Nightshade is found in moist ground where it has other plants on which to grow. It may not matter if the host has a different growing schedule. For example, jewelweed and nightshade are often found together. In early spring, you are apt to see nightshade growing a foot higher than the young jewelweed hosts, but a month later, the jewelweed may outstrip the nightshade. They remain companions for the rest of the summer, the clinging nightshade sometimes becoming twice as long as its hosts, but spreading over several feet so that it does not look nearly its size.

As the nightshade matures, its hairy green stalks become smooth and woody, like a shrub, and turn grayish; in England, the plant is often called woody nightshade. Though shrublike, nightshade is a perennial herb, which means that its above-ground parts die at the end of its season and new stalks come up in spring.

The plant is considered a pest by some farmers and a danger by agricultural inspectors who have rejected whole truckloads of beans because a few nightshade berries were found mixed in, reports Richard Spellenberg, author of *The Audubon Society Field Guide to North American Wildflowers: Western Region.*

Other names for our common climbing nightshade include: blue bindweed, felonwood, felonwort, poisonflower, snakeberry, scarletberry, dulcamara, and violet bloom. A felon—a blister or boil especially around fingernails—was once treated with this plant. Felon is an interesting word; both this sense and the meaning of an evildoer are believed to have come from the same origin—a word that meant someone or something that is full of bitterness.

## *Other Nightshades*

True deadly nightshade (*Atropa belladonna*), the plant with which our subject is sometimes confused, is native to central and southern Europe and is very rarely seen on this continent. Every part of *A. belladonna* is extremely poisonous and dangerous.

An American plant, black or garden nightshade (*Solanum nigrum*), is sometimes called deadly nightshade because the leaves and the unripe berries are thought to be somewhat poisonous and, like belladonna, the berries are black. However, black nightshade's toxicity is not nearly that of its European cousin. In fact, midwesterners used to add ripe black nightshade berries to pies. Children in South Africa are especially fond of them, as are African witch doctors, who use them in a rain-making concoction. Since cattle will not eat the greens, it is possible that the poisonous qualities, if any, lie only in those parts. Yet, the boiled leaves of black nightshade have been widely used for food, from our own continent through Europe and even on the distant island of Mauritius in the Indian Ocean.

Black nightshade, which bears white flowers of the same shape as climbing nightshade, ranges from the East into the Rockies. It was for centuries employed to treat dropsy, gastritis, skin eruptions and injuries, and as a narcotic for nervous afflictions. American Indians, such as the Rappahannocks and the Houmas, used it to treat worms, sores, and insomnia. In Central Europe, mothers used to hang the plant over their babies' cradles as a hypnotic inducement to sleep. The narcotic or hypnotic effects of various nightshades on the mind may have inspired its name, the "shade" being a dark hallucination. True deadly nightshade has long been associated with the devil, and so has night. In general, it is a gloom and doom name, no matter how you look at it.

Drier parts of California support several other nightshades, including white nightshade (*S. nodiflorum*) which, as its name suggests, has white flowers. White horsenettle (*S. elaeagnifolium*), is a prickly plant with violet flowers and yellow berries; the name probably refers to the grayish leaves. Purple nightshade (*S. xanthi*), has green berries. Buffalo bur (*S. rostratum*) is another prickly variety found throughout the West. Its golden prickers are useful, too, for they discourage animals such as cattle from eating its very toxic leaves.

*Solanum* is one of the world's largest plant genera, containing more than 1,000 species, mostly in the tropical Americas; only about 40 species live wild in North America. Some species are quite familiar to us, such as *S. melongena*, a native of northern India, which we call the eggplant. Another sibling, *S. tuberosum*, was first domesticated by Indians on the slopes of the Andes Mountains centuries ago. Brought to Europe, the common potato has become one of the most widely eaten vegetables in the Western world. However, true to its genus, the potato contains a bit of poison in its skin. Don't worry about eating your entire baked potato, though; cooking removes the toxicity.

This genus is in turn a member of the Nightshade or Potato family (*Solanaceae*) of some seventy-five genera worldwide, and about twenty in North America. Among the most recognized members is the tomato (*Lycopersicum esculentum*), believed also to be a native of the

Andes or perhaps of Mexico. Few people would eat tomatoes when the plants were first taken to Europe. The fruit, sometimes called love apple, was considered poisonous and the plant was mostly used ornamentally. The Italians eventually started making spaghetti sauce from the fruit, and appreciation of its culinary value is said to have spread from there.

Another popular member of the family is the genus *Nicotiana*, or tobacco, with some fourteen species on this continent. And while experts may question whether our common nightshades are very poisonous, just read the little box on a package of cigarettes. There is no doubt expressed in its warning.

**Purple Loosestrife**
*(Lythrum salicaria)*

# *Summer's Purple Glow*

"One who has seen an inland marsh in August aglow with this beautiful plant is almost ready to forgive the Old Country some of the many pests she has shipped to our shores in view of this radiant acquisition," wrote Mrs. William Starr Dana nearly a century ago. Indeed, many wetlands seem to burn with the tall purple spikes of loosestrife, which begin blooming around the Fourth of July, peak in August, and remain flowering as late as mid-September in the Northeast. But the plant that made Charles Darwin "almost stark, staring mad" is making others angry.

Purple or spiked loosestrife (*Lythrum salicaria*) is a member of the Loosestrife family (*Lythraceae*), consisting of about twenty-one genera and more than 400 species worldwide. Most are tropical, and only seven genera and about 25 species are found in North America. Nearly a dozen species are of the *Lythrum* genus, and probably the most common is our purple loosestrife, found widely east of the Mississippi from Tennessee and Virginia north into Canada, and in the Pacific Northwest. It is yet another European immigrant that has struck it rich in America, though not everyone is pleased about it.

## *Gore and Peace*

Purple loosestrife is a true loosestrife, as opposed to the genus of primroses, also called loosestrife (such as yellow loosestrife and whorled loosestrife, both natives of eastern North America). As if to confuse us more, those plants bear the Latin name *Lysimachia*, which literally means "loose-strife." Our purple loosestrife has a less-than-peaceful Greek name. *Lythrum* means "gore," of the blood-and-guts kind that would result from a battle. While the name probably stems from the color of the flowers, it seems incongruous for a plant at once to be called loosestrife in English and gore in Greek. There is some history of the plant's being used as a styptic poultice for wounds, however, and the connection with the primrose loosestrifes was probably drawn from that association.

Purple loosestrife was once in widespread use to treat dysentery and diarrhea, and was also a respected treatment for fevers, liver diseases, constipation, and cholera. It has also been employed as an eye-freshener and a gargle for sore throats.

*Salicaria* means "willow"; the leaves are similar in shape to willow leaves. In France, the common name for the purple loosestrife is *salicaire*, which has given rise to such English folk names as red sally and flowering sally.

Plants run from three to five feet tall, and sometimes hit eight or ten feet in height. They grow in meadows, along stream banks and ponds, and near swamps. They also prefer full sunlight, although I have found them growing in a wet area that gets direct sun for less than half the day. This species is, incidentally, one of the relatively few plants whose seeds require light for germination; seeds of most plants seem indifferent to light.

Purple loosestrife, like most wetland species, is easily transplanted because its roots are not too deep. The plant is easy to find in wet waste places, and snatching one or two from a colony would probably go unnoticed. It is hardly an endangered species.

### *Aggressive*

In fact, some authors warn that purple loosestrife is downright pushy, adding that it spreads rapidly and makes a pest of itself. My experience has been that it spreads slowly, at least in my semishaded wetland. However, Lawrence J. Crockett, author of *Wildly Successful Plants*, points out that while purple loosestrife may not be weedy in the sense that it pops up all over the place, it can tend to crowd out native plants.

After I once wrote about purple loosestrife in a newspaper column, I received an angry letter from a nature center director, decrying loosestrife as a scourge of native plant life that should be destroyed on sight. Indeed, many naturalists are concerned about the rapid spread of purple loosestrife and the choking effect it has on native plant life. Efforts to eradicate it seem doomed to failure, however. Like the Europeans who arrived in North America, displacing many of the natives, purple loosestrife has gained a foothold on soil it likes and will not easily give up. If you are trying to grow cardinal flowers or other sensitive species in your meadow or at your water's edge, do not put loosestrife in with them. If, however, you are looking for long-lasting, sizable, and colorful plants in such a situation, you may want to give purple loosestrife a try.

One other word of warning: Japanese beetles will feast on them, both flowers and leaves, and it is possible that those voracious eaters could be attracted to your property by loosestrife, though usually gardeners already have other plants, like roses, that appeal to these invaders.

In Europe, where it is widely distributed, purple loosestrife has acquired many folk names, such as spiked soldiers, purple grass, killweed, willowweed, purple willowherb, grass polly, foxtail, and salicare. One of its more common old names in England was long purples, which has led some authors to wonder about a line from *Hamlet*. Shakespeare, considered almost as expert in floral culture as in playwrighting, wrote in Ophelia's death scene:

*There with fantastic garlands did she come*
*Of crow-flowers, nettles, daisies, and long purples.*

All but the long purples are spring flowers in England, leading some authors, such as Neltje Blanchan, to suggest that Shakespeare made a mistake. It could also be that Shakespeare simply had some other flower in mind or employed the famous poetic license.

### *Trimorphic*

Although at casual inspection, purple loosestrife flowers seem ordinary enough, they are actually trimorphic, that is, they come in three forms: long-styled, in which the pollen-catching stigma is on a long style, and the stamens, bearing pollen-producing anthers, are medium and short; medium-styled, in which the style is middle length, and the stamens are both long and short; short-styled, in which the style is short and the stamens medium and long.

Each plant has flowers all of one kind. The pollen produced by the long-stamened anthers is large; the medium length has smaller pollen, and the short ones, smaller still. Pollen from anthers on long stamens will fertilize only the stigma on long styles. Medium-length stamens fertilize only medium length stigma. And so for the short ones.

Thus, when a bee enters a flower, it picks up one size of pollen on one part of its body and another size elsewhere. The insect must move on to other flowers with different configurations in order to unload the pollen. This trimorphism, which guarantees that inbreeding will not take place, amazed Charles Darwin, who studied it at great length. He once wrote to the noted American botanist, Asa Gray: "I am almost stark, staring mad over Lythrum. . . . For the love of Heaven, have a look at some of your species, and if you can get me some seeds, do!"

**Heal-All**
*(Prunella vulgaris)*

# *The Once-prized Weed*

Many are the lowly creeping flowers that gain little more than a glance from the average person. They are the plants with small blossoms that weave through fields and into lawns; they are the weeds targeted in pesticide commercials. Such is heal-all, a plant of odd and untrue name and rather ordinary existence, but one worth knowing nonetheless.

Heal-all or self-heal is another of the European herbs brought over because it was widely believed, as its names suggest, to have healing powers. While it is common in its native Europe as well as in Asia, heal-all is abundant here from coast to coast, another immigrant that took so well in its new homeland that it seems native. There is a difference between Old and New World editions, however. John Burroughs and other travelers noticed that the flower varies in color. "Prunella was much deeper purple there than at home," Burroughs wrote of the European expedition. Some 400 years ago John Gerard wrote that heal-all flowers around Heningham Castle in Essex were all white.

Our *Prunella vulgaris* is a beautiful shade of light purple, particularly at the top of the flower hoods—features of the blossoms that are typical of members of the large Mint family. Much admired by Thoreau for their color, which he said deepened toward night, these handsome flowers are attractive enough in both hue and form that they would surely be coveted by gardeners, were they only five or six times larger. The flowers, which appear from June through fall, are densely packed in a head. After the flowers die, the rusty brown, boxy calyxes remain in whorles on the stem, colorful in their own right.

This dense flower arrangement minimizes travel for bees, and helps heal-all compete with other flowers. It has been estimated that a bee can drink one flower's worth of nectar in two seconds, and can clean out—and pollinate—a whole flower head in thirty seconds.

Later, four neatly packed seeds form at the base of each calyx. When the wind bends the head, the ripe seeds spill out to begin a new generation.

## *A Creeper, Too*

Survival of this perennial is also aided by the plant's vine-like stems that spread *Prunella* quickly and thoroughly wherever it is happy. Like other successful plants, it is not very particular about its habitat, living in fields, lawns, roadsides, and woods—in full sun and even in some rather shady locations, all usually poorly drained. If all is well, it will grow up to two feet high; in other spots, such as lawns that are frequently mowed, it will not get much more than two or three inches high and is more apt to gain size by creeping along the ground.

Like many other weedy and successful plants, it has acquired quite a collection of names, including all-heal, slough-heal ("slough" means "skin"), heart of the earth, blue curls, Hercules woundwort, panay (a corruption of *panax*, Latin for "all-healing" as in the generic name for ginseng), brownwort, prunella, brunella, sicklewort (viewed sideways the flower resembles a sickle), and thimbleweed (probably the shape of the flowerless head).

*Prunella vulgaris* is one of a small genus of mints, none of which is probably native to this continent (though some people maintain heal-all is a native). *Vulgaris* means "common," a fitting title, while *prunella* has an origin in an old affliction of soldiers. The name is a variation of the German word, *Brunella.* A man named Cole, who wrote *Adam in Eden* in 1657, reported, "Brunella [is] from Brunellen, which is the name given unto it by the Germans because it cureth that inflammation of the mouth which they call *die Breuen.*" This disease, he said, "is common to soldiers when they lye in camp, but especially in garrisons." Now called *die Braeuen*, or quinsy, the disease was cured by wrapping the neck in heal-all leaves. Ben Charles Harris, in *The Compleat Herbal* (1972), says the plant was popular for mouth and throat diseases because each flower had a mouth and throat, another application of the "doctrine of signatures."

## *None Better*

Gerard wrote, "There is not a better wound herbe in the world than that of self-heale is, the very name importing it to be very admirable upon this account." According to an old French saying, "No one wants a surgeon who keeps Prunelle." Thus we have several names for the plant connected with the tradesmen or instruments whose wounds it cured: carpenter weed or herb, hookweed, and hook-heal (as in the wounds suffered by fishermen), and perhaps sicklewort. It was used for treating wounds "both inward and outward," for mouth and throat ulcers, for internal bleeding, piles, bruises, and diarrhea, wrote Gerard. "The juice used with oil of roses to anoint the temples is very effectual to remove the headache," said Nicholas Culpeper.

As was often the case with plants that arrived from Europe to fill colonial herb gardens, it did not take long for American Indians to find uses for it. The Chippewas used heal-all to treat "diseases of women," the Delaware and Mohegans concocted a soothing body wash for fevers, and several tribes used the leaves to make a refreshing tea and to treat dysentery in babies.

Most modern practitioners of herb medicine either ignore or discredit heal-all as a valuable medicine, and it has generally fallen out of common use. Nelson Coon said in his *Dictionary of Useful Plants* (1974) that all indications are that the plant's values have been largely psychological. In *A Field Guide to Medicinal Plants* (1990), however, Steven Foster and James A. Duke say research indicates that the plant has antibiotic qualities and that it contains ursolic acid, an antitumor compound.

An amazing number of our common wildflowers, like heal-all, have a history of use as herb medicines. It is hard to know which species may or may not have medicinal value. It is interesting that in a July 1978 article, *The New York Times* reported that nearly half the drugs used in medicine today are based on substances first discovered in nature. Yet, less than ten percent of the world's plants have been screened for medically useful substances.

"Somewhere on the face of the earth," wrote *Times* reporter Boyce Rensberger, "perhaps in a Brazilian jungle or on a Cambodian mountainside, or maybe by the banks of the Congo River, a nondescript little plant may be growing, synthesizing in its leaves a substance that can cure cancer or prevent heart attacks."

**Yarrow**
*(Achillea millefolium)*

## *Of Livers and Lovers*

As soon as March rolls around, when the sun is higher in the sky and the air is a tad warmer, northern wildflower fanatics hit the trail in search of some sign of life. Among the earliest greens are tiny combs that sprout from the earth almost as soon as the snow has melted. These early leaves of yarrow are tantalizing, but it will be several months before the plant spreads its white flowers.

The Chippewas had an appropriate name for yarrow, calling it *adjidamowano*, which meant "squirrel tail." The feathery tails, so small in March, are the finely segmented leaves that earned *Achillea millefolium* its name, *millefolium*, or milfoil as it is widely known. The name may be an exercise of poetic license. Though I've never taken the time to confirm it by counting, there probably are not a thousand leaves on the plant, just as there are not a thousand feet on a millipede or a hundred on a centipede. Nevertheless, the name well suits the appearance, as does a popular Spanish name in the Southwest, *plumajillo*, which means "little feather."

Botanists, no poets when it comes to description, call these leaves bipinnate, which means leaflets branch off the stem, and from them, smaller subleaflets branch off, giving an overall lacy effect. Ferns with this appearance would be called twice-cut, and indeed casual observers of plant life sometimes mistake the flowerless yarrow for a fern.

### *Fit for Survival*

Yarrow, though, is a member of the Composite family and thus is among the highest rather than the more primitive forms of plant life. Each flower is composed of disk and ray florets. Yarrow has only five rays per blossom, much like a simple, five-petaled flower. The sparsity of rays is balanced by a plenitude of flowers. While daisies or sunflowers have a few large blossoms composed of many disk and ray florets, yarrow has many small blossoms each of which are composed of a few tiny disk and ray florets.

It is yarrow's way of surviving. The plant puts out flat-topped clusters of flowers, flashing a sizable and bright display to passing insects, which find the wealth of closely packed blossoms easy pickings. It offers those flowers from May or June through the summer and sometimes into November, virtually guaranteeing pollination despite the floral competition. A feeding insect will easily fertilize many flowers with pollen since all are so close together.

The perennial can also spread from underground runners that are difficult to eradicate. Farmers consider yarrow a pest because animals shun the bitter leaves. (If forced by hunger to eat yarrow, cows will give milk with an off flavor.) Because it survives in poor soils that little else of commercial or ornamental value would live in, though, yarrow can serve the useful ends of preventing erosion and decorating an otherwise bleak landscape. One of its favorite haunts is the roadside, where doses of sand, salt, and petroleum pollution fail to daunt its annual appearance.

### *Rust of Achilles*

Like so many other sun-loving weeds of summer, *A. millefolium* is not native. At least, that is what most botanists think, though a few feel the plant was here long before the Europeans arrived. Its Old World connections might be guessed from its generic name, which recalls the Greek hero. Among the six species of *Achillea* occurring in North America, four are natives, though they are not nearly as well known and widespread as *A. millefolium*, which is now found coast to coast and even in New Zealand and Australia. Most of the genus's hundred or so species live in Europe and Asia, and the only other import that has made any name for itself here is the sneezewort or white tansy (*A. ptarmica*), so called because it was once dried and used as snuff to encourage sneezing as a headache remedy.

With a name like *Achillea*, you can bet a few tales have been told about yarrow. In the most popular, Chiron, the centaur, is supposed to have taught Achilles about the virtues of yarrow. When Achilles and the Greeks were on their way to attack Troy, Telephus, a son-in-law of King Priam, tried to stop them. Clumsy Telephus tripped over a vine; Achilles caught him and seriously wounded the interloper with his spear. Later an oracle told Telephus that his worsening wound could be cured only by "Achilles," meaning the herb yarrow. Telephus misunderstood and went straight to Achilles, the person, promising to conduct his army to Troy if he would heal the wound. Agreeing, Achilles scraped some rust off his spear and from the filings arose a yarrow plant, with which he treated Telephus's wound. (Ancient tribes that settled what is now Hungary and Finland also believed that the scrapings from a weapon that caused a wound could cure the wound—more of the old "hair of the dog that bit you" theory.)

Yarrow supposedly helped Achilles win Troy, but according to legend, it also helped keep his men fit for fighting. Achilles was widely known for his use of yarrow to cure the wounds of his soldiers. Consequently the plant has been called not only *Achillea*, but also by such names as soldier's woundwort and *Herba militaris*.

## *The Woundwort*

Through the centuries, curing wounds has been yarrow's chief use. From the Greeks before Christ to the American Indians of the West, yarrow has been a medicine for the injured. The medieval English called it woundwort (wound plant), the same name used by the Utes in their own tongue. In fact, the word "yarrow" is said to have come from the Anglo-Saxon *gearwe*, a name used as early as 725 A.D. that may have meant "to repair," reflecting the plant's healing applications.

Herbals and herb histories go on at length about the medicinal uses to which the dried flower tops of yarrow have been put throughout centuries and across continents. Indeed, the ancients claimed its thousand-parted leaves were a sign from above of its thousand uses, and it has been eaten, drunk, smoked, snorted, rubbed on, and bathed in by many peoples. Its wound-healing ability is said to stem from a substance that speeds up the clotting of blood, and it has even been studied as a possible cancer-preventing agent. All sorts of skin problems—from ulcers and burns to the eruptions of measles and chicken pox—have been treated with yarrow ointments, although some sensitive people can wind up with skin irritations from its use. In 1640 herbalist John Parkinson recommended putting the leaves in the nose to stop bleeds. A short time later, in 1649, Culpeper wrote, "An ointment of the leaves cures wounds, and is good for inflammations, ulcers, fistulas, and all such runnings as abound with moisture." In 1633 Gerard noted, "The leaves of yarrow doe close up wounds, and keep them from inflammation, or fiery swellings. . . . The leaves being put into the nose, do cause it to bleed, and ease the paine of megrim"—a rather messy way of dealing with a headache.

Yarrow or milfoil tea was well known as a treatment for stomach problems. The plant's content of iron, calcium, potassium, and other minerals led to its use as a tonic. It has been used to treat hypochondria, cramps, dysentery, hemorrhoids, diabetes, and disorders of the lungs, kidneys, and liver. The leaves were chewed to relieve toothaches. American Indians employed it for many problems, including balding, earaches, and sprains, and as a contraceptive, sweat herb, cold medicine, and appetizer. Its wide use may vouch for its status as a native plant. The Iroquois, Micmac, Chippewa, Chickasaw, Delaware, Menomini, Objibwa, Mohawk, Ute, Meskwaki, Piute, Zuni, Miami, Illinois, Winnebago and other tribes all used yarrow. Despite this wide use, the *British Pharmacopoeia* dropped yarrow as an official medicine back in 1781 and the *U.S. Pharmacopoeia* did so in 1882.

Yarrow is not without other uses. The leaves are pungent—it was called old man's pepper—and it was once used to pep up salads and as a snuff. The Swiss made a vinegar from a variety from the Alps. An extract obtained from the flower heads is used as a flavoring for soft drinks, and liqueurs have been made from several European species. The Swedish, who call it field hop, once used it in making beer; Linnaeus maintained yarrow-brewed beer was more intoxicating than hop-brewed.

## *Good and Evil*

Speaking of spirits, the forces of both good and evil have put yarrow to use. Witches employed it for spells, prompting such names as devil's nettle and bad man's plaything. On the other hand, the plant was woven into garlands that were hung in homes and churches to ward off evil spirits. People hung some yarrow in cribs to discourage baby-stealing witches. The Chinese cast yarrow stems like lots to divine the future, a technique described in the *I Ching*.

Love, too, was closely connected with yarrow. For example, in a rather odd custom, country folk in England would tickle the inside of the nose with yarrow leaf while chanting:

*Yarroway, Yarroway, bear a white blow,*
*If my love love me, my nose will bleed now.*

Country girls practiced a less messy system to find out who their future husband would be. Wrapping an ounce of dried yarrow in flannel, they'd place it under their pillow at night, saying:

*Thou pretty herb of Venus' tree,*
*Thy true name is Yarrow;*
*Now who my bosom friend must be,*
*Pray tell thou me to-morrow.*

Some maidens believed that if they cut the stem crossways, the initials of their future husband would appear. Once a maiden found and married him, she might give him yarrow to chew at the wedding, for then he would not leave her—for seven years, at least.

Yarrow's unusual leaves and many uses have earned it many names, among them knight's milfoil, thousand weed, thousand seal, nose bleed, bloodwort, staunchweed, sanguinary, noble yarrow, and dog daisy. Since carpenters were apt to cut themselves in their work, it was also called carpenter's weed, especially in France, where it was *herbe aux charpentiers.*

Yarrow makes a bright addition to a wildflower garden of daisies, black-eyed Susans, St. Johnsworts, goldenrods, and asters. Its fragrance, said to be like chamomile, is fresh and the flowers are long-lasting in summery bouquets. It is easily transplanted to well-drained, well-sunned spots.

*A. millefolium* will often produce pinkish flowers, especially at higher altitudes. Bright pink and red varieties, *A. millefolium rosea* and *A. millefolium rubra,* are popular with gardeners. Wild yarrow is even used sometimes as a ground cover that can be walked upon, though not heavily. As such, the bright green leaves, not the flowers, are wanted, and the plants must be mown regularly. Imagine how soft and luxurious yarrow grass would feel to the barefoot stroller!

**Motherwort**
*(Leonurus cardiaca)*

## *A Wort for Mom*

*W*ort is a word that often confuses people who begin to take an interest in wildflowers. Names like liverwort, mugwort, lungwort, and milkwort may make you wonder whether you will get lumpy skin if you touch the plant. However, "wort"—as opposed to "wart"—is from the Old English *wyrt,* and means only "plant" and nothing dire.

Notwithstanding that comforting assurance, motherwort has been known to cause dermatitis in some people with sensitive skin. But the problem is not common and the plant, which is common, has long had a reputation as a friend of mankind—or womankind, as the case may be.

Which brings to mind John Burroughs's wonderful comment on weeds: "One is tempted to say that the most human plants, after all, are the weeds. How they cling to man and follow him around the world, and spring up wherever he sets foot! How they crowd around his barns and dwellings, and throng his garden, and jostle and override each other in their strife to be near him." Burroughs also found that some weeds "are so domestic and familiar, and so harmless withal, that one comes to regard them with positive affection. Motherwort, catnip, plantain, tansy, wild mustard—what a homely, human look they have! They are an integral part of every old homestead. Your smart new place will wait long before they draw near it."

## *Blithe and Merry*

Colonists carried motherwort from its native Europe and Asia to northern North America, where it is now found coast to coast. Motherwort was much admired for its medicinal qualities and it was a standby in early American gardens. It rapidly spread and it is particularly common in waste places and disturbed places. It found our countryside more to its liking; in England its qualities were much praised, but it is apparently less common.

In 1597, John Gerard reported, "Divers commend it against infirmaties of the heart. Morever, the same is commended for green wounds; it is also a remedy against certain diseases in cattell [whence the old name, cowthwort] as the cough and murreine, and for that cause diverse husbandmen oftentimes much desire it."

"There is no better herb to drive melancholy vapours from the heart, to strengthen it and make the mind cheerful, blithe, and merry," wrote Nicholas Culpeper in 1649, making it sound like some sort of drug that would be forbidden by federal authorities today. "It cleanseth the chest of cold phlegm, oppressing it, and killeth worms in the belly."

## *Female Weaknesses*

"Motherwort is especially valuable in female weakness and disorders—hence, the name, allaying nervous irritability and inducing quiet and passivity of the whole nervous system," wrote Maude Grieve. Culpeper maintained that the plant made mothers joyful and settled the womb, which was why it was called motherwort.

Practitioners of folk medicine in America considered it an important tonic and stimulant. *Ladies' Indispensable Assistant*, an 1852 manual for housewives, said of motherwort: "It is excellent in all nervous and hypochondriacal affections, dizziness in the head, etc. A strong tea, made of it and drank freely, will raise the spirits and impart new life and vigor to the whole system." Both the Delaware and Mohegan Indians brewed motherwort tea for "diseases and complaints of women." So respected was motherwort as a tonic that those with knowledge of plants, psychology, and humor used to say, "Drink motherwort and live to be a source of continuous astonishment and grief to waiting heirs."

Of course, these are all views of people who appreciate the plant. Modern gardeners, who usually favor large, fancy, or colorful flowers, are not as appreciative. Even in the last century, some writers forgot how motherwort was imported to plant in colonial gardens. For example, Peter Henderson in his *Handbook of Plants and General Horticulture* (1890) dismissed motherwort with nine words: "A worthless weed, common in neglected and waste places." At least he didn't call it a pest.

## *Lion's Tail*

*Leonurus cardiaca* is a member of the large Mint family. There are no native species of this genus, all of whose ten members come from

Europe and Asia. Three species, including motherwort, have established themselves on our continent, though neither of the other two is nearly as common as motherwort, which can be found in all states east of the Rockies as well as in Washington, Arizona, and southern parts of most Canadian provinces.

As in many mints, the plant is pleasantly but pungently scented. The flowers bloom in midsummer and are typical of the mints—they are tubular with a single-lobed lip or hood above and a three-lobed lip below. They are small, clustered at the junctions of the stem and opposing leaf-stalks, and are a pretty purple and white; in England, they may take on a more pinkish or reddish hue. (The plant is sometimes called throwwort, possibly a corruption of "through-wort," because the stem seems to run through the flowers and the opposing leaf stalks.) For mints the plants are tall, reaching five feet if sun and soil conditions are right.

*Leonurus* means "lion's tail," apparently because someone thought the whole plant or its three-pointed leaves bear some resemblance to the tip of a lion's tail. In England, the plant is sometimes also called lion's ear or herb of life. *Cardiaca* is based on the old Roman word for the plant, and refers either to the general heart shape of the leaves or to their supposed ability to treat physical afflictions of the heart.

**Queen Anne's Lace**
*(Daucus carota)*

## *The Queen's Carrot*

Queen Anne's lace is another of those hardy, weedy, but attractive wildflowers that will inhabit places most plants disdain. In full bloom it is among our most handsome flowers. It is also among the most hated. But loved or hated, Queen Anne's lace is an interesting plant whose ancestry has been much debated.

*Daucus carota*, also commonly called wild carrot, is a native of the Old World that, like the daisy, dandelion, and other sun-loving imports, spread across the continent with ease and abundance. It favors the edges of sunny roads and will also fill dry fields with its flat-topped clusters of tiny, white flowers. It earned its common name from the lacelike delicacy of these circular umbels, which bloom from late June into October. Queen Anne, who ruled England from 1702 to 1714, was said to have been fond of wearing lace on her dresses. A close look at the umbels shows they are actually composed of many smaller clusters of flowers or umbellets, all lacily laid out and probably quite as exquisite as anything the queen wore.

This huge mass of tiny flowers is a flashy display to passing insects. More than sixty kinds have been found visiting the blossoms, including flies, bees, butterflies, wasps, and beetles, some perhaps drawn by the somewhat strong smell of the plant.

*Daucus*, the generic name, is from the Greek, *dais*, to burn, descriptive of the acrid taste of the root and leaves. *Carota* comes from a Greek word for "carrot" that may in turn have been based on the word for "head," a reference perhaps to the showy display of flowers. Maude Grieve says the word is Celtic for "red of color."

### *One of a Kind?*

Is Queen Anne's lace the cultivated carrot run wild or the wild parent of the cultivated carrot? Or is it neither? Various authorities report that the carrot we grow in the garden or buy in the market is really the same species as this wild carrot. Cultivated carrots carry the scientific name *Daucus carota sativa*, indicating they are a subspecies of wild carrot. The cultivated carrot, said to have originated from the area of Afghanistan, has spread around the world to every continent and was in North America by 1609. Known to the ancient Greeks and Romans before Christ, it was prized by them for medicinal virtues—it is rich in vitamin A, among other things. Though it has long been eaten, the root was not too popular as a food until fairly modern times, and was not widely consumed raw until this century. (However, E. Lewis Sturtevant reported that in the nineteenth century, "So fond of carrots are the Flathead Indians of Oregon that the children cannot forbear stealing them from the fields, although honest as regards other articles.")

Some authorities believe the eating variety was cultivated from the wild while others believe just the opposite—that Queen Anne's lace is merely some bastard offspring of cultivated carrots gone wild.

Other authorities disagree with both contentions. "Still another fiction," wrote Neltje Blanchan in 1900, "is that the cultivated carrot, introduced to England by the Dutch in Queen Elizabeth's reign, was derived from this wild species. Miller, the celebrated English botanist and gardener, among others, has disproved this statement by utterly failing again and again to produce an edible vegetable from the wild root. When the cultivation of the garden lapses for a few generations, it reverts to the ancestral type—a species quite distinct from Daucus carota." Nonetheless, Dr. Sturtevant said, "Vilmorin-Andrieux obtained in the space of three years roots as fleshy and as large as those of the garden carrot from the thin, wiry roots of the wild species."

While the garden and wild carrots have very similar fernlike leaves, underground parts are noticeably different. Wild carrot has a white root that burrows deep into the rather dry ground in search of water. The roots of cultivated carrot are red-orange outside (the bark) and yellowish inside (the wood). By the intention of the cultivators, the roots do not go nearly so deep and favor rather richer soils. Mrs. Grieve, a turn-of-the-century herbalist, said that the wild carrot has a "strong aromatic smell and an acrid, disagreeable taste" while the garden carrot has a "pleasant odor and peculiar, sweet, mucilaginous flavor."

### *Poisonous Relatives*

Queen Anne's lace is one of only two members of the *Daucus* genus in North America. Rattlesnake-weed (*D. pusillus*) has smaller flower heads and is found in the southern and western states. They are in turn members of the Carrot or Parsnip family (*Umbelliferae*) of about fifty genera in North America, including cicelies, parsleys, parsnips, pimpernels, and fennel. While many of these plants have been used as foods, two genera include the highly poisonous water hemlock (*Cicuta maculata*), summer bloomer of wetlands, and the poison hemlock (*Conium maculatum*), found throughout the United States and southern Canada, and said to be one of the most poisonous plants in the world.

Because Queen Anne's lace and poison hemlock have very similar leaves and somewhat similar flowers, it is best to make certain you know the plant's identity before handling or sampling it. In many cases, identification in this family is difficult and can be done only by studying the seeds. Queen Anne's lace is quite like some other less common members of the clan, but can usually be identified with certainty by the one or several tiny deep purple flowers that appear in the center of the white-flowered umbel. No one knows for certain why these purple flowers appear, but children used to be told that Queen Anne pricked her finger, causing a drop of her blood to stain the lace. Poison hemlock has no purple flower, but does have purple-spotted stems, which are lacking in Queen Anne's lace.

### *Bird's Nest*

After the flowers die, the umbel curls up so that each head forms what looks almost like a bird's nest, which is one of the folk names for the plant. The shape of this nest or basket has led some to believe that certain insects are specially adapted by nature to make their homes there. Certainly, spiders find it handy, but one well-circulated story—and probably only a story—was that a species of bee would dwell only in the dried umbels of wild carrots.

These baskets often fall off and roll away in the breeze, like tumbleweeds. If they roll across or come to rest in the right environment, the seeds that fall out will eventually germinate. Thus the nests may actually be a clever evolution of nature that provides vehicles to carry loads of seeds for establishing new colonies.

Over the centuries, wild carrot has been used to treat a wide selection of ailments, everything from kidney problems and gout to hiccoughs and flatulence. "Though Galen [a second-century Greek physician] commended garden carrots highly to break wind," wrote Nicholas Culpeper in 1649, "yet experience teacheth they breed it first, and we may thank nature for expelling it. . . . The seeds of them expel wind indeed, and so mend what the root marreth." In many cases just the plant's seeds, which are plentiful, were used to obtain the medicinal essences and oils. Spicy like celery seed, they can be used to season soups and poultry, herb bread, or campfire stew. To collect them, simply shake the brown baskets into a small paper bag or a can. (Make sure, of course, that you're not shaking one of those poisonous hemlocks.) To clean the seeds, rustle them in a light breeze.

Wild and cultivated carrots also had an odd use during the reign of King James I when it was the fashion for ladies to decorate their hats with leaves, in the manner of feathers. "One can picture the dejected appearance of a ballroom belle at the close of an entertainment," observed Mrs. William Starr Dana.

One could also picture the dejected look on the belle who used a once-popular concoction of questionable efficacy. Boiled in wine, the flowers were supposed to be a love potion that was also a contraceptive.

Transplanting flowering Queen Anne's lace is difficult because by maturity, the plant's root has sunk itself so deep in the ground that extracting it without breaking it and killing the plant is almost impossible. These deep roots were one reason the plant was among the most hated of weeds; farmers could not eradicate it from fields and often called it devil's plague. Dairy farmers especially dislike the Queen Anne's lace because it is said to give an unpleasant taste to the milk of cows that eat it.

If you want some of these flowers in your wildflower garden or field, it is best to dig the very young plants—easily identified by the distinctive, feathery leaves—early in the season or gather the seed in late summer. Once you have them growing you can try an entertaining trick that country folk used to do. Cut the flowers and stick the stems in cans of water to which vegetable dyes of various colors have been added. After six or eight hours, the white flower heads will turn to pretty shades of color, suitable for some interesting bouquets.

Other names for Queen Anne's lace include crow's nest, lace-flower, parsnip, and rantipole. The last—an old word for a wild, reckless, or ill-behaved person—was undoubtedly first applied by a farmer, not a flower fan.

**Asiatic Dayflower**
*(Commelina communis)*

# *An Embarrassing Memorial*

Stacey Wahl, who wrote a children's book that uses flower petals to teach number groups, told me that one of the most troublesome numbers to represent was "two" because there are so few two-petaled flowers.

"How about the dayflower?" I asked her.

"That would be cheating," she replied. "I would never cheat a child."

Indeed, while at first glance it seemed to be our only two-petaled flower, the Asiatic or common dayflower (*Commelina communis*) has a third petal, barely visible below the main part of the blossom. Unlike the pair of larger sky blue petals, the lower one is whitish and wan, looking as if it were a useless mistake of nature.

This petal arrangement, a characteristic of the whole dayflower clan of some ninety-five species worldwide, inspired an eighteenth-century botanist to employ some humor in naming the genus *Commelina*. According to Neltje Blanchan, "Delightful Linnaeus, who dearly loved his little joke, himself confesses to have named the dayflower after three brothers, [named] Commelyn, Dutch botanists, because two of them—commemorated in the two showy blue petals of the blossom—published their works. The third, lacking application and ambition, amounted to nothing, like the inconspicuous whitish third petal!" Linnaeus himself was less blunt in his own explanation, saying only that the Commelina are "flowers with three petals, two of which are showy while the third is not conspicuous, from the two brothers Commelin, for the third died before accomplishing anything in botany."

### *Odd Flowers*

Our dayflowers are interesting not only for their name, but also in their odd form and habits. No plentiful flowers in the northern states and Canada look anything like the dayflowers, which seem as if they would be more at home in a jungle. Each flower rises from boatlike bracts, with the two large petals looking like blue Mickey Mouse ears. The flowers remain open long enough to be fertilized by passing bees. They then close, usually by midday, never to open again—hence, dayflower. (If the sky becomes cloudy after a flower opens, the blossom may last longer, sometimes all day.)

The bright petals, almost the color of many of our gentians, are probably what prompted the importation of the Asiatic dayflower in the nineteenth century. However, they are attractive not only in their hue but in their large numbers, their long blooming season (June to October), and their peculiar tendency to sparkle in the sunlight. Examine one closely and you will see hundreds of tiny shiny spots, like so many miniature diamonds or dewdrops set off nicely by the blue. Under a microscope these appear to be clear cells scattered through the more plentiful blue-tinted ones. The sparkle occurs when sunlight hits the juice in the colorless cells. The petals are very succulent; crush one in your fingers and you'll find much moisture and little substance—and a blue tint on your skin. It is possible that these sparkles act as beacons to distant bees, luring them in so that they will notice and be attracted to the blue color of the flowers.

### *A Second Chance*

The flowers, incidentally, give the bees two chances to dine. When the petals whither in late morning or early afternoon, they collapse into a gelatinous mass that remains blue but mixes with the remaining nectar. Bees love this sweet mixture and while dining on it, may leave a bit of pollen on the pistil, still erect and able to be fertilized.

Almost as odd as the flowers are the leaves, which clasp or wrap around about a half inch of the plant stem before spreading out in normal leaf fashion. If they were not so common outdoors, the exotic Asiatic dayflowers would probably be a popular and prized houseplant.

And they are common, almost ubiquitous in parts of the continent and particularly around older established properties. Dayflowers can be found growing out of cracks in sidewalks, around the bottoms of utility poles, and almost anywhere there is a bit of fairly moist soil. They can spread quickly, forming an eight- to twelve-inch-high ground cover in sunny or even somewhat shady locations, such as the edges of lawns, where they make a nice transition between the grass and shrubs. They spread easily because the stems flop over and creep along the ground, sinking new bunches of roots from their joints. (If you should use dayflowers as ground cover, keep them away from territory inhabited by delicate plants.)

Members of the small Spiderwort family (*Commelinaceae*) of twenty-five genera and 350 species, all with three-petaled flowers, dayflowers are among the few temperate-zone members of their genus and family. Named in error for another plant (*Phalangium*) that was supposed to cure the bite of a poisonous spider, most spiderworts are natives of the tropics. Only three genera have members in North America. One genus, called spiderwort (*Tradescantia*), has the unusual ability to register the level of nuclear radiation. Under exposure, the stamen hairs turn from blue to pink, the degree of change reflecting the strength of the radiation.

*Commelina* species include two common natives. Virginia dayflower (*C. virginica*), whose minipetal is blue and bigger than the Asiatic dayflower's, has a tremendous range—Pennsylvania south to Florida and Texas through Central America into South America as far down as Paraguay. The slender dayflower (*C. erecta*) has a white minipetal, but stands upright and does not flop over like its Asiatic sibling. Eight *Commelina* species live in North America, mostly in the southern states, and only the Asiatic dayflower can be expected to be found in the northern tier of states and Canada. It, too, ranges into Central America, where it is known as *hierba de pollo*, or herb of cooked chicken, a possible reference to its use as a flavoring. The western dayflower (*C. dianthifolia*) occurs in the Southwest and has a third petal that is larger and bluer than most of the others.

### *Nature's Makeshift*

Dayflower is so widespread that it can be considered a weed. The term does not mean that it is necessarily a pest or worthless. Weeds can be admirable plants, covering the soil with vegetation to prevent erosion and flooding. John Burroughs, the American naturalist, had high praise for weeds in 1881:

> *Weeds are nature's makeshift. She rejoices in the grass and the grain, but when these fail to cover her nakedness, she resorts to weeds. It is in her plan or a part of her economy to keep*

*the ground constantly covered with vegetation of some sort and she has layer upon layer of seeds in the soil for this purpose and the wonder is that each kind lies dormant until it is wanted. . . .*

*Ours is a weedy country because it is a roomy country. Weeds love a wide margin, and they find it here. You shall see more weeds in one day's travel in this country than in a week's journey in Europe. Our culture of the soil is not so close and thorough, our occupancy not so entire and exclusive. . . . The European weeds are sophisticated, domesticated, civilized; they have been to school to man for many hundred years, and they have learned to thrive upon him: their struggle for existence has been sharp and protracted; it has made them hardy and prolific; they will thrive in a lean soil, or they will wax strong in a rich one; in all cases they follow man and profit by him. Our native weeds, on the other hand, are furtive and retiring; they flee before the plow and the scythe, and hide in corners and remote waste places. Will they, too, in time, change their habits in this respect?*

Certainly the Asiatic dayflower, from a faraway continent, has found its niche in North America and is doing its best to clothe nature when and where she needs it.

## LATE SUMMER AND FALL

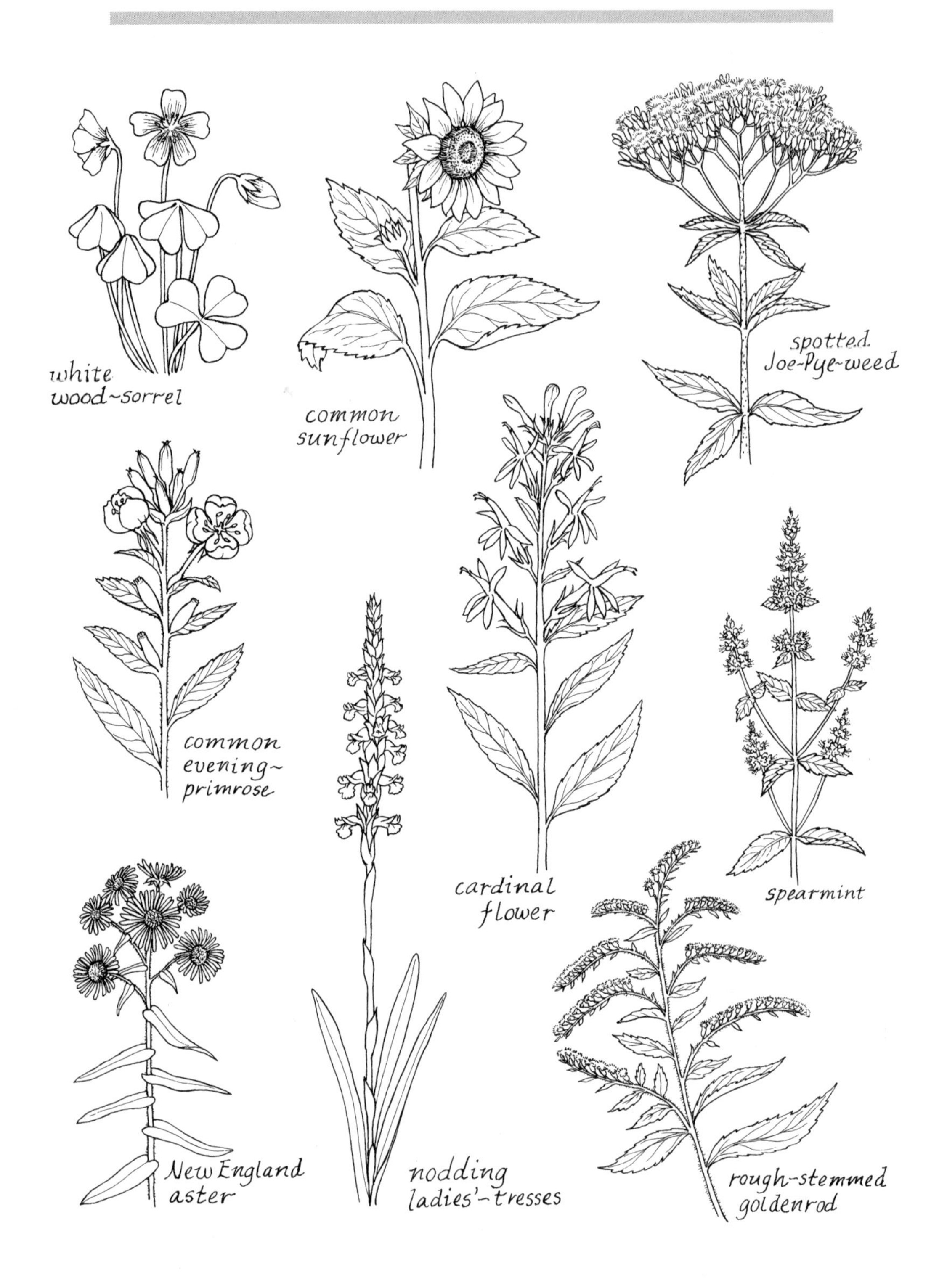

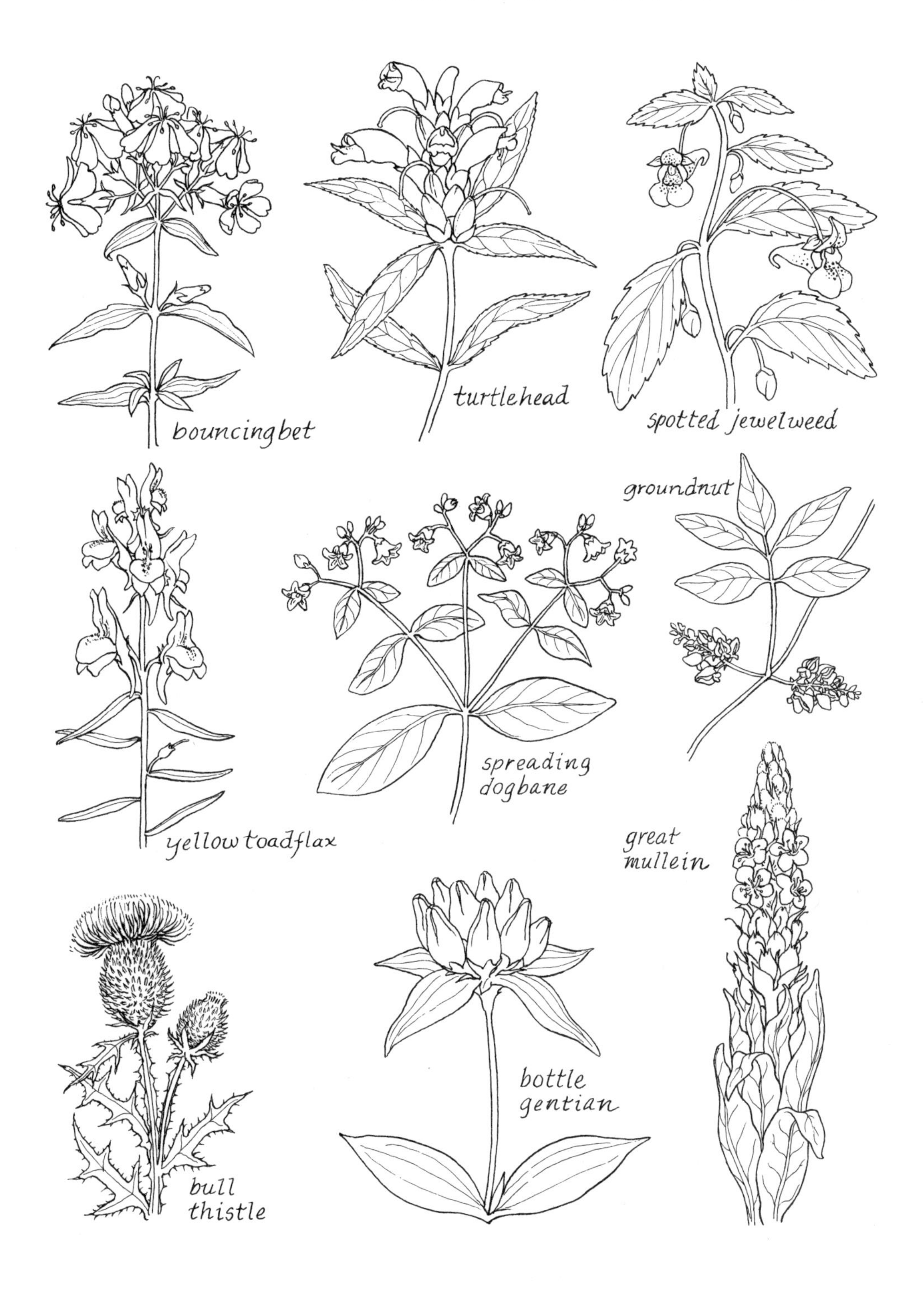
bouncingbet
turtlehead
spotted jewelweed
groundnut
yellow toadflax
spreading dogbane
great mullein
bull thistle
bottle gentian

**Pink Knotweed**
*(Polygonum pensylvanicum)*

# *It Loves the Human Foot*

Knotweeds are known by many different names, including smartweed, water-pepper, and persicary. One is even called smartass. But the names I like best—names that recall friendly, old, ramshackle farmhouses—are doorweed and doorgrass.

"[Knotgrass] carpets every dooryard and fringes every walk, and softens every path that knows the feet of children, or that leads to the spring, or to the garden, or to the barn. How kindly one comes to look upon it! . . . It loves the human foot, and when the path or place is long disused, other plants usurp the ground." Thus John Burroughs spoke of *Polygonum aviculare*, common knotgrass, one of the many polygonums that inhabit North America and much of the world.

The Germans called it W*egtritt* or literally "path step," for these plants are so often underfoot. Like flies, mice, and roaches, they seem to follow humans wherever they go. Unlike vermin, however, they are not necessarily pests—except to the finicky gardener who does not see or appreciate their miniature beauty when the plants invade the flower or vegetable beds.

Polygonums are a widespread and botanically elementary genus of more than 100 species worldwide, and some 70 on this continent. Everyone has seen them, though few people bother to notice them, much less learn their names, because the flowers are so small. As Burroughs urged, however, "Examine it with a pocket glass and see how wonderfully beautiful and exquisite are its tiny blossoms."

## *Tiny Flowers*

In most polygonum species, the flowers are pink; a few species have whitish or greenish flowers. Although they are but an eighth of an inch or less long, they are often clustered in groups of from a few to fifty or more. Thus, their pink color, sometimes bright and rich in hue, often stands out nicely against the green foliage of leaves and nearby grass. Their color is especially appreciated because, in many areas, the polygonums and Deptford pinks are about the only common pink wildflowers in the late summer or autumn. And since they thrive in hard, well-packed soil, such as paths, they are often the only vegetation that will color the more downtrodden parts of our planet.

If you take Mr. Burroughs's advice and inspect the flower cluster closely, you will find the vast majority of the blossoms closed, as if they were all just buds. One or two flowers at a time among the dozens in spikes or scattered around the plant will open up, usually at random and without order. When they finish blooming, the polygonums do not wither away. Instead, the five-part, petal-like calyx closes back up and a black-shelled, elliptical seed case begins growing inside the flower, still pink and budlike outside. Thus, a cluster of knotweed flowers can be a collection of buds, blossoms, and seed-hiding calyxes, all looking alike from a distance and retaining their color for weeks. These clusters may be the source of the name knotweed—the flowers appearing to be so many little knots.

### *Buckwheats*

Polygonums are members of the Buckwheat family (*Polygonaceae*) of some forty genera and 800 species around the world, including rhubarbs and docks. Buckwheat itself (*Fagopyrum esculentum*) may be found throughout the northern United States and in much of southern Canada as an escape and as a descendant of cultivated plants brought over from Europe. Americans have for years been fond of buckwheat pancakes, a traditional winter meal made from its grain. The Russians are fond of buckwheat honey. The Chinese, Hindus, and Japanese have long cultivated this central Asia native. The English, however, grew it only as food for pheasants.

Many kinds of birds, especially game birds and waterfowl, eat knotweed seeds. *Aviculare* means "of the birds," and the plant has been known as birdgrass, birdweed, and goosegrass for centuries. Probably from seeing how birds sought out the knotweeds, American Indians collected the seeds to add to others to grind into flour. Many polygonum species also offer a nectar that attracts bees, and beekeepers consider the genus an important honey source.

Because most of these plants are a foot or less tall, the nectar stores of polygonums are subject to attack by ants and other pedestrian insects that are not apt to pollinate flowers. Consequently, many species have evolved effective defenses. For example, the long-bristled smartweed (*P. cespitosum*—"of the ground") has long white hairs situated just below the spike of flowers or intermixed with the bottom few blossoms. These hairs discourage crawlers from passing to the flowers above.

### *Characteristic Sheath*

In this species and many others, distinctive sheaths wrap around the junctions of each stem and stalk, almost like tape that is holding the two together. In the long-bristled smartweed and in some others, long hairs project from the top edge of the sheath, again discouraging crawlers.

Common knotgrass does not have these hairs since its flowers produce no nectar to attract insects. Instead, it fertilizes itself to create seeds. Nonetheless, the flowers carry the necessary equipment for cross-pollinating, in case an indiscriminate insect pays a visit. Its reproductive systems obviously work well, for the plant is an annual, relying on the seeds for the survival of the species.

Though it has few flowers, common knotweed has many names. Aside from the three previously mentioned, it has been called bird's tongue or sparrow tongue because of the shape of its little leaves; allseed, because it was, like its cousin buckwheat, used as a grain; armstrong, because it's hard to pull up from invaded gardens; pigweed, pigrush, swine's grass, hogweed, and cowgrass, because livestock eat it; centinode, ninety-knot, and nine-joints, because of its characteristic stem joints; red robin because of its flowers; beggar grass, because it usually inhabits poor soils; wild buckwheat, because of that cousin; and wire weed, because it's wiry.

Swamp, or shoestring, smartweed (*P. muhlenbergii*) is a peculiar polygonum that also does not need the services of bees. This species relies so much on its pervasive shoestringlike roots to spread its numbers that it rarely puts forth many flowers. In fact, acres of these wetland plants may be seen in season without a single flower. The species is named for the Rev. Heinrich

Muehlenberg, a minister who was also a noted naturalist. His name is more commonly seen in connection with an endangered turtle, called Muhlenberg's, or bog, turtle.

Another common variety is Pennsylvania smartweed or pinkweed (*P. pensylvanicum*), whose pink clusters on one- or two-foot stems are found around house foundations, paths, and roadsides from the Atlantic to the Rockies. "Its erect pink spikes direct attention to some neglected corner in the garden or brighten the field or roadside," wrote Mrs. William Starr Dana.

Throughout spring and early summer, long-bristled and Pennsylvania smartweeds are low, barely noticeable weeds. In mid-August, however, they stand up and show off their colors—in the process growing over plants that are past flowering. I have grown long-bristled smartweed in a spot reserved in the spring and early summer for daisies, black-eyed Susans, yarrow, and hawkweeds. The smartweed gains height just in time to surround and cover over the unattractive dying or dead remains of its predecessors.

### *Smarting Weeds*

Smartweeds have been put to less decorative uses. Russians have experimented with and used various smartweeds for tanning leather and for feed grain, going so far as to irradiate the seeds to increase the percentage of protein in them. Because of its high nitrogen content, Pennsylvania smartweed has been recommended by agricultural experts as an excellent fertilizer for poor soils; it is grown and then plowed under.

The name smartweed comes from the bitter taste of the leaves of some species. One of the smarting smartweeds you are apt to see around pond edges is often called mild water-pepper (*P. hydropiperoides*—"water-pepper-like"), one of our common native species. Amphibious swamp smartweed (*P. coccineum*) can live on dry land, on land sometimes submerged, and in water with its leaves floating. The terrestrial form, often seen around summer-dry drainage ditches, has striking stems striped with crimson or scarlet (*coccineum*). This native plant possesses a characteristic of many polygonums—swollen joints where the leaves join the stem. Hence, the generic name, *polygonum*, which means "many knees." Some authorities feel that these joints are the source of the "knots" of knotweed.

Several polygonums are called tearthumbs (such as the arrow-leaved tearthumb, *P. sagittatum*—"arrowlike") because they have rows of tiny prickles on their leaves and stems. If rubbed across the skin, the prickles might make a weak scratch, but hardly a true tear.

Though most polygonums are low-lying plants, one species is a giant, reaching ten feet in height. In fact, the Japanese knotweed (*P. cuspidatum*) is so big and bushy that it is often mistaken for a shrub. (This edible but often bothersome plant is covered in Japanese Knotweed: An Oriental Invader.)

*P. persicaria*, another common weed and an import from Europe that is found coast to coast, is edible as a salad green and was once used to produce a yellow dye. It is called lady's thumb, either because the spike of flowers bears some resemblance to a woman's fingernail painted with polish or because the leaves carry a design that some people thought looked like a delicate thumb print. Its specific name, *persicaria*, means "peachlike," and many polygonums were formerly classified under a genus, *Persicaria*, because their leaves resemble those of the peach tree. Though it was not native, lady's thumb quickly spread across the continent and was so established by the late nineteenth century that American Indians in the Midwest were using it to treat stomach ailments.

### *A Medicine Chest*

Among the most interesting and widely known of the polygonum clan is *P. hydropiper*, another European immigrant, which has a myriad of names and medicinal uses. Its folk names include water-pepper (the translation of the

Latin name), biting persicaria, bity tongue, ciderage, red knees (the color of the joints), bloodwort, snakeweed, redshanks, sickleweed, and pepperplant.

Packaged for each of its traditional herbal uses, this water-pepper could probably fill a pharmacist's whole shelf. In various solutions, it was used to treat epilepsy, gravel, dysentery, gout, mouth sores, dropsy, jaundice, colds, coughs, and bowel complaints. It was also used as an antiseptic and a stimulant. Extracts of the plant were applied to ulcers and hemorrhoids (hence, two of its more earthy folk names, arsesmart and smartass).

According to the "doctrine of signatures," because water-pepper had joints, it should be used to treat sore and swollen joints. "It is very good for sciatica, gout, or pains in the joints, or any other inveterate disease," said Culpeper, "if the leaves are bruised and mixed with hog's grease and applied to the place, and kept on four hours in men and two hours in women, the place being afterwards bathed with wine and oil mixed together, and then wrapped up with wool or skins, after which they sweat a little." Another signature found on many polygonum species is spotted leaves; these leaves were used to doctor pimples and acne.

Americans treated cholera by wrapping the patient in a sheet soaked in water-pepper tea. Mexicans used it as a diuretic and for rheumatism. People who believed that a certain kind of worm caused earaches used to apply a few drops of the juice to the ear as a cure. Some herbals recommended the plant for getting rid of fleas, and maintained that chewing the leaves would eliminate toothaches—perhaps because the irritation it would cause to the mouth would divert attention from the tooth.

There are even more ailments for which it was used, but suffice it to say that among practitioners of folk medicine, this polygonum was a staple. Even equestrians of old found the plant useful. If the plant was placed under the saddle, a horse would be able to travel faster than usual without stopping for food or water. At least, that is what the ancient Scythians believed. Pity the horse!

**White Wood-Sorrel**
*(Oxalis acetosella)*

# *The Sour Wood-Sorrels*

A television commercial for mail-order houseplants once offered a package of seemingly exotic varieties, including one billed as the amazing Prayer Plant. Its amazing quality was the fact that its leaves folded up at night, somewhat in the shape of hands folded in bedside prayer. Yet, anyone who has ever weeded a shady garden has probably run across a plant that has the same amazing characteristic, but is so common that it is more pest than blessed.

Yellow wood-sorrel has three-part, cloverlike leaves that fold up each evening. According to Charles Darwin, who studied wood-sorrels extensively, the action protects the plant from the cold by mutual radiation—not unlike the old New England custom of bundling. Other authorities add that it provides security against excessive collection of dew that might break the fragile leaf stalks. Wood-sorrels are plants of shady ground, and the leaves will also fold up if they are exposed to direct sunlight. In this case, their position of prayer protects the thin leaves from excess heating and from too much transpiration, the loss of moisture through evaporation. Variations in the intensity of the sunlight will cause the plant to vary the amount of leaf exposure to the sun. In daytime rain or too much cold, the leaves will also fold up, and people in rural England used to use the folded leaves during the day as a signal of an approaching storm or shower.

How does the wood-sorrel make food through photosynthesis if it shuns the sun? Much of its food making takes place in the spring and the fall, when the leaves are off the trees, but when the angle of the sun's radiation is not as strong as in summer. In addition, it has been found that the carbon dioxide content of the air near the ground in a forest is about twenty-five percent higher than that of open ground. Both sunlight and carbon dioxide are used in the process of assimilation—the plant's incorporation of nutrients through photosynthesis—and the extra carbon dioxide is said to make up somewhat for the lower light level.

Wood-sorrel flowers come in many colors, including yellow, white, pink, and violet. The plants are members of their own little family (*Oxalidaceae*), very closely related to the Geranium and Flax families, yet not even closely connected with the true sorrels (*Rumex*). The only similarity with *Rumex* may be the sour taste of the leaves, believed to be a defense against snails and other little herbivores.

That taste explains both its scientific and common names. The generic name, *Oxalis*, is from the Greek for "sharp" or "acid," while sorrel is from the French, *surelle*, or Low German, *suur*, both meaning "sour." It is not surprising that they are sour, since they contain potassium binoxalate, a salt of oxalic acid related to chemicals used to clean car radiators, bleach wood, and whiten clothing. In fact, in Europe the plant was once collected to make an oxalic acid extract, called Salts of Lemon, which was used as a stain remover. Country folk employed the acidic leaves to curdle milk and make junket.

### *Salts of Lemons*

White wood-sorrel (*Oxalis acetosella*), with white petals veined red or deep pink to guide insects, has been used for such varied ailments as heartburn, liver disorders, fevers, and mouth ulcers; it was once an ingredient in a popular spring tonic. Because its leaves are heart-shaped, herbalists used it to treat cardiac ailments. "[It is] effectual in hindering the putrefication of the blood," wrote Nicholas Culpeper. "It quenches the thirst, strengthens a weak stomach, stays vomiting, and is excellent in fevers."

Peter Kalm found *O. acetosella*, a European native, in the woods of Quebec in 1747. The species has spread in northern North America, but it is not as common here as it is in Europe. *Acetosella* is from the Latin word for vinegar, and many people find the vinegar-flavored leaves a tasty addition to salads. The plant has also been boiled like spinach, cooked like applesauce, baked with butter in a pot, turned into a rhubarblike pie, and simmered into soup.

Modern herbals, however, generally warn against consuming too much of the plant, which in excess can cause hemorrhaging, diarrhea, and kidney damage. It can also upset the calcium balance in the blood stream, and inhibit the body's ability to absorb calcium for bones. To someone susceptible to the gout, even a little can cause a flare-up. There are reports that cows have been made ill and sheep have died from eating wood-sorrel. "It is recorded that the milk of cows after having eaten it is with difficulty converted into butter," wrote John Hutchinson.

White wood-sorrel, which blossoms in spring and summer, was popular not only as a medicine and tonic, but also as a decorative plant—both Fra Angelico and Botticelli placed it in the foreground of some of their paintings. They and other Christian artists considered it a wonderfully symbolic plant, with the cloverlike leaves representing the Trinity and the red-stained flower symbolic of Christ's death on the cross.

Some believe that white wood-sorrel is the true shamrock, an ancient Druidic symbol that St. Patrick employed to explain the Trinity when he arrived to spread Christianity in Ireland in 432. A half-dozen plants found in America and Europe are also called shamrock, however, and at least one authority says that it is the least hop clover (*Trifolium dubium*) that is the true shamrock. In England, white wood-sorrel has also been called cuckoo-sorrel and cuckoo's meat because it was believed that bird ate the plant to clear its voice or because flowers appeared in the season that the cuckoo was most full of song. Monks knew it as halleluia flower because it blooms around Easter in England. The Welsh named it fairy bells, believing that its bell-like flowers summoned elves to moonlit revelry. English country folk called it green sauce because they made a sauce, said to improve the appetite, by mushing the leaves. (British naturalist G. H. Copley found the leaflets to be "a most beautiful pale green. I know of no leaf in which this shade is more perfectly brought out.") Other old names include trefoil, wood-sour, stubwort, and cuckoo bread and cheese.

White wood-sorrel bears normal flowers and cleistogamous flowers. The latter, produced near the ground, look like buds, but they never open and they have no odor, nectar, or entrance for bees. Yet they self-fertilize and bear seeds, particularly in the early spring when insects may not be available to pollinate. To guarantee against excessive inbreeding, the plants also bear normal insect-attracting flowers later in the season.

## *Lowly Siblings*

Its lowly siblings, yellow wood-sorrels, are represented by more than a half-dozen species. Among the most common may be *Oxalis stricta* and *O. europaea*, both of which look much alike and are called simply yellow wood-sorrel. They are considered annoying weeds, managing to creep into any fertile and fairly moist plot of land. Because they are so delicate, they are easily picked. They are nonetheless hard to eradicate, however, for in picking them, one usually leaves behind the roots that are not so delicate and quickly shoot up new plants. Yellow wood-sorrel has found its way into salads and into the cold summer drinks of those whose palates enjoy its acidic touch. They are also called sheep-sorrel, poison-sheep-sorrel, toad-sorrel, sour grass, and ladies' sorrel.

Redwood sorrel (*O. oregana*) is a rose-ink variety found in redwood forests from California to Washington.

The *Oxalis* genus has some 31 species in all parts of North America, and some 600 species worldwide, many of them weedy. Exotic varieties of *Oxalis* from the Falkland Islands, Bolivia, Mexico, southern Australia, and other southern areas are sold as garden flowers. One such plant is named Bermuda buttercup, despite being a native of South Africa. No doubt the Prayer Plant advertised on television was an *Oxalis*, bigger-leaved than our common varieties.

The oca (*O. tuberosa*), a tuberous variety found in the high Andes, is as important a crop as the potato in parts of Peru and Colombia. Before being eaten it is dried in the sun for several days to remove the calcium binoxalate.

**Spotted Jewelweed**
*(Impatiens capensis)*

# *Nature's Toy and Salve*

Hey, Dad, wanna look for poppers?"

When he was three or four years old, my son asked that question several times during the summer. Since he had been barely able to walk, Ben had hunted poppers in our backyard, and later his younger brother Mike joined in the quest for these entertaining toys of nature.

Poppers, a word coined by Ben, are the energetic little pods of the jewelweed. The seeds are wrapped in an ingenious case which, when mature and disturbed, suddenly pops as the covering lets go like an uncoiling spring. The action sends the seeds flying as far as four or five feet. No wonder the plant is also known as touch-me-not and no wonder it is so widespread.

Some people say jewelweed is so called because the colorful orange flowers dangle like earrings or pendants from the plant. Others say it is because the edges of the leaves, when wet with dew or rain, hold tiny drops of water. "[They look like] scintillating gems, dancing, sparkling in the sunshine," wrote Neltje Blanchan. "It is, indeed, a jewel," said William Hamilton Gibson. "Upon the approach of twilight each leaf droops as if wilted, and from the notches along its edge the crystal beads begin to grow, until its border is hung full with its gems. It is Aladdin's lantern that you set among a bed of these succulent green plants, for the spectacle is like a dream land."

### *Poison Ivy*

Jewelweed is most famous as a balm to relieve the itching caused by poison ivy. I have found that it both relieves the itch and helps to clear up the rash, and many other people have had equally good results. It is also supposed to prevent the rash from breaking out if you have touched the plant, apparently by attacking and dissolving poison ivy's oil before it can adhere long enough to cause blistering.

To make a jewelweed solution for poison ivy, pick leaves, stems, stalks, flowers—any part of the plant—and put them in a large pot with enough water to cover the vegetation. Stuff in as much as you can fit. Boil the plants until the color of the water becomes deep orange. This may take a half hour to an hour, depending on how much vegetation you have in the pot. Bottle and refrigerate the liquid. The decoction may be preserved for long periods by freezing it. When you have a case of poison ivy, just spread the fluid on the irritated area.

If you have a good supply of jewelweed in the yard, simply rub freshly picked leaves or, better, crushed stalks on the irritation. Ironically, jewelweed is often found growing with or near poison ivy since both plants like similar situations, semishade and rich, moist soil.

Various American Indian tribes put the plant to extensive use as a skin salve, treating athlete's foot, other fungi, and all sorts of itches in general. The Nanticoke of Delaware also made leaves into a poultice for wounds. The juice of the jewelweed was used by our ancestors to dye wool yellow, and the leaves were eaten as a pot herb.

### *Hummingbird Heaven*

Though people with the itch have long been fans of jewelweed, its biggest admirer is the ruby-throated hummingbird, which thrives on these flowers in midsummer. In fact, nature—more precisely, evolution—has designed the flowers to be pollinated by the bill of the hummingbird, which picks up the grains of white pollen from just inside the top front of one flower and deposits them on the inside top of the next.

Bumblebees, which also frequent these flowers, rarely pollinate them and cannot reach to the back to collect all of the nectar. Some bees and wasps of sneaky bent will chew through the back of the flower to rob the nectar without even coming near the pollen.

In many places, hummingbirds are not common. Jewelweed can produce seeds anyway because it has cleistogamous flowers. In fact, Charles Darwin found that in England, where this native American was taken and spread, only about one in twenty plants put out showy flowers; there are no hummingbirds in England and bees are unlikely to pollinate the flowers there. This two-flower characteristic of jewelweed led to its former specific name, *Impatiens biflora.*

*Impatiens* is a genus of succulent herbs that has about ten other native members in North America, and more than 200 species worldwide, mostly in the mountains of Africa and Asia. Spotted jewelweed may be found in most states east of the Rockies, and in the Pacific Northwest to Alaska. Among the more common of the other species is the pale touch-me-not (*Impatiens pallida*), which favors northern climes and is common in southern Canada. The genus, in turn, belongs to the tiny Touch-Me-Not family (*Balsaminaceae*), which includes only one or two other genera.

### *Pick a Name*

Jewelweed's most commonly used scientific name is misleading, and two other names have been employed right up to modern times. For more than 150 years, spotted jewelweed was known in most botanical circles as *Impatiens biflora.* The generic name is an allusion to the easily triggered seedpods, as if they were impatient to do their job. Most, but not all, authors now refer to the plant as *Impatiens capensis.* The specific name here has the meaning, "of the Cape of Good Hope." Also, several authors refer to the plant as *I. fulva*, a name that dates from 1818; *fulva* means "tawny," referring to the flower's color.

Why would botanists, who had a perfectly good name in *Impatiens biflora*, use one recalling the southern tip of Africa more than 8,000 miles from the plant's homeland? The Brooklyn Botanic Garden provided the answer: "The name *I. capensis* was published by Meerburgh in 1775, thirteen years earlier than Walter's *I. biflora.* It has priority of publication and is therefore the correct name. Meerburgh described it from material cultivated in European gardens. He mistakenly thought it had been introduced from the Cape of Good Hope. The International Code of Botanical Nomenclature, in the interests of stability, does not permit changes in the specific epithet merely on the grounds that it is 'inappropriate.' Thus, *Impatiens capensis* remains the correct name."

Plants in the *Impatiens* genus have picked up many folk names, including silver-leaf, speckled jewels, silverweed, silver cap, slipperweed, ladies'-slipper (from the slipperlike shape of the flower), snapweed, quick-in-the-hand, ear-jewel, pocketdrop (as in a watch fob), ladies' ear-drop, wild or brook celandine, solentine, snapdragon, shining-grass, cowslip, weather-cock (pods burst in the wind and leaves wilt in the hot sun), kicking-colt, and wild balsam (the old-fashioned balsam of nineteenth-century gardens is in the same genus, though the flowers are completely different in shape). According to eighteenth-century botanist Peter Kalm, the American Indians called it a crowing cock because of its shape.

Names like silverweed and shining-grass come from an interesting characteristic of the plant. If you turn a leaf upside down and dip it in water, it will take on a silvery or shiny appearance, probably because some coating on the surface holds a thin film of air.

### *It "Evaporates"*

Jewelweed's blooming season in the Northeast is generally from mid-July to mid-September, although in years with mild winters, flowers—both showy and cleistogamous—will be out in middle to late June. The plants quickly wilt and die at the first appearance of cold weather; in fact, anything below 40 degrees Fahrenheit seems to do them in. Because such a high percentage of this succulent plant is water, once jewelweeds die, they quickly dry up and there is virtually no sign of them a few weeks later, almost as if they had evaporated.

It is no surprise then that jewelweed likes moist ground and is especially common around streams and woodland ponds, although it will sometimes spread into fairly dry shaded areas where its growth will be stunted. In ideal conditions, plants will grow almost five feet tall, even though the roots are short, relatively thin, and would seem to be unable to support such height in a plant. The trick is its hollow stem, a design at once light and strong.

Although the root systems are not very extensive, it is somewhat difficult to transplant jewelweed. If you should want to try it, use small, young plants and put them in wet, loose mulch. The best way to introduce them is by seeds, which you literally catch. Cup your hand around the quarter-inch pod and touch it. The pod will explode and shoot the seeds into your hand. Only the mature pods will pop, but it will not take you long to recognize which ones are ready to fly. Place the seeds into moist ground. If you do it early enough, the plant could mature and produce more seeds in the same season.

### *A Warning*

Be forewarned, however. Once, after I had written a newspaper column about jewelweed, I quickly heard from an irate wildflower gardener who cursed the existence of this plant, which had overrun some of her nicest flowers. Indeed, jewelweed is a mover and a rabbitlike reproducer, so keep it in areas where it will not spread into your finer flowers.

The plant can be fairly easily eradicated if it becomes a pest. Just pull it out of the ground before it goes to seed; the small and shallow root system is easy to extract.

Jewelweed makes a nice annual hedge and mixes well with blue flags, nightshades, and certain woodland sunflowers that are not intimidated by its numbers. Of course, it is always handy to have around for first aid in case you run into some of that all-too-common but often unnoticed poison ivy.

**Yellow Avens**
*(Geum aleppicum)*

# *Both Blessed and Cursed*

Few people recognize plants in the *Geum* genus, but many people notice their seeds after a walk in fields or woods. Avens relies on mammals—from woodland wildlife to humans—to spread its population. The fruits appear in summer, usually as little green clusters of seeds. At the end of each seed is a tiny hook that grabs on to fur or clothing to get a free ride to a new home. "Whoever spends an hour patiently picking off the various seed tramps from his clothes after a walk through the woods and fields, realizes that the by-hook-or-by-crook method of scattering offspring is one of Nature's favorites," wrote Neltje Blanchan.

The hooks are actually transformed styles. The style connects the pollen-catching stigma to the seed-producing ovaries in the pistil. In most plants the style withers away after fertilization, but in the avens it becomes stronger and develops into a hook. I once heard the inventor of Velcro report that he got his inspiration for the device after a walk in the woods when he observed how some hooked seedpods—quite possibly a species of avens—had attached themselves to his clothing.

## *Natural History*

The genus *Geum* comes in several common and distinct varieties in North America, including white avens (*Geum canadense*), also called redroot; rough avens (*G. virginianum*,) which has cream-colored flowers; yellow avens (*G. aleppicum*), probably the most common species; purple or water avens (*G. rivale*), perhaps the best known; large-leaved avens (*G. macrophyllum*), a yellow-flowered variety widely found in the Pacific states; prairie smoke (*G. triflorum*), an odd-looking variety with bell-shaped pink flowers found in the sagebrush plains of North America; and bennet (*G. urbanum*), a native of England that is now found on this continent.

Most avenses are small flowers, about the size of a nickel, and bear five rounded petals and a bushy green center that later becomes the seed cluster. There are some fourteen species across North America, most favoring cool climates. Showier species are found in Europe and South America; the hybrids of these avenses have become garden flowers.

The flower has the aspect of a wild rose, which is not surprising since it is a member of the Rose (*Rosaceae*) family. Other members of the Rose family, like wild strawberries, blackberries, and cinquefoils, are closely related to avenses and have similar-looking flowers. In most cases, these plants are low or shrubby while avenses run two to three feet tall and are quite herblike or, as some would say, weedy looking.

The small flowers and weedy habits of this perennial have left the avens clan ignored by many modern wildflower writers. Yet the genus is rich in history, both botanical and ecclesiastical.

### *Folklore*

Known to the ancients as a medicinal herb, avens was called by the Romans *avencia*, a word whose origin is obscure and that meant simply "avens." *Geum*, the generic name, is from the Greek, *geno*, which means "to yield an agreeable fragrance" or possibly from the Greek, *geuein*, which means "to give a taste of." Either origin would probably stem from the fact that, when pulled from the ground, especially in the spring, the roots of some species give off a clovelike scent.

Perhaps because of the fragrance, the plant was worn as an amulet. *Ortus Sanitatis*, a medieval guide to good health published in 1491, maintained, "Where the root is in the house, Satan can do nothing and flies from it, wherefore it is blessed before all other herbs, and if a man carries the root about him, no venomous beast can harm him." If you think that superstition is far-fetched, try this one: In an article in *The American Botanist* in 1918, Lucinda Haynes Lombard reported that some people believed that friends who held in their hands the leaves of avens were able to converse telepathically over many miles.

In America and in England, *G. urbanum* is called bennet or herb-bennet. These terms are a corruption of either *Herba benedicta* "blessed herb" or "St. Benedict's herb." The latter name was applied to several plants used as antidotes. According to legend, the name comes from St. Benedict, who founded the Benedictine order of monks. A fellow monk once gave a cup of poisoned wine to St. Benedict, but as the saint blessed the drink, the poison—likened to a devil—flew out of it with such power that the cup disintegrated, thus disclosing the murder plot.

Most avenses bear leaves of three. In medieval times, these leaves and the five golden petals of the blossoms symbolized the Holy Trinity and the five wounds of Christ. By the fourteenth century, the plant was often used as an architectural decoration for church columns and walls.

### *Medicinal Uses*

Avenses, particularly *G. urbanum*, have been used to treat diarrhea, sore throats, skin afflictions, agues, bronchial catarrh, and fevers. "The root in the spring-time, steeped in wine, doth give it a delicate flavor and taste, and being drunk fasting every morning, comforteth the heart, and is a good preservative against the plague or any other poison," said Culpeper. Bennet has been used to remove freckles, treat bad breath, and flavor beer and ale, including Augsburg ale. It is also supposed to preserve such drinks.

Our own *G. rivale*, which has similar constituents, was once well known across America as Indian chocolate because its roots were used to concoct a drink that looked somewhat like hot chocolate, though its taste was more like that of cloves. Mixed with sugar and milk, it was used for dysentery, colics, stomach problems, as well as many of the ailments listed above. It was also commonly called throatwort from its uses as a gargle.

**Spearmint**
*(Mentha spicata)*

# *An Old and Lively Scent*

Spearmint is better known as a chewing-gum flavor than as a wildflower. Without its odor, the plant would hardly be noticed at all. Only two dozen or so species of flies and a few desperate bees visit the tiny flowers of *Mentha spicata*. Yet its aromatic leaves have earned spearmint a fame that began before Christ and extends until today, when it is still popular as an ingredient in many forms of food and refreshment.

Mints are a large family of 3,200 species in 160 genera worldwide. The genus *Mentha* has 30 species; about a dozen of these species can be found in the United States and only one of them is native. *Mentha*, the Latin, and *Minthe*, the Greek, are words based in mythology. Minthe was a sweetheart of Pluto, but like many relationships, it led to trouble. Proserpine, Pluto's properly jealous wife, turned Minthe into the plant that bears her name.

Wrote Ovid:

*Could Pluto's queen, with jealous fury storm*
*And Minthe to a fragrant herb transform?*

She could. What's more, "Proserpine certainly contrived to keep her rival's memory fragrant," said Neltje Blanchan. "But how she must delight in seeing her under the chopping knife and served up as a sauce!"

Indeed, spearmint is usually the variety of mint used in concocting mint sauce or jelly, a condiment that is almost as much a part of a lamb dinner as cranberry sauce is of a turkey dinner. A popular recipe for mint sauce calls for mixing two tablespoons of chopped fresh spearmint, one-half tablespoon of sugar, one tablespoon of warm water, and the juice of two lemons. So long have such sauces been used with lamb that one of the plant's common folk names is lamb mint. Its use for flavoring seafood dishes earned it two other names, mackerel mint and fish mint.

### *Paying Tithes*

Before Christ, the Pharisees were paying tithes with mint, anise, and cumin. "In Athens, where every part of the body was perfumed with a different scent, mint was specially designated to the arms," reported Maude Grieve.

Virgil maintained that deer injured by hunters sought out spearmint to heal their wounds, but Gerard warned that injured men should not consume it because "whoever eat mint when wounded will never be cured." The Romans, who introduced it into Britain, cultivated spearmint for food preparation (Ovid recommended scouring food service platters with the green leaves), for preventing coagulation of milk, for love potions, and for an old-time Alka-Selzer—a use to which many of the mints have been put.

The Arabs and Persians were the first to use spearmint to flavor drinks. In fact, the word julep is from the Arabic, gulab, which means "rose water," another plant-flavored drink. A fine and flavorful tea can be brewed by steeping the dried leaves in hot water. Euell Gibbons liked to add a little spearmint to a tea made from the dried flowers of red clover.

Amatus Lusitanus reported in 1554 that the plant was always found in gardens. Later, Gerard wrote, "The smelle rejoiceth the heart of man, for which cause they used to strew it in chamber and places of recreation, pleasure and repose, where feasts and banquets are made." Spearmint was for centuries added to bath water "as a help to comfort and strengthen the nerves and sinews," wrote John Parkinson in 1629. "It is much used either outwardly applied or inwardly drunk to strengthen and comfort weak stomackes." Nicholas Culpeper, another herbalist, cited forty different ailments treated with spearmint, including something that would please Mr. Wrigley—sore gums. (Even today, children enjoy picking and chewing the leaves for the flavor.) But be warned: Culpeper also claimed that the plant "stirs up venery, or bodily lust."

Spearmint probably first arrived with the Pilgrims. It is mentioned in a list of plants brought over to Plymouth, demonstrating the esteem in which it was held. Although a native of southern Europe and Asia, the plant was widespread in America by 1739 when a botanist found it growing wild in various parts of Virginia, suggesting that it had also been popular in early colonial gardens. Its general popularity prompted one of its most common titles, garden mint.

### *Carvone*

Mint has been used to whiten teeth, to perfume soaps, flavor toothpaste, cure chapped hands, and relieve stings. "Mice are so averse to the smell of mint, either fresh or dried, that they will leave untouched any food where it is scattered," Mrs. Grieve maintained. Pennsylvanians used to pack bundles of spearmint with their grain to keep out rodents.

Spearmint should be picked just before it blooms in August or September. The herbs should be hung in bunches and once dry, the leaves are then removed and ground into a powder. The powder can be stored and used as needed, or it can be mixed with corn sugar syrup to form a basis for various mint sauces.

So popular was spearmint as a flavoring that by 1930 some 50,000 pounds of it was being grown annually, primarily in Michigan and Indiana. Ten to twenty pounds of spearmint oil could be obtained from an acre of plants. Though its flavor is as popular as ever, the plant itself is not consumed commercially as much as it used to be because carvone, the oil in spearmint that creates the attractive flavor, is now being produced synthetically and more cheaply from waste orange and grapefruit peels.

In North America spearmint is a weed, a garden escape that will grow almost anywhere that is moist enough. Like its sibling, wild mint (*M. arvensis* or *canadensis*), it favors moderately shady situations, but will survive in full sun if the ground is not dry. The plant propagates by sending out underground runners that produce new plants, forming colonies. Although the plant is difficult to start from seed, acquiring spearmint for your own garden is easy, once you have found a colony. Just dig up several plants and move them to your yard. They normally grow about two feet in height.

A warning, however. Like wild mint, spearmint can become a nuisance, spreading like a weed into parts of the garden where it is not wanted. If you introduce it, either select a spot where it can spread without causing problems, or set up borders around the plants. The border can consist of one-by-six-inch boards buried upright, bricks placed end-up, or fairly deep stone. Spearmint also does well in boxes.

Another possible problem with spearmint is a form of rust, peculiar to mints and for which there is no cure. Afflicted plants should be pulled up and destroyed to prevent the disease from spreading.

### *Many Names*

Among the many names applied to spearmint over the centuries are common mint, sage of Bethlehem, brown mint, Our Lady's mint, green mint, spire mint ("spear" and "spire" refer to the plant's tall, narrow shape), and St. Mary's herb. Some authors list it as *Mentha viridis*, a name applied by the noted American botanist, Asa Gray. However, most modern authorities call it *M. spicata.* The specific name means "spike," again referring to the shape.

If you have spearmint, plan to have it, or have access to it, you might want to try this old-fashioned mint punch: Pick a quart of fresh spearmint leaves, wash and dry them, then mash them till soft and cover with freshly boiled water. Set aside for ten minutes. Strain, cool, and chill. Add two cups of cold grape juice plus lemon juice to taste. Mix in sugar till sweet enough and add a quart of ginger ale. Spike it with what you wish, if you wish.

But watch out for venery.

**Cardinal Flower**
*(Lobelia cardinalis)*

## *America's Favorite*

America's favorite. That is how Roger Tory Peterson described the most stunning of our midsummer bloomers. Found along streams and in moist pastures, cardinal flower shocks passersby with its brilliant red.

Mr. Peterson's evaluation, contained in a field guide almost void of comment, has a sound basis. In the 1940s, Dr. Harold N. Moldenke, curator and administrator of the herbarium at The New York Botanical Garden, surveyed more than 1,000 botanists and naturalists throughout North America, asking them to list the dozen most showy, conspicuous, and interesting wildflowers in their regions. More than 500 people responded, and the tally left little question as to which was the favorite. Cardinal flower, *Lobelia cardinalis*, amassed 213 votes, while showy lady's slipper received only 155.

"There is no other wild flower which approaches it in color," said F. Schuyler Mathews, who studied floral colors in the late nineteenth century. Some people have said that the name was inspired by the native bird, but even our handsome cardinal does not match the flower in the brilliance and magnificence of its fire-engine red. The name almost certainly came from the color of the vestments of the princes of the Roman Catholic Church. Ironically, the first European garden to have a blooming specimen of this plant belonged to one Cardinal Barberini in seventeenth-century Rome.

The North American native had arrived in Europe in 1626, collected by John Tradescant, who was sending back plants for the botanical gardens of England. Once it was discovered, cardinal flower quickly became a popular addition to the gardens of wealthy Europeans who coveted and collected exotic flowers of the new lands being opened up by explorers and traders.

### *Survival*

Today, however, cardinal flower may be counted among our uncommon and perhaps endangered wildflowers. Its beauty is so captivating that the unknowing or thoughtless admirer is tempted to pick it—and too often does. Overpicking can spell disaster for the cardinal flower. The seeds have a good germination rate, and the plant tends to be a short-lived perennial that relies a good deal on its seeds for survival.

Cardinal flower does, however, have another method of spreading. The mother plant sends out little shoots that, in their first year, rise only as basal rosettes of leaves. The next year, these shoots mature to flowering plants three to four feet high. Left alone, a fairly good-sized colony can establish itself by shoots and seed.

Because they are such attractive plants, cardinal flowers are in considerable demand. Naturally, they should not be picked or transplanted. The best way to obtain them is by collecting seeds from the wild, or acquiring seeds, rootstock, or plants from a reliable nursery. For all their exotic beauty, cardinal flowers are not particularly fussy about soil pH or richness. It is essential, however, that the ground be moist and the location fairly sunny. Cardinal flower's usual haunts are stream sides and wet meadows. Some authorities have found the plant sensitive to winter kill, perhaps in the northern reaches of its range, and it is said to do best in ground that does not freeze hard. I have seen a ten-year-old plant growing alongside a subdivision house—right next to the downspout of a roof gutter that apparently provided the kind of dampness it wanted.

### *A Blue Sibling*

Great lobelia is more common and hardier than its sibling, cardinal flower. It has striking deep blue flowers that blossom in late August and September. The rather tubelike flower is about an inch long and has an upper and a lower lip. The upper lip is divided into two petals while the bottom has three petals marked with white. This shape has prompted some botanists to suggest that lobelia may be an important evolutionary link between the simpler tubelike flowers and the more complex and advanced Composites, which usually have a center disk of tubular florets surrounded by florets that have turned into rays. Lobelia petals, experts say, are on their way to becoming rays. In fact, botanists have classified lobelias just below the Composites, reflecting a high degree of evolutionary development.

Some botanists believe that blue is at the high end of the evolutionary progression of floral coloring, which started with green, then went through phases of white and yellow, then developed reds, and finished at bright blue. Blue attracts bees best, and it is probably no coincidence that bees are among the most highly evolved of the insects.

The beauty, size, and hardiness of great lobelia have made it popular with some gardeners here, and with more in Europe. Lobelias are easy to start from seed and to transplant, and though they look rare, they are not.

Great lobelia is named *Lobelia syphilitica*, a rather unattractive title reflecting its former use as a treatment for syphilis. It was also a medicine for dropsy, diarrhea, and dysentery.

### *Indian Tobacco*

Indian tobacco (*L. inflata*) is a small-flowered species common east of the Rockies. The plant was once widely known as a medicinal herb. Even though grazing animals will not touch it because of its acrid taste, and the plant sometimes proves poisonous, quacks of the last century concocted potions from it because it was believed that anything that set the insides on fire was beneficial to health. Even serious physicians used Indian tobacco for all sorts of ailments and more modern experts suspect that the plant's narcotic effect may have been the actual cure. In the last century, one odd herbalist named Samuel Thomson was so enamored of its powers that he used the plant to treat almost any ailment and succeeded in poisoning one of his own patients. He was arrested for murder, but got off by maintaining the victim was simpleminded for having taken such silly medicines as ram-cats, well-my-gristle, and Indian tobacco in the first place. The court did not seem to mind that all of these medicines had been prescribed by Thomson himself, an herbal example of *caveat emptor*—let the buyer beware.

American Indians were perhaps more skilled at its use, and employed it to treat sore eyes, breast cancer, and coughs. The Creeks used it to ward off ghosts, and the Meskwakis considered both red and blue lobelias as magical, especially when used as love potions. As its name suggests, Indians also smoked the leaves as well as chewed them, and it is said the effect was to induce drowsiness. About its only real value was as an emetic, whence it picked up such unappetizing names as vomitroot, puke weed, and gagroot. "If yer ever wants to get rid of what's inside yer," a Canadian farmer told an interviewer in 1879, "jist make a tea of lobelia leaves and I'll bet my team of hosses out there it'll accommodate you."

### *Bellflowers*

Cardinal flower, great lobelia, and Indian tobacco are members of the genus *Lobelia*, which is named after Matthias L'Obel (1538–1616). L'Obel was a Flemish botanist and herbalist who became physician to James I of England and was known as Lobelius. The genus has about 30 species in North America, mostly east of the Rockies, and some 250 species worldwide. It is a member of the Lobelia subfamily (*Lobelioideae*) of the small Bellflower, or Bluebell, family (*Campanulaceae*), which is said to have some twenty genera and more than 600 species worldwide, including exotic tropical and mountain plants. Among the many lobelias that appear in summer is one that provides a rare example of humor, or at least punning, in a plant name. The native *L. spicata*, which is among the tallest of the genus, is called the highbelia.

### *Red Lobelia*

Cardinal flower is also called red lobelia, red Betty, slinkweed, and hog's physic. It is reported to have many of the same chemical properties as the popular medicinal species, but has seen limited use as a medicine, perhaps because of its beauty. It was once employed as a nervine and some American Indians rid themselves of worms by eating it. Cherokees, however, used it instead of great lobelia in a concoction to treat syphilis. The plant may be found from New Brunswick to Florida and west into Texas and Colorado, and parts of California. Great lobelia has about the same range, though it is not found as far west.

Red is a color that is particularly attractive to hummingbirds. (One friend of mine had a hummingbird come right up to inspect the red flower print on her dress as she was sitting near her garden one day.) Cardinal flower's shape, a long tube at the bottom of which is a pool of nectar, is well suited to this long-billed, hovering bird. The flower's reproductive organs, the pistil and stamen, project from the mouth of the flower tube so that they will touch the head of the visitor. In great lobelia and most other species, these parts are tucked safely inside to touch only bees that can climb in.

It has been said that the relative rarity of hummingbirds is due to the relative rarity of red flowers, or vice versa. Whichever way, both hummingbirds and red flowers are much more common in tropical America than they are in temperate regions. However, if you can gather in your garden cardinal flowers, bee balm, trumpet flowers, and jewelweed (or such cultivated varieties as nasturtiums, salvia, gladioli, red phlox, and verbenas), you are apt to have one or more of those fascinating birds as a regular visitor or even a resident of your yard.

A plant endowed with so much beauty has, to no one's surprise, won the praises of almost every writer of natural history, not the least of whom was John Burroughs. "The cardinal [flower] burns with [an] intense fire, and fairly lights up the little dark nooks where it glasses itself in the still water," he wrote. "One must pause and look at it. Its intensity, its pure scarlet, the dark background upon which it is projected, its image in the still darker water, and its general air of retirement and seclusion, all arrest and delight the eye. It is a heart-throb of color on the bosom of the dark solitude."

At least a half-dozen other writers have noticed the beauty of the flower reflected in nearby water. Justice Oliver Wendell Holmes put it into poetry:

*The cardinal, and the blood red spots*
*Its double in the stream:*
*As if some wounded eagle's breast*
*Slow throbbing o'er the plain,*
*Had left its airy path impressed*
*In drops of scarlet rain.*

**Bouncing Bet**
*(Saponaria officinalis)*

## *Some Soap with Bounce*

Many of our most abundant summer wildflowers are natives of Europe that were brought over to fill colonial gardens, or that snuck over with crop seeds. Bouncing bet falls in the first category, and it was probably used for both practical and decorative reasons. Today, however, few gardens display its pinkish blossoms. Like so many other imports, bouncing bet has run wild and become a weed, growing along railroad tracks, along roadsides, around parking lots, and in other waste areas. Just like human immigrants, it found much freedom in America.

The one- to three-foot-tall perennial bears clusters of five-petaled phloxlike flowers, whose color was described by F. Schuyler Mathews as "the most delicate crimson pink imaginable—a tint so light that we might call it pinkish white." Unfortunately, because the plants are often found in dusty waste places, the flowers frequently turn out to be dirty pink.

## *Purpose of Color*

The natural color has a purpose. The petals are attached to a long tube, at the bottom of which is a pool of nectar. Only a creature with a long tongue can easily reach the pool. While light pink is not particularly attractive to butterflies, which have long tongues but which are usually drawn to brighter colors, the shade is perfect for attracting the large sphinx and other night-flying moths. It is no accident that the flower's scent is strongest just after sunset.

That sweet, almost spicy scent is responsible for one of bouncing bet's more unusual folk names, London pride. It is said that the plant's nocturnal perfume helped mask the unpleasant odors of sewerless London in centuries past.

*Saponaria officinalis* is a member of the Pink family, which includes such common summer plants as evening lychnis, ragged-robin, catchflies, and campions. Within the genus *Saponaria* are about three dozen species, all natives of Europe, Asia, and northern Africa. Bouncing bet is the type species, the only one found in North America, and certainly the most widespread variety of the genus. On this continent it can be found in just about every state and province.

## *Cleaning Up*

*Saponaria* is from the Latin word *sapo*, soap. The plant is usually called soapwort in England, where it was probably introduced by the Romans. One of its constituents is a juice called saponin, a glucoside that appears when the leaves are bruised. Saponin not only produces suds, but also dissolves oils, fats, and grease. Farmers—and it was around farms that the plant was most often found wild—would use the leaves as soap, whence such names as latherwort, bruisewort, scourwort, crowsoap, soaproot, and soapwort gentian. A decoction obtained from the root has been used as an ingredient in homemade toothpastes and shampoos.

The plant was called *herba fullonum*, fuller's herb, by Medieval monks who used it to clean cloth. A fuller was someone who increased the weight and bulk of cloth by such techniques as shrinking, beating, and pressing. Well into the nineteenth century, North American fullers were using bouncing bet as a cleaning agent, and they often planted fields of it near their mills. Today, long after the fulling mills have disappeared, bouncing bet plant is still found around old mill sites. It is also common along old canals because the immigrants who worked their boats in the 1800s often planted it along the banks for a ready soap supply, wherever they were.

Centuries ago, brewers would slip some of the juice of bouncing bet into their beer, to improve the frothiness of the head. Brewers still do that kind of thing today, but use more modern head-builders.

Like so many other plants of old-time gardens, bouncing bet served as a medicine as well as a decoration. As might be expected, it was used as a skin wash for the likes of dermatitis, itching, poison ivy rashes, and tumors. Gerard said it would "beautifie and cleanse the skin." It has also been used as an expectorant for respiratory congestion, as a cure for venereal diseases such as syphilis and gonorrhea, and for treating jaundice. However, most modern authors warn of the poisonous or at least very irritating effect of saponin on the stomach. Cows and other livestock avoid it as well as its sibling, cow cockle (*S. vaccaria*), which has been known to make animals ill.

Bouncing bet is a widespread August bloomer. As Neltje Blanchan remarked, "A stout, buxom, exuberantly healthy lassie among flowers is the bouncing bet." Naturalist John Burroughs appreciated its name and admired its "feminine comeliness and bounce." Actually, bet is a version of "betty," an old term for a laundress, and is supposed to reflect a resemblance of the flowers to a washer-woman, seen from the rear as her flounces bounced while she scrubbed the clothes up and down the washboard—presumably in a solution of soapwort.

The plant has also been called sweet betty, hedge pink, old maid's pink, Boston pink, chimney pink, sheepweed (from its pastoral settings), wild sweet William, lady-by-the-gate, wood's phlox, mock-gilliflower, and dog's cloves.

Bouncing bet multiplies by producing many seeds and by forming colonies via thick underground runners. If your wildflower garden or yard is in need of some bounce, you can easily transplant it. Or, if you would like more refined flowers, several cultivated double-flowered varieties of *Saponaria officinalis* are available in either pink or white.

**Indian Pipe**
*(Monotropa uniflora)*

## *Ghosts of Summer's Woods*

There is something eerie about seeing a cluster of Indian pipes, flowers downturned, on a warm summer day. They are ghostly and pale; their flesh is freakish; they look more like some oddly formed fungus than wildflowers.

Because of their unusual appearance, Indian pipes are once seen, never forgotten. I can remember finding them as a child on Nantucket Island and being told their name. Indian pipes, daisies, black-eyed Susans, dandelions, and violets were probably the only wildflowers I could name till well into adulthood.

Indian pipes are white or bluish white (rarely pink or red), almost leafless plants bearing a single five-petaled flower that, when young, tilts downward. The shape of the plant resembles a clay pipe whose stem has been stuck in the earth, and the flower is not unlike the bowl. This albino of the flowering plant world is, surprisingly, loosely related to dogwoods, heaths, and even evergreen laurels and rhododendrons.

Scientists call it *Monotropa uniflora*, meaning "once-turned" and "single-flowered." "Once-turned" refers to the fact that the flowers, which are at first bent down, turn straight upward once they begin producing seeds (though you'd think the plant would be straight first and bent second, in order to spill out the seeds). Indian pipes are one of our few native wildflowers that can be called transcontinental. They range across southern Canada and into Alaska, then south to Florida and California, then even farther south into Mexico. In most areas they appear in midsummer.

Indian pipe is a member of a tiny genus of only three or four species. Only it and pinesap are found in North America. Another member inhabits such faraway places as Japan and the Himalayas (where our own Indian pipe may also be found). Still another, called bird's nest, is found in Britain and Europe.

*Monotropa* is in turn a member of the Wintergreen family (*Pyrolaceae*), a small clan of only ten genera in North America, their chief habitat. They include the equally unusual pinedrops and beech-drops.

## *The Saprophytic Plant*

Indian pipe is strange not only in appearance, but in habit. It is a saprophyte (from the Greek, "rotten plant"), living chiefly on the decaying roots of other plants, particularly trees. Indian pipes are most often found near a dead stump in deep woods, although they will sometimes pop up in a lawn near dead tree roots. They favor beech woods, but will live in other areas, and it is said that the best time to find them is after a heavy, soaking midsummer rain.

Some botanists believe that the roots, working in symbiosis with certain soil fungi such as mushrooms, also obtain food from live tree roots, which would make the plant a parasite as well as a saprophyte. If this is true, Indian pipe certainly has a small enough appetite that it can do no harm to large trees, most of whose roots are well beyond its reach. Most authorities, however, now believe *Monotropa* species are parasitic only on the soil fungus that helps them get food and water from the rotting vegetation. As Alastair Fitter observes in *New Generation Guide to the Wild Flowers of Britain and Northern Europe*, species like yellow bird's nest (*M. hypopitys*) have turned the tables on the usually parasitic fungi, and live off a fungus without apparent benefit to the fungus.

Since the plant obtains all the nutrients it needs from other plants via the cooperating fungus, it requires neither leaves nor chlorophyll, both of which it has lost during the process of evolution. The only remaining vestiges of leaves are the white, scalelike appendages on the stems.

The plant cannot be picked for display—not that anyone would want it as a decoration—because its flesh turns black and oozes a clear, gelatinous substance when it is cut or bruised. These unattractive characteristics have earned Indian pipe some unflattering names, like ghost flower, corpse plant, and American iceplant. Another name, though, is pretty—fairy-smoke.

"This curious herb well deserves its name of corpse plant, so like is it to the general bluish waxy appearance of the dead," wrote Dr. Charles F. Millspaugh. "Then, too, it is cool and clammy to the touch, and rapidly decomposes and turns black even when carefully handled."

"It is the weirdest flower that grows, so palpably ghastly that we feel almost a cheerful satisfaction in the perfection of its performance and our own responsive thrill, just as we do in a good ghost story," said Alice Morse Earle.

## *For Bright Eyes*

Its use as a medicine has earned it other names. Indians employed it as an eye lotion—whence the name, eyebright—as well as for colds and fevers. Americans of the last century treated spasms, fainting spells, and nervous conditions with it, giving rise to the names convulsionroot, fitroot, and convulsionweed. Mixed with fennel, it was once also used as a douche.

Dr. R. E. Kunze, writing more than a century ago in *The Botanical Gazette*, told this story:

> *Fourteen years ago—it was in the early part of July—I went woodcock-shooting with two friends, near Hackensack, New Jersey, and while taking some luncheon in a beech grove along the course of Saddle River, I found a large patch of ground literally covered with* Monotropa uniflora *in full bloom; it covered a space some five feet wide by nine feet long, a beautiful sight of snow-white stems and nodding flowers. Being in need of some just then, I proceeded to fill my game-bag; and to the question, what it was used for, answered: 'Good for sore eyes'; little thinking that the party addressed was suffering from a chronic inflammation of the eye-lids, the edges of which had a very fiery-red appearance. No sooner said than he proceeded to take in his game-bag a supply also, and he made very good use of it, as I ascertained afterwards. His inflamed lids were entirely cured in four weeks' time, and he has had no further trouble since, by applying the fresh juice of the stems he obtained while it lasted.*

## *Whose Pipe?*

Its common name comes, of course, from the shape of the plant and probably from the fact that it was first known as an Indian herb. However, naturalist F. Schuyler Mathews disliked the name. "Why should it have been named Indian pipe?" he wondered. "It occurred to me once, when I was climbing the slopes of South Mountain in the Catskills and came across a pretty group of the ghostly Indian pipes, that they were wrongly named; they should have been called the Pipes of Hudson's Crew. Those of us who have seen the ghostly crew in [Washington Irving's] Rip Van Winkle can easily imagine the gnome-like creatures smoking pale pipes like these." Perhaps Mathews did not know that the plant has also been called Dutchman's pipe.

It is difficult to start Indian pipe from seed because the plant requires precise conditions, including the decaying matter it feeds on and the fungus with which it coexists. Clarence and Eleanor Birdseye (yes, the frozen-foods folks) wrote a book, *Growing Woodland Plants*, in which they said it is virtually impossible to transplant because its delicate root system is intermixed with the humus and other decaying material in the ground. One can try by digging up a big shovelful from soaking-wet ground, and moving it to a hole lined with wood compost, they said. However, even if it succeeds and reappears the next year, odds are such tamed Indian pipes will not have the charm they do in the wild.

## *Bad Press*

Indian pipe has gotten some bad reviews from nature writers who prefer showier plants. Explaining its colorless and parasitic qualities, Neltje Blanchan wrote a lengthy attack, including: "No wonder this degenerate hangs its head; no wonder it grows black with shame on being picked, as if its wickedness were only just then discovered. . . . To one who can read the faces of flowers, as it were, it stands a branded sinner."

However, a nineteenth-century poet named Mary Thacher Higginson offered the following pleasant description of these unusual plants:

*In shining groups, each stem a pearly ray*
*Weird flecks of light within the shadowed wood,*
*They dwell aloof, a spotless sisterhood.*
*No Angelus, except the wild bird's lay,*
*Awakes these forest nuns; yet night and day,*
*Their heads are bent, as if in prayerful mood.*
*A touch will mar their snow, and tempests rude*
*Defile; but in the mist fresh blossoms stray*
*From spirit-gardens, just beyond our ken.*
*Each year we seek their virgin haunts to look*
*Upon new loveliness, and watch again*
*Their shy devotions near the singing brook;*
*Then mingling in the dizzy stir of men*
*Forget the vows made in that clustered nook.*

From a wicked degenerate to a saintly nun: These are the extremes of human imagination.

**Stinging Nettle**
*(Urtica dioica)*

# *Our Stinging Friends*

Nothing is all bad, and even a wildflower varmint with a name like stinging nettle has its virtues. In fact, this almost worldwide weed has been used for food, clothing, medicine, and even as a salve for its own stings.

Various plants are called nettles, but the true nettles (*Urtica*), especially the stinging nettle (*U. dioica*), all bear hypodermiclike hairs on leaves, stems, and flowers that can deliver painful stings. Some 30 species of *Urtica* exist worldwide, and the genus is so well known that it has lent its name to its family (*Urticaceae*), which includes about forty genera and 600 species, most of them with stinging hairs. The Nettle family in turn is closely related to both mistletoes and hemps, including the infamous marijuana.

A native of Asia that favors waste places, *U. dioica* made its way to Europe and then to America, and is now distributed coast to coast. It spreads quickly by underground runners, and can become a pest by sneaking into gardens. Stinging nettle is not attractive or showy; the summer-blooming flowers are small and green, and are not likely to invite a curious, unknowing hand—unless it is that of a gardener weeding. This drab plant offers little warning of the stings that await the person who brushes by or pulls it.

Though dull in color, the flowers are interesting in design. They are either male or female; sometimes, both appear on one plant, but usually a whole plant is either one sex or the other, whence the name *dioica*, which means "two houses." What insect would be attracted to such a dull-looking flower? Except for specialized caterpillars that love its leaves, probably none, for the nettle does not need any creature to transfer its pollen. When the male flowers open, the coiled pollen-bearing anthers suddenly spring loose, firing pollen into the air. It thus casts its fate to the wind and, it hopes, to the awaiting pistil of nearby females.

The seedpods that result from the union are sticky and apt to get caught up in fur or clothing, so they are easily transported to new localities.

## *Food and Clothing*

Although they would seem pure and simple pests, nettles have had almost as long a history of helping people as of stinging them. Long before flax was introduced, Germans and other northern Europeans were using nettles to make fine silklike cloths, as well as coarser items such as sails, sacks, fishnets, twine, and even a high-quality paper. The word "nettle" is said by one authority to stem from the old Germanic root, *ne* or *na*, meaning "to sew or bind." (It may also have come from the German or Dutch words for "needle," because of the stingers.) Before World War I, the Germans were harvesting up to 60,000 tons a year to produce clothing for their soldiers.

The Scots have long been fans of the nettle. Complaining that the English ignored the plant, a poet named Campbell once wrote, "In Scotland, I have eaten nettles. I have slept in nettle sheets, and I have dined off a nettle tablecloth. The young and tender nettle is an excellent potherb. The stalks of the old nettle are as good as flax for making cloth. I have heard my mother say that she thought nettle cloth more durable than any other species of linen." Nettle pudding, a traditional dish in Scotland, was made of plant tops, leeks, onions, oats, sprouts, and seasoning, and served with butter or gravy.

The young shoots and cooked leaves, rich in Vitamins A and C plus protein and iron, have for centuries been used as a food in Europe; boiling or drying removes the sting and acidic irritants. In his diary in 1661, Samuel Pepys reported visiting a friend who served some very good nettle porridge. Nettle beer was popular once in the British countryside. Even an herb wine can be made from it, reports Nelson Coon, whose recipe includes leaves of nettles, dandelions, burdock, plus peels of lemons, tangerines, and oranges, with the usual sugar, yeast, and water. The Swedes used dried nettles as fodder to improve the milk and butter of cows and make horses "smart and frisky," wrote C. S. Rafinesque in 1828. He added that the seeds make "good food for fowls and turkeys," and in humans they are "said to cure goitre and excessive corpulence."

A medicine since ancient times, stinging nettle has served as an astringent, diuretic, tonic, and a galactagogue (an agent that encourages milk production in mothers, both among humans and cattle). Nettle tea was consumed to ease the pain of rheumatism. Urtication, a rather odd treatment for rheumatic or paralyzed limbs, consisted of flogging the affected arms and legs with nettle plants to stimulate them. While the practice has disappeared, the word remains, now meaning any sensation of stinging or itching.

Quick to enjoy the benefits of imports, the Mohegans, Iroquois, and other tribes ate the greens. As the nettle moved west, the Chippewas and Ojibwas discovered it and started treating urinary disorders and dysentery with the plant.

If you should ever try any of these concoctions, take warning from the Latin name, which comes from the word "to burn." The hairs are said to contain formic acid, the same substance that red ants use in their sting. Wear gloves when harvesting nettles, or you may be wearing Band-Aids—unless you believe the sexist, old English rhyme:

*Tender-handed touch a nettle,*
*And it stings you for your pains,*
*Grasp it like a man of mettle,*
*And it soft as silk remains.*

If you get stung, rub alcohol, juice of jewelweed (see Jewelweed: Nature's Toy and Salve) or juice of dock on the skin for relief. In one of his tales, Chaucer quoted an old country adage, "Nettle in, Dock out." Ironically, the juice of nettle is an antidote for its own sting and, according to Maude Grieve, "affords instant relief."

Also called hokey pokey and devil's leaf, stinging nettle has been widely used in magic. In parts of England, it was employed to drive the devil away. Pulling a plant up by the roots while uttering a sick person's name was supposed to cure a fever. Blowing through a hole in a nettle leaf into a youngster's eye would improve poor eyesight—but the blower had to be a "woman who had never seen her father."

Nettles have also been called naughty man's plaything. While first day of April is now known as April Fool's Day, the last day of April in Ireland was called Nettlemas-night. Boys would go about after dark, carrying bunches of nettles and trying to sting one another. Also, wrote Marcus Woodward, "Young and merry maidens availed themselves of the privilege to sting their lovers, with the best of goodwill, a noteworthy way of warming affection."

Perhaps there is more to this custom than meets the eye, for Galen, a Greek physician who lived more than 2,000 years ago, claimed that the nettle seeds mixed with wine were a treatment for impotence and would "excite to games of love."

Another reason to be careful in the garden?

**Great Mullein**
*(Verbascum thapsus)*

## *Wonderful Weeds*

Weeds they are—common around the world, often found in places where little else will grow. Nonetheless, mulleins are wonderful weeds, both in form and in utility. Mulleins are represented in North America chiefly by two plants: great mullein, known for its leaves, and moth mullein, known for its flowers.

Great mullein, the more common of the two, has become so famous over the centuries that it has developed more than forty folk names and a long list of uses, from a torch to a hair color restorer. Practically everyone has seen great mullein, although few people know its formal name or its reputation as anything but a weed. A tall plant of from five to eight feet in height, it bears thick, velvety, grayish leaves that have earned it such names as ice leaf, Our Lady's flannel, Adam's flannel, beggars flannel, velvet dock, blanket herb, velvet plant, woolen, feltwort, fluffweed, and hare's beard. Because of its stance, it has been called shepherd's club, Aaron's rod, Jacob's staff, or Jupiter's staff (depending, no doubt, on caller's religious persuasion).

### *Hag's Torch*

The genus has been appreciated since ancient times. It was said that Ulysses used great mullein, long believed to ward off evil spirits, to protect himself against the wily Circe.

The Romans and subsequent civilizations dipped the dried plant in fat and lit it. These torches, called *candelaria*, were often used in funeral processions and other ceremonies. Later civilizations that used mullein in this manner called the plant high taper, hedge taper, torches, and candlewick plant.

The colorful name, hag's taper, may have come from the belief that witches used mullein to illuminate sinister ceremonies. Some people say the name was sparked by the taper's use to repel hags, and others maintain hag is just a corruption of the Old English, *haege*, meaning "hedge."

The down on the leaves and stems was once gathered as tinder; when dry, it would ignite at a spark.

Great mullein has for centuries been used to treat diseases of the lungs, earning it the names lungwort and ag-leaf. Europeans, colonial settlers, and many groups of American Indians smoked the dried leaves to obtain relief from coughs due to consumption and asthma, though one wonders how smoke could ameliorate breathing problems.

"The seeds, bruised and boiled in wine and laid on any member that has been out of joint, and newly set again, takes away all swelling and pain," wrote Nicholas Culpeper. The *Ladies' Indispensable Assistant* in 1852 said steeped mullein "is good for a lame side, and internal bruises." The leaves were used to relieve soreness; like flannel, they were rubbed on rheumatic joints, the gentle friction creating a soothing warmth. The plant was also used for diarrhea, colic, piles, gout, mumps, toothaches, ringworm, burns, migraines, earaches, and warts, and even for removing slivers.

Of all the medicinal and cosmetic forms of mullein, none is more noted than mullein tea, used for coughs and colds, or simply as a tonic. In England, it is concocted by mixing a cup of boiling water with a teaspoon of leaves that have been dried and powdered. Euell Gibbons recommended cough syrup made from red clover, white pine, mullein, and wild cherry bark. Before you run out and brew some tea or syrup, though, be aware that cows and other grazing animals shun mullein because its hairs are irritating to the mucus membranes. To be safe, the tea should be filtered through fine muslin or a similar material.

## *Exotic Uses*

The plant had some rather exotic uses, too. The seeds, considered somewhat narcotic, were thrown into water to intoxicate fish and make them easier to snare. Figs and other fruits were wrapped in its leaves to prevent rotting, a use that has led to some modern speculation that mullein contains an antibiotic, inhibiting the growth of various bacteria. The velvety leaves were placed inside socks or shoes to warm the feet and increase circulation—and perhaps to act as a sort of natural Odor Eater.

From the yellow flowers, Roman women obtained a dye to give them blond hair. The plant's ashes were made into a soap that was said to restore gray hair to its original color (possibly true, if the original color was black). "Pale country beauties rub their cheeks with the velvety leaves to make them rosy," noted Neltje Blanchan in 1900.

The spring rosettes of leaves are used today by professional flower arrangers at the base of displays. In *Using Wild and Wayside Plants*, Nelson Coon says the leaves make fine blankets for children's dollhouses. In nature, the hair has a curious use. Hummingbirds have been seen gathering the down to line their tiny nests.

One would think that with all those features, mullein would be a popular plant. It was, once. Years ago, many gardens contained great mullein to provide not only medicine, but also beauty. The statuesque plant was admired both for its plentiful yellow flowers and for its handsome foliage. In fact, it was widely grown in the British Isles and especially in Ireland around the turn of the century. "I have come 3,000 miles to see the mullein cultivated in a garden and christened the 'velvet plant,'" wrote a surprised John Burroughs, the American naturalist, on a trip to Great Britain.

## *Inhospitable Places*

Great mullein's ability to live in inhospitable places—full bright midsummer sunlight and dry, poor soil—is due in part to its ingenious design. The long leaves wind around the stem in whorls that point upward, an arrangement that captures every drop of rain possible and directs it down the stem to the thirsty roots. These roots are found both near the surface, to catch the sprinklings of showers, and deep in the earth, to collect the more consistently available bits of moisture far below the heat of the sun.

The hair that covers both leaves and stem serves several purposes. One, apparently, is to discourage animals and other creatures from eating the plant—although slugs, usually hair haters, are able to chew up mullein. The hairs also discourage crawling insects, especially ants, from making the long climb up to the flowers, where they could rob the nectar without pollinating the stigmas.

The hairs are also believed to make a barrier against the harsh sunlight that might damage the delicate cells in the leaves or simply sear the plant's flesh. The hairs may also serve as a barrier to dust particles, plentiful in the dry soils in which mullein is often found; dust might become layered enough on a leaf to prevent the cells from receiving the sunlight and carbon dioxide needed to function properly.

### *Moth Mullein*

Moth mullein is a rather different sibling whose leaves are not unusual, but whose flowers possess a strikingly delicate beauty. Field guides usually list moth mullein under yellow flowers, but this is one of a handful of wildflowers that will play tricks on you. As often as not, moth mullein's flowers will be white or even light pink. In all color forms, however, the blossom is purple toward its center, where it bears what appears to be a little ball of purple wool. This purple-on-white or purple-on-yellow combination, probably aimed at guiding insects to the nectar and pollen, is unusual in flowers of midsummer, and a roadside stand of moth mullein will easily catch and hold the eye.

Like dayflower or chicory, moth mullein opens in the early morning, but usually wilts by midday. Each blossom lasts one day, sometimes two, then drops off to leave a rounded seedpod with a long tail on it. (I've seen some blossoms open for a second day, but only after having fallen away from their connection with the plant; they were merely dangling from the seedpod tail on which they had been snagged. Unlike the proverbial chicken without its head, it was a head without its chicken!)

Like its great sibling, this mullein is a biennial that sends up a low, nonflowering rosette of leaves the first year and the tall flowering stem the second. Consequently, mulleins are prolific producers of seeds and these, obtainable later in the summer (if such birds as goldfinches do not beat you to them), are the best way to introduce the plants to your property. Particularly in the case of great mullein, transplanting is difficult because of the deep roots.

Some people believe that moth mullein is so called because it attracts moths. Other observers point out, however, that the flower is not designed for moths and that the blossoms are closed at night when most moths are about. I have seen bees and particularly pollen- and nectar-gathering flies on the flowers (which can, in a pinch, fertilize themselves), but never a moth. It is more likely that the name came from a fancied resemblance of the white or pinkish flowers to the insect. The purple hairs, which appear in tufts on the stamens and may be protection against rain diluting the nectar, could be likened to the furry body of a moth.

If the plant bloomed in large numbers and if the flowers lasted longer, moth mullein would no doubt be popular with gardeners. However, what pleases the gardener is not necessarily best for the plant. Mullein must rely on seeds to keep the species alive and therefore it produces prodigious numbers of them. To do this most efficiently, the plant puts out a few fresh flowers a day rather than many at once. It thus spreads over several weeks the effort needed to provide an attractive display for potential pollinators and to get many flowers fertilized. The pods in turn ripen successively over a period of weeks, increasing the chances for nature—via showers, wind, birds, or other means—to disperse the seeds.

Such untamed flowers are always a challenge to cultivators, who have managed to develop mullein hybrids that are available in a variety of colors and that are long blooming. Most of the hybrids are offspring of purple mullein (*Verbascum phoeniceum*), a Mediterranean species.

Mulleins are members of the genus *Verbascum*, a word that is probably a corruption of *barbascum*, from the Latin, *barba*, "a beard" (whence barber). This meaning could refer either to the hairy leaves of the great mullein or to the tufts of fibers in the center of mullein flowers of many kinds.

Great mullein is *Verbascum thapsus.* Some sources say it was named for an obscure Greek island, Thapsos, where the plant is supposed to have originated, while others maintain it refers to the city of Thapsus in the North African nation of Tunisia. (It was there that Julius Caesar defeated the partisans of Pompey in 46 B.C., reportedly killing 50,000 people.) Whatever the geographical origin of the name, the plant is widely spread around the Mediterranean and is also found in Asia and, on this continent, in all forty-eight lower states and most provinces. Its journey across North America was apparently rapid; one explorer reported in 1802 that he could not find it west of the Alleghenies, and another seventeen years later saw it growing along the Missouri River on trails frequented by westward-traveling settlers and trappers. "[It] follows closely on the footsteps of the whites," wrote Edwin James in 1819.

Moth mullein's scientific name is *Verbascum blattaria. Blatta* is Latin for "cockroach," an insect that this plant was once believed to repel. Though less common, moth mullein is equally widespread in North America.

The origin of the word mullein itself has been subject of considerable speculation. Some people say it is from the French, *melandre,* meaning "leprosy" or, generally, diseases of cattle or the lungs. The plant is sometimes called cow's, or bullock's, lungwort because it was used to treat ailments of those animals. However, other authorities say the name is from the Old French, *moll,* meaning "soft," referring to those flannelly leaves. Still other writers say that it is a corruption of the Old English *wolleyn,* meaning "woolen." The venerable *Oxford English Dictionary* suggests it might come from *molegn,* an Old English word for curds. But it doesn't say whey—oops, why.

The genus *Verbascum,* with nearly 300 species worldwide, is a member of the Figwort family, which consists of about 165 genera and 2,700 species, including butter-and-eggs, snapdragons, turtleheads, beard-tongues, speedwells, monkey flowers, betony, and louseworts. The discovery of the rare and now famous Furbish's lousewort along a river in Maine once helped halt a multimillion dollar dam project. Such respect the mulleins will doubtlessly never attain.

**Common Evening-Primrose**
*(Oenothera biennis)*

# *An Owl-like Sweet*

Some of the most parched patches of earth are home to the evening-primrose, an often overlooked but useful and decorative weed with somewhat unusual blossoms. Each four-petaled yellow flower opens handsomely to form a cross, echoed by a cross-shaped stigma. But people usually do not appreciate the flowers, much less the plants. As its name suggests, evening-primrose blooms as the sun is going down. By late the next morning, when the sun's rays have beaten down on the delicate blossoms, the flowers are a ratty collection of wilted petals.

Mrs. William Starr Dana, a turn-of-the-century writer on wildflowers, waxed almost poetic when she described the flowers' nocturnal habits. "Along the roadsides in mid-summer, we notice a tall rank-growing plant which seems chiefly to bear buds and faded blossoms. And unless we are already familiar with the owl-like tendencies of the evening-primrose, we are surprised some dim twilight to find this same plant resplendent with a mass of fragile yellow flowers, which are exhaling their faint delicious fragrance in the evening air."

Though chiefly a night-bloomer, the flower stays open a bit longer in late summer and early fall. Mrs. Dana suspected the flower's tendency to remain open for part of the following day may be due to the diminished strength of the sun as the winter solstice approaches.

Mrs. Dana and others suggest that the plant's internal clock was designed to set forth flowers by night because day-flying insects would not pollinate them. The service is instead provided chiefly by the pink night-moth and many miller and sphinx moths, attracted to the plant both by the lemony scent and the color, a yellow that is striking to the eyes of night-flying insects. Occasionally, a moth will even be found sleeping in daytime within the tent formed by the wilted evening-primrose petals.

For Burroughs, who did not mind pulling himself out of bed for a sunrise stroll, the evening-primrose was a "coarse, rankly growing plant; but, in late summer, how many an untrimmed bank is painted over by it with the most fresh and delicate canary yellow." And Neltje Blanchan added: "Like a ballroom beauty, the evening-primrose has a faded, bedraggled appearance by day. . . . But at sunset a bud begins to expand its delicate petals slowly, timidly—not suddenly and with a pop, as the evening primrose of the garden does."

## *Sunlight Battery?*

Some botanists of a century ago believed that the flowers of evening-primrose were unusually visible at night because the petals were phosphorescent, able to produce light if stimulated by some source. Writing in 1894, Charles Millspaugh said that technically speaking, the petals did not generate light, but merely stored sunlight absorbed during the day. He compared this process to that occurring in calcium sulfide (obtained from crushed oyster shells), which was used at the time for luminous clock faces. Modern authorities do not seem to mention this luminous quality so it may have been imagined by the nineteenth-century beholders.

Its fragrant breath is apparently produced inconsistently. Naturalist John Burroughs observed, "Our evening-primrose is thought to be uniformly sweet-scented, but the past season, I examined many specimens, and failed to find one that was so. Some seasons, the sugar maple yields much sweeter sap than in others; and even individual trees, owing to the soil, moisture, and other conditions where they stand, show a difference in this respect." A Dutchman named Hugo de Vries, who lived from 1848 to 1935, was interested in that variability. de Vries was suspicious of Darwin's theory that all changes in species occurred exceedingly slowly, requiring thousands of years. He studied some 50,000 evening-primrose plants and the hundreds of thousands of flowers they produced, and very occasionally discovered odd blossoms, such as ones that were much bigger or smaller than usual, or that bore more or fewer petals. He found that in breeding these errant forms together, the unusual characteristics survived. He called the variant forms mutants and their different characteristics mutations. Thus, he theorized, major changes in evolution could be caused suddenly by these occasional accidents of nature.

## *Contradictions*

Evening-primrose's name seems full of contradictions. The plant is neither a rose nor a primrose, but an evening-primrose, a botanical family all of its own that is not even closely related to either of the other two clans.

The derivations for primrose do not fit evening-primrose. "Prim" is from *primus* or *primula*, Latin for "first," because some true primroses bloom early in the season—usually in April—and are among the first garden-type flowers to appear. "Rose" is probably not a reference to the flower. The Old English word for primrose was "primrole" or "pryme rolles," which was a corruption of the French, *primevere*, which meant "first of spring." Evening-primrose, though, begins blooming in July, reaches its peak in August, and can bloom into early October.

The Evening-Primrose family (*Onagraceae*) consists of about forty genera and 400 species distributed worldwide, but mostly in the Americas. Although only thirteen genera are known on this continent, the evening-primrose genus, *Oenothera*, alone has at least 100 species living in North America, mostly in the central and western states and Mexico. Our common evening-primrose (*Oenothera biennis*) is common and widespread, found coast to coast, from southern Canada south. Most evening-primroses are yellow- or white-blossomed, though one beautiful species—the rose sundrops (*O. rosea*) of the Southwest—is rosy purple. In the West the better-known varieties often inhabit sandy locations, such as deserts and beaches, and many are called primroses instead of the more accurate evening-primrose.

Like the common name, the plant's scientific name has ancient roots. One authority said that *Oenothera* is Greek for "wine-scenting," because the roots of the plant were once used for that purpose. Another authority said it means "wine-hunting" or "wine-drinking" and referred to another, apparently similar plant eaten to create a desire for wine (just as peanuts or olives are eaten by some people for that end). There is also a story that the plant dispels the effects of too much wine. *Biennis* means "biennial," which the plant is.

Other English names include night willowherb, four-o-clock, king's cure-all, feverplant, scurvish, wild beet, and scabish. As is apparent from some of the names, the plant was used in folk medicine, especially as a cough treatment and for skin irritations. Although the French in Quebec as well as some American Indians such as the Ojibwas considered it excellent for healing wounds, the plant seems to have been largely ignored by other American Indians. Modern science, though, is delving into the possible values of evening-primrose. Since the 1960s, Yugoslavian researchers have been experimenting with the oil from the seed, finding it rich in essential fatty acids (EFAs) and using it as a treatment for burns and other skin wounds. Scientists in England in the 1970s were looking into using a seed extract to prevent heart attacks by reducing the blood's ability to clot. Researchers in Europe and Canada were also finding this extract of some help to multiple sclerosis patients.

### *Sweet and Nutritious*

Mule deer and pronghorns are especially fond of evening-primrose, and many kinds of birds seek the plentiful seeds. Humans have also appreciated evening-primrose as a food. The plant was first transplanted to Italy and then, by 1614, to England where it is still cultivated as a garden and food plant. First-year roots were boiled to create a dish described as both nutritious and sweet, with a taste similar to that of parsnips, though it is said that if the roots are not pulled at the right time, the flavor can be peppery.

Both the French and the Germans used the young shoots in salads, and the Germans treated it like scorzonera, a European vegetable. In fact, this native American plant was once so popular among Germans that an American writer on gardens called it German rampion in an 1863 book.

Though it is called wild beet, that name probably reflects the shape of the biennial's first-year root more than its taste. It is fat and round, full of food stored to give it strength to send up the flowering plant in the second year.

If you want to taste the plant, find some of these first-year roots, peel them, boil them in two changes of salt water, and serve them with butter. Several authors even recommend evening-primrose french fries (peel, boil twice, dip in batter, and pan fry).

If their taste does not interest you, you can always wait until the plant forms dried seedpods, which have long been popular for decorations in flower arrangements and herb wreathes.

### *Hardy*

The common evening-primrose is a hardy plant, able to survive in unpleasant places and preferring dry, sandy soils—perhaps this is why so many others of the genus are widespread across the dry plains and deserts of the West. I once found a sizable plant growing in about two inches of sand on top of a large roadside culvert; the thick root crept inside that thin coating around the pipe for about two feet until it could wind its way down into more substantial soil, still sandy and only sometimes wet during the summer.

That ability to live where the water only occasionally appears is typical of such species as *O. clavaeformis*, which is found in desert washes. Almost all members of the genus require sandy soil, whether it is in the desert, the suburbs, or along an ocean beach.

Even in the common evening-primrose, which usually lives in sandy soils far from deserts, the root appears to have the ability to store water for quite a spell. In this connection, it is interesting to note that the evening-primroses are only a couple of families removed from the Cactus family.

The evening-primrose sows so easily that the simplest way of obtaining some for your backyard is to gather the seeds in September and October and plant them. New plants should self-sow for years afterward. Since evening-primrose is a biennial, it takes two years to get a mature plant from seed. The first-year plant consists only of what Ms. Blanchan called "exquisitely symmetrical complex stars"—the basal rosette of leaves.

Of course, unless you are a night person, a sunrise walker, or a lover of parsnips, you may not want to bother with such a coarse, rank creature.

**Japanese Knotweed**
*(Polygonum cuspidatum)*

## *An Oriental Invader*

There it stood, nearly five feet tall, bushy, and loaded with sweet-smelling, tiny white flowers. The kids and I had watched it grow from the day in the spring when we first noticed its asparaguslike shoots at the edge of our road. Now, in late August, it was big and spreading and unlike anything I had seen before.

What was this mysterious plant?

There were clues. One of the first things we had noticed about the plant was its hollow stems. When it was little more than several shoots, two feet or so high, the boys had broken one and, noticing the empty middle, stuffed a stick into it. They wanted to see how long it would remain, stick in shoot. It was still there three months later, but hidden by a luxurious growth of large oval leaves and many drooping branches of small white flowers.

We had also noticed that the stalks were wrapped here and there by paperlike bands, not unlike those found at the joints of knotweed. Knotweeds grow all over the place and, in midsummer, bear hundreds of little pink buds. But this mystery plant was as an elephant would be to a mouse.

After looking in a couple of field guides without luck, I picked some leaves and flowers and took them to another wildflower enthusiast.

"I know what that is," she said. "I just can't think of the name."

### *Mystery Solved*

But the next day, she had it: *Polygonum cuspidatum*, Japanese knotweed.

My helper used *The Shrub Identification Book* (1963) by George W. D. Symonds. Technically speaking, Japanese knotweed should not have even been in the book. As Mr. Symonds explained, the plant is not a woody shrub, but a perennial herb, and he included it in his text because it looks more like a shrub than an herb.

Perhaps that was why I had not noticed it before—I had mistaken it for a shrub, and paid no attention to it. Once I had identified it, however, I soon spotted more of it in other locations, and so did my wife. Our eyes had been opened.

Where did this plant come from? A Belgian botanist took it from Japan to England in 1864, and it probably made its way to America soon after. Keepers of gardens, perhaps Oriental gardens, probably used the plant because of its sweet scent or simply because of its abundance of flowers and leaves. Whatever the reason for its arrival, it has spread to such a degree that Nelson Coon, in *The Dictionary of Useful Plants*, calls it the worst of the *Polygonum* weeds. It is spreading steadily and it is almost impossible to eridacate. In the Northeast, Japanese knotweed may be seen growing along miles of railroad track.

Japanese knotweed is also called Japanese or Mexican bamboo because the hollow stems are similar to those of bamboo, and both Japanese knotweed and bamboo are weedy. Knotweeds, however, are not even closely related to bamboo, which is a grass. Japanese knotweed is actually a member of the large Buckwheat family, *Polygonaceae.* This family has about forty genera and 800 species worldwide, including sorrel, dock, and the knotweeds—all weedy characters (see Knotweed).

The genus, *Polygonum,* has about 100 species worldwide, and more than 70 can be found north of Mexico. Almost all are low-lying, but one other Asian import—the pink-flowered princess feather (*P. orientale*), found east of the Rockies—reaches nine feet in height. *Polygonum* means "many knees," referring to the swollen joints appearing in so many of the species, including Japanese knotweed (and that unrelated bamboo). *Cuspidatum,* from the Latin, means "having a cusp or point," probably referring to the point of the leaf. The word is from the same root that gives us cuspid and bicuspid, our one- and two-pointed teeth.

### *Good Eating*

Although Japanese knotweed may be a pain in the green thumb to gardeners who suddenly find it spreading rapidly through their prized hybrids, Euell Gibbons saw in it a source of a considerable variety of foods. In his best-selling *Stalking the Wild Asparagus* (1962), Mr. Gibbons devoted a full chapter to Japanese knotweed, treating it as a combination fruit and vegetable. He maintained that the young shoots make a pleasant vegetable, boiled like asparagus and served with butter and maybe a little sugar to counteract the tartness. He also gave recipes for aspic salad, a sweet-and-sour sauce, Japanese knotweed jam, and *Polygonum cuspidatum* pie. If you wish to sample some of these dishes, Japanese knotweed should be easy enough to find. Resist the temptation to forage for it along railroad tracks since most are sprayed with herbicides to inhibit plant growth.

Whether you want this food factory on your own property is questionable. As noted above, it can spread rapidly and extensively and it is difficult to eradicate. Some people consider Japanese knotweed the most serious plant pest around today, a threat to many native wild species. What's more, the sweet though not overpowering scent of the flowers seems to attract many stinging insects—not so much bees, as yellowjackets and sundry species of wasps and hornets. A bush-full of those could unnerve someone who is sensitive to insect venom.

In general, gardeners would rather eliminate the plant than introduce it. Most chemicals are ineffective because the rootstock—up to five feet deep—is difficult to kill. One technique is to cover the invaded area in the spring with sheets of black plastic. Do that for a year or two and you will starve the root. Of course, you will also kill everything else under the plastic, but in war, desperate measures are sometimes necessary.

**Blue Vervain**
*(Verbena hastata)*

# *A Favorite of Priests and Witches*

Slender blue candles rise from meadows, brooksides, and pond shores in the heat of mid- to late summer. Dozens of little flowers open at the bottom of the spikes and slowly the bloom moves upward, like a flame burning from the base of a candle.

Perhaps it is unfortunate that blue vervain's spikes do not bloom all at once, giving us long, blue wands instead of green ones with blue rings, buds above, and seeds below. What the plants lack in showy beauty, though, they make up for in legend and lore. American vervain and its European sibling belong to a clan of plants that has had magical, mystical, and medicinal qualities attributed to it for thousands of years.

*Verbena*, the principal genus within the Vervain family (*Verbenaceae*), includes from 100 to 200 species, found mostly in the tropics. (The Burmese teak tree, one of the hardest woods in the world, is a member of the Vervain family.) All but a few species are natives of North or South America, yet the type species is European vervain, *Verbena officinalis*, which is now also found in North America. Vervain grows to four or five feet tall.

### *Name Theories*

Theories about the origin of the plant's name are almost as numerous as its species. Some authorities say that *verbena* is a corruption of *herba veneris*, "herb of Venus," a name used because the ancients thought vervain was an aphrodisiac able to rekindle the flames of dying love. Other writers say the name was simply the Latin word for altar plants, and that vervain was so called because it was frequently used in connection with Roman religious ceremonies. *Webster's New International Dictionary* traces the word to the Latin *verber*, meaning "rod" or "stick," describing the shape of the plant, which country children use as toy swords and arrows.

Still others, especially Italians, believe *verbena* is a variation of the Latin *herbena* or *herbeus*, which means "green." Or it could be a corruption of *herba bona*, "good plant." And there are those who feel that vervain and perhaps *verbena* are connected with the ancient Celtic word, *ferfaon* or *ferfaen*, meaning "to drive away stone," reflecting a former use in treating bladder disorders.

## *Colorful Past*

Vervain has many folk names, like herb grace, holy herb, enchanter's plant, Juno's tears, frog's feet, pigeon grass, herb of the cross, and simpler's joy. Our native variety is also called American vervain, wild hyssop, ironweed, and purvain. Many of these names recall vervain's colorful past.

The Druids were supposed to have put vervain in their lustral water, used in rites of purification. Their priests gathered it "when the dog-star arose from unsunned spots," according to one authority, and held it between their hands during ceremonies. When they picked it from the ground, they would have to leave fresh honey on the spot to make amends for having robbed the earth of so sacred a plant.

The priests of early Rome believed the flowers were formed from the tears of Juno. They called it *Herba sacra* and employed it in decorating sacrificial animals, altars, and headdresses. Roman ambassadors carried it as a symbol of peace and friendship when visiting other nations. Vervain also figured in ancient Jewish ceremonies, and Christians used it as well as hyssop as an aspergillum, a device for sprinkling holy water.

Christians in the Middle Ages believed it a cure for many ailments because it was found growing on Mount Calvary. An old legend said it was used to dress Christ's wounds—hence such names as herb of grace or herb of the cross. When gathering vervain, people used to chant a song that began:

*Hallowed be thou, Vervain*
*As thou growest in the ground*
*For in the Mount of Calvary*
*There thou wast first found.*

On the other hand, vervain was believed to be a common ingredient in the brews of witches. Magicians and sorcerers were supposed to use it in sundry rites and with incantations. For example, magicians taught that smearing the juice of vervain on the body would guarantee that a wish would come true, or would make the worst enemies friendly. John Gerard did not think much of such goings on: "Many odde wives fables are written of Vervaine tending to witchcraft and sorcery, which you may reade elsewhere, for I am not willing to trouble your eares with reporting such trifles, as honest eares abhorre to heare." In fact, he believed the Devil himself deceived physicians into believing vervain was good as a medicine for the plague.

Vervain was also thought to repel evil spirits and bring good fortune. English peasants in the seventeenth century hung vervain and dill, along with a horseshoe, over doorways to keep the devil out. "Vervain and dill hinders witches from their will," it was said. The plant was worn around the neck as a charm against headaches, snake bites, insect stings, and "blasts" (sudden infections); it was also carried for good luck. When French peasants went courting, they presented vervain to young ladies, believing it would help win their hearts. In Germany a hat made of vervain was given to a bride to protect her from evil.

Culpeper listed many uses for the plant in the seventeenth century. "Used with lard," he said, "it helps swellings and pains in the secret parts." But it also "causes a good colour in the face and body." So valuable was vervain a few centuries back that simplers, people who gathered herbs from the wild, were always assured of buyers; thus, the name simpler's joy.

## *Nerves to Worms*

The medicinal uses of European blue vervain were legion. *V. hastata*, the American blue vervain, has also been popular in folk medicine, and is listed in several modern herbals. Vervain tea, made from our vervain, was famous not too many years ago as a tranquilizer and as a relief for symptoms of fevers and colds, and for chest congestion. The herb has been used to treat insomnia and to drive out intestinal worms; it has been used as a poultice for external wounds and sores.

Indians in California made a flour from the roasted, ground seeds (of a western species) whose bitterness can be reduced by soaking them in several changes of cold water. Chippewas "snuffed" the dried flowers to treat bloody noses.

### *Other species*

While the blue vervain found in New England tends to have tiny blossoms, *V. canadensis,* found in the Midwest and South, bears large blue or purple flowers. *V. canadensis* has been used as the parent of several garden hybrids of vervain known for their color, longevity, and ease in growing.

Also fairly common in the eastern half of North America is white vervain, *V. urticifolia,* much like blue vervain in size and shape of the plant, except that the flower spikes are taller and the blossoms are small and white. The flowers are not considered very pretty, and weed expert Edwin Rollin Spencer calls the species the homeliest of the genus; he adds that it is also sometimes a pest to farmers. White vervain can be found in pastures, but it favors thickets and the edges of woods.

One of the more spectacular natives is western pink vervain (*V. ambrosifolia*), found blooming in the Southwest much of the year and covering vast areas with clusters of pink to purple flowers. The Mexicans call it *moradilla,* or "little purple."

If you have some moist open land, a colony of vervain would blend in well with the other flowers of the season, such as Joe-Pye-weed, boneset, early goldenrods, and ironweed, all of which favor moist ground. Vervain is easily transplanted and spreads readily from seed.

If its various qualities and uses are not enough to convince you to acquire some blue vervain, perhaps one last ancient practice will. If you believe the Latin writer, Pliny, you will give better parties. "If the dining chamber be sprinkled in water in which the *herba verbena* has been steeped," Pliny wrote, "the guests will be merrier."

**Yellow Toadflax**
*(Linaria vulgaris)*

## *Old Toad Face*

Yellow toadflax, also called butter-and-eggs, is one of our common and handsome imports, found widely in sunny, dry, waste places from June until early fall. Botanists call it *Linaria vulgaris. Linaria* is from the Latin, *linum,* meaning "flax." From the same root comes linen, a cloth made from flax. Before it blooms, toadflax's slender, stringy leaves look much like flax, although the flowers bear no resemblance. *Vulgaris* simply means "common."

And common it is, as long as it can find the sandy, sunny spots it favors. The plants produce thousands of seeds to start future generations, and its creeping rhizome can establish sizable colonies.

### *The Bees*

The flower itself is very attractive, shaped much like garden snapdragons (*Anthirrhinum*), to which it is closely related. While most of the blossom is yellow, the area around the closed lips is bright orange. Orange attracts bees, particularly bumblebees, and various researchers have reported that bumblebees and large honeybees are about the only insects strong enough to open the lips and large enough at the same time to reach down inside the lower spurlike tube to obtain the nectar. In the process, they rub against the stamens, which dust the backs of the bees with pollen.

This closed-door policy is a marvelous example of having your cake and eating it, too. Unlike so many flowers, toadflax does not have to waste energy opening and closing each day or night, or when it rains. It is always closed to pilferers, and yet always open to the right insects.

No system, however, is perfect. Certain butterflies and moths, also drawn to orange, are sometimes able to dip their long tongues inside the flower to steal nectar without pollinating the flower. These thefts do not really do any harm, for toadflax can fertilize itself—one more reason for its success at survival.

The flower's lips, incidentally, probably led to its peculiar and ancient name. As far back as sixteenth-century England, the plant was called toadflax because the orange mouth is shaped somewhat like that of toad. Children sometimes take the flowers, squeeze them just behind the lips, and make the toads "talk."

There is also an old story that the name originated from an observation that "toads will sometimes shelter themselves amongst the branches of it," reported William Coles, a seventeenth-century herb expert. The plant's slender, grasslike leaves could not provide much shelter from either sun or rain, however, and the first explanation seems more believable. (Some people say the name comes from the whole flower's form, which resembles a tadpole, but the explanation may be stretched too far.)

Mary Durant, in *Who Named the Daisy? Who Named the Rose?*, reports that toadflax is also called ranstead (ramstead or ramsted) because it was said to have been introduced to America by a Welshman named Ranstead, who settled near Philadelphia and planted it in his garden. From there—and probably other sources—it headed for the wide, open spaces, from coast to coast.

### *Many Names*

Today, the plant has spread across not only this continent, but the temperate zones of the world. Such a widespread flower is bound to generate many folk names, and there are no fewer than thirty recorded for *Linaria vulgaris*, including: fluellin, patten and clogs, flaxweed, snapdragon, churnstaff, dragon-bushes, brideweed, toad, yellow rod, larkspur, lion's mouth, devil's ribbon, eggs-and-collops, eggs-and-bacon, bread-and-butter, devil's head, pedlar's basket, gallwort, rabbits, doggies, calve's snout, impudent lawyer, Jacob's ladder, rancid, wild flax, wild tobacco, devil's flax, devil's flower, deadman's bones, continental flower, and rabbit's weed.

Several names refer to the shape of the flower, which some liken to a dragon's face, or shoes, or things familiar around a farm. Gall was a disease of chickens, treated with the plant. The colors yellow and orange recall sulfur, and sulfur recalls the down-under fellow, giving rise to so many devilish names. The imagination strains at a reason for impudent lawyer, unless it is the expression on the face of the flower. But why a lawyer? The origin of fluellin is discussed in another chapter, Speedwells: Diamonds in the Rough.

Like so many other imports, toadflax may have been brought here as a source of medicine as well as beauty. Through the ages it has been used to treat several ailments including jaundice, liver diseases, dropsy, hemorrhoids, and eye difficulties. The plant was added to bathwater to relieve skin rashes and diseases and it is said to be a diuretic. "This is frequently used to spend the abundance of those watery humours by urine, which cause the dropsy," said Culpeper. Herbalist John Lust, however, suggests that toadflax is rather powerful and warns against internal use without medical supervision. Since its juice, mixed with milk, was widely used as a fly poison centuries ago and cattle will not eat the plant, there is reason to heed the warning. Germans, incidentally, obtained a yellow dye from the flowers.

Toadflax may bloom rather variably, apparently depending on climatic conditions. One year I found plants in bloom in a high part of my hometown on July 4, while the next year, on July 17 in the same place, the buds were not even out. Yet, that year in a warmer valley, hundreds flowered on July 15. Some authors describe them as flowers of the late summer, although they clearly can bloom earlier in my part of the Northeast.

Transplanting them is easy—just dig up a bunch and place it in an arid, sunny spot. Unless they get strong sunlight, however, the plants will fail to produce blossoms each year. Toadflax should also be intermixed with some other plants, such as grasses, that are not too tall and overpowering. Toadflax needs neighbors because it is one of our few common parasitic herbs. Its roots tap into the roots of other plants to steal both water and salts. Its thieving, however, is done in moderation—it does not want to kill its hosts and lose the assistance they supply.

Toadflax is a member of the Figwort family (*Scrophulariaceae*), which in North America includes about sixty herbaceous genera as well as some shrubs and trees. Among the figworts are foxgloves, mulleins, turtleheads, monkeyflowers, and speedwells. More than 150 species of *Linaria* grow around the world; some 14 may be found on this continent. Several European and North African species, mostly purple-flowered, have been popular with gardeners and rock gardeners. A native member of the genus, almost as widespread but not as common as yellow toadflax, is blue, or wild, toadflax (*L. canadensis*), found coast to coast, as well as in Central and South America. It, too, has slender leaves. Dalmatian toadflax (*L. dalmatica*), a Eurasia variety now found widely coast to coast, has ovate, clasping leaves.

**Spotted Joe-Pye-Weed**
*(Eupatorium maculatum)*

# *A Noble Lummox*

Folklorists tell us that Joe Pye, sometimes written Jopi, was a traveling Indian medicine man or, as the early New Englanders would have called him, a "yarb man." One tale says he came from a Maine tribe and sold his herb wares around the Northeast at about the time of the Revolution. Another had it that Joe Pye owned much land near Salem, Massachusetts, in early colonial times, and though he befriended European settlers with his herbal medicines he was eventually chased off his land and forced to live in an Indian village in western Massachusetts. He is said to have used his "weed" as a treatment for typhoid fever, possibly because it induced a great deal of sweating in those who consumed it. He must have had some success—or at least a lucky batting average—for the plant has borne his name for more than two centuries.

Actually, Joe-Pye-weed refers to several different weeds, all members of the genus *Eupatorium*, although there has been confusion over whether some plants are distinct species or just variations of others. At least three Joe-Pye-weeds—spotted (*E. maculatum*), sweet (*E. purpureum*), and hollow (*E. fistulosum*)—are widespread, found in most states east of the Rockies. *E. maculatum* has crossed the Great Divide and can be found on the West Coast, both in the U.S. and Canada.

Some botanists suspect spotted Joe-Pye-weed, identified by its spotted stem markings, may be a race of sweet Joe-Pye-weed. The ovate hairy leaves grow in whorls of four or five, and the many flower heads are in several bunches of six or seven, all so jammed together that the plant often seems to have one flat-topped cluster. Sweet Joe-Pye-weed, considered rare and treasured in some of its range, is easily identified by the vanillalike odor of its crushed leaves. While all species attract butterflies, sweet Joe-Pye-weed's scent and color probably make it the most attractive of the lot. Hollow Joe-Pye-weed has a hollow stem, absent in the other varieties.

### *Huge Genus*

*Eupatorium* is a huge genus, with some 500 species around the world. In North America, there are 50 species, including the several kinds of Joe-Pye-weeds, a few bonesets (see the next chapter), sundry snakeroots, and a thoroughwort or two. Among the most famous and certainly the most notorious of the clan is white snakeroot (*E. urticaefolium*), which may have killed thousands of Americans in the eastern half of the United States, including Nancy Hanks Lincoln, Abraham Lincoln's mother. White snakeroot, which cows ate only when there was no other fodder available, tainted milk with a poison that caused an often fatal disease called milk sickness. For decades people did not know the source of the disease and suspected everything from poison ivy to bacteria and vapors from under the earth. So devastating and feared was milk sickness, especially in the first half of the nineteenth century, that whole villages were sometimes permanently abandoned after it struck.

Joe-Pye-weeds are members of the Composite family. Unlike typical Composites such as daisies, asters, and sunflowers, Joe-Pye-weeds have no rays and are composed only of the tubular disc flowers, favored by the long-tongued butterflies and bees. Although these insects do pollinate some flowers while dipping for goodies, Joe-Pye-weed can pollinate itself. Because the flowers are so closely packed, pollen-bearing stamens of one flower head can come in contact with the long pollen-catching stigma of a neighboring head, accomplishing the job that insects usually have to do in Composites.

The plants can be found in moist or wet lowlands, especially in meadows near ponds and streams, and can grow to twelve feet, making them one of our tallest herbs. Their flowers range from pink to light purple, coloring that inspired F. Schuyler Mathews to write in the 1890s, "A good patch of Joe-Pye-weed under a hazy August sky produces one of those delicious bits of cool pink, set in dull sage-green, such as an impressionist likes to paint."

Purple-shaded Joe-Pye-weeds—one author likens their color to crushed raspberries—are a sort of transition from midsummer to fall, a harbinger of the cooler weather to come. If you mark the passing of the seasons with the color of flowers, you might shiver just a little in the heat of August when you see Joe-Pye-weed. Although I have seen the plants in bloom as early as July 15 in Connecticut, the great groves of them are not out in true color and height until mid-August. The flowers are usually gone by mid-September.

Many people enjoy Joe-Pye-weed indoors and out. Country inns in New England often display bouquets of Joe-Pye-weed in August or early September. The purple clusters liven up tables and counters, and one fancy Connecticut inn used to fill a whole corner of its dining room with the tall flowering stalks.

### *More Blood*

*Eupatorium* means "of a noble father." Mithridates Eupator, also called Mithridates the Great, was ruler of the Asia Minor kingdom of Pontus from 120 to 63 B.C. Why him? Some authorities say it is because he was the first to use one of the genus as a medicine. Others tell the story of how Mithridates had discovered that a species of *Eupatorium* was an antidote to poison, and he consumed it regularly to protect himself from poisoning by his enemies—including his mother. He was eventually captured, however, and since he preferred death to being a prisoner, he tried to poison himself. He had so much antidote in his system that nothing worked and he finally had to have a comrade stab him to death.

If that tale seems farfetched, there are those who believe the name recalls this warrior's penchant for bloodshed—shed blood being somewhat similar in color to European varieties of our weed. Mithridates once ordered the massacre of all Roman and Italian cities in Asia, and it is said that 80,000 people were killed in one day in the winter of 88 B.C. Thus, like the purple loosestrife discussed elsewhere, this plant's name may have a gory origin, making one wonder whether botanists—or at least taxonomists—are a bloodthirsty lot.

Sweet Joe-Pye-weed has several folk names. It is called queen of the meadow (sometimes "king," more in keeping with the meaning of *Eupatorium*), trumpet flower (if you have a good imagination, the upward-pointing whorl of leaves could look like the end of a horn), kidney root, gravel root (it was used to treat kidney ailments), marsh milkweed (no relation to true milkweeds), quillwort, and motherwort.

### *Medicinal Uses*

Indian Joe may have found a medicine for typhus in this plant, but nineteenth-century Americans used it chiefly to treat kidney and urinary illnesses. One Indian tribe—maybe Joe's—even favored it as an aphrodisiac. Perhaps less interested in its libidinous virtues, the Chippewas employed solutions of Joe-Pye-weed to treat inflamed joints. The Potawatomi made poultices for burns from its leaves and considered the flower heads to be good luck charms, especially when gambling. The Ojibwas believed that washing a papoose up to the age of six in a solution made from the roots would strengthen the child. Children who were fretful and could not sleep were put in a bath to which a Joe-Pye-weed decoction had been added, and they were supposed to have relaxed and gone to sleep.

Wildflower gardener and former U.S. senator George D. Aiken called Joe-Pye-weed "a good natured lummox, willing to grow anywhere for anyone." It makes an excellent border flower or pond-edge plant, self-sowing readily. All that is needed is some wet soil and good sunlight and they can be transplanted easily.

Mixed with goldenrod and some of our earlier tall white asters, Joe-Pye-weed creates a colorful, late-summer hedge, especially in front of a wood. And you can always use it to fire your imagination, as did a *New York Times* editorial writer some years ago: "Those eddying mists of this [August] morning could have been more than a swirl of vapor. If old Joe Pye's spirit was there, he must have been appraising the season's yield."

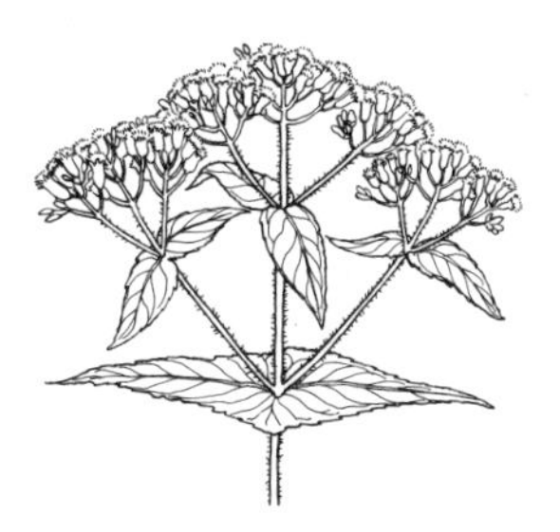

**Boneset**
*(Eupatorium perfoliatum)*

## *A Bitter Tea for What Ails You*

It was not too long ago that attic rafters were jammed with the dangling, drying leaves of boneset, one of the most widely used and widely hated medicinal herbs of old America. Boneset tea, the scourge of children who dreaded its bitter taste, was extensively used as a febrifuge, a fever reducer, from the seventeenth and eighteenth centuries well into the twentieth century.

Boneset is a July and August flower of wet sunny meadows and waste places. Although it has been likened to milkweed, with which it often grows, boneset is no relation and is, in fact, a member of the huge Composite family. Its white (rarely blue), rayless blossoms are packed in rounded heads, with long white threads projecting far beyond each floret, giving a fuzzy appearance to the clusters.

The leaves, not the flowers, are the more distinctive feature of *Eupatorium perfoliatum.* The leaves clasp and entirely surround the stem, making it appear as if the stem perforated one long leaf with pointed ends.

### *Uses*

"It has always been a popular remedy in the United States," wrote British herbalist Maude Grieve. "Probably no plant in American domestic practice [has had] more extensive and frequent use." At one time it was listed in the *U.S. Pharmacopoeia* as an official medicine.

Many is the old-timer who can recall grandfather's or grandmother's attic with dozens of boneset plants, hanging to dry and awaiting use. "To one whose childhood passed in the country some fifty years ago, the name or sight of this plant is fraught with unpleasant memories," wrote Mrs. William Starr Dana in 1893. "The attic or woodshed was hung with bunches of the dried herb, which served as many gruesome warnings against wet feet, or any overexposure which might result in cold or malaria." A friend who grew up in the 1930s remembered its being collected and dried by her grandmother. Much to her chagrin, the friend was also fed its tea for colds and fevers.

Mrs. Dana described the taste of boneset tea as nauseous. Mixing boneset extract with candy such as taffy made the medicine more palatable to ailing children. Yet Alice Morse Earle, author of books on early American life, recalled boneset tea as having "a clear, clean bitter taste, no stronger than any bitter beer or ale."

Whatever the taste, the tea was a common and inexpensive method of relieving fevers, and was especially popular among blacks in the South. When medical supplies were short during the Civil War, boneset tea was given to Confederate troops instead of quinine. Many drug stores carried the leaves by the middle of the nineteenth century.

### *Bones of Contention*

The name "boneset" may have come from one of its varied uses. Boneset tea was used to treat dengue, a disease once common in the South. The disease was also called break-bone fever because the pains were so severe that bones seemed broken. Perhaps as a consequence, the plant that relieved the pain was called boneset.

Another theory has it that the name came from the "doctrine of signatures." People believed that because the opposing leaves of boneset were joined together at the stem, a poultice of the plant would help broken bones to knit. Still another theory—perhaps the most reasonable—was that boneset tea was given as a pain reliever to people who had broken bones.

The herb was also used to treat constipation, rheumatism, catarrh, pneumonia, influenza, and ringworm. Boneset tea was given to snakebite victims and crushed boneset leaves used for a poultice on the bites. Boneset was also used for expelling tapeworms. Perhaps because of its "thoroughness" as a medicine, it was also popularly known as thoroughwort. Some authorities believe that boneset's only real value was in causing fever victims to sweat; it was popularly known as sweating plant and feverwort.

Charles F. Millspaugh described one dramatic case of boneset's effectiveness:

> *When a young man, living in the central part of this state, he was attacked with intermittent fever, which lasted off and on for three years. Being of a bilious temperament, he grew at length sallow, emaciated, and hardly able to get about. As he sat one day, resting by the side of the road, an old lady of his acquaintance told him to go home and have some thoroughwort "fixed," and it would certainly cure him. (He had been given, during the years he suffered, quinine, cinchonine, bark and all its known derivatives, as well as cholagogues, and every other substance then known to the regular practitioner, without effect; the attacks coming on latterly twice a*

*day.) On reaching home, with the aid of the fences and buildings along the way, he received a tablespoonful of a decoction of boneset evaporated until it was about the consistency of syrup and immediately went to bed. He had hardly lain down when insensibility and stupor came on, passing into deep sleep. On awaking in the morning, he felt decidedly better, and from that moment improved rapidly without farther medication, gaining flesh and strength daily. No attack returned for twenty years, when a short one was brought on by lying down in a marsh while hunting.*

## *Charming Deer*

American Indians used boneset as a medicine, calling it a name equivalent to ague-weed, but the Chippewas used it in a most unusual manner, as a charm for calling deer. The hunters used special whistles that they believed would work properly only if rubbed with boneset root fibers.

Other names for boneset include crosswort (the pairs of leaves whorl around the stem so that, as you look down on them, each pair crosses the next below), wild sage (the leaves bear some resemblance in shape), Indian sage, thoroughwax, thoroughgrow, and throughstem. In some cases "thorough" may be a variation of "through," as in "throughstem," because the stem projected through the leaves.

## *Culture*

There are about fifty species of Eupatorium in North America, mostly in the East, and several of them are called boneset. Only *E. perfoliatum*, however, has the distinctive perforated leaves, and this species is among the most common and widespread, ranging from Nova Scotia to Manitoba and down into Florida and Louisiana. East Texas has a variety, *E. compositifolium*, whose white flower clusters are more pyramid-shaped than flat-topped and that carries the suspicious name, Yankee weed. The plant does not come from the land of the Yankees, so the Texans must hold the weed in such contempt that they named it after their favorite "enemy."

Although F. Schuyler Mathews found the flowers "dull and uninteresting," healthy plants are attractive, even desirable, according to Edwin Steffek in *Wild Flowers and How to Grow Them.* The handsomely shaped leaves often turn yellowish in the wild, however, and are frequently attacked by leaf-eating insects that do not have children's tastes. To maintain healthy-looking plants, the ground should be continuously moist, and you may have to spray for insects. Transplant stock in late spring or early summer, as soon as the plants are recognizable. The short-lived perennials self-sow readily, and you will soon wind up with enough plants to load up your rafters and fill many a cup of tea.

**Common Sunflower**
*(Helianthus annuus)*

# *Beauty and Bounty*

If ever a clan of flowering plants were put on this earth to help humans, it would be the sunflowers, whose golden-rayed blossoms seem so symbolic of late summer. Sunflowers have been used to feed people, birds, pigs, and bees; to clear swamps; and to encourage egg laying. They have been an ingredient in paper and cigars. In one species nearly every part of the plant is or has been of economic value, even its ashes.

Sunflowers are New World plants. *Helianthus*, the genus name, is from the Greek *helios*, "sun," and *anthus*, "flower." Sunflowers, in turn, are members of the large Composite family. About seventy species are known in the Western Hemisphere, but fifty to sixty of them are North American. More species are found in the Midwest and West than in the East. Because so many sunflower seeds are purchased to feed wild birds, odd species and hybrids can pop up almost anywhere. Identification is often difficult for this reason and because, even among the wild native species, hybridizing is possible.

## *A Popular Style*

Neltje Blanchan observed at the turn of the century that one-ninth of all the then-known flowering plants in the world belonged to the Composites. Over 1,600 Composites were found in North America north of Mexico, and more than half of these were of the "daisy pattern," wrote Mrs. Blanchan. She called this pattern "the most successful arrangement known." And of these, the majority are wholly or partly yellow.

Of the yellow daisylike Composites, the sunflowers are the most conspicuous. In many cases their flower heads are the largest and their stalks the tallest. Tall, or giant, sunflower (*H. giganteus*) and common sunflower (*H. annuus*) can reach twelve feet in height. These features help assure survival: bright yellow flags waving high above the masses easily attract pollinating bees. Later, the seedy heads still wave high, readily attracting hungry birds who help disperse the seeds.

The king of the genus is common sunflower, although in parts of the continent, other varieties may be more common. It is royal both in its history and as the parent of most garden and agricultural sunflowers grown for their seeds. One scion, the mammoth, or Russian, sunflower, has a head up to a foot wide that bears 2,000 or more good-sized seeds.

## *Early History*

Because there is virtually no written record of pre-Columbian North and South America, fairly little is known about the early history of this popular plant. Natives in Mexico and Peru used the flower, so similar in form and color to the sun, in ceremonies honoring the sun god. Aztec priestesses wore the flowers in their hair, and the conquistadores found many representations of sunflowers, wrought in pure gold, embellishing Aztec and Incan temples.

Although common sunflower is probably native to western North America, trade among American Indians made the species well known and widespread across the continent by the time European explorers arrived. Champlain found the Huron growing them in 1615 to use the stalks as a source of fiber for cloth, much as flax was used. They used its leaves as fodder, the flower rays as a yellow dye, and the seeds for both food and hair oil. Some tribes made black and purple basket dyes from the seeds. The Senecas roasted the seeds and boiled them with water to make a coffee. Some tribes believed that to eat the seeds improved the eyesight. The Ojibwas made a poultice for blisters from the leaves.

Lewis and Clark found that the Plains Indians, who often grew sunflowers intermixed with their corn crops, added the ground seeds to marrow of buffalo bones to form a sort of hard pudding. (Euell Gibbons mixed boiled beef marrow, sunflower seed meal, and salt to make a tasty spread for bread or crackers.) Peter Kalm reported that by 1749 Indians in Loretto, Canada, were cultivating sunflowers and mixing the seeds in maize soup. Indeed, in Russia and elsewhere, powdered sunflower seed is today often used as a thickening agent for soups.

Early settlers, especially in Canada, quickly saw the plant's value and fed it whole to livestock. They also sent it to Europe, where it became very popular. John Gerard, the seventeenth-century herbalist who experimented extensively with discoveries from the New World, wrote: "We have found by triall that the buds before they be flowered, boiled and eaten with butter, vinegar and pepper after the manner of artichokes, an exceeding pleasant meet, surpassing the artichoke far in procuring bodily lust." He also found broiled buds tasty.

## *Many Uses*

Over the years common sunflower and its hybrids have been used in dozens of ways. The seed has been for centuries ground into meal and used to make a palatable and nutritious bread. Sunflower seeds have a high food value, containing vitamins A, B, calcium, phosphorus, and other minerals.

With sixteen percent albumen and twenty-one percent fat, the seeds have been valued for feeding and fattening chickens, hogs, and milking cows. With hogs, all the farmer needs to do is plant the seeds of *H. tuberosa*; the animals will root out the tasty underground tubers themselves. Sunflowers are said to encourage the egg-laying ability of poultry. The leaves also make an excellent fodder. The stems and seedless heads, when dried, have served as litter in poultry houses.

The pith of the sunflower stalk is the lightest natural substance known, having a specific gravity of 0.028, compared to 0.24 for cork. Consequently, it was used to stuff life preservers. The stalks also were burned in heaps to obtain large quantities of potash from the pith to use as fertilizer. Well into this century, and perhaps still, the Chinese used the stalk fiber to blend with the silk cloths. This fiber has also been used to make paper in fairly modern times. The shells were once ground and made into blotting paper.

Seeds are pressed cold or under moderate heat to obtain a vegetable oil that is much like olive oil and is readily available in supermarkets today. It has been and is used in food preparation, including the manufacture of margarine. The oil was also used as fine lamp fuel, as a lubricant, for soap- and candle-making, and as a drying oil in paints. Sunflowers are now Argentina's most important oil-producing seed.

They are also said to be the only major crop plant to have originated in the United States, and are still widely grown on the Plains. (The sunflower is the state flower of Kansas, a fact noted on at least two U.S. postage stamps bearing its likeness.)

The seeds, raw or roasted, have been eaten by humans in many forms, and today are still popular as a snack food. One manufacturer's product, roasted in soybean oil and seasoned with sea salt, contains more than 200 calories an ounce—not exactly the stuff of diets. In Russia, where they are as popular as peanuts are here, large bowls of hybrid sunflower seeds are often found on tables in restaurants, or the seeds are sold on street corners. Roasted seeds have also been used to brew a coffeelike drink, particularly in Russia and in Hungary, where sunflowers are also a popular crop.

In herb medicine, various parts of the plant have been employed to treat bronchial and pulmonary diseases, malaria, and fevers. Linoleic acid, extracted from the oil, has been used by modern herbalists to slow the progress of multiple sclerosis.

The carefully dried leaves have been used as a tobacco substitute in cigars and, according to one author of the last century, "the flavor . . . is said to greatly resemble that of mild Spanish tobacco." The leaves have been smoked both as a medicine and for enjoyment, especially in sections of Germany.

The plant is said to have a remarkable ability to dry damp soils. "Swampy districts in Holland have been made habitable by extensive culture of the sunflower," reported Maude Grieve. Research has found that a sunflower's leaves transpire six gallons of water over its eighteen-week growing season.

In nature, bees find sunflowers useful for obtaining not only large quantities of nectar, but also wax for their hives.

### *Our Artichoke*

Among the many varieties of sunflowers found in America, *H. tuberosum* is probably the least known as a sunflower, though it is well known as Jerusalem artichoke, Canada potato, or earth apple because of its starchy tuber. Various nations of Indians cultivated Jerusalem artichoke. The Chippewas, who simply dug it up and ate the tuber uncooked, called it by a name that translates as "raw thing." The Indians passed the plant on to European settlers, who sent it to Europe as early as 1617. By 1630, it was widely used as a vegetable.

Italians cultivated it and called it *girasole aricocco*—"sunflower artichoke"—and it is believed that a mispronunciation of *girasole* led to the popular but geographically incorrect name, Jerusalem. The plant was as well used as the potato, to which it is about equal in food value, until the latter was introduced into Europe in the eighteenth century and became more popular.

### *Stronger Than Cement*

Obviously, sunflowers have many attributes. One of their strangest is their strength. Naturalist John Burroughs described an unusual seedling back in the early part of the twentieth century:

> *One of the most remarkable exhibitions of plant force I ever saw was in a Western city where I observed a species of wild sunflower forcing its way up through the asphalt pavement; the folded and compressed leaves of the plant like a man's fist, had pushed against the hard but flexible concrete till it had bulged up and then split, and let the irrepressible plant through. The force exerted must have been many pounds. I think it doubtful if the strongest man could have pushed his fist through such a resisting medium. . . . It is doubtful if any cultivated plant could have overcome such odds. It required the force of the untamed hairy plant of the plains to accomplish this feat.*

Although large-flowered varieties, the bird food kind, are readily available, Frank C. Pellett, who set up a large wildflower sanctuary in Iowa back in the 1940s, shunned the mighty annuals and hybrids in favor of smaller wild varieties whose flowers he found more delicate and numerous. The plants can be relied upon to send up flowers in larger numbers each year. They require very little care, he said, and are not fussy about their situation, as long as it is sunny.

My favorite wild variety is tall, or giant, sunflower (*H. giganteus*), which likes semi-shaded moist territory and which each year produces many delicate and long-lasting flowers, about 2½ inches in diameter.

In the nineteenth century, Alice Morse Earle reported, "The sunflower had a fleeting day of popularity, and flaunted in garden and parlor. Its place was false. It was never a garden flower in olden times, in the sense of being a flower of ornament or beauty; its place was in the kitchen garden, where it belongs." Nonetheless, more than two dozen garden hybrids of *H. annuus*, with petals bearing shades of red, pink, maroon, and red, have been developed in this century.

Whether or not you choose to grow wild or cultivated varieties for their beauty or your kitchen, you are providing food naturally for many wild birds; more than forty-five species have been observed eating them. If you feed birds, you probably cannot help having a few of the cultivated sunflowers spring up from seeds dropped or cached by birds or buried by feeder-robbing squirrels. You can either let the birds pick away at the heads as they stand on the stalk, or after the stalk has fallen to the ground, or you can cut the heads—with mature seeds—dry them, and save them for winter when food is scarcer. The larger heads may be suspended from trees or the house in such a way that squirrels have difficulty pilfering the seeds. For an added treat, the head can be coated with melted suet, wrapped with pieces of suet, or dabbed with peanut butter.

Thus, everyone—humans and beasts—can enjoy the beauty and the bounty of the amazing sunflowers.

**Turtlehead**
*(Chelone glabra)*

# *The Talking Heads*

"We're going to look for some turtleheads," I told my three-year-old son as we got into the car.

He looked at me, puzzled, and asked: "Just the heads?"

"They're flowers," I replied. "They look sort of like the head of a turtle."

He paused again and asked: "Do they have eyes?"

"No," I said, "but they have big mouths and

you can make them talk."

He seemed to accept that explanation, and once we reached the edge of the swamp where I had seen the flowers in years past, he began asking where the turtleheads were. When we finally found some mixed among tall grasses and cattails, he stared for a moment at their peculiar shape.

"What do they say?" he asked.

I picked one blossom from a cluster, squeezed its sides, and played ventriloquist as its mouth opened and closed.

"That's pretty funny, Daddy," he said. And for the next ten or fifteen minutes, he insisted that the turtlehead "say something."

### *Masticating Flowers*

Unfortunately, he did not get to see a more natural performance that is both funnier and stranger than his father's. Turtleheads rely almost exclusively on larger bees for pollination. Fluffy furlike hairs on the lower lip keep out crawlers, and few flying insects are strong enough to push their way between the lips and past an armlike sterile stamen that must be moved aside to reach the nectar. When bees squeeze between the closed lips, then wiggle and twist around the one- to two-inch-long flower tube, searching for food, they cause the front lips to open and close as if the flower were chewing its own food instead of providing it. To come upon one of these flowers "masticating" is a most entertaining sight that we missed that day for lack of bees.

Turtlehead is a fairly common flower of wetlands, swamp fringes, and stream banks that blooms in August, September, and sometimes into October. *Chelone*, its generic name, is from the Greek for "tortoise," referring to the shape of the top of the flower which is like a tortoise's shell. *Glabra*, its specific name, means "smooth" and describes its smooth, hairless stems and leaves.

It is a member of the Figwort family (*Scrophulariaceae*), a clan whose members include the butter-and-eggs, or toadflax, covered in another chapter, and the garden snapdragons. The similarity between these and the turtleheads can easily be seen in the construction of the flowers.

While there are four North American species of *Chelone*, *C. glabra* is probably the most widespread, found from southern Canada to Alabama, and from the Atlantic to the Mississippi and into Missouri. In the South, there are attractive purple and pink species. *C. glabra* is generally known as a white flower, but pink-tinged specimens are not unusual.

### *Dining Spot*

A nectar-loving butterfly makes use of the turtlehead, not for food, but as a place to lay eggs. The Baltimore checkerspot, a black-and-white species with brick red or orange spots along its wing edges, may be found over a wide area of the Northeastern United States, but is extremely local in its living habits. In fact, guidebooks tell butterfly collectors who are hunting the Baltimore to look for turtleheads and to expect the butterfly to be not more than 100 yards away.

The Baltimore lays its eggs on the leaves and the resulting spiny orange-and-black caterpillars feed exclusively on the leaves. If you see a turtlehead with holes in its foliage, odds are a Baltimore caterpillar was there for dinner. In the fall, groups of the caterpillars spin thick webs over the plant and spend the winter inside together. The next spring the caterpillars feed and then construct their blotched, grayish chrysalises on the underside of the turtlehead or other leaves.

Though odd of shape and plain of color, turtlehead is nonetheless a handsome flower, and its tight clusters produce many blossoms over many weeks. The perennials grow from one to six feet high. You might consider starting some if you have a moist sunny spot on your property, though the late Vermont senator George D. Aiken maintained that they also do well in dry soils. While you can transplant them in the spring, they are not common enough to be removed from the wild and should be left alone, unless they are threatened with destruction. They can be started from cuttings taken in the summer, but the best method of establishing turtleheads is from their seeds, which have a good germination rate. Seeds should be easy to obtain in September or October, if you know where to find the plants.

### *Fish and Snakes, Too*

Among *Chelone glabra*'s popular names, most of which are derived from the flower shape, are turtlebloom, snakehead, codhead, fishmouth, bitterherb, salt-rheum weed, and shellflower (probably from the tortoise shell, but there is a genus of common seashell called the Chelone clams). It has been called hummingbird tree because those long-billed birds seek out its sweets. Some people call it white closed gentian because of a similarity to the blue closed gentians, but there is no botanical relation.

The plant has also been called balmony among people who practice folk medicine and have used the leaves to make a salve for a variety of skin irritations, such as tumors and ulcers. It was popular among some tribes of American Indians as a tonic and a laxative, although the leaves from which the medicines were concocted have a markedly bitter taste. The Malecite Indians of Canada's Maritime Provinces somehow used the plant as a contraceptive. Other medicinal uses included treatment of worms, jaundice, consumption, and dyspepsia.

Not one to mince words, herbalist Ben Charles Harris says the turtlehead is good for "the removal of toxic sludge from the stomach and intestines."

Personally, I'll stick with using it for puppetry.

**Spreading Dogbane**
*(Apocynum androsaemifolium)*

## *A Fly's Worst Friend*

September is the season of seeds. The flowers of summer send forth their annual bounty, which flies, floats, pops, and drops onto a foothold for next year's growth. Dogbane sports one of the more unusual of the season's seed containers. The long, slender seed cases come in pairs, looking like the pajama bottoms of long-legged elves. They contain seeds attached to fluffy fibers, like those of the milkweed. In fact, dogbane was once classified as a milkweed. Today, it is in a family (*Apocynaceae*) and a genus (*Apocynum*) of its own, one step away from the milkweeds.

Dogbane is a common shrubby herb whose pink flowers bloom in July and early August, and whose green pods disperse their seeds at the beginning of fall. *A. androsaemifolium*, spreading dogbane, is both the type species and the most common species of this small genus. It is found throughout the United States and southern Canada. *Apocynum* means "dogbane" while *androsaemifolium* refers to the similarity of the leaf to that of the androsaemon, a kind of Old World St. Johnswort.

In all the world, there are only a dozen species in the *Apocynum* genus; 6 are found in North America. The dogbane family consists of 130 genera and 1,100 species, mostly tropical. Only 9 genera are found in North America, 4 of them in the Northeast.

### *Like Rubber*

Spreading dogbane is peculiar in a couple of ways. One is its feel. Touch the leaves, stems, and especially the pods, and they feel like rubber. Perhaps it is not surprising that the milky white juice inside the plant dries like soft rubber when exposed to the air.

Spreading dogbane, which grows to four or five feet in height and is usually found in colonies, bears small pinkish flowers that resemble lilies of the valley. F. Schuyler Mathews, author of *Familiar Flowers of Field and Garden*, wrote,

> *The flowers are quite as beautiful as many small garden favorites and in my estimation, they are individually more attractive by reason of their delicious dainty pink flush than the lily of the valley.*
>
> *This seems flat heresy, but in defense of the preferences for a common wild flower, I would venture to predict that if some horticulturist should succeed in producing a lily of the valley with the dainty pink coloring of dogbane, such a flower with its charming perfume would be wildly admired by every lover of flowers. Such is the disadvantage of the wild flower that its beauty is discounted if it has not reached an abnormal development, and its charms are unheeded if it does not throw out a perfume strong enough to entice the passerby.*

### *Bane of Bugs*

These flowers, so admired by Mathews, may be the bane of dogs, but they are certainly the bane of flies and various smaller insects. Dogbane flowers are designed to attract butterflies, whose tongues are dabbed with a cement-and-pollen mixture as they dip for the nectar. Bees may also feed and then transfer pollen. However, flies and other weak flying insects that are not valued as pollen carriers are unwelcome and often wind up dead for their trespassing.

Neltje Blanchan describes the process this way:

> *Suppose a fly falls upon this innocent-looking blossom. His short tongue, as well as the butterfly's, is guided into one of the V-shaped cavities after he has sipped; but getting wedged between the trap's horny teeth, the poor little victim is held prisoner there until he slowly dies of starvation in the sight of plenty. This is the penalty he must pay for trespassing on the butterfly's preserves! The dogbane, which is perfectly adapted to the butterfly and dependent upon it for help in producing fertile seed, ruthlessly destroys all poachers that are not big or strong enough to jerk away from its vise-like grasp. [Another author maintains that scales are actually triggered by touch and bend inward to clasp the victim.]*
>
> *One often sees small flies and even moths dead and dangling by the tongue from the wicked little charmers. If the flower assimilated their dead bodies as the pitcher plant, for example, does those of its victims, the fly's fate would seem less cruel. To be killed by slow torture and dangled like a scarecrow simply for pilfering a drop of nectar is surely an execution of justice medieval in its severity.*

## *Poisonous*

Dogbane is considered poisonous, to humans as well as to dogs, and in that sense it could be considered a bane of any mammal foolish enough to eat it. The name probably stems from a related or similar European species or genus. The only apparent connection between the American plant and dogs was its occasional use to treat people who had been bitten by mad dogs.

Besides, what self-respecting dog would be foolish enough to eat the leaves? Dogbane, like milkweed, leaves have an acrid taste—the plant was formerly commonly called bitterroot.

A 1939 text on poisonous American plants reported that only fifteen to thirty grams of dogbane leaves could kill a horse or cow. Subsequent investigation, however, found that this statement was based on erroneous data published in 1922 by a New Mexican agricultural experiment station, which had confused dogbane with the related and very poisonous oleander. In other words, while dogbanes are poisonous, they may not be as potent as experts once thought.

The caterpillar of the monarch butterfly and other milkweed butterfly larvae are not affected by the poisonous chemical. These insects feed on the leaves and build their chrysalises under them. Some authorities believe that the acrid juices of dogbane and milkweeds, ingested by the caterpillar, make the insect unattractive to birds and thus form a natural chemical defense against predators.

Dogbane is called flytrap, honeybloom, rheumatismwood, wild ipecac, western wallflower, and wandering milkweed. Apocynum, one of the digitalis group of medicines that is a powerful drug for slowing the pulse, was extracted from this plant. Dogbane has also been used to treat rheumatism, syphilis, and scrofula. As the name wild ipecac suggests, it has been employed to induce vomiting.

## *Popular with Indians*

American Indians, including the Crees and more western tribes, used to peel the skin off the outside of the stems of white-flowered dogbane, called Indian hemp (*A. cannabinum*), and use its fibers in making string. They frequently manufactured fishing lines and nets from it, and sometimes wove cloth with the fibers. Swedes who settled in New Jersey and Pennsylvania two centuries ago favored dogbane over other materials for bridles and nets, and traded with local natives for Indian hemp rope. "The Swedes usually got thirty feet of these ropes for one piece of bread," reported a contemporary author. Some traders!

Because dogbane flowers are so rich in nectar, both American Indians and settlers used to procure small quantities of sweetener from the blossoms when sugar was not available. Such sweetness notwithstanding, the Chippewas of Minnesota and Wisconsin, who used it as a medicine and a charm, called spreading dogbane *makwonagic odjibik*, which translates into the rather unattractive "bear entrails root."

Spreading dogbane is a fairly handsome plant with smooth dark green leaves and reddish stems. You may wish to consider it for areas that are sunny, fairly dry, with poor soil and lots of space. You can transplant, divide, or sow seeds collected in September and October. But be forewarned that this perennial can spread and choke out smaller, more delicate plants. In addition, if you have small children who might be tempted to taste its leaves or seedpods, it would be best to avoid having this somewhat poisonous plant around.

If you like butterflies and hate flies, though, dogbane may be right for you.

**Common Ragweed**
*(Ambrosia artemisiifolia)*

# *The Season for Sneezin'*

The end of summer is the season for sneezin', when the breezes bear pollens that bring tears to eyes and tickles to noses of millions of hay fever sufferers. Most of the blame is properly laid on the ragweeds, though some unfortunately has been placed on innocent goldenrods.

Ragweed pollen is a substantial source of the irritants that cause late-summer hay fever. Although there are some fifteen species of the ragweed genus, the main culprits are common ragweed (*Ambrosia artemisiifolia*) and great ragweed (*A. trifida*).

Many people have found it strange that such devilish plants should be called ambrosia, which was the food of the Greek gods. (If he consumed both ambrosia and nectar, the drink of the gods, a man could become immortal.) However, *ambrosia* was ragweed's ancient classical name, first applied no doubt to a finer-flowered or better-tasting member of the clan.

*Artemisiifolia*, sometimes spelled *artemisiaefolia*, means that the leaves are like those of wormwoods, members of the genus *Artemisia.* Artemisia was the wife and sister of Mausolus, a Persian satrap and ruler of Caria and Rhodes, who died in 353 B.C. Artemisia erected a huge and elaborate tomb in her husband's memory. The edifice became one of the seven wonders of the ancient world, and the satrap's name became our word for an above-ground burial place, mausoleum.

Common ragweed is found coast to coast, from Canada to Brazil, especially in colonies along roadsides. If cows are hungry enough, they will eat ragweed, producing bitter milk (whence the name bitterweed). Experiments in the Midwest in the 1940s found that cattle favored—even over alfalfa—hay made by harvesting ragweed before it bloomed and curing it with a little salt. Sheep and pigs like the plant fresh (whence another name, hogweed). For them, at least, it is ambrosia.

Common ragweed's fernlike leaves are actually quite attractive, and a grove of the plants looks almost like a stand of ferns. Wands of dangling, green male flowers rain down the pollen on the less numerous females, hidden in clusters of bracts below. Because ragweed does not use the services of insects, it has not had to evolve showy, scented blossoms. The flowers are green, the same as the rest of the plant, and have no sweet scent to woo passing bees.

The pollen is tiny and light, designed to be borne by air and not by insects. The pollen is manufactured in massive amounts so that at least a few grains will pollinate a female flower somewhere. If you are a hay fever sufferer, you know how successful such a system can be. Just consider your nose to be a flower. When you start sneezing, you have been well pollinated.

### *Pestiferous Pollen*

Ragweed pollen is no worse than the airborne pollen of some other weeds, but ragweeds are the most prolific producers in many areas from August through September. Nationwide, ragweeds spew a quarter of a billion tons of pollen into the air each season. A single plant can produce several million grains of pollen and, spread by the wind, these can easily travel a mile or two from the parent plant.

Annihilating the weed is almost impossible, according to an official of the Connecticut Lung Association. While setting up pollen-counting stations around Connecticut some years ago, the official was dumbfounded at the number of ragweed plants he saw. "It was everywhere—in fields, cracks in driveways, along sidewalks, in flower gardens." While the pollen can be borne over long distances by air, he said, the highest concentrations are within a few hundred yards of the plant, so destroying them could bring some relief to nearby sufferers.

In some places, it is illegal to allow ragweed to grow and you can be fined for not destroying plants that appear on your property. Law or no law, pulling up any ragweed you see does some service to the many hay fever sufferers. Often when my family is out walking, we will yank up any plants we run across. They establish themselves very easily and quickly, so ripping up one may prevent a colony of dozens from forming over a couple years.

Between five and ten percent of the population is allergic to pollen, and some seventy-five percent of those individuals are allergic to ragweed pollen. The lung association calls it the single, most important pollen in causing hay fever. The allergic reaction can include repeated and prolonged sneezing, stuffy and watery nose, redness, swelling and itching of the eyes, and various breathing difficulties. Over some years of exposure, people can develop chronic sinusitis and even asthma.

Other plant pollens or spores can be equally annoying to sensitive people. In the spring, certain tree and grass pollens can cause symptoms, while into the summer and early fall, there are mold spores and airborne pollens from cockleburs, plantains, sheep sorrel, and some other plants.

Goldenrods, which bloom extensively at the same time that ragweed flowers bloom, are often blamed for hay fever, a sort of guilt by association. In fact, the heavier goldenrod pollen is designed to be bee-borne, not air-borne, and is not considered among the culprits affecting hay fever sufferers.

Common ragweed's other names, many as unattractive as the problems it causes, include stickweed, stammerwort, blackweed, carrotweed, Roman wormwood, tasselweed, and hay-fever weed. Hay fever, incidentally, is a misnomer, since neither hay nor fever is involved.

Ragweed has had some medicinal uses. The Delaware Indians used the plant as a poultice to prevent blood poisoning, and in the 1800s the leaves were rubbed on poison ivy inflammations to provide relief. Cheyennes treated bowel cramps with ragweed tea and the Nanticoke considered it a laxative. Old herbals recommended it as an antidote for hay fever—a little hair of the dog that bit you—and today scientists are developing new hay fever medicines employing the pollen to help increase the body's tolerance. The Mexicans recognized it early in this century as an official drug for reducing fevers. Its leaves have been used to produce a long-lasting green dye. And its use as hay may become more extensive when farmers realize that some weeds can be their friends as well as foes.

Perhaps its greatest value, however, is as a natural soil preserver and conditioner. Ragweed is quick to arrive and patch up the earth's wounds, such as swathes cut by floods, fires, or even bulldozers, thus helping to prevent erosion. The nutrients and especially the fibers contained in the above- and below-ground parts of the plant enrich and condition the soil, paving the way for other plants.

### *The Great One*

Great ragweed (*A. trifida*) is almost as common as *A. artemisiifolia*, and its name aptly describes its size, though not its popularity. While the green flowers are very similar to those of common ragweed, the leaves are trifid—three-lobed—and quite different. A fan of rich soils, it often grows from ten to fifteen feet tall, and naturalist William Hamilton Gibson claimed to have measured an eighteen-foot, four-inch specimen in the 1800s. F. Schuyler Mathews said it is the tallest member of the huge Composite family, though some of the related sunflowers and wild lettuces can get quite tall. Great ragweed ranges from the entire East Coast to Manitoba to New Mexico.

Although it is a prolific producer of sneezy pollen, this plant has also had its friends. Smart wheat farmers used to appreciate its arrival after their spring crop was harvested. Rich in nitrogen and other nutrients, great ragweed would be allowed to grow until just before blooming time and then plowed under as a green manure.

The plant has also been called horseweed and horse-cane because those animals supposedly like it (or perhaps because it is as tall as a horse). Either explanation may also apply to its name of buffalo weed, more common in the Midwest. Unless you are an equestrian, buffalo herder, or a wheat farmer, however, you would do as well to yank it from the ground early in its career before it gives you or a neighbor the sneezes and wheezes.

**New England Aster**
*(Aster novae-angliae)*

# *The Stars of Autumn*

Asters, someone once said, "are stars fetched from the night skies and planted on the fields of day." Indeed, it sometimes seems as if there are as many asters as stars when September and October roll around. And to those who have studied the subject a little, it seems almost as if there are as many aster species as there are asters, for perhaps no genus of wildflowers has more North American members than this one does.

Aster is the Latin generic name, one of the few that has caught on as a common English wildflower name as well. Aster means "star," as in "astronomy" and "astronaut"; asters were once more frequently called starworts and still are so called in England.

Although some 250 species of asters grow around the world, the majority, at least 150, are natives of North America, and about 50 might be considered common and widespread. While so many of our common wildflowers have come from Europe, none of our asters is an immigrant. In fact, Europe has relatively few asters. *The Oxford Book of Wild Flowers* lists only one species of note in the British Isles, and most of the European varieties are rather unimpressive. Donald Culross Peattie said in 1935, "Europe has no asters at which an American would look twice."

## *The Hunt*

Of our native species, most of which are perennials, some 75 are found east of the Rockies and 55 of them in the northeast United States and southeast Canada. The Pacific states and British Columbia seem to have fewer of them, but those few include the widespread leafy aster (*A. foliaceus*), with beautiful purple- or lavender-rayed flowers. Since there are so many species, aster hunting is almost an autumnal subhobby of wildflower hunting. With so many varieties, some exceedingly rare, the amateur flower sleuth could spend many hours, not only in finding, but then in identifying them.

This is sometimes no simple task, for most wildflower guides do not pretend to list every species you might come across. Even when armed with an extensive catalog, such as Britton and Brown's three-volume set, *An Illustrated Flora of the Northern United States and Canada*, identification can be tedious and technical, requiring close inspection of the leaves, seeds, or other parts. What's worse, asters in the wild tend to form hybrids and create tiny races that sometimes become distinct enough to be classified by some botanists as species. For example, you could stalk the elusive crimson-disk aster (*A. carmesinus*), which in 1913 was known to exist only on shaded rocks near Yonkers, New York. Britton and Brown describe it as distinguished from the common white wood aster by having "dense glomerules subtended by large short-elliptic leaves." Or you might look for *A. gravesii*, which had been found only around Waterford, Connecticut, early in this century and was separated from *A. dumosus* (bushy aster) by its oblong-lanceolate leaves, acuminate at both ends.

These are extreme examples and most asters can be identified by people not holding a botany degree. Actually, it is fun and challenging and, in the process of trying to separate similar species, you can learn a good deal about plant identification and structure.

The season for aster hunting starts in August when the white wood asters and other early species appear. September is the best month, since virtually every variety is in bloom sometime during the month. The flowers are a prelude to autumn's bright colors. John Burroughs observed: "How rich in color before the big show of the tree foliage has commenced, our early roadsides are in places in early autumn—rich to the eye that goes hurriedly by and does not look too closely—with the profusion of goldenrod and blue and purple asters dashed upon here and there with the crimson leaves of the dwarf sumac."

Blues, purples, and variations thereof are common colors among asters. However, many white varieties are also common, though often the white species will produce blossoms with subtle pastel tints of violet, pink, or blue. In many species the center disks start out yellow, but turn to purple or brown later on.

## *Success Story*

Members of the huge Composite family, the asters are one of the most typical and successful examples of Composite construction—a center disk of fertile florets (almost always yellow), surrounded by rays that, while they look like petals, are actually sterile florets lengthened through evolution in a design to attract insects.

Neltje Blanchan wrote an interesting essay on the Composites that is fitting to pass on here because, according to some botanists, asters are among the most successful Composites and hence among the most successful flowers.

*Evolution teaches us that thistles, daisies, sunflowers, asters, and all the triumphant horde of Composites were once very different flowers from what we see today. Through ages of natural selection of the fittest among their ancestral types, having finally arrived at the most successful adaptation of their various parts to their surroundings in the whole floral kingdom, they are now overrunning the earth.*

*Doubtless, the aster's remote ancestors were simple green leaves around the vital organs, and depended upon the wind, as the grasses do . . . to transfer the pollen. Then some rudimentary flower changed its outer row of stamens into petals, which gradually took on color to attract insects and insure a more economical method of transfer. Gardeners today take advantage of a blossom's natural tendency to change stamens into petals when they wish to produce double flowers.*

*As flowers and insects developed side by side, and there came to be a better and better understanding between them of each other's requirements, mutual adaptation followed. The flower that offered the best advertisement, as the Composites do, by its showy rays; that secreted nectar in tubular flowers where no useless insect could pilfer it; that fastened its stamens to the inside wall of the tube where they must dust with pollen the underside of every insect, unwittingly cross-fertilizing the blossom as he crawled over it; that massed a great number of these tubular florets together where insects might readily discover them and feast with the least possible loss of time—this flower became the winner in life's race. Small wonder that our fields are white with daisies and the autumn landscape is glorified with goldenrod and asters.*

### The Celebrity

Asters are found in all kinds of situations: fields, dry sand, salty beaches, swamps, forest, leaf-mold, thickets, limestone cliffs, and, of course, along roadsides. Some thrive in bright sun while others favor shade.

Among the most beautiful of the genus is the New England aster, about which the experts seem to agree:

"Probably no [aster] is more striking," wrote Mrs. William Starr Dana in 1893.

"Surely this is the most admirable of all the asters," said Mabel Osgood Wright, in 1901.

"The flower-heads . . . shine out with royal splendor," noted Neltje Blanchan in 1900.

"Our most showy wild aster," observed Roger Tory Peterson in 1968.

Even the staid, scientific Britton and Brown called it "one of the most beautiful of the genus." And in that poll of naturalists and botanists in the 1940s, New England aster ranked as the third most popular flower in North America.

From late August to early October, New England aster colors moist roadsides with varying shades, including violet, magenta-purple, violet-purple, pink-rosy-lilac, and reddish purple. Occasionally, a red or white bloom is found. The 40 to 100 rays on each flower are stunningly set off by the center disk of yellow, creating a blossom an inch to an inch and a half across. Were these only solitary flowers on single stems, they would probably be much admired. As it is, up to fifty blossoms may appear in a single two-to-five-foot tall plant, making quite an impressive show.

*Aster novae-angliae* translates literally as "star of New England." Though its name is geographical, this aster is by no means limited in range to New England, and can be found across southern Canada to the Rockies, and south in the United States to the Gulf Coast.

This perennial likes plenty of sun and fairly rich, moist soils, and spreads slowly by roots and by seeds. Because it is such a common, hardy, and easy-to-grow flower, it is well worth trying to establish in your yard or garden. The best way is to transplant in late spring or early summer. Since the plants are usually found in large colonies, removing a few individuals will do little harm, either to the scenery or to propagation. The experts say that the most successful time to transplant is June, but I have moved them in late July without trouble. Transplanting in fall is risky unless you get a complete clod of roots.

Planting seed is easier, but less likely to succeed because the germination rate in asters is not great. If you give it a try, use many seeds, gathered and sown in October or November.

The lower leaves on the New England aster tend to die and dry up, making the plants somewhat ratty looking by blooming time. To prevent this, mulch the plants heavily over the winter, remove the mulch in the spring, and replace it once the new growth has hardened. Mulching also produces better-quality flowers.

New England aster is the parent of many garden asters, cultivated widely especially in Europe. Among the more common hybrids are Barr's Blue and Barr's Pink, Crimson Beauty, Snow Queen (a white variety), and Harrington's Pink. The similar and beautiful New York aster (*A. novi-belgii*) is parent of the famous and widely grown Michaelmas daisies, which have escaped from gardens in Europe and are considered wildflowers in places like Great Britain.

## *Useful Stars*

Among Europeans and the colonists, asters were never famous as medicinal herbs, although the Shakers brewed solutions from them that supposedly cured skin rashes and the ancient Latins were said to have used some species to treat snakebites and sciatica. Culpeper recommended a couple of European varieties for such things as fevers, asthma, and "swellings in the groin."

American Indians found plenty of uses for asters, treating problems such as skin rashes, earaches, stomach pains, intestinal fevers, and insanity with various species. The Meskwakis used aster smoke in their sweat baths. By feeding the smoke into a paperlike cone fitted into a nostril, they revived unconscious people. The Ojibwas of the Midwest smoked the New England aster and other asters in pipes as a charm to attract game, especially deer. The Objibwas and settlers in Maine and Quebec ate the young leaves of large-leaved aster (*A. macrophyllus*).

While European asters did not do much to perk up ailing patients, they were recommended as a sort of medicine for bees by no less than Virgil, the great Latin poet. Book IV of his *Georgics* is devoted to the natural history and care of bees, and therein Virgil offers a suggestion for ailing colonies, using a European aster (probably *A. amellus*):

*The meadows know a flower, yclept by swains*
*"The Starwort": 'tis an easy one to find*
*For from one root it rears a mighty forest.*
*Its disc is gold; its many petaled fringe*
*Pale purple shadowed with dark violet.*
*Often the altars of the gods are decked*
*With chaplets wreathed of it; 'tis rough to taste;*
*In sheep-clipped dells and near the winding stream*
*Of Mella shepherds gather it. Take thou*
*And seethe the roots in fragrant wine, and serve*
*Full baskets in the doorway of the hive.*

Although they may have little practical value, asters have long been recognized as decorations. The flowers of most species last several days after being picked and put into vases, though many, like New England asters, close up at night. Mixed with plumes of goldenrod, what finer bouquet can adorn a table than these two handsome and colorful autumnal natives?

**Groundnut**
*(Apios americana)*

## *Sweet from Tip to Toe*

Those who have read John Greenleaf Whittier's idyllic celebration of youth may recall that "The Barefoot Boy" knew not only the ordinary wildflowers, but also the groundnut vines with their hidden treats:

*Oh for boyhood's painless play,*
*Sleep that wakes in laughing day,*
*Health that mocks the doctor's rules,*
*Knowledge never learned of schools*
*Of the wild bee's morning chase,*
*Of the wild-flower's time and place,*
*Flight of fowl and habitude*
*Of the tenants of the wood;*
*How the tortoise bears his shell,*
*How the woodchuck digs his cell,*
*And the ground-mole sinks his well;*
*How the robin feeds her young,*
*How the oriole's nest is hung;*
*Where the whitest lilies blow,*
*Where the freshest berries grow,*
*Where the ground-nut trails its vine,*
*Where the wood-grape's clusters shine;*
*Of the black wasp's cunning way,*
*Mason of his walls of clay,*
*And the architectural plans*
*Of gray hornet artisans!*
*For, eschewing books and tasks,*
*Nature answers all he asks;*
*Hand in hand with her he walks,*
*Face to face with her he talks,*
*Part and parcel of her joy, —*
*Blessings on the barefoot boy!*

Unfortunately, some wildflower watchers miss vines like groundnut because they are so intent on the ground that they ignore shrubs or even fences for interesting blossoms. Groundnut is a plant worth noticing, both for its strong, sweet scent, and the bounty below the ground.

Groundnut is a member of the Pea family and, as every barefoot boy once knew, frequents moist thickets. The vines bear distinctive fronds, consisting usually of two or three pairs of opposite leaves and one end leaf at a right angle to the rest. The more distinctive feature of the plant is its flowers. Blooming in tight clusters of a dozen or two blossoms from July through September, they are of an unusual color. Some describe it as purplish brown or even chocolate.

The flowers look almost good enough to eat, especially after you smell them; the scent is among the strongest and the sweetest in our wildflower world. "Although too inconspicuous in itself to be called a landscape flower," wrote

Mabel Osgood Wright in 1901, the groundnut "pays its tithe in fragrance."

Since the flowers are often hidden behind the vine's own leaves or that of the host plant, their existence must frequently be betrayed by the scent. Mrs. Wright added that groundnut vines help to add fullness to greenery in that each vine "brings into uniformity much that would otherwise be unsightly, straggling growth."

### *Tasty Roots*

The sweetness does not end with the flowers. American Indians, explorers, and barefoot farm boys alike cherished the tuberous rootstock, which has pea- to egg-sized lumps linked like big beads on a chain. These tubers have a sweet, somewhat nutty taste recalled in its common name. Among many American Indian tribes, including the Sioux, Delaware, and Wampanoags, it was considered an important food and was cultivated at many villages. Groundnuts may be eaten raw, boiled, roasted, or fried, but several authorities say they taste best if you peel and parboil the tubers with salt, and then roast them or chop and fry them. The meat should always be eaten while hot; a cold groundnut is said to be about as tasty as a wet towel.

Europeans knew of the plant by 1590 when Thomas Hariot, writing about Sir Walter Raleigh's early but unsuccessful attempt to establish a colony in Virginia, told of "openask," with its "very good meate." Gosnold found Indians of Martha's Vineyard eating them in 1602, and Massachusetts Bay Indians introduced the plant to the Pilgrims, who ate them to help get through that first difficult winter at Plymouth. Early Swedish immigrants in the mid-Atlantic colonies used groundnuts for bread in the 1700s. Once, when his potato crop failed, Henry David Thoreau dug up groundnuts and found them quite tasty. (Nelson Coon says that for diabetics they make a good substitute for potatoes.)

Explorers and soldiers on long trips through the Midwest sought out groundnut; one trick was to look for the burrows of field mice, which collected them and stored them for winter food. One expedition reported finding a peck of roots from the stores of mice.

It is said that Raleigh was impressed enough with the groundnut that he brought it back to England as a "potato," though in taste it is more often likened to a turnip. Dr. Asa Gray, the noted nineteenth-century botanist, was of the opinion that had civilization started in the New World instead of the Old, the groundnut would have centuries ago been cultivated and developed as a commercial crop and would now be an everyday vegetable. Some American farmers in the past made an attempt at cultivating the groundnut but were never successful at gaining a wide enough market to profit from growing them. Perhaps that's because the European palate simply did not like groundnuts as much as it did other discoveries from the Americas, such as the true potato and the tomato.

### *Many Names*

The plant is also called wild bean. It is a relative of our garden beans and produces small, edible bean seeds in the fall. (The name is confusing because several related plants are also called wild bean.) Other folk names include hyacinth bean, Indian potato, pig potato, bog potato, potato bean, white apple, ground pea, trailing pea, and Dakota potato. French settlers in Canada called it *pomme de terre* or "earth apple."

Its scientific name, or names, are almost as plentiful as its common ones. In 1753 Linnaeus named the plant *Glycine apios*; *glycine* means "sweet" and apios is Greek for "pear," referring to the shape of the tuber. By the 1800s it was being called *Apios tuberosa* by some, including Dr. Gray. By the 1890s, it was *Apios apios*. In 1913 Britton and Brown called it *Glycine apios* again, but today it is known as *Apios americana*, probably the most suitable of the lot since it is a widespread native, at home from eastern Canada to Florida and west into Texas and Colorado. The only other member of the genus in North America is quite rare, found only in rocky woods of Tennessee and Kentucky. Only five *Apios* species were known in the world in 1913; two were in China and one, the Himalayas.

### *For Your Own*

Perhaps because its flowers are not huge, *Apios* species or cultivars have not been popular with gardeners, except in France during the nineteenth century. (The closely related wisteria has fared better.) Groundnut is easy to grow from tubers transplanted in the spring or from seeds collected in September or October. It needs moist, rich soil, a host plant or fence, and not too much sun. Although it does not spread rapidly and overrun an area, it is difficult to eradicate once established, so select planting places with care. One nineteenth-century gardener, writing in the *Canadian Horticulturist*, suggested planting them with tall summer roses: "It would do them no harm, but lend a beauty to them after they had done blooming."

In your garden it may be picked freely to bring its fragrance into the home, but avoid picking it in the wild. While not an endangered species, groundnut is not as common as it once was and should be encouraged to self-sow seeds where it is not being a pest.

After all, barefoot boys—and girls—of the future should have a chance to find its trailing vine.

**Rough-stemmed Goldenrod**
*(Solidago rugosa)*

## *The Glorious Goldenrods*

Goldenrods, wrote Mabel Osgood Wright, "are a byword among plant students, who say that if a botanist is ever condemned to the severest punishment that the underworld can mete, the penalty will be to write a monograph, accurately describing and identifying all the known goldenrods."

To describe goldenrods in terms of torture seems a shame, but the point is well taken. Throughout the world, 125 species of goldenrod are known; of these, around 90 are found in North America. The Northeast and particularly New England is home to up to 50 kinds. They vary from widespread species found from Newfoundland to California, to species of very restricted ranges, such as one found only on the shaded cliffs of the Wisconsin River in Sauk County, Wisconsin. "To name all these species, or [those of] the aster, the sparrows, and the warblers at sight is a feat probably no one living can perform," observed Neltje Blanchan.

There is a certain challenge to being able to identify goldenrods—with the help of a good guidebook, of course. While many are distinctive, many others are similar to each other and quite a few kinds may be found in one location. F. Schuyler Mathews tells of finding no fewer than fifteen varieties in a quarter-mile length of road in Campton, New Hampshire.

### *Visual Delight*

Goldenrods, however, are better as visual delights than objects for cataloging. In late summer and autumn, their tall wands and plumes wave over fields and roadsides in such profusion that they are perhaps the dominant ground coloring of the season. In eastern North America, they are so common and adaptable that there is almost no spot—outside an inner city—where one can stand outdoors in September and not see their bright color.

"Goldenrod, collectively, is a delight to the eye, for its color and indispensable factor in the landscape," said Mrs. Wright in 1901. "For decorative purposes it is eminently satisfactory, sought out and beloved by all men, as is amply proved by 'goldenrod weddings,' and by the numerous jars, pitchers, water cans, and bean pots filled with it that decorate suburban stoops." In Europe, where only a couple of not very showy species are found as natives, some of the more luxuriant American varieties have been carefully cultivated in gardens and have been popular as border plants.

Certain goldenrods, as well as steeplebush, are unusual among plants with spikes of flowers in that the blossoms at the top open first and the blooming creeps downward. In most other plants, the bottom-most flowers open first and the blooming moves upward. (However, John Burroughs found that in teasel, "The wave of bloom begins in the middle of the head and spreads both ways, up and down.") The top-to-bottom flowering of the spike-shaped goldenrods may be connected with their competition for insect attention. When the plant first blooms, many of the late-summer flowers are competing to attract bees, and thus the highest, most visible flowers come out first. Later, as the competition fades in the cooling breezes of fall, goldenrod is one of the few flowers left, and it has no trouble flagging down hungry bees with its lower-blooming blossoms.

Another creature attracted to goldenrods is the praying mantis, the large green insect that eats so many garden pests. The fire chief in our town, who is also a trained entomologist, told me one fall day that the best place to find mantis egg cases is on the dead stalks of goldenrod. To prove his point, a few hours later the chief showed up in my office with a dry stalk of goldenrod, mantis eggs attached. I kept the stalk outdoors over the winter and when spring arrived, the mantises hatched and headed out, presumably to devour local pests. Why do these Mantids favor goldenrods? Possibly because the mother mantises spend a lot of time late in the season on goldenrods. They await prey among the many flying insects drawn by the color and scent to the wealth of nectar in the goldenrod fronds, clusters and wands of flowers. When they are done hunting and ready to lay eggs, they pick the nearest handy place.

### *Sun Medicine*

Though not nearly as plentiful in the Old World as here, goldenrods have been long recognized as important plants by European herbalists and physicians. Even their generic name, *Solidago*, means "to make whole," referring to their supposed medicinal benefits. The Chippewa Indians had an even better name for the goldenrod family in general, calling it *gizisomukiki*, which translates as "sun medicine." The plant has been used to calm stomachs, allay nausea, pass stones, and cure wounds, and to treat diphtheria, bronchitis, and tuberculosis. Old-time Californians employed the appropriately named *S. californica* to treat sores and cuts, calling the plant *oreja de liebre*, which means "jackrabbit's ear," supposedly the shape of the leaf. "It is a sovereign wound-herb, inferior to none, both for inward and outward use," wrote the herbalist Nicholas Culpeper centuries ago, referring to the European species, *S. virgaurea*. It has been used to treat so many maladies that it is as much a panacea as any plant could be, says Donald Law, a modern English herbalist.

The Great Saladin (1137–1193), the poor boy who rose to be caliph of Egypt and fought King Richard in the Third Crusade, was said to have greatly treasured goldenrod as a medicine and introduced its cultivation into the Middle East, where it long remained an important crop. When Mediterranean-grown *S. virgaurea* was first introduced into Elizabethan England as a medicinal herb, it was much sought after and commanded high prices—as much as a half-crown an ounce. When people discovered that the very same species could be found growing wild in parts of English countryside, however, its monetary value plummeted and so did its popularity among herb users. The reversal prompted John Gerard to observe: "This verifieth our English proverb: 'Far fecht and deare bought is best for ladies.'"

### *Ancient Brews*

Brews of goldenrod were popular on many fronts. Witches were said to have used goldenrod in potions. In Europe, the leaves were sometimes concocted into what was called Blue Mountain wine. Teas made from several species, especially the more aromatic ones, have been brewed in both Europe and in North America, particularly by the Indians. Culpeper said, "No preparation is better than a tea of the herb made from the young leaves, fresh or dried." Medicinal extracts and tea leaves made from such aromatic American species as fragrant goldenrod (*S. odora*) were exported in the nineteenth century to China, where they were much admired and commanded high prices.

Bees also drink goldenrod products, harvesting its nectar in great quantities in the flower-starved autumn. In fact, goldenrods are considered one of the most important bee plants. And if you should bug one of those drinking bees, you could try the sting lotion that was once concocted by the Meskwaki Indians from the flowers of stiff goldenrod (*S. rigida*).

The flowers of various species of goldenrods have been used to make reliable yellow dyes for cloth. While their excellence as dyes has been recognized for several centuries, goldenrod colorings for some reason were little used professionally and were popular mostly in the home. Thomas Edison experimented with using goldenrods as a source of rubber. Ancient diviners believed the plant could be used to point the way to underground sources of water, hidden springs, and even to troves of silver and gold.

With so much beauty and so many uses to its credit, it is not surprising that two states—Kentucky and Nebraska—have named it their state flower.

While it has long been known as a curative, goldenrod has inappropriately been blamed as a chief cause of hay fever, probably because it blooms in such great numbers at the height of the hay fever season (see Ragweeds: The Season for Sneezin').

### *Common Species*

Goldenrods are members of the Composite family—a fact given away by their tight clusters of tiny florets. There are many widespread species, several of which are worth noting.

- Blue-stemmed goldenrod (*S. caesia*), also called wreath goldenrod, has tufts of blossoms on bluish or purplish stems. "None is prettier, more dainty, than this common species," says Mrs. Blanchan.
- Canada goldenrod (*S. canadensis*), with spreading plumes, may grow five feet tall or higher and is unusually widespread; it can be found from Labrador to the Pacific states, where it is more commonly called meadow goldenrod. Its roots are among the deepest of common American herbs—growing as many as eleven feet down in the prairies of Nebraska—enabling it to obtain deep subterranean water in very dry seasons. The Meskwakis, who believed that some children were born without the ability to laugh, would boil this goldenrod in water

with the bone of an animal that died when the child was born. Washing the baby in this concoction supposedly guaranteed that the child would be cheerful and blessed with a good sense of humor.

- Early goldenrod (*S. juncea*), a small and common variety with comparatively few blossoms, is true to its name by blooming as early as the last week in July, an occurrence that some New Englanders take—without cause—to presage an early winter. Nonetheless, its appearance does put a psychological chill into the viewer, warning that despite all this warmth, the cold is not so far off. Years ago this plant was dried as a winter decoration, and the Chippewas used it to treat convulsions and women's ailments.
- Gray goldenrod (*S. nemoralis*) is a two-foot-high species found mostly in sterile eastern fields. This species was considered by Mathews as "the most brilliantly colored of all goldenrods." Probably following the "doctrine of signatures," the Houma Indians made a tea from its roots to treat jaundice.
- Lance-leafed goldenrod (*S. graminifolia*), a very fragrant and common variety in the East, has a flat top of flower clusters and is sometimes confused with tansy.
- Rough-stemmed goldenrod (*S. rugosa*) is another tall variety, whose specific Latin name means "with wrinkled leaves." The word "rugged" is based on the same root; apparently something that is rough and wrinkled was considered rugged or tough. Since this species likes dry soils and dusty roadsides, the name is doubly appropriate.
- Sharp-leaved goldenrod (*S. arguta*) is sometimes reported as the earliest goldenrod, with full bloom in mid-July. Flowers appear greenish yellow.
- Narrow goldenrod (*S. spathulata*), another wide-ranging species found on both the East and West Coasts and across Canada, is interesting in that it thrives in such variant locations as coastal sand dunes and mountain slopes. It is so called because its flower heads are composed of narrow clusters.
- Sweet goldenrod (*S. odora*), also called Blue Mountain tea, is noted for its strong anise scent. During the Revolution it was frequently used as a replacement for British teas. Charles Francis Saunders, in *Edible and Useful Wild Plants*, calls it "a pleasant and wholesome drink," and Euell Gibbons recommended its sweet-aromatic flavor and aroma. This was the only goldenrod ever to make the *U.S. Pharmacopoeia*, but it was dropped by 1882.
- Tall goldenrod (*S. altissima*) may reach eight feet in height and can be found from the Atlantic to Wyoming and Arizona. The Chippewas, who called this squirrel tail, used it to relieve cramps.
- White goldenrod (*S. bicolor*) is more colorfully called silverrod. Its flowers are white or creamy and so unlike typical goldenrods that few people recognize them as such. Silverrod is also called belly-ache-weed from its use as a carminative—an herbal Gas-X.

All goldenrods are perennials. Most are showy and long-lasting enough to make fine border flowers, and are easily established by transplanting or gathering and spreading the seeds. Their decorative blossoms remain fresh in bouquets for several days, and I can't imagine an autumn flower arrangement without goldenrods.

Nor can I imagine a late fall walk without seeing the dried, gray, fuzzy-topped wands that John Greenleaf Whittier recalled in "The Last Walk in Autumn":

*Along the rivers summer walk,*
*The withered tufts of asters nod;*
*And trembles on its arid stalk*
*The hoar plume of the golden-rod.*

"The goldenrod is certainly our representative American wildflower," wrote Mathews in 1895. A few years before, when the subject of a national flower was widely discussed, a Boston man published an essay suggesting that either arbutus or goldenrod be chosen, and asking the people to make known their preference. "The response was decisive," Mathews reported. "And the vote was cast by an overwhelming majority for the goldenrod." Were it not for its misrepresentation as causing hay fever, goldenrod might well be in the running today as our national flower.

**Nodding Ladies'-Tresses**
*(Spiranthes cernua)*

# *Orchids of the Autumn*

To many of us, the word "orchid" conjures up images of large, showy flowers of fine color and exquisite form. Ladies'-tresses may not be large, finely colored, or particularly showy, but their form has made them a favorite of those who hunt for the seeming handful of early autumn flowers that do not fall within the aster or goldenrod clans.

Ladies'-tresses are one of the last of the Orchid family to bloom in the Northeast and some say they are the most common variety of wild orchid in the eastern United States. In my territory, they are hardly common—none of the wild orchids is—and I once got a call from an orchid enthusiast visiting the area who wanted to know where he could view some ladies'-tresses, even if it took a good bit of hiking.

To the casual wildflower observer, such interest may seem odd, for none of the ladies'-tresses species gets to be more than eighteen or so inches in height. Their spikes of small white flowers are slim and often difficult to pick out from their surroundings, which frequently includes small white asters. Yet, the delicate, cleverly designed flowers are well worth seeking out and inspecting, even if doing so requires a magnifying glass.

## *Nodding and Slender*

Some twenty-five species of ladies'-tresses can be found throughout North America. In the eastern half of the continent, the genus is most apt to be represented by two species, the nodding ladies'-tresses (*Spiranthes cernua*) and the smaller-flowered slender ladies'-tresses (*S. gracilis*). The former inhabits the typical haunt of the genus, swamps and wet fields. The latter favors dry, sandy places, particularly hillsides; I have see them happily growing amid the ugliness of an old sandpit. Both are widespread, found from Newfoundland to Florida, and westward to New Mexico. The largest-flowered of the genus, fragrant ladies'-tresses (*S. odorata*), has a scent that hints of vanilla; this species is found in the South. Pacific states representatives include hooded ladies'-tresses (*S. romanzoffiana*) and western ladies'-tresses (*S. porrifolia*), both of which are summer rather than autumnal bloomers. Some authorities say the hooded ladies'-tresses may be found throughout northern North America as well as in Europe, especially Ireland.

The genus got its name from the way in which the flowers are displayed. They seem woven into the stem, giving it the appearance of a woman's braid—which is an old meaning of "tress." The plants have also been called ladies'-traces, "trace" being another form of "tress." *Spiranthes* comes from *speira*, a "spiral," and *anthos*, "flower," Greek words descriptive of the manner in which the flowers wind their way around the stem like a spiral staircase. Actually, the flowers appear on only one side of the stem, but the stem twists to make them seem to be attached spirally. Britton and Brown called this genus *Ibidium*, from a fancied resemblance of the flowers to the head of an ibis. The genus has also been called *Gyrostachys*, Greek for "twisted stalk." *Cernua* means "nodding," because the flowers are downward-turned; *gracilis* means "slender" or "graceful"; *porrifolia* suggests its leaves are leeklike; and *romanzoffiana* refers to a person, possibly a botanist or perhaps the whole Russian royal family.

## *The Climbing Bees*

Despite their size and lack of vivid color, ladies'-tresses attract many bees, without which they and half the other flowers in the world would disappear. Thus, it is important that flowers have something—be it size, color, or scent—to attract the interest of these insects. In this case, it is a strong, sweet fragrance.

The complex relationship between bees and ladies'-tresses fascinated Charles Darwin, Asa Gray, William Hamilton Gibson, and other noted students of nature. If you observe a bee visiting a colony of the plants, you will find that the insect always starts at the bottom of the spiral spike of flowers and works its way up to the top, then flies to the bottom of the next plant's spike, works upward, etc. Why the bee uses this bottom-to-top system is uncertain. Darwin suspected it is just easier for bees to climb up than back down. "I believe," he wrote, that "bumblebees generally act in this manner when visiting a dense spike of flowers, as it is the most convenient method—on the same principle that a woodpecker always climbs up a tree in search of insects."

More important, however, it is a system that enables the plants to survive and to which the ladies'-tresses probably adapted themselves during their long evolution. In a maturing spike, the lower flowers are older, and have grown to the point where they are designed to be receivers of pollen. The blossoms toward the top are newer, less developed, and can only give pollen. Thus, having picked up grains from the top flowers of one plant, the bee moves to the bottom of the next to deliver the pollen and fertilize those flowers. Gradually, the ability to receive pollen moves up the spike so that most of the flowers—perhaps with the exception of the uppermost—are fertilized.

## *Goo for Pollen*

Even the method of dispensing pollen is unusual. As the bee inserts its tongue into a new flower to sip the nectar, it splits a little disk inside, releasing a very sticky glue that dries almost instantly and that helps assure that a tiny "boat" carrying pollen adheres to the bee. Apparently, having little pods of pollen on their tongues does not annoy the bees too much, for they continue to visit other flowers. When a bee visits the lower, older flowers, it finds the channel for his tongue has widened a great deal as the flower has matured. This allows the pollen-catching stigma to be exposed to the bee's pollen-bearing tongue, effecting pollination.

Ladies'-tresses have seen limited use in the practical world. A European species was once thought to be an aphrodisiac, and has been used to treat eye, kidney, and skin ailments. A Chilean variety is considered a diuretic.

Other names for these plants include wild tube-rose and screw-auger for *S. cernua* and green-lipped ladies'-tresses, twisted-stalk, and corkscrew-plant for *S. gracilis*. Fragrant ladies'-tresses have also been called simply fragrant tresses as well as tidal tresses.

These plants grow from tuberous roots. They should be transplanted only if they are in certain danger of destruction. Like most orchids, they're fussy about their surroundings, and they probably require the presence in the soil of certain kinds of fungus that help the young plants to grow. If you are patient, you can try planting from seed. In the case of *S. gracilis*, you'll have to wait three years before flowers will appear.

**Bull Thistle**
*(Cirsium vulgare)*

## *Watch Your Step*

Thistles are so well known for their prickly nature that many people call any plant with stickers a thistle. Yet, thistles are important, often attractive plants that have many points—other than sharp ones—worth appreciating.

Many varieties of thistles are covered with thorns from head to foot, a defense against insects as well as two-footed or four-footed animals. The stickers that adorn the thistle heads are designed to discourage grazing animals from eating them and to keep crawling insects, such as ants, away from the unusually sweet nectar in the flowers.

The blooms of the flower heads, which range from the size of a marble to almost as big as a tennis ball, burst from the tops with thin hairlike petals of bright purple or deep pink. Some species are yellow and a few star-thistles (*Centaurea*) are blue.

### *Poor PR*

Though brilliantly colored, thistles have suffered from some pretty poor PR over the millennia. "Cursed is the ground because of you," the Lord told Adam in the Garden of Eden. "Thorns and thistles it shall bring forth to you." Shakespeare called them "rough thistles" in the same breath with "hateful docks." In his book, *All About Weeds*, biology professor and farmer Edwin Rollin Spencer labeled Canada thistle (*Cirsium arvense*) "perhaps the worst weed of the entire United States. The plant does not have a single virtue so far as man is concerned."

So despised have thistles been that Australia passed an Act of Parliament around the turn of the century, imposing stiff fines on persons who failed to destroy the plants, which were taking over thousands of square miles of fields Down Under. The government even appointed inspectors to search out scofflaws. England enacted a similar measure, and no fewer than thirty-seven states have officially declared Canada thistle *planta non grata.*

With such an unpleasant history, there would seem to be no redeeming value to this prickly family, whose very name is said to come from an ancient Saxon word for "to stab." Thistle has been well appreciated, however, in both fact and legend. Many varieties of birds love thistle seed, as do bird fans, who will pay several dollars a pound for it. And a pound of tiny thistle seed is not much.

Butterflies love its nectar and bees make fine honey from it. When thistle leaves have been crushed to destroy the thorns, they have been found to be excellent food for livestock, and were once widely used for that purpose in Scotland. Stripped of their spines, the young leaves of many *Cirsium* species make fine salad greens and cooked vegetables. The peeled stems are said to be tasty either cooked or raw, and the roasted root is sweet. From the flower heads, the British have made golden thistle wine, which is supposed to taste like dry sherry. The seeds have been pressed to obtain oil; perhaps that was what Theophilus Thistlebottom of tongue-twisting fame was planning to do after successfully sifting thistles.

"Two or three of our native species are handsome enough to be worthy of a place in gardens," wrote British herbalist Maude Grieve. Indeed, some years ago, it was common in the British Isles to find Scotch or Scots thistle naturalized about the ruins of old castles in whose gardens it had been cultivated. It and members of its genus are still mentioned as border plants in a few gardening books.

Then, there is the scent. The despised Canada thistle is as fragrant and sweet as the most delicate and cultivated of garden flowers. One plant's perfume fills the air for yards around. The pasture thistle (*C. pumilum*), a large pricker-studded fellow, is also called the fragrant thistle and once had the scientific name *C. odoratus* because of its fine scent.

## *Thistle Clans*

About a dozen thistle genera occur in North America, all members of the large Composite family. Many species were unintentionally imported from Europe with crop seeds. Canada thistle did so via Canada, whence the name; back home in Europe it is usually called creeping thistle.

*Cirsium* is one of the larger thistle genera, with some ninety-two species in North America, and its name comes from a Greek word that reflects the fact that one of the species was once used as a medicine to treat swollen veins. The Chippewas used native species to treat back pain during pregnancy. The Mohegans of Connecticut employed the imported *C. arvense* as a mouthwash for infants.

Much of the farmers' hatred for thistles stems not so much from the fact that they are prickly as from their being prolific and persistent, able to take over fields and stay there. In fact, their taste for good-quality soil is legend, and the British used to tell of the blind man who was choosing land to buy for his farm. "Take me to the thistle," he said. A sixteenth-century poet, writing on husbandry, advised:

*If thistles so growing proove lustie and long,*
*It signifieth land to be hartie and strong.*

The perennial Canada thistle has roots that not only go deep but also creep along just under the surface, sending up many new shoots. If left alone for a couple of years, a single plant can establish a sizable colony. *C. arvense* is a dioecious species, having both males and females, and unless plants of the opposite sex are close by, fertile seeds will not be produced. A male plant will produce only colonies of males via the underground runners, and females will make only females. But, to the dread of farmers, a colonizing male near a colonizing female can soon wind up producing scads of seeds, which the goldfinches and other birds scatter everywhere.

Though thistle heads are equipped with a generous supply of down that one would think was designed to lift away seeds in the wind, relatively few seeds find their way aloft. Most reach the ground when the flower head dies and falls off. While the down may do little for future generations of thistles, it kept past generations of Americans warm. Thistle-down quilts were great for snuggling under in winter and the fluff was also popular with woodsmen, who used it as tinder for their campfires.

The tall or roadside thistle (*Cirsium altissimum*), is a closely related species that, as both the English and Latin names suggest, is one of our loftier herbs. It can reach ten feet in height.

### *Blessed Among the Cursed*

Among the other alien species that grow in North America is the blessed thistle (*Cnicus benedictus*), a seeming contradiction in terms. It may have been so called because of its extensive reputation and use as a cure for many maladies in the Middle Ages, when religion and medicine were closely connected. There is also a legend that the plant's veins were made white by the Virgin Mary's milk as she fed the infant Jesus. It was considered so powerful that it was used to treat the plague. *Cnicus* is the Latin word for "bastard saffron" or "mock saffron," perhaps reflecting some ancient use of the plant, which is found throughout the United States and southern Canada.

Scotch thistle (*Onopordum acanthium*) is found from the East Coast to Montana and Texas and in the Pacific Northwest. *Onopordum* means "asses' thistle," an ancient name possibly indicating that "stupid asses" would eat it, thorns and all. *Acanthium* means "thorny."

It may be the "true" thistle of Scotland, emblazoned on coins, flags, coats of arms, and the like. It was originally the emblem of the House of Stuart—so ordered by James IV, on the occasion of his marriage to Margaret Tudor ("The Thistle and the Rose" of poet Dunbar). In 1540, James V created The Order of the Thistle for knights of Scotland. Its motto, *Nemo me impune lacessit* ("No one attacks me with impunity") became the motto of Scotland and might well be the motto of the thistle itself.

The Scotch thistle is a tall, erect, single-flowered, and very thorny plant of open fields. Legend has it that when the Danes or Norsemen invaded Scotland a thousand years ago, the soldiers stole up to a Scottish camp one quiet night by marching barefoot. However, one hapless Dane inadvertently stepped on a thistle and let go a loud yelp that aroused the sleeping Scots, who thereupon slaughtered the Danes and saved themselves and their country from being conquered. Hence, the respect paid in Scotland to the thistle.

Even in England and elsewhere, thistles have long been valued as a medicine for convulsions and cricks of the neck, as a spring tonic, and to restore hair. "Though it may hurt your finger, it will help your body," advised Culpeper. Country maidens in England believed they could use thistles to determine who would be the best candidate as a husband. They'd place thistle heads, one for each suitor, in the corners of their pillow at night, and the head that had grown a shoot by the next morning represented the most faithful admirer.

Perhaps the thistle was better used as a prognosticator of the weather. If the flower head closed during the day, it was a sign of impending rain. Later, the down was a forecaster: "If the down flyeth off coltsfoot, dandelyon, or thistles when there is no winde, it is a signe of raine," wrote a seventeenth-century Englishman.

Thistles have worked their way into history in many ways, both good and bad. Perhaps the most creative and nefarious use for the plants was discovered by some evildoers in South America. When Charles Darwin was in Argentina on the *Beagle*, he asked a native whether robbers were numerous in one outlying district he wished to explore.

"The thistles are not up yet," the fellow replied.

Darwin was quite rightly confused by the answer. But later on during his visit, he learned that the fields of the "great thistle . . . were as high as the horse's back" in some parts of the territory. "When the thistles are full-grown," he said, "the great beds are impenetrable, except by a few tracks as intricate as those of a labyrinth. These are only known to the robbers, who at this season [late summer] inhabit them, and sally forth at night to rob and cut throats with impunity."

**Field Sow-Thistle**
*(Sonchus arvensis)*

# *When Hares Go Mad*

Few North American books on wildflowers even mention the sow-thistle, probably because it is not showy, not rare, and not native. Yet this increasingly common import from Europe was highly regarded among ancient civilizations. And for certain animals today, it represents a much-desired delicacy.

Common weeds found in most parts of the world, sow-thistles bloom from July into November. I have seen the spiny-leaved sow-thistle (*Sonchus asper*) flowering as early as mid-July one year in the same spot I saw one in bloom November 7 the year before. That unusually long season gives this annual plenty of opportunity to produce seeds, carried on fuzzy dandelionlike tufts or pappi by the wind, to help assure there will be a crop the next year.

The genus *Sonchus* is a member of the Composite family, and very closely related to the dandelion, as well as to the chicory, goatsbeard, and hawkweeds—whose kinship with the sow-thistle is clear from the similarity of the flowers in form and color.

## *Body Strengthener*

*Sonchus* is a Latin word based on the Greek for "hollow," descriptive of the stem, and it was the ancient Roman name for sow-thistles. That an old name became the modern generic name indicates that the plant likely was well known and used in ancient civilizations. Both the Greeks and the Romans thought highly of the sow-thistle, which was believed to strengthen the body. Pliny wrote that an old woman treated Theseus, the Greek prince, to a dish of sow-thistles just before he went out to single-handedly slay a furious bull that had been ravaging the countryside at Marathon.

The ancients also believed that sow-thistles were valuable in treating a variety of ailments, but by the 1500s they had fallen out of use for such purposes. Another ancient use, however, continues today in some parts of the world. Common sow-thistle is called *S. oleraceus*, a specific name meaning it was used as a pot-herb. The leaves were boiled like spinach and were sometimes added to soups. Even now, in some parts of Europe, the young leaves of *S. oleraceus* are mixed into salads.

Milkweed, milk-thistle, and milky tassel are other folk names that refer to the milky juice that *S. oleraceus* contains.

### *Bunny Food*

Common sow-thistle has been widely used well into this century as a food for rabbits, which are said to favor its leaves above all others. Such names as hare's thistle, hare's lettuce, and hare's colewort, refer to the hare's and the rabbit's liking for the plant. It was even believed that if a rabbit sat under the plant, no predator could touch it, for which reason the plant has also been called hare's palace and hare's house.

A naturalist a couple of centuries ago maintained, "When hares are overcome with heat, they eat of an herb called hare's lettuce," and that when ill, rabbits sought out the plant. Another writer said, "If a hare eat of this herb in the summer when he is mad, he shall become whole."

Other animals are fond of sow-thistles. One, obviously, is the pig—whence the common name and another folk name, swinies. Sheep and goats also devour it, although horses will not touch it.

### *Three Species*

*S. oleraceus*, a native of Europe and Asia, made its way to other parts of the world by following Western civilization. It is found in North, Central, and South America. J. D. Hooker, a naturalist who studied the botany of Antarctica, reported in 1847 that the natives of New Zealand were already using the import as food.

Spiny-leaved sow-thistle (*S. asper*), which lives in similar situations, is also found in most parts of the cultivated world. Its names, both English and Latin, refer to the prickers along the edges of the leaves; *asper* means "rough."

Corn, or field, sow-thistle (*S. arvensis*) can be found from New England to the Rockies in cooler climates. A perennial with creeping roots, it invades corn or wheat fields—*arvensis* means it likes cultivated fields. Thus it favors the luxurious, though dangerous and unpopular, life of a farm weed.

**Bottle Gentian**
*(Gentiana clausa)*

## *The Royal Family*

If there were ever a royal family of wildflowers, it would be the gentians. Most are brilliant in color, extraordinary in dress, finicky in situation, and few in number. Even their name has an origin that is regal.

If you discover a fringed or a closed gentian on an early autumn trek through field or wood, you will not soon forget it. The color of the fringed gentian has been described by Thoreau as "surpassing that of a male bluebird's back" and by William Cullen Bryant as "heaven's own blue." The several closed, or bottle, gentians, less sung by poets, are almost as blue but tend toward purple and are not as showy.

Although their seasons coincide—late August through early October—and they share similar hues, little else about our two most common eastern gentians seems the same. The fringed variety likes sunny meadows while the closed favors the forest's shade. Fringed is biennial, appearing two years after the parent plant spreads its tiny seeds; closed is a perennial, long-lived and often forming large colonies. Fringed is showy, among our most beautifully shaped flowers; closed is more conservative, so much so that it never opens its petals—hence its name.

### *The Nun of Flowers*

"A bud and yet a blossom!" wrote John Burroughs. "It is the nun among our wild flowers, a form closely veiled and cloaked." Burroughs and other naturalists have marveled at the closed gentian's ability to reproduce itself without opening its petals to pollen-transferring insects. Burroughs, in fact, long believed that the flower could not be pollinated by bees. "The buccaneer bumblebee sometimes tries to rifle it of its sweets," he once wrote. "I have seen the blossom with the bee entombed in it. He had forced his way into the virgin corolla as if determined to know its secret, but he had never returned with the knowledge he had gained."

Burroughs later learned that larger bees and bumblebees do indeed know how to safely extract the flower's nectar, though it is with considerable effort that they force their way inside. Although their petals are ever-closed, the flowers are actually designed to attract and serve the bee. Being closed protects the nectar from rain and pilfering insects of lesser strength, and the flower tips are specially coded to let the bees know which ones have already been drained of their sweets.

William Hamilton Gibson once watched a bee as it made the rounds of some asters, and then moved over to a closed gentian. There, it pushed its way into only one of the five blossoms on the plant, and then moved on to more asters. Curious as to why the bee stopped at only one, he examined the blossoms and found that the flower the bee visited was a young one, marked with white where the bee entered at the tip of its corolla. Older flowers—from which the nectar had been extracted—had turned purple around the opening. They had lost their honey guides, as botanists call them; it was the plant's way of telling the bee not to bother with these blossoms.

In the 1920s a German botanist named Knoll experimented with similar honey guides. On a dark blue piece of flat paper, he drew white circles; in the middle of each was a hole through which sugar-water was available. A hummingbird hawk-moth, which in the wild feeds at a European flower with a white ring on a dark blue background, quickly learned to go to the circle to find its treat. The shape of the "flower" had nothing to do with the moth's interest—it was all color. The insect ignored other combinations, such as white rings on yellow or gray paper. Knoll later placed a sheet of glass over the blue paper. The moth still went to the rings, and little tongue-marks remained on the glass where it tried in vain to dip into the hole at the center.

It is not always easy to see bees entering closed gentians. Possibly bees will not expend the energy needed to get at the nectar unless they are fairly desperate for food. Bees burn much fuel simply flying about on their nectar quests, and must be careful not to use up more than they collect. F. Schuyler Mathews spent many seasons watching closed gentians in a vain effort "to catch the robber in the act."

Mathews, however, may have lived with lazy bees. When I once wrote an article on gentians for *The New York Times* and mentioned the infrequent bee visitations, I received a letter from a clergyman in upper Wisconsin who not only often observed bees opening closed gentians, but also enclosed pictures as proof. "Maybe these bees are Scandinavians—industrious and all that sort of thing," the priest wrote.

### *Uncommon but Plentiful*

Closed gentian is not commonplace, but in its place, it can be common. I have seen the plant in the wild in only one spot in my hometown, and there it grows by the hundreds. When I first saw this colony in 1972, it consisted of several dozen plants. Ten years later, there were a thousand or more of them.

The sight was made all the more satisfying by the fact that this grove of uncommon flowers is thriving in the middle of dirt roads that had been cut through woods for a huge housing development. Before the subdivision ever got to be more than dirt roads, however, our wise town fathers decided to purchase the 550-acre woodland as a refuge. So often developments destroy wildlife and their habitats. How nice to see the flowers, for once, having the last laugh!

The closed, or bottle, gentian (*Gentiana andrewsii*)—also called blind, or barrel, gentian—is named for Henry C. Andrews, a noted English painter of flowers at the turn of the nineteenth century. It is found from Canada to Georgia and out to the states along the Mississippi. Much like it in shape, color, and range is the slightly smaller *G. clausa*, also called bottle, or closed, gentian.

These closed gentians are not difficult plants to grow. The seeds, which can be gathered in October or purchased from a specialty nursery, should be spread on damp soil and lightly tamped into the surface. Be careful not to plant on ground that is either too wet or that will dry out. *G. andrewsii* will grow from one to three feet high, but the taller ones often lie down along the ground, as if unable to bear the weight of the clusters of up to a half-dozen flowers at the top.

Edwin F. Steffek, author of *Wild Flowers and How to Grow Them*, says that bottle gentian is less finicky about soil than its fringed cousin, and will grow in most damp, shaded places. Perhaps it is because we have lost so much of our old forests, whose fringes are the favored haunt of the bottle gentian, that the flower is not as common as it could be.

### *Fringed Gentian*

Fringed gentian is considered by many to be our most attractive wildflower. Indeed, in the wildflower poll, it ranked eighth of the most beautiful wildflowers.

The four petals of the vase-shaped flowers each end in long, fine fringes. While these add to the flower's showy beauty and may help attract passing bees, they probably evolved chiefly to keep crawling insects away from the plentiful supply of nectar. Some thieves become tangled in the fringe and give up their expedition while others, surprised by the fringe's lack of support as they try to climb over it, simply slip off and fall to the ground. So characteristic are these fringes that the eastern fringed gentian has been named *Gentiana crinita*, the specific name meaning "hairy" or "with long hair."

When the sun is not shining, the tops of the petals wrap themselves tightly around each other, forming a pointed cap and protecting the interior from rain that might dilute nectar or from night-flying insects that might steal the bait without providing pollination. The flowers are plentiful and large, two inches tall on a healthy plant, which may itself reach three feet. A single plant may bear from one to an impressive one hundred blossoms.

Fringed gentian is probably the fussiest and least predictable of our well-known flowers. These characteristics, combined with the fact that it is a biennial and its flowers tempt wildflower gatherers, have made it rather rare. The seeds need just the right moisture (not too wet and never dry), neutral to moderately acid soil, and, some authorities say, the presence in the soil of a certain kind of root bacteria. Thus, transplanting is almost always a waste of time and removes the plants—and the seeds—from a natural habitat, eliminating future generations from proven ground.

### *From Seeds*

The acquisition of some seeds, either from a plant (they must be fresh) or from a nursery, is the safest method. You can try spreading them in a wet meadow, as nature does, or you can follow one of the several indoor planting methods outlined in books on wildflower cultivation. Former U.S. senator George D. Aiken of Vermont, one of the best authorities on the horticulture of fringed gentian, devoted a full chapter to the subject in *Pioneering with Wildflowers.* The senator maintained that the flower is easy to grow.

In nature, the plant is not necessarily stable in situation. Being a biennial "with seeds that are easily washed away, it is apt to change its haunts from time to time," wrote Mrs. William Starr Dana. "So our search for this plant is always attended with the charm of uncertainty. Once having ferreted out its new abiding place, however, we can satiate ourselves with its loveliness, which it usually lavishes unstintingly upon the moist meadows which it has elected to honor."

There is a spot in my town where fringed gentians appear each year. Some years only three or four plants will show up, possibly because conditions, such as the amount of rainfall, were not good. Other years, more than two dozen plants will bloom. Since one pod can contain hundreds of seeds, the future crop each year for this meadow depends on the success of the plants two years earlier. If a big rainstorm hits at seed-spreading season, the next generation may disappear down the drain—the site is only a few feet from a well-traveled highway.

Although Mrs. Dana found them to be transient, this reliable site perhaps bears out the poetic impression had by one S. R. Bartlett more than a century ago:

*I know not why but every sweet October*
*Down the fair road that opens to the sea*
*Dear in the wayside grasses tinging sober*
*Blooms my blue gentian faithfully for me.*

### *Royal Medicine*

Gentian, the name of several species of flowers and a small family of plants, recalls King Gentius of Illyria. This country, where Shakespeare set *Twelfth Night*, is now roughly where Albania and what was formerly called Yugoslavia are located. The king supposedly discovered that some species cured a strange illness that had infected his troops. Nonetheless, it was not powerful enough to deal with a worse problem, and he and his men were conquered by the Romans in 168 B.C.

Old herbals describe the use of European gentians for a myriad of ailments such as colds, skin itches and ulcers, worms, kidney stones, ruptures, bruises, and even stitches in the side. "A more sure remedy cannot be found to prevent the pestilence than it is," said Culpeper. "It strengthens the stomach exceedingly, helps digestion, comforts the heart, and preserves it against faintings and swoonings." It was also good for "the biting of mad dogs and venomous beasts." Gentian leaves are supposed to be a refrigerant, an agent that lowers abnormal body heat; the leaves were placed on open wounds and inflammations to cool them.

In modern times yellow gentian (*G. lutea*), native of Eurasia, has been used to stimulate the appetite and to treat a variety of stomach problems and other ailments. In Switzerland and the alpine regions of Austria and Germany, several liqueurs and cordials are made from a sugar obtained from its roots. A European concoction known as gentian bitters is sold today in better American food markets as an after-dinner drink to aid digestion.

Fringed gentian apparently possesses chemicals similar to the yellow gentian, for American Indians, including the Delaware, used to brew a tea from its roots to purify the blood and strengthen the stomach. The mountain folk of Appalachia made a similar tonic from the marsh gentian (*G. villosa*) and would even wear the root for strength.

The Gentian genus (*Gentiana*) is part of the Gentian family (*Gentianacea*), which includes the marsh pinks, sabbatias, centauries, columbos, felworts, pennyworts, and other obscure types. Of the fifty-six North American members of the genus, only the fringed and bottle gentians are widespread east of the Mississippi. Many gentians favor colder climates, such as high mountains—particularly the Rockies—and some are very particular about where they settle. In 1900 one species had been found only on Nantucket Island and at Portsmouth, Virginia, while another, only rarely seen even in the nineteenth century, was occasionally sighted in the Grand Rapids section of Saskatchewan.

At least twenty species of *Gentiana* live in the Rocky Mountains, and at least a half-dozen live in the Pacific Northwest, especially in wet places. Most common varieties are blue or purple, though there are some yellow species. One of the most striking in the Rockies is the western fringed gentian (*G. thermalis*), similar to the eastern variety, which is the official flower of Yellowstone National Park. *Thermalis* refers to the fact that it likes warmth, and while it can live in mountains more than two miles high, it favors wet spots, particularly warm springs.

The clan is more common in European uplands. Ms. Blanchan wrote, "Fifteen species of gentians have been gathered during a half-hour walk in Switzerland where the pastures are spread with sheets of blue. Indeed, one can little realize the beauty of these heavenly flowers who has not seen them among the Alps."

Notwithstanding that lofty report, the fringed gentian has hardly gone unappreciated in its homeland. Bryant's praise of it is perhaps best known:

*Thou waitest late, and com'st alone*
*When woods are bare and birds have flown,*
*And frosts and shortening days portend*
*The aged year is near his end.*
*Then doth thy sweet and quiet eye*
*Look through its fringes to the sky,—*
*Blue—blue—as if that sky let fall*
*A flower from its cerulean wall.*

**Common Burdock**
*(Arctium minus)*

## *The Hitchhikers*

"Weeds," wrote John Burroughs, "are great travelers; they are, indeed, the tramps of the vegetation world. They are going east, west, north, south; they walk; they fly; they swim; they steal a ride; they travel by rail, by flood, by wind; they go under ground, and they go above, across lots and by the highway. But, like other tramps, they find it safest by the highway: in the fields they are intercepted and cut off; but on the public road, every body, every passing herd of sheep or cows, gives them a lift."

The experts at getting a free ride are the clingers-on, the sticker-studded models of late summer and fall. Although these wildflowers are much disparaged, it is not the flowers but their aftermath that is so annoying. Still and all, the burdocks, beggar-tickets, tick-trefoils, avens, and other clingy plants of wood and field are flattering in that they look to us mammals for their autumnal migrations. All produce sticky seedpods or seeds designed to attach themselves to the fur or clothing of passersby and thus find their way to new places to colonize. In so doing, they are somewhat unusual in the plant world, living commensally with the highest forms of life.

### *Tick-Trefoils*

Tick-trefoils are among the most wide-spread of the mammal riders. They make up a large family of low-and-bushy to tall-and-slender weeds that are found in wet places and woodlands. The flowers are among the most attractive of the hitchhiking set; in some common varieties they are brilliant magenta or pink, and can be quite showy, if the Japanese beetles do not wipe them out as buds.

Their seedpods, or loments, which appear in September, are rather like flattened miniature pea pods—not surprising since the plants are members of the Pea family. Some two dozen species of *Desmodium*, a genus found only in the New World, live east of the Rockies. *Desmodium* is from the Greek for "chain," referring to the segmented pods, which tend to break apart into individual seed cases. The common name comes from the fact that the hairy body of the pod sticks to clothing or hair like a tick, and that the plant has three-leaf ("trefoil") clusters, typical of peas.

Writing in 1900, Neltje Blanchan observed, "As one travels hundreds or even thousands of miles in a comfortable railway carriage and sees the same flowers growing throughout the length and breadth of the area, one cannot but wonder how ever the plants manage to make the journey." One method is animal transportation; Charles Darwin raised more than sixty wild plants from the seeds found in a single piece of mud taken from the leg of a single partridge.

Tick-trefoil has a "by-hook or by-crook system," Ms. Blanchan wrote. "The scalloped, jointed pod, where the seeds lie concealed, has minute crooked bristles, which catch the clothing of man or beast, so that every herd of sheep, every dog, every man, woman or child who passes through a patch of trefoils gives them a lift. After a walk through the woods and lanes of summer and autumn, one's clothes reveal scores of tramps that have stolen a ride in the hope of being picked off and dropped amid better conditions in which to rear a family."

Despite this annoying habit of hitching rides, some tick-trefoils, like the wetland-loving panicled tick-trefoil (*Desmodium paniculatum*), are worth growing for their clusters of colorful flowers. Rich in protein, the pods have been used as an ingredient in chicken feeds. In the West Indies, a species of tick-trefoil is grown as a hay and forage crop.

### *Beggar-Ticks*

Beggar-ticks. What an appropriate name for this group of little freeloaders! Also called the tickseed sunflower, stick-tight or bur-marigold, the beggar-tick "is so constantly encountered in late summer, and yet so generally unknown, that it can hardly be overlooked," wrote Mrs. William Starr Dana by way of an excuse for including an unattractive plant in her turn-of-the-century wildflower guide.

In fact, the flowers of one of the most common natives, annual beggar-tick (*Bidens frondosa*), look like daisies robbed of all their white rays. Only a border of green leaves—actually bracts—seems to surround the lonely yellow disk, but a close inspection will often reveal tiny yellow rays. Others among the thirty or so North American species of *Bidens* have large and handsome yellow rays, such as the bur marigold (*B. cernua*), common in the Pacific states, and are more sunflowerlike. Indeed, being Composites, beggar-ticks are related to sunflowers, daisies, and asters.

The flowers bloom in August and September and the seeds appear in late September and through the fall. These seeds each have two barbed prongs that are difficult to extract from clothing or fur. The clan is named *Bidens*, Latin for "two-toothed," though a few species have four prongs like, one author says, a devil's pitchfork. Thoreau suggested that both beggar-tick and tick-trefoil inhabit only places that have been frequented by man or animal, and that they "prophesy the coming of the traveler, brute or human, that will transport their seeds on his coat" to yet another settlement.

In the Midwest vast fields full of golden Spanish needles (*B. bipinnata*) occur. Some farmers take advantage of them as a green fertilizer. Their pollen, however, is said to contribute to the agonies of hay fever sufferers.

### *Burdocks*

Burdocks are often mistaken for thistles and, like thistles, are members of the Composite family. Burdocks are also called stick-buttons, cockleburs, cuckoo-buttons, beggar's buttons, cockle-buttons, hardock, bardane, fox's clote, and a host of other folk names. About six species are found in Europe and Asia, and three have made it across to colonize North America.

The most common species is called, appropriately enough, common burdock (*Arctium minus*). A large-leaved plant that grows on roadsides and in other waste places through much of the United States and southern Canada, common burdock is fairly tall (to five feet); its close sibling, *A. lappa*, can reach nine feet. Both produce purple and white thistlelike flowers in August and early September, with the bright tubular florets appearing at the very tip of the needled, green head.

They are biennials, sending up only a basal rosette of large, rhubarblike leaves in the first year. This rosette makes and stores food in the roots for the big shrublike plant and flowers that show up in the second season. When you consider that one plant can produce 300,000 to 400,000 seeds, it is no wonder it lasts only two years, dying, as Edwin Rollin Spencer put it, of exhaustion.

After the flowers blossom, the heads dry up to form brown balls more than a half-inch in diameter. Their long, hooked stickers readily latch on to any passing creature and are one of the hardest to extract from clothing. Because of the rough, brown appearance of the seed balls, the genus has been named *Arctium*, from the Greek for "bear." *Minus* means "smaller" while *lappa* is a "bur," possibly based on the Celtic *llap*, "hand," as in something that can grab.

The color and weak-but-sweet scent of burdock attract a good many late-season butterflies. It has other friends, too. "The plant is so rank that man, the jackass, and the caterpillar are the only animals that will eat of it," wrote Charles F. Millspaugh, no doubt with a smile. Both roots and stems can be eaten—if you have ever had real sukiyaki at a Japanese restaurant, you probably ate some of the sliced, first-year burdock roots called "gobo." According to Euell Gibbons, Hawaiians believed these roots were an aphrodisiac as well as a body strengthener and, as a joke, friends of a bride and groom would present the couple with a bunch of burdock roots as a wedding present. The Iroquois dried the root to save as a winter food.

Peeled flower stems were boiled as a tasty asparaguslike green, though they are said to have a laxative effect. If simmered with some sugar, the pith in the flower stalks becomes a syrup, which turns into a sweet and tasty candy when rolled in granulated sugar.

As a medicine, burdock has been widely used for scrofula, psoriasis, scurvy, venereal diseases, rheumatism, gout, sties, and sundry other ailments, and was once listed in the *U.S. Pharmacopoeia* of approved drugs. It has long been used as a blood purifier and tonic, and some herbalists claimed that it would promote the growth of hair. Witches of Europe used it, with appropriate incantations, to treat burns.

Indian medicine men were quick to use the fast-spreading import. The Chippewas, who called the plant *wisugibug* (meaning "bitter leaf"), used it as a cough medicine. The Delaware brewed a tea from it to treat rheumatism while the Mohegans bound the leaves to rheumatic joints. The Nanticoke of Delaware steeped the leaves and put them on boils. The Ojibwas used it for stomach pains and the Meskwakis for labor pains. The Otoe drank the tea to treat pleurisy, and the Cheyennes and Dakotas made it a part of rituals.

Less practical but equally popular were the toys that children made of the burs. Girls used them to concoct chains, baskets, and bird nests, and boys used them to torment girls; through the generations, many a young mischief-maker has stuck cockleburs in many a young lady's tresses. Three centuries ago, Culpeper reported that the plant is "well known even by the little boys who pull off the burs to throw at one another." A worse practice of youth was to throw the burs at flying bats in an attempt to foul their wings and cause them to crash.

### *The Enchanter*

Two other common plants usually go unnoticed until their pods becomes stowaways. Enchanter's nightshade (*Circaea quadrisulcata*) is found in shady places throughout southern Canada and the eastern United States to Oklahoma and North Dakota, and smaller enchanter's nightshade (*C. alpina*) is common across the northern part of the continent and, at higher altitudes, in the Southwest and in California.

In summer bloom, the flowers of enchanter's nightshade are tiny and white, probably noteworthy only for the fact that they are among our very few two-petaled flowers. These deeply cleft petals sit on a fat green base, whose hairs later harden to become Velcro-like hooks that cling to fabric or fur. *C. quadrisulcata* grows one to two feet tall, while *C. alpina* grows only three to eight inches tall.

*Circaea* is from Circe, the enchantress who turned Ulysses' men into pigs and who later became his lover. The English name is said to reflect the legend that Circe used a poisonous member of this family in one of her magical potions. Enchanter's nightshades, however, are neither nightshades nor very enchanting. They are members of the Evening-primrose family and annoy more woodland walkers with their pods than they enchant with their flowers.

# Bibliography

The following publications were consulted for this book. Starred entries (*) are particularly recommended for further reading or as field guides.


Addison, Josephine. *The Illustrated Plant Lore.* London: Sidgwick and Jackson, 1985.

Ahmadjian, Vernon. *Flowering Plants of Massachusetts.* Amherst: University of Massachusetts Press, 1979.

*Aiken, Senator George D. *Pioneering with Wildflowers.* Englewood Cliffs, N.J.: Prentice-Hall Inc., 1968.

Anderson, A. W. *How We Got Our Flowers.* New York: Dover Publications Inc., 1966.

Angier, Bradford. *Feasting Free on Wild Edibles.* Harrisburg, Pa.: Stackpole Books, 1972.

Bailey, L. H. *How Plants Get Their Names.* New York: Dover Publications Inc., 1963.

Baker, Herbert G. *Plants and Civilization.* Belmont, Calif: Wadsworth Publishing Company, 1965.

Baldwin, W. T. *The Orchids of New England.* New York: John Wiley and Sons, 1884.

Balls, Edward K. *Early Uses of California Plants.* Berkeley & Los Angeles: University of California Press, 1965.

Birdseye, Clarence, and Eleanor Birdseye. *Growing Woodland Plants.* New York: Dover Publications Inc., 1972.

*Blanchan, Neltje. *Nature's Garden.* New York: Doubleday, Page and Company, 1900.

Bliss, Anne. *North American Dye Plants.* New York: Charles Scribner's Sons, 1979.

Britton, Lord Nathaniel, and the Honorable Addison Brown. *An Illustrated Flora of the Northern United States and Canada.* New York: Dover Publications Inc., 1970.

*Brown, Rowland W. *Composition of Scientific Words.* Washington: Smithsonian Institution Press, 1991.

Burroughs, John. *The Writings of John Burroughs.* 19 vols. Cambridge: The Riverside Press, n.d.

Chase, Agnes, et al. *Old and New Plant Lore.* Smithsonian Scientific Series. Washington, 1934.

Cocannouer, Joseph A. *Weeds: Guardians of the Soil.* New York: The Devin-Adair Company, 1950.

*Coon, Nelson. *The Dictionary of Useful Plants.* Emmaus, Pa.: Rodale Press, 1974.

Coon, Nelson. *Using Wild and Wayside Plants.* New York: Dover Publications Inc., 1980.

Copley, G. H. *Wild Flowers and Weeds.* London: John Crowther Ltd., n.d.

*Craighead, John J., Frank C. Craighead Jr., and Ray J. Davis, *A Field Guide to Rocky Mountain Wildflowers.* Peterson Field Guide Series. Boston: Houghton Mifflin Company, 1963.

Crispeels, Maarten J. *Plants, Food and People.* San Francisco: W. H. Freeman and Company, 1977.

*Crockett, Lawrence J. *Wildly Successful Plants: A Handbook of North American Weeds.* New York: Collier Books, 1977.

Crow, Garrett E. *New England's Rare, Threatened, and Endangered Plants.* Washington: United States Department of the Interior, 1982.

Culpeper, Nicholas. *Complete Herbal.* Philadelphia: David McKay Company, n.d.

Dalton, Patricia A. *Wildflowers of the Northeast in the Audubon Fairchild Garden.* Greenwich, Conn.: National Audubon Society Inc., 1979.

Densmore, Frances. *How Indians Use Wild Plants for Food, Medicine, & Crafts.* New York: Dover Publications Inc., 1974.

Durant, Mary. *Who Named the Daisy? Who Named the Rose?* New York: Dodd, Mead and Company, 1976.

Earle, Alice Morse. *Old-Time Gardens.* New York: The Macmillan Company, 1902.

*Erichsen-Brown, Charlotte. *Use of Plants for the Past 500 Years.* Aurora, Ontario: Breezy Creeks Press, 1979.

*Fernald, Merrit Lyndon, and Alfred Charles Kinsey. *Edible Plants of Eastern North America.* Cornwall-on-Hudson, N.Y.: Idlewild Press, 1943.

*Fitter, Alastair. *New Generation Guide to the Wild Flowers of Britain and Northern Europe.* Collins New Generation Guide. London: William Collins Sons & Company Ltd., 1987.

Forey, Pamela. *Wild Flowers of North America.* Limpsfield, Surrey: Dragon's World Ltd., 1990.

*Foster, Steven, and James A. Duke. *A Field Guide to Medicinal Plants: Eastern and Central North America.* Peterson Field Guide Series. Boston: Houghton Mifflin Company, 1990.

*Fox, Helen Morgenthau. *Gardening with Herbs for Flavor and Fragrance.* New York: Dover Publications Inc., 1970.

Gibbons, Euell. *Stalking the Wild Asparagus.* New York: David McKay Company, 1962.

*Gibson, William Hamilton. *Our Native Orchids.* New York: Doubleday, Page, and Company, 1905.

*Graham, Ada, and Frank Graham. *The Milkweed and Its World of Animals.* Garden City, N.Y.: Doubleday and Company, 1976.

Gray, Asa. *The Manual of the Botany of the Northern United States.* New York: American Book Company, 1889.

*Grieve, Mrs. M(aude). *A Modern Herbal.* 2 vols. New York: Dover Publications Inc., 1971.

Griffin, Diane. *Atlantic Wildflowers.* Toronto: Oxford University Press, 1984.

Grounds Committee of the National Society of Colonial Dames of America in the State of Connecticut. *Simples, Superstitions & Solace.* Hartford, 1970.

Hall, The Rev. Charles A. *Wild Flowers and Their Wonderful Ways.* London: A. & C. Black Ltd., 1926.

Harris, Ben Charles. *The Compleat Herbal.* New York: Larchmont Books, 1972.

Headstrom, Richard. *Suburban Wildflowers.* Englewood Cliffs, N.J.: Prentice-Hall Inc., 1984.

Healy, B. J. *A Gardener's Guide to Plant Names.* New York: Charles Scribner's Sons, 1972.

Hedrick, U. P., ed. *Sturtevant's Edible Plants of the World.* New York: Dover Publications Inc., 1972.

Hill, Jeff. *Friendly Weeds.* Mount Vernon, N.Y.: The Peter Pauper Press, 1976.

Hodgins, James L., ed. various issues. *Wildflower* (magazine). Toronto, Ontario, 1985–1992.

Hoehn, Reinhard. *Curiosities of the Plant Kingdom.* New York: Universe Books, 1980.

Houk, Rose. *Wildflowers of the American West.* San Francisco: Chronicle Books, 1987.

House, Homer D. *Wild Flowers.* New York: Macmillan, 1934.

Hutchinson, E. *Ladies' Indispensable Assistant.* New York, 1852.

Hutchinson, John. *Common Wild Flowers.* Middlesex, England: Penguin Books, 1945.

Hutchinson, John. *More Common Wild Flowers.* Middlesex: Penguin Books, 1948.

Hutchinson, John, and Ronald Melville. *The Story of Plants.* London: P. R. Gawthorn Ltd., 1948.

Johnson, C. Pierpoint. *Useful Plants of Great Britain.* London, 1862.

Jordan, Michael. *A Guide to Wild Plants.* London: Millington Books, 1976.

Kalm, Peter. *Travels in North America.* 2 vols. New York: Dover Publications, 1966.

*Kavasch, Barrie. *Native Harvests.* New York: Vintage Books, 1979.

Kerr, Jessica. *Shakespeare's Flowers.* New York: Thomas Y. Crowell Company, 1969.

Kieran, John. *An Introduction to Wild Flowers.* Garden City, N.Y.: Doubleday and Company, 1952.

Kingsbury, John M. *Deadly Harvest.* New York: Holt, Rinehart, and Winston, 1965.

Kluger, Marilyn. *The Wild Flavor.* Los Angeles: Jeremy P. Tarcher Inc., 1984.

Law, Donald. *The Concise Herbal Encyclopedia.* New York: St. Martin's Press, 1973.

*Lust, John B. *The Herb Book.* New York: Bantam Books, 1974.

*Mathews, F. Schuyler. *Familiar Features of the Roadside.* New York: D. Appleton and Company, 1897.

*Mathews, F. Schuyler. *Familiar Flowers of Field and Garden.* New York: D. Appleton and Company, 1915.

Medsger, Oliver Perry. *Edible Wild Plants.* New York: The Macmillan Company, 1966.

Meyer, Joseph E. *The Herbalist.* Glenwood, Ill.: Meyerbooks, 1960.

Millspaugh, Charles F. *American Medicinal Plants.* New York: Dover Publications Inc., 1974.

*Mohlenbrock, Robert H. *Where Have All the Wildflowers Gone?* New York: The Macmillan Company, 1983.

Moldenke, Harold N. *American Wild Flowers.* New York: D. Van Nostrand Company Inc., 1949.

Moore, John. *The Season of the Year.* London: Collins, 1954.

Morris, Frank, and Edward A. Eames. *Our Wild Orchids.* New York: Charles Scribner's Sons, 1929.

Muenscher, Walter Conrad. *Poisonous Plants of the United States.* New York: The Macmillan Company, 1939.

*Newcomb, Lawrence. *Newcomb's Wildflower Guide.* Boston: Little, Brown and Company, 1977.

Nicholson, B. E., et al. *The Oxford Book of Wild Flowers.* London: Oxford University Press, 1960.

*Niehaus, Theodore F., and Charles L. Ripper, *Pacific States Wildflowers.* Peterson Field Guide Series. Boston: Houghton Mifflin Company, 1976.

*Niehaus, Theodore F., Charles L. Ripper, and Virginia Savage. *Southwestern and Texas Wildflowers.* Peterson Field Guide Series. Boston: Houghton Mifflin Company, 1984.

*Niering, William A., and Nancy C. Olmstead. *The Audubon Society Field Guide to North American Wildflowers.* New York: Alfred A. Knopf, 1979.

Nutting, Wallace. *Connecticut Beautiful.* Framingham, Mass.: Old America Company, 1923.

Parker, A. C. *Iroquois Uses of Maize and Other Food Plants.* Albany: New York State Museum, 1910. Reprint. Iroqrafts, Oshweken, Ontario, 1983.

Pellett, Frank C. *Success with Wild Flowers.* New York: A. T. de la Mare Company, 1948.

*Peterson, Lee Allen. *A Field Guide to Edible Wild Plants (Eastern and Central North America).* Boston: Houghton Mifflin Company, 1977.

*Peterson, Roger Tory, and Margaret McKenny. *A Field Guide to Wildflowers.* Boston: Houghton Mifflin Company, 1968.

Philipson, W. R. *Wild Flowers.* Black's Young Naturalist's Series. London: Adam and Charles Black, 1950.

Potterton, David, ed. *Culpeper's Color Herbal.* New York: Sterling Publishing Company Inc., 1983.

Rishel, Dr. Jonas. *The Indian Physician.* New Berlin, Pa., 1828. Reprint. The Ohio State University Libraries Publications Committee, 1980.

Santillo, Humbart. *Herbal Combinations from Authoritative Sources.* Provo, Utah: NuLife Publishing, 1982.

Saunders, Charles Francis. *Edible and Useful Wild Plants of the United States and Canada.* New York: Dover Publications Inc. 1976.

Schery, Robert W. *Plants for Man.* Englewood Cliffs, N.J.: Prentice-Hall, Inc., 1952.

Skene, MacGregor. *The Biology of Flowering Plants.* London: Sidgwick and Jackson Ltd., 1947.

*Spellenberg, Richard. *The Audubon Society Field Guide to North American Wildflowers: Western Region.* New York: Alfred A. Knopf, 1979.

Spellenberg, Richard. *Familiar Flowers of North America: Eastern Region.* New York: Alfred A. Knopf, 1986.

*Spencer, Edwin Rollin. *All About Weeds.* New York: Dover Publications, 1974.

Stark, Raymond. *Guide to Indian Herbs.* Surrey, British Columbia: Hancock House Publishers, 1984.

Stary, Dr. Frantisek, and Dr. Vaclav Jirasek. *Herbs.* Prague: Artia, 1973.

Steffek, Edwin F. *Wild Flowers and How to Grow Them.* New York: Crown Publishers Inc., 1954.

Stefferud, Alfred. *The Wonders of Seeds.* New York: Harcourt, Brace and Company, 1956.

Stevens, John E. *Discovering Wild Plant Names.* Aylesbury, England: Shire Publications Ltd., 1979.

Swain, Ralph B. *The Insect Guide.* Garden City, N.Y.: Doubleday and Company, 1948.

Tantaquidgeon, Gladys. *Folk Medicine of the Delaware and Related Algonkian Indians.* Harrisburg: The Pennsylvania Historical and Museum Commission, 1977.

*Taylor, Kathryn S., and Stephen F. Hamblin. *Handbook of Wild Flower Cultivation.* New York: Collier Books, 1963.

Turner, Mrs. Cordella Harris. *The Floral Kingdom.* Chicago: Moses Warren, 1877.

Venning, Frank D. *Wildflowers of North America: A Guide to Field Identification.* New York: Golden Press, 1984.

Virgil (Publius Virgilius Maro). *The Eclogues and Georgics of Virgil.* Translated into English Verse by T. F. Royds. New York: E. P. Dutton and Company, n.d.

*Vogel, Virgil J. *American Indian Medicine.* New York: Ballantine Books, 1973.

Weed, Clarence M. *Ten New England Blossoms and Their Insect Visitors.* Boston: Houghton, Mifflin and Company, 1895.

Weslager, C. A. *Magic Medicines of the Indians.* New York: Signet, 1974.

Wood, Alphonso. *The New American Botanist and Florist.* New York: American Book Company, 1870.

Woods, Sylvia. *Plant Facts & Fancies.* London: Faber and Faber, 1985.

Woodward, Marcus. *How to Enjoy Wild Flowers.* London: Hodder and Stoughton, 1927.

Woodward, Marcus. *Leaves from Gerard's Herball.* New York: Dover Publications, 1969.

Wright, Mabel Osgood. *Flowers and Ferns in Their Haunts.* New York: The Macmillan Company, 1901.

# Plant Index

## *T*



## *U*



## *V*



## *W*



## *Y*



# *Subject Index*

## *A*



## *B*